SPRACHWISSENSCHAFTLICHE
STUDIENBÜCHER

2

D1492904

MANFRED GÖRLACH

A Textual History of Scots

Universitätsverlag
C. WINTER
Heidelberg

Die Deutsche Bibliothek – CIP-Einheitsaufnahme
Ein Titeldatensatz für diese Publikation
ist bei der Deutschen Bibliothek erhältlich.

COVER PICTURE
Edinburgh Castle

ISBN 3-8253-1073-6

© 2002 Universitätsverlag C. Winter Heidelberg GmbH
Imprimé en Allemagne · Printed in Germany
Druck: Strauss Offsetdruck GmbH, 69509 Mörlenbach

Gedruckt auf umweltfreundlichem, chlorfrei gebleichtem
und alterungsbeständigem Papier

Den Verlag erreichen Sie im Internet unter:
www.winter-verlag-hd.de

List of Contents

List of Abbreviations

/ / = phonological transcription
[ ] = phonetic transcription
< > = grapheme
{ } = morpheme
' ' = meaning
C = century, consonant
> = becomes
< = derived from
* = reconstructed form
Ø = zero
BrE = British English
CSD = *Concise Scots Dictionary*
DOST = *Dictionary of the Older Scottish Tongue*
EDD = *English Dialect Dictionary*
EDS = English Dialect Society
EETS = Early English Text Society
EL = English Linguistics reprint series
EModE = Early Modern English
ESc = Early Scots
GVS = Great Vowel Shift
IrE = Irish English
Lat = Latin
LModE = Late Modern English
LSS = Linguistic Survey of Scotland
ME = Middle English
MSc = Middle Scots
OE = Old English
OED = *Oxford English Dictionary*
OSc = Older Scots
p.c. = personal communication
PDE = Present-day English
RP = Received Pronunciation
Scand = Scandinavian
ScE = (Standard) Scottish English
SLRC = Scots Language Resource Centre
SND = *Scottish National Dictionary*
St EngE = Standard English English
STS = Scottish Text Society
SVLR = Scottish Vowel Length Rule
TPS = Transactions of the Philological Society

List of Figures

List of Texts

T1   BARBOUR, John, *The Bruce* (1375-77)
T2   BLIND HARRY, *Wallace* (1470s)
T3   HENRYSON, Robert, *The Testament of Cresseid* (late 15th cent.)
T4   DUNBAR, William and KENNEDY, Walter, *The Flyting* (c1500)
T5   DUNBAR, William, *Lament for the Makaris* (c1505)
T6   DOUGLAS, Gavin, *Virgil's Aeneid* (1515)
T7   THE CHANCELLOR AND THRIE ESTATIS, *Letter to Henry VIII* (1522)
T8   BELLENDEN, John, *The Chronicles of Scotland* (1531)
T9   GAU, John, *The Richt Vay to the Kingdom of Heuine* (c1533)
T10   WEDDERBURN, Robert, *The Complaynt of Scotland* (1549)
T11   LYNDSAY, David, *Ane Exclamatioun to the Redar* (c1554)
T12   KNOX, John, *History of the Reformation of Scotland* (1559-66)
T13   SKEYNE, Gilbert, *Ane breve descriptiovn of the pest* (1568)
T14   LINDSAY, Robert, *The Historie and Cronicles of Scotland* (1570s)
T15   BUCHANAN, George, *Letter to Thomas Randolph* (1577)
T16   JAMES VI, "Ane Short Treatise Conteining Some Revlis and Cautelis to Be Obseruit and Eschewit in Scottis Poesie." (1584)
T17   JAMES VI, *Letter to Elizabeth I* (1588)
T18   JAMES VI, *Basilicon Doron* (1599-1616)
T19   MELVILLE, James, *Scotland* (1601)
T20   ANON., *Education Act* (1616)
T21   HUME, Alexander, *Of the Orthographie and Congruitie of the Britan Tongue* (c1617)
T22   FERGUSSON, David, *Scottish Proverbs* (1641)
T23   ANON., *The Minute Book of Tyninghame* (1634)
T24   PITCAIRNE, Archibald, *The Assembly* (1692)
T25   RAMSAY, Allan, *Elegy on Maggy Johnston* (1712)
T26   RAMSAY, Allan, *The Gentle Shepherd* (1725)
T27   RAMSAY, Allan, *Dedication to Proverbs* (1737)
T28   MRS McLINTOCK, *Receipts for Cookery and Pastry Work* (1736)
T29   HUME, David, *Scoticisms* (1760)
T30   BEATTIE, James, *Scotticisms* (1779)
T31   MAYNE, John, "Glasgow. A Poem." (1783)
T32   FERGUSSON, Robert, *To Andrew Gray* (1773)
T33   BURNS, Robert, *Epistle to W.S. Ochiltree* (1785)
T34   BURNS, Robert, *Letter to William Nicol* (1787)
T35   KEITH, Charles, *An Address in Scotch* (1788)
T36   SCOTT, Sir Walter, *The Twa Corbies* (1802)
T37   SCOTT, Sir Walter, *The Heart of Midlothian* (1818)
T38   HOGG, James, *The Brownie of Bodsbeck* (1818)
T39   GALT, John, *Annals of the Parish* (1821)
T40   MOIR, David Macbeth, *The Life of Mansie Wauch* (1828)
T41   ANON., 'Maansie o' Slushiegarth', *"Letter to the Editor"* (1838)
T42   ANON., 'Peter Hardie', *"Letter to the Editor"* (1858)
T43   ANON., *"Family Dialogues. Household Taxation"* (1850)
T44   ALEXANDER, William, *Johnny Gibb of Gushetneuk* (1871)
T45   STEVENSON, Robert Louis, *Thrawn Janet* (1881)
T46   MACLAREN, Ian, *Beside the Bonnie Brier Bush* (1890s)
T47   ANON., *Thrums on the Auld String* (1890)
T48   MURRAY, Charles, *The Whistle* (1906)
T49   BROWN, George Douglas, *The House with the Green Shutters* (1901)
T50   BELL, John Joy, *Wee Macgreegor* (1901)
T51   CAMERON, Henry P., *Genesis in Scots* (1921)

Foreword

This textbook is the first to combine selected texts with a linguistic history of Scots since Grant & Dixon's classic collection (1921). In fact, the history of the Scots language has never received more than a fraction of the attention that it deserves on the basis of its complex history and the fascinating coexistence of present-day varieties (cf. Görlach 1985a). The scholarly interest in Scots, one might argue, should be almost as great as that in the Big Brother, English – part of whose history is of course also part of the Scottish heritage. However, whereas dozens of books deal with historical aspects of English, there has never been a comparable range of publications on Scots. It is only very recently that the picture has begun to change, with the substantial survey written by McClure (1994) and the large but not quite comprehensive collection of papers edited by Jones (1997a).

My own plans to write this book go back almost twenty years to a time when the publication of the two titles above was not yet envisaged. However, even now there seems to be room for a book like this, for the following reasons:

1) A textbook should be accessible to students, that is, a book whose size, price and the scholarly methods employed should be adapted to a student audience. It should also include details such as exercises and take into account various didactic considerations.

2) The book should have a generous selection of texts to illustrate the development of the (written) language in its various forms and functions. Such carefully selected excerpts also permit students to develop a feeling (*sprachgefühl*) for the language they study, and to test their newly acquired knowledge on textual analysis, guided by study questions.

The experience gained in writing a set of textbooks on Early Modern English (Görlach 1978/94, 1991a), on English in 19th century England (Görlach 1999) and on English in the 18th century (Görlach 2001a) has been helpful in writing this manual; a few texts have in fact been reprinted in part from my *Introduction to Early Modern English* (T6, 8, 13, 16, 18, 20).

Since the book is devoted to the textual history of Scots I have not included much material on spoken Scots (although in a few subchapters the present-day situation of Scots is discussed and illustrated by excerpts). If such material were represented in a significant quantity, the book would have grown to a size beyond that appropriate for a student handbook (for regional treatments combining written and spoken data cf. Macafee 1983a and McClure 2002).

The introductory chapters 1-9 are related to the texts as closely as possible; the excerpts themselves are reprinted with brief introductions explaining their status. I have not provided a glossary, because this would have taken up too much space and excellent dictionaries such as the *Concise Scots Dictionary* (Robinson 1985) are available. Since the texts are chosen from a large variety of periods and dialects, numerous cross-references would also have been needed. Instead, I have supplied an index of the most important words which covers both the introduction and the text section.

As frequently happens in the history of philological disciplines, I am greatly endebted to scholars who went before me. This intellectual debt, also indicated by the number of quotations from their work, is due in particular to Jack Aitken, James Main Dixon, William Grant, Tom McArthur, J. Derrick McClure, James A.H. Murray, James Wilson and the contributors to the book edited by Charles Jones (1997a). A great number of colleagues were kind enough to go through this book in draft form and have made very valuable suggestions and comments. I wish to thank in particular Fiona Douglas, Paul Johnston, Caroline Macafee, Ronald Macaulay, J. Derrick McClure, Iseabail Macleod, Colin Milton and Graham Tulloch. Katja Lenz has accompanied the writing of the book with memorable acumen and energy, and has given generous comments as well as bringing in her technical expertise; I regret that the book proved impossible to publish as a joint venture as originally planned. The final version has profited a great deal from the knowhow of Sirka Laass, Angela Reck and Ruth Möhlig.

Publishers have generally permitted me to reprint excerpts from copyright texts; these are mentioned in the introductions to T1-75. In particular I wish to acknowledge the willingness of the following authors to reprint their texts: Dauvit Horsbroch (T73), John Kirk (T75), Tom Leonard (T67) and Stephen Mulrine (T60,61) and the widows of W.L. Lorimer (T69b) and W. Tait (T59).

Eilert Erfling of C.Winter Universitätsverlag has supported the project all through its complex history and accepted the awkward delay in its publication.

My personal relations with Scotland, with Scottish friends and the Scots language have been long and fruitful; German-speaking scholars have contributed a great deal to the study of Scots, in particular in the present century, and I am glad to be able to continue this tradition into the new millenium. I hope that some of my enthusiasm will be shared by the students who may discover how attractive the field of study here presented is.

Going through the texts selected for this volume I have become aware of how many authors with whom I have been in close contact over the years, who wrote translations for me and helped me with many instances of excellent advice, are no longer with us. It is, I think, a fair tribute to their memory to dedicate this book to them: A.J. Aitken, J.K. Annand, Flora Garry, John Thomas Low and Robert McLellan.

1 *Introduction*

1.1 *The subject matter, or the identity of Scots*

In a field in which the boundary lines are as vague and as fluid as they are in the case of the Scots language, writers have to take controversial decisions. Among the most important questions are to decide

1) What constitutes a Scots utterance, and how the identity of Scots should be defined. A major point at issue is that many scholars include Scots in descriptions of *English*, whether they discuss the problematic nature of their decision (Görlach 1991a), or not (Cusack 1998). Also, compare McClure (1994), who wrote on Scots under the title of "English in Scotland" in a book devoted to Englishes, and Jones, who mainly discusses Scottish Standard English (ScE) in a book on Scots (1995) and disregarded the distinction between Scots and ScE in another (2002).
2) How far regional diversity should be included in a book on a language which is made up more or less of individual dialects.

I have tried to provide a balanced view in both respects: thus I do not ignore the coexistence of English and Scots, especially where both occur in the same texts (contrast the purist solution adopted in Grant & Dixon, 1921, where English passages are omitted from 'mixed' texts), and I include a few specimens of local dialects of Scots, ranging from the Borders to Shetland.

1.1.1 *Why Scots matters*

Why Scots Matters is the title of one of McClure's more popular books ([2]1997). First and foremost, Scots matters to the Scots. Although the existence of a well-defined linguistic variety, clearly distinct from the most closely related languages, is not a necessary precondition for national identity, it often emphasises the cultural and political distinctiveness of a group of speakers.

It can be argued that Scottish Standard English (ScE), the variety spoken by most, and written by all, people in Scotland is sufficient for identification. Yet, some Scots consider ScE as an import, and as depleted of much that makes sense in a Scottish situation. Moreover, ScE introduces a middle norm intermediate between St EngE and Scottish dialects. On the other hand, seen from the perspective of ScE, braid Scots is often either stigmatized as uneducated, dated or odd, or seen as part of a nostalgic world which is not relevant to present-day concerns.

This view is beginning to change. Scots has recently reached official recognition (though not as an 'official' language in British legislation), when it was classified as one of Europe's minority languages by the European Bureau of Lesser Used Languages in 1993 (cf. Macleod & MacNeacail 1995, McGugan 2001 and 2.3.4). And for many speakers in Scotland Scots certainly fulfils identificational functions. To put it in the words of Billy Kay, writer and broadcaster (Kay 1986, [2]1993):

t1 The guid Scots tongue... a slovenly debased dialect... the Doric... corrupt English... artificial Lallans... uncouth gutturals... the National Language... an unintelligible dialect of English... Braid Scots... coarse slang... a language that never existed – every one of those terms and epithets has been used to describe the language I was brought up to speak – Scots.
  5 Its sounds are still the ones which rise most naturally to my lips and therefore haunt the very

writing of this book. The ideas often come in Scots, and the previous passage could just as easily be transcribed as: every ane o thae terms an epithets has been uised tae describe the language I wes brocht up tae speak, an its soonds is aye the anes that rise maist natural tae ma lips. Thinking in Scots and writing in English, switching from Scots to English when the social situation calls for a change of register, getting into a muddle or "puttin yer fuit in it" when the switch is not a clean one and Scots invades the English – all are part of the linguistic experience of most Scots raised in the Lowlands – and that covers the great majority of the population.   ([2]1993:17)

His book ends with a powerful appeal not to let Scots die:

t2   Because language itself helps form the thoughts we have about our environment, Scots has a unique role as the tongue which is rooted deeply in the physical landscape we inhabit and has expressed our relationship with it for hundreds of years. If Scots were to disappear we would lose part of our sensitivity to our environment, because no other language can describe it with the same "feel"; a snell founeran wind that wad gar yer banes chitter, a dreich haar happin aa thing alang the coast, a douce simmer's gloaming that's saft an bonnie, a thrang city street wi fowk breengin aboot an joukin atween ane anither. It is also the language that describes perfectly the human types that inhabit this landscape; a wice-like bodie ... a sleekit scunner ... a braw, sonsie lassie ... a gleg wean ... a sapsie muckle hertit sumph ... a thrawn besom ... a shuilpit wee nyaff ... a bachle wi no eneuch sough tae sprachle oot a sheugh ... a fushionless craitur ... a kenspeckle child ... a gallous chancer ... in fact, the haill jingbang o sister an "brither Scots frae Maidenkirk tae John O' Groats".

     Scots is as essential to Scotland as her folk, her towns, her fields and rivers. It is a mirror of Scotland's soul. That is why it, and the values it expresses, will endure. It's comin yet for a that...
     For we hae faith in Scotland's hidden poo'ers
     The present's theirs, but a' the past and future's oors.   ([2]1993:189)

Apart from these reasons, the study of Scots is not only a concern for speakers of Scots, but is also of relevance to anyone interested in sociolinguistics. With its long history, its close relationship with a sister language of different status and the strong linguistic attitudes towards its varieties it has often been seen as a kind of linguistic laboratory, a test-case for various linguistic models and concepts.

1.1.2 *Language and nation*

Does a nation state need a language of its own? (Görlach 1997b) The United States came closest to implementing their linguistic independence in the 1780s, when names like 'Fredonian' were suggested for the newly defined American language. However, the Americans finally decided that independent norms within a shared pluricentric language were good enough. Similar reactions to questions of linguistic identity arose in Canada, Australia and New Zealand. On the continent, the German-speaking Swiss believe that a national form of a spoken dialect suffices, but that written norms can be (largely) shared, whereas Luxembourg has created a new standard language on the basis of its historically German dialect.

     In approaching the topic for Scotland, we must not forget that the concept of a unitary nation-state based on cultural and linguistic identity is a development mainly of the 18/19C. To make such a general claim for earlier periods would be somewhat anachronistic (cf. Grant 1994). Consequently, the largely inconsistent attitudes towards Scots in the 16C should not come as a surprise. Even seemingly contrasting views of Protestants (English) and Catholics (Scots) may not be ascribed to these groups in general, but apply only to some individual writers like Winzet, who in 1563 "attacked Knox on the grounds of his unpatriotically anglicised language":

t3　Gif ze, throw curiositie of nouationis, hes forzet our auld plane Scottish qhuilk zour mother lerit
　　zou, in tymes cuming I sall wryte to zou my mind in Latin, for I am nocht acquyntit with zour
　　Southeroun.　　　　　　　　　　　　　　　　　　　　　　　　　(quoted from Corbett 1999:59)

When the identification of nations with national languages came to be relevant in the 19C, Scotland had just opted for anglicization also of the spoken standard (7.1.2). In consequence, there was no institution or educated elite that could have demanded and implemented a return to total linguistic independence on the basis of a standardized Scots – when a great fraction of the population was trying to give the language up. This question has indeed not been raised again in the context of political devolution or independence, for instance on the agenda of the SNP. The status of Scots as a supplementary language in the new parliament and the possible introduction of a question on Scots into the next census, however, are being discussed (cf. McLeod 1998, Scott 1998, Máté 1996, Horsbroch 2000, 2001, McGugan 2001).

　　For a long time, then, ScE, rather than Scots, has served Scotsmen (and served them well) as a badge of national identity; it has the advantage of being both of high international prestige and of general intelligibility. Having the same OE roots as EngE it also can claim historicity to an extent that not many national languages can.

1.1.3 *Attitudes towards Scots and English*

Attitudes toward Scots and English have, then, largely determined the functional and structural history of the minority language. We might wish to claim that the development, range of functions and degree of standardization of Scots has depended on the native speakers' attitudes towards it all through its history. However, it is difficult to substantiate such a large claim empirically. Did the practice of 15C and 16C makars who borrowed styles, topics, genres – and along with them the pertinent vocabulary – from English models reflect their faith (or lack of faith) in Scots as an independent literary language? How are we to judge Gavin Douglas's compromise (cf. T6 and 8.2.5)? How different were the atittudes of 16C Protestants and Catholics concerning the vernacular? Was James making a moderate claim to Scottish identity when using Scottish spellings (but largely avoiding Scots lexis) in his letters to Elizabeth (T17), and did he change his attitudes between 1595 and 1602 (as perhaps illustrated by the decreasing density of the specifically Scots element in his *Basilicon Doron*, cf. T18 and 8.2.8)? Such uncertainties continue in later centuries, as is evident from the linguistic practice of 18C writers like Ramsay. In addition, many early statements are not quite precise since 'Scots' might refer to ScE or to Scots (or in earlier periods even to Gaelic).

　　Scots clearly did not suffer from the patronising view educated Englishmen kept of Irish English (cf. Bliss 1979). While the latter came to be the stock dialect of the stage bumpkin, Sawney did not suffer the same sneers from John Bull as Paddy did. Criticism of ScE was admittedly harsh enough – but it frequently came from Scotsmen themselves, especially from the educated middle-classes from 1750 onwards (cf. for instance David Hume's remarks about the 'corrupt' dialect of English spoken in Scotland, e.g. in Grieg 1961:255).

In the critical late 18C, even the decidedly Scotophile English grammarian Adams in his spirited defence of Scots as an expression of Scottish identity describes the ScE treatment of /x/ as follows:

t4   We [the English] suppress the harsh gutturals, or convert them into single consonants. The Scotch
     retain them; and when they affect to soften them, the articulation or sound resembles that of a deep
     asthma, or last rattling of a deep quinsey   (1799:153)

Still, he prefers ScE to local Scots dialects and distinguishes clearly between various types of Scots of different acceptability:

t5   besides the above corruptions, every word has some peculiar twang, and twist discordant with
     received classical English sounds, and that there is a dialect of dialect in different quarters, and it is
     this kind of local dialect alone that locally sinks into vulgarity amongst the illiterate Scotch, and
     may rank with our provincial corruptions.   (1799:154)

He is even more explicit in another passage:

t6   This original Dialect manifests itself by two extremes. The one is found in the native broad and
     manly sounds of the Scoto-Saxon-English [= Scots]; the terms of coarse and harsh are more
     commonly employed. The other is that of a tempered medium, generally used by the polished class
     of society. To attempt to vindicate the first will be deemed not only singularity, but madness, by
   5 some of my countrymen, so strong is the flow of prejudice. The vindication of the second will meet
     the ideas of liberal observers of men and manners.   (1799:156-7)

The 19C, with its general interest in local dialect, brought forth a new vernacular revival in the literature of the North-east in particular, while the Burnsian tradition was kept up in a wide range of popular writing, along with more local varieties (Donaldson 1986, 1989). At the same time, the acceptance and spread of English continued to grow, with the threat for the vernacular being significantly increased by the introduction of compulsory education in 1872. Reactions to the use of Scots became even more complex in the 20C, when both 'mainstream' and local forms of literary Scots came to be looked upon very critically by MacDiarmid and the *Scottish Literary Renaissance* (cf. Milton 1983).

Attitudes largely account for the dramatic loss of broad rural dialect from the 19th century onwards in everyday speech. In this, Scotland is not much different from the erosion of dialects and minority languages elsewhere in Europe – with admitted contrasts in the speed of the process. Robinson & Crawford repeat the oft-told story of parents' attitudes being largely responsible. They are likely to tell their children "if folk are to get on the world nowadays, away from the ploughshafts and out of the pleiter, they must use English, orra though it be" (quoting from Gibbon's *Sunset Song*, 2001:13).

In particular, attitudes diverge between the acceptance of rural and urban speech (as is in fact widespread in W Europe) – whereas the latter is associated with poverty and even with brutality and crime and sometimes labelled 'gutter Scots', the rural varieties tend to be seen as reflexions of a pre-industrial Golden Age. That this situation can be changed is seen in the covert prestige that urban Glaswegian has for many (not just in the football stadium or in the music hall). Playfully the situation can even be reversed, as in Tom Leonard's *If Only Bunty Was Here* (1979), where fun is made of the "Bannock-an'-But-an'Ben Preservation Society".

Attitudes are possibly most strongly expressed in poetry, and in the 20C in particular. A first line like "The heicht o the biggins is happit in rauchens o haar" in A. Scott's excellent "Haar in Princes Street" signals unmistakably that the poem is intented to be in *Scots*. It is also remarkable how often Scottish writers make reflections on the language appropriate for literary diction the topic of their poems and prose. Compare poems like Soutar's "The makar", Garioch's "A makar's prayer" and T54, 55, 67a on poetry and T56, 57 and 67b on prose.

Ex 1 Compare attitudes to linguistic independence in present-day Scotland with those in German-speaking Switzerland and Luxembourg.

1.1.4 *Language labels*

Up to the late 15C, the term 'Inglis' was used to refer to Anglo-Saxon derived speech forms current in Lowland Scotland and Southern England. 'Scottis' as a name for the non-Celtic language of the Scottish Lowlands is first recorded to have been used in 1494 (McClure 1995d:44) and Gavin Douglas, in his translation of the *Aeneid* (1513, T6) explicitly distinguished between 'Scottis' and 'Inglis' or 'Sudron'. The distinction was kept from then on, but where differentiation was not needed (or wanted), 'Inglis/English' continued to include both English and Scots. Earlier on, the name 'Scottis' was generally applied to the Gaelic language of the ancient Scots of Dal Riada in Ireland, sometimes also to contemporary Scottish Gaelic. The more common name for the latter was 'Irische' or 'Ersche', which continued to be used.

The term 'Sudron' or 'Southeron' for the English language came into use when Scots and English were beginning to be distinguished. This was not only less ambiguous than the word 'Inglis', "it might also have been convenient for some, perhaps, in having stronger negative connotations" (McClure 1995d:50). It is still used today, especially in the vocabulary of language activists, and has kept (or rather increased) its pejorative flavour.

Further labels denoting Scots or a variety of Scots were introduced later on, especially from the 18C. Several of them are clearly positively charged, among them 'braid Scots' and the 'auld leed/leid'. Both names refer to Scots in general, though ususally excluding its contemporary urban varieties, whereas another positive term, 'the Doric' is even more clearly restricted to rural dialects, especially to those of the North-east. The same is true for 'Buchan', which is not necessarily limited to the district of that name.

The term 'Lallans', used in an affectionate way by Robert Burns in the 18C to refer to the language of the Lowlands, i.e. to Scots, changed its meaning slightly in the 1940s when it came to be applied to the variety of literary Scots used by writers of the *Scottish*

Literary Renaissance. Its connotations are therefore not always positive today, because it is often felt to be artificial and pretentious.

A humorous, affectionate name for Glaswegian speech is 'the Patter'. More commonly, this dialect – like other urban forms of Scots – is not well liked and has been called 'demotic Scots', or even 'corrupt' or 'gutter Scots'.

Ex 2 Describe how the words *Scot/Scots/Scotch/Scottish* have been understood over the centuries (*CSD*, *OED*, McArthur 1992).

1.1.5 *Sources*

Every description of historical stages of a language is restricted by the available data; the absence of oral evidence is a serious impediment, but the quantity and quality of the surviving written and printed records are also obstacles to a comprehensive and correct description. All grammars and dictionaries of earlier periods can be little more than adequate descriptions of the texts they are based on. In particular, we will have to take into account (cf. Görlach 1991a:2-5):

1) *Gaps in the transmission of texts*. Personal documents, such as letters, diaries or household books, tended to be destroyed, as were ephemeral printed texts, such as broadsides or newspapers. Entire text types are thus incompletely documented, in particular those of the more informal type. However, the survival of the unique copy of Nisbet's *New Testament* of ca. 1520 shows that texts of eminent historical importance could easily be lost, too.

2) *The authenticity of the surviving texts* (cf. Görlach 2002e). The question of how 'real', authentic or representative a text is depends on the specific text type, which can account for artificial usage in some poetic genres, fossilization in legal and religious texts, and so on. In the manuscript tradition, surviving versions tend to be copies of copies (cf. 8.2 and 8.2.2 for James I in particular), and are sometimes even transcriptions from intervening printed texts. Thus most of the early Scottish poetry survives in a few large collections, such as the Bannatyne MS (compiled ca. 1565-8), the Maitland Folio MS (ca. 1570-86), the Maitland Quarto MS (1586) and the Asloan and Reidpeth MSS – and in fragmentary Chepman and Millar imprints of 1508. In many cases even ascriptions are uncertain. What is the total corpus of Dunbar's poetry? Were the *Morall Fabillis of Esope* (printed by Charteris and Bassandyne in 1570/71) thus arranged by Henryson, who died around 1490? This patchy tradition makes it impossible to establish what a poet like Dunbar actually wrote (cf. Mapstone 2001). Such decisions are even more difficult in a time when we must take both possible Scottization and Anglicization of texts into account; moreover, a few texts, such as Henryson's *Fabillis*, contain corruptions, of which some may be due to Protestant censorship. In addition, the linguist's use of modern editions will distort the linguistic analysis even further, especially as far as spelling and punctuation is concerned. By contrast, diplomatic transliterations such as those in Cusack (1998) need a great deal of philological competence to make them interpretable in sociolinguistic analysis.

However, even in data collected by linguists who are, one assumes, committed to real language, authenticity is not guaranteed. Dialectologists were often (mis-)led by concepts of ideal, pure dialect, and sociolinguists prefer (often isolated) items that can be quantified. We may get closer to real language where collectors pursue less academic objectives: Robinson & Crawford originally wanted "to offer guidance to actors working on Scots accents" and accordingly "did not seek out the strongest examples but selected more mainstream speakers" (2001:9; cf. T74).

1.2   *Synchronic and diachronic description*

A synchronic description of a language accounts for its structure on the levels of phonology, morphology, syntax and lexis and for written languages also the orthography. The analysis is valid only for the system under investigation, i.e. findings cannot be expected to be true for other subsystems (dialects, sociolects or chronolects), let alone for more than one language. This conclusion is particularly relevant for the investigation of Scots. It warns us not to equate linguistic items or structures
a) across dialects (mixing evidence from, say Shetland and the Central Belt);
b) across language boundaries (not distinguishing between data from English and Scots
    – in so far as the two systems can be considered distinct);
c) over time (combining evidence from 15C and 20C texts).
Note that in poetic diction such differences are sometimes intentionally disregarded so that a poet may create a new system of his own. It is even doubtful how far individual items from different styles (spoken vs. written, formal vs. informal etc.) can be assumed to correspond. Variation must therefore be carefully considered in structural analysis, which, however, is ideally undertaken with material from a homogeneous system.

The reconstruction of each of the linguistic (sub-)systems used by Scottish writers in the course of history can only be as good as the quantity and quality of the surviving evidence permits. It is necessary to reflect that non-literary written sources are rare, even for the period up to 1900 (only few such texts were written down or printed, and of these only a minimal proportion survived). Moreover, of the documents still extant, not all have been analysed for linguistic purposes. These limitations are grievous when it comes to compiling a grammar of, say, 15C Scots, but they are much worse when linguists undertake to write a diachronic account of the language on its individual levels. These restrictions may be summarized as follows (adapted from Görlach 1995e:67):
1) There is no complete written grammar of the language, and there has never been one in its entire history – in contrast to English, where almost all grammar books from at least Lowth (1762) onwards comprise comprehensive lists of what the author prescribed as the correct forms.
2) The Helsinki Corpus (cf. Meurman-Solin 1993b) is too small for a comprehensive coverage of all linguistic features, and what is more, it has no post-1700 equivalent to permit a comparison with modern conditions. The forthcoming Glasgow Scottish Corpus of Texts and Speech (SCOTS) will hopefully remedy the situation, but is still in the planning stage (F. Douglas, p.c.).

3) Of the historical dictionaries, the *Dictionary of the Older Scottish Tongue* (*DOST*, Craigie *et al.* 1937-, the inclusive dictionary of words used in Scottish texts up to 1700) is not yet published in full, and the *Scottish National Dictionary* (*SND*, Grant *et al.* 1931-76) is restricted to exclusively Scots words and meanings after 1700. Neither includes full lists of recorded forms, nor can information on their distribution and frequency be retrieved in a satisfactory way. The *Concise Scots Dictionary* (*CSD*, Robinson 1985), draws on historical data, being based on *DOST* and *SND*, and includes more recent 20C material, written and spoken texts, and both 'standard' (in the literary tradition) and dialect sources. But even the evidence found in the *CSD* is too scanty to permit reliable conclusions for the following reasons:

    a) words also found in English with the same meaning are not included at all;

    b) regular inflectional forms are frequently omitted, so that only the by-forms are mentioned as "also..."; therefore, many verbs, for instance, have no forms listed at all – because they behave like their English equivalents;

    c) only incomplete information can be extracted from the entries on the individual forms' currency or acceptability.

(For the restrictions in reconstructing historical pronunciation cf. 4.1 below.)

Ex 3 Contrast the limits of a linguistic reconstruction for English and Scots, summarizing the evidence for a particular century.

1.3 *Demographic background*

The relationship between English and Scots is partly determined by the relative political, economic and demographic weight of the two nations. Although the following description of the population of the whole of Scotland does not account for the proportion of the Gaeltacht and its Gaelic-speakers, it may give an idea of general tendencies. In the period from 1801 to the present, the population of Scotland has formed a steadily declining proportion of the total population of mainland Britain:

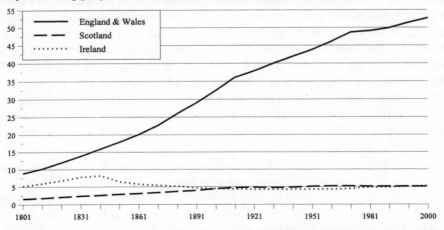

Fig. 1 Development of the population in England & Wales, Ireland and Scotland, 1800–2000 (in millions).

In 1801 there were 1.6 m Scots against 8.9 m in England and Wales (1 in 5.6), but in 1994 the ratio was only 1 in 10 (5.1 m against 51.4 m). This decline has been continuous, whereas for Ireland it was even more dramatic, sinking from 1 in 1.7 in 1801 to 1 in 10 today; this was especially so between 1841 and 1901, when the population was halved in Ireland, but doubled in England and Wales.

The following figures establish that in 2000 the ratio of the populations remains at 1: 9.5 (while the relationship between the sizes of territories is 1: 1.7 – which shows how much more sparsely Scotland is settled):

	population	%	area (in sq km)	%
Great Britain	59,501	100	242,910	100
England	49,753	83.6	130,422	53.7
Scotland	5,119	8.6	78,133	32.2

Fig. 2 Populations and size of territory in England and Scotland today (*Fischer Weltalmanach 2002*)

A ranking of the biggest towns in Great Britain shows similar results: Glasgow comes fourth with 619,700 inhabitants, followed by Edinburgh in eighth place (450,200) and Aberdeen, which reaches only the thirty-sixth position (218,000). The Central Belt is in fact the only Scottish region that is densely populated.

1.4   Book production, education and literacy
1.4.1 Book production

The number of books printed in 16C Scotland (compared with imports from England) and the language used in them (Scots as against English) was one of the major factors that determined the fate of Scots. In Scotland, book printing started as late as 1508, the number of titles and of the copies printed was very small (and the total circulation was soon superseded by imported English books); moreover, the density of the Scots used even in Scottish productions decreased in the course of the 16C. Bald (1926) counted the books printed in Scots and English in Edinburgh before the early 17C. The modest number produced before 1560 was all in Scots, but the predominance ceased after 1580 and the publication of works in Scots came to an end after 1625 (cf. Görlach 1991a:19):

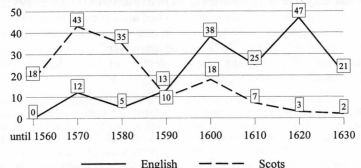

Fig. 3 Number of books printed in Scots and English in Edinburgh before the early 17C (total in English: 161, in Scots: 136)

This decline was partly because important printers like Waldegrave came from England, and partly because there was no institution supervising the purity of Scots employed in Scottish books – how could there have been when the most important book, the Bible, was in English from 1560 onwards?

In the 18C and 19C, Scottish publishing saw a new peak – but this was exclusively in St E. Macfarquhar printed and sold the *Encyclopædia Britannica* in 1768, and companies like Constable, Oliver & Boyd, Collins, Chambers, Blackwood, A. & C. Black, and Nelson established Edinburgh (and Glasgow) as a second centre of book publishing after London. Many firms concentrated on school books, thus making correct English available to increasing numbers of learners and effectively spreading the southern, national language among 'North Britons'.

Ex 4 Try to assess the share Scottish publishers had in the production of grammars and dictionaries of English in the 19C (cf. Görlach 1998b).

1.4.2 *Education*

The fact that Scotland had three universities in 1500 – when there were only two in England – underlines the high standard of learning in the country. In the schools, too, education was excellent and available to the landowning classes, although the Act of 1496 probably paints too positive a picture:

t7 It is statute and ordanit throw all the realme, that all barronis and frehaldaris, that ar of substance put
   thair eldest sonnis and airis to the sculis, fra thai be aucht or nyne yeiris of age, and till remane at the
   grammar sculis, quhill thae be competentlie foundit and haue perfite latyne. And thereftir to remane
   thre yeris at the sculis of art and Jure, sua that thai may haue knawlege and vnderstanding of the
5 lawis   (quoted from Daiches 1981:109)

Figures for school attendance are very uncertain until the 19C, but Scotland appears to have equalled standards in England. In 1826 the Statistical Account for Scotland stated:

t8 However humble their condition the peasantry in the southern districts can all read and are generally
   more or less skilful in writing and arithmetic, and under the disguise of their uncouth appearance
   they possess a laudable zeal for knowledge ... not generally found among the same class of men in
   other countries in Europe   (from Daiches 1981:111)

Again the estimate seems too generous; contrast George Lewis, a Dundee minister who said in 1834 that only one in 12 were enrolled in day schools (Daiches 1981:111). The particular linguistic problems Scottish children had are not even mentioned.

By the turn of the century, the establishment of a national inspectorate in 1845 and the Education (Scotland) Act of 1872, which introduced compulsory education (in English), had taken effect, speeding up the decline of Scots dialects (Williamson 1982/83). Sir James Wilson commented as early as 1915:

t9 There is no doubt that here, as elsewhere, the native dialect of the people is rapidly disappearing,
   and as each generation passes away, some of the good old pithy words and phrases pass away with
   it. Books and newspapers are teaching the people, even in remote villages, to think and speak in
   something like standard English. But the chief enemy of local dialects is the schoolmaster. He
5 rightly holds it one of his first duties to teach the village boys and girls to read, write, and speak as
   correct standard English as he can, and in pursuit of this aim discourages the use of local
   peculiarities of pronunciation and idiom.   (Wilson 1915:13)

Also compare Eugen Dieth's description of the situation in Aberdeenshire (1932:xviif., quoted in 2.4.6 below). Since the erosion of Scots has continued all through the 20C, the practical problems of teaching more Scots in schools – quite apart from the more difficult question of how to implement such plans – are immense (cf. 9.2).

1.4.3 *The model function of French and Latin*

French and Latin had been the major media for advanced teaching in the Middle Ages. The importance of French decreased in the 16C, although it remained considerable until the end of the Auld Alliance in 1560. For instance, it has been reported that of the "books printed down to 1560 which survive from identifiable Scottish libraries, well over 500 were printed in France, but only five are of English origin" (Simpson 1979: 16). However, the knowledge of French and its societal functions must have declined rapidly after 1560; even French emigrants went to London rather than to Edinburgh. This did not, however, stop cultural contacts – much of the intellectual climate in 18C Edinburgh appears to have been stimulated by France, including the 1768 *Encyclopædia Britannica* which was modelled on Diderot's *Encyclopédie* of 1751.

Latin was, by contrast, the dominant and permanent source of educational advancement. It was the medium in grammar schools and in the universities, so that James VI's utterance can be assumed to be representative: "they gar me speik Latin or I could speik Scottis" (quoted from Jack 1988:125). As regards scientific and scholarly texts, it is also clear that the problem of how to render terminology in a vernacular not equipped for this was the same in England and in Scotland. Skeyne, writing a treatise on the pestilence in 1586 and justifying the use of Scots for the uneducated readership he addressed, complained:

t10 And howbeit it become me rather (quha hes bestouit all my Zouthe in the Sculis) to had vrytin the samin in Latine, Zit vnderstanding sic interpryses had bene nothing profitable to the commoun and wulgar people, thocht expedient and neidfull to express the sam in sic langage as the vnlernit may be als weil satisfyit as Masteris of Clargie.   (quoted from Görlach 1991a:365)

Humanism in Scotland saw some of the most learned scholars in Europe, in particular historians, who naturally wrote in Latin. Although the relevance of Latin in education decreased in the 17C, and it was no longer used as a language for books printed in Britain, the knowledge of the language remained an unquestioned element in a gentleman's education and a necessary qualification for many professions, such as medicine or law (the latter discipline has, in Scotland, a remarkably large number of unadapted loanwords from Latin to the present day).

The excellence of Latin remained largely unquestioned. It is rare to find critical remarks relating to its inadequacies. John Corbett points to an aside made by John Bellenden who complained about the limitations of his Latin sources:

t11 I wate nocht gif I war to do ane profitabill werk, gif I wrate þe dedis of romanis sen the first begynnyng of rome; peraventure I dar nocht write þe samyn þocht I could. And ȝit I se þare werkis of lang begynnyng and richt divulgate to þe pepill, sen new authoris belevis Ilk day owthir to write þe said history with mair faith and sikkernes, or ellis be þare crafty eloquence traistis to vincuss the
5 rude langage of anciant authoris.   (1531, quoted from Corbett 1999:53)

1.4.4 *Translation*
    (Corbett 1999, Görlach 2002c)

Translation was, in Scotland as elsewhere, an important element of cultural exchange; it helped substantially to expand the functions and the expressiveness of the vernacular. A few illustrations will indicate its relevance for Scottish culture and the Scots language.

In the 16C, Douglas's rendering of the *Aeneid* (T6) and Bellenden's of *Livy* were the first proper translations of these works undertaken in Britain – long before there were English translations of these classic authors straight from the original languages. Both renderings set high standards of linguistic and rhetorical quality, but because of the political state of Scotland they did not give rise to literary traditions.

There were also important cases of 'internal' translation between Scots and English: Murdoch Nisbet produced the first full version of a Scots *New Testament* (c1520), basing his version on the ME Wycliffite text (which he adapted to make it intelligible to 16C Scots readers, 8.1.2). In contrast, the Earl of Surrey used for his translation of the *Aeneid* Gavin Douglas's (although it would be going too far to say that he 'translated' the Scots text), and William Harrison's famous Scottish *Chronicle*, Book V of Holinshed and source of Shakespeare's *Macbeth*, was largely based on Bellenden's translation of Boethius (Fig.17 and T8). The main purpose of 16C Scots translation was, as in England, to make encyclopedic information and classical and contemporary poetry and drama available to those without Latin – and refine the vernacular in the process. Sir David Lyndsay (T14) in particular stressed the need to supply religious texts in the mother tongue (which for him might have included an *English* Bible). European poetry was translated in great quantity (and excellent quality) at the court of James VI (cf. McClure 1993b).

It is significant that Scots largely ceased to be a medium for respectable literature after 1603 – there was no courtly culture and national language to be refined by foreign patterns adapted and adopted from translated texts. Translating, however, did not stop: William Drummond of Hawthornden gave us portions of Ovid (in ScE!), Sir Thomas Urquhart translated Rabelais (8.2.9), Allan Ramsay parts of Horace, La Motte and La Fontaine, and Struan Robertson also parts of Horace. But there was nothing comparable to the output of English translators – with excellent English renderings being easily available, most Scotsmen would not have seen any point in repeating the laborious exercise in their vernacular. However, it was the Scotsman Tytler who read his papers on translation in the Royal Society in 1790 and thus produced the earliest substantial treatise devoted to the discipline in Britain.

There was a fresh upsurge of translation activity in Scotland – and into *Scots* – in the 20C. The apparent motivation for authors like Alexander Gray, Hugh MacDiarmid, Douglas Young, J.K. Annand, Robert Garioch, Edwin Morgan and many others (cf. France & Glen's anthology, 1989) was to create a literary medium from a neglected Scots, by making it fit for rendering world literature, ranging from Ancient Greek to Russian, and from Latin to German. Such efforts culminate in one of the greatest prose works in 20C Scots, W.L. Lorimer's *New Testament in Scots* (T69). English sources were less frequently used, but there have of course been Scots versions of Shakespeare, most notably and appropriately of *Macbeth* (T72). Many modern 'translations' of foreign texts (especially theatre plays) into Scots are, however, Scotticizations of existing English translations.

The use of local Scots dialects in translation is comparatively rare. Robert Forbes's translation from Ovid's *Metamorphoses* (1742) is one of the earliest sustained attempts at a piece of writing in a distinctively NE dialect. The language of the poem features both semi-archaic literary words and NE vocabulary items, for several of which Forbes's (t12) is the first attested use.

The wight an' doughty Captains a'
Upo' their doups sat down;
A rangel o' the common fouk
In burachs a' stood roun.
5 *Ajax* bangs up, whase targe was sught
In seven fald o' hide;
An' bein' bouden'd up wi' wrath,
Wi' atry face he ey'd
The *Trojan* shore, an' a' the barks
10 That tedder'd saft did ly
Alang the Coast; an' raxing out
His gardies, loud did cry:
O Jove! The cause we here do plead,
An' unco' great's the staik;
15 Bat sall that sleeth *Ulysses* now
Be said to be my maik?
Ye ken right well, fan *Hector* try'd
Thir barks to burn an' scowder,
He took to speed o' fit, because
20 He cou'd na' bide the ewder.
Bat I, like birky, stood the brunt,
An' slocken'd out that gleed
Wi' muckle virr, an' syne I gar'd
The limmers tak' the speed.
25 'Tis better then, the cause we try
Wi' the wind o' our wame,
Than for to come in hanny grips
At sik a driry Time.
At threeps I am na' sae perquire,
30 Nor auld-farren as he,
But at banes-braken, it's well kent,
He has na' maughts like me.
For as far as I him excel
In touilzies fierce an' strong,
35 As far in chaft-taak he exceeds
Me, wi' his sleeked tongue.
My proticks an' my doughty Deeds,
O Greeks! I need na' tell,
For ther's nane here bat kens them well:
40 Lat him tell his himsel:
Which ay were done at glomin time,

Or dead hour o' the night,
An' deil ane kens except himsel,
for nae man saw the sight. (...)
45 Bat gin my wightness doubted were,
I wat my gentle bleed,
As being sin to *Telamon*,
Right sickerly does plead:
Wha, under doughty *Hercules*,
50 Great *Troy's* walls down hurl'd,
An' in a tight *Thessalian* Bark
To *Colchos'* harbour swirl'd.
An' *Æacus* my gutcher was,
Wha now in hell sits jidge,
55 Where a fun-stane does *Sisyphus*
Down to the yerd sair gnidge.
Great *Jove* himsel owns *Æacus*
To be his ain dear boy,
An' syne without a' doubt I am
60 The neist chiel' to his oye.
Bat thus in counting o' my etion
I need na' mak' sic din,
For it's well kent Achilles was
My father's brither sin:
65 An' as we're cousins, there's nae scouth
To be in ony swidders;
I only seek fat is my due,
I mean, fat was my brither's.
Bat why a thief, like *Sisyphus*,
70 That's nidder'd sae in hell,
Sud here tak' fittininment,
Is mair nae I can tell.
Sall then these arms be deny'd
To me, wha in this bruilzie
75 Was the first man that drew my durk,
Came flaught-bred to the toulzie?
An' sall this sleeth come farrer ben,
Wha was sae dev'lish surly,
He scarce wou'd gae a fit frae hame,
80 An' o' us a' was hurly?

(t12, Forbes 1742/1869: 2-5)

This experiment is parallelled by Benjamin B. Rogers' use of NE Scots for the speech of Spartans in his 1911 rendering of the *Lysistrata* (cf. excerpts in Bailey & Robinson 1973:113-4). By contrast, Stephen Mulrine's translation of Ronsard into Glaswegian (T60) and William J. Tait's into Shetlandic (T59) provoke questions of decorum and linguistic appropriateness – contrast the successful translations into these dialects of Wilhelm Busch's children's classic *Max und Moritz* (T71) or the perfect match achieved by Gilbert McKay who translated the Low German fairy tales of the Brothers Grimm into the dialect of a Banffshire fishing community (in Luke 1982). A similar problem is deliberately raised by Jamie Stuart's 'translation' of the Gospel into Glaswegian (1992). By contrast, non-standard originals seem to be particularly well suited for translation into local Scots (cf. Bill Findlay's translation of Gerhard Hauptmann's Silesian version of *Die Weber* (1998) or his and Martin Bowman's several adaptations of Michel Tremblay's playtexts written in Quebecois, e.g. 1991).

1.5   *Historical background and periodization*
(McClure 1994:24-46; Lynch [2]1992)

The coexistence of Gaelic, Scots and English in Scotland is the result of a complex history which is here summarized with particular reference to developments which had linguistic consequences.

79-83	First Roman invasions of Scotland
501-503	The Scots from Ireland, a Gaelic-speaking people, Christian in religion establish their kingdom of Dalriada in Argyll on the West coast and Isles of Scotland.
7C	First Anglo-Saxons (i.e. speakers of the OE ancestor of Scots) arrive and settle in what is now Southern Scotland; the area of Anglo-Saxon occupation remains limited to South-Eastern and Southern Scotland until the 12C
9C/10C	Scandinavian/Viking raids and settlements on Orkneys and Shetlands (Northern Isles), the Hebrides (Western Isles) and on the mainland; introduction of Norse/Norn to these areas
1058-93	Malcolm (III) Canmore introduces the feudal system, founds burghs and in 1066 marries the Anglo-Saxon princess Margaret (of Wessex); Anglo-Saxon becomes additional court language along with Gaelic
1072	William the Conqueror invades Lothian and Fife as a reaction to Malcolm's aggressions;
1240-66	Lordship of the Western Isles (= Hebrides) and the Isle of Man (later lost to England, 1286, and recaptured 1457) is taken from the Scandinavians; the Northern Isles and parts of Caithness remain Norwegian
1292-96	John Balliol is elected king with the support of Edward I of England and has to pay homage to his English liege lord at Newcastle
1295	'Auld Alliance' with France against England (until 1560)
1296	Edward I of England ('Hammer of the Scots', 1272-1307) begins his campaigns against Scotland (first 'War of Scotland' 1296-1304). The castles of Roxburgh, Edinburgh and Stirling fall; King John Balliol is taken prisoner at Montrose. The realm of Scotland is annexed
1297	Battle of Stirling Bridge; the Scots under Sir William Wallace defeat the English
1298	The Scots are defeated at Falkirk
1305	Wallace, as military leader of the defeated Scots, is executed in London.
1306-29	Robert I (the Bruce)
1309-28	Renewed warfare with England under Edward II (1307-27); 'War of Independence'.

1314	Battle of Bannockburn; the Scots under Bruce defeat the English
1320	Declaration of Arbroath addressed to the Pope requests the lifting of the sentence of excommunication on Robert and declares Scottish independence
1371	Beginning of the Stewart dynasty with Robert II (1371-90)
1376	Beginning of permanent written records in Scots with John Barbour's *Bruce*
1406-1437	James I (*1394), scholar and poet king; captive in England for the first 18 years of his reign (1406-1424); in 1437 murdered by his own nobles
1411	St Andrews University founded
1472	Full rights to Orkney and Shetland finally ceded to Scotland by Norway, since the dowry for Margaret (the daughter of Christian I of Denmark and Norway, who was married to James III of Scotland in 1469 in order to settle the dispute between the two states over the Western Isles) was not paid
1488-1513	James IV succeeds when aged only 15; scholar king and patron to William Dunbar, Gavin Douglas and other Renaissance makars.
1496	Education Act encourages grammar school attendance (acquisition of 'perfyte Latyn') for sons of barons and freeholders
1503	James IV married to Margaret of England (the "Marriage of the Thistle and the Rose").
1507	Printing starts in Edinburgh by Chepman and Millar
1513	New campaign against England results in the disastrous Battle of Flodden; James IV killed in battle and Scots defeated
1513-42	James V (comes to the throne in 1528, aged 16)
1542	Defeat of the Scots at Solway Moss; James V dies shortly afterwards
1542-67	Mary (assumes the throne in 1561, aged 19)
1560	Beginning of the Reformation: Protestant Church founded by John Knox.
1567-1625	James VI (assumes the throne in 1585, aged 19)
1587	Execution of Mary, Queen of Scots
1603	Union of the Crowns: James VI, King of Scots, becomes James I of England and Scotland
1609	Statutes of Iona: a deposition by James VI to 'civilize' the Highlands, directed against Catholicism and the use of Gaelic.
1610-25	Ulster Plantation: Scots settle in N Ireland
1616	Education act ratifying the Statutes of Iona: contains a much more explicit stricture on the 'barbarity' of Gaelic; see T20
1688	'Glorious Revolution'
1692	'Massacre of Glencoe' (attempt to force the Highland chiefs to submit to governmental control by force)
1707	Union of the Parliaments: The Treaty of Union, uniting the Parliaments of England and Scotland, creating the United Kingdom of Great Britain, but keeping separate the state religions, educational systems, and laws of the two kingdoms.
1712	First literary club, the Easy Club, founded in Edinburgh by Ramsay (writer and editor) and Ruddiman (Jacobite printer).
1715 & 1745	Unsuccessful Jacobite rebellions of the Stewart line against Hanoverian succession
1746	Charles (Bonnie Prince Charlie), the Stewart Pretender, is defeated at Culloden
1750-80	The Scottish Enlightenment and Age of 'Improvement'
1754	The Select Society is formed in Edinburgh (David Hume, 1711-77, founder member); active until 1763.
1760-3	Macpherson's 'translations' of the poems of 'Ossian'
1768-71	*Encyclopædia Britannica* published in Edinburgh
1800s-30s	Highland Clearances: expulsion of Highlanders from their small farms (enforced emigration) to introduce large-scale sheep farming
1843	Disruption splits Established Church of Scotland; Free Church of Scotland founded; results in new organisation of schooling and poor relief

1872	Education Act introduces compulsory education (equivalent bill passed in England in 1870)
1920s	Beginning of the *Scottish Literary Renaissance* (Hugh MacDiarmid 1892-1978, and others)
1979	Devolution referendum secures a narrow majority of 51% but the bill fails because of insufficient turn-out at the election (thus, less than 40% of total electorate support devolution)
1997	Labour win general election and hold referendum, in which a decisive 76% vote in favour of a Scottish parliament
1998	Scots is included in the European Charter of Minority Languages
1999	Scottish parliament elected; SNP comes second after Labour, who form a coalition government with the Liberals; the vote is interpreted as a defeat of the separatists

Ex 5 Which of the historical dates listed can be assumed to have had the most important consequences for the use of Scots and attitudes towards it?

Germanic invaders from the continent conquered parts of what is now Scotland from c600 onwards, founding the kingdom of Bernicia in the 7C. The border region remained linguistically mixed, but the Ruthwell Cross (close to Dumfries) documents that the Anglian dialect of OE was used in the region. Scandinavian settlers of the 9/10C changed the character of Anglian, so that when new Germanic expansions from further South into Scotland came in the 11/12C, they spread 'Northumbrian English' with a strong Scandinavian component, hence the linguistic similarity of northern English and Scots. As this expansion continued, the Gaelic speech of Dalriada (which had incorporated the Pictish kingdom further north under Kenneth McAlpin in the mid 9C) receded.

Several members of the Anglo-Saxon royal family and some of their followers fled to Scotland after the Norman Conquest of 1066; the marriage of Malcolm of Scotland with Margaret of Wessex established English more permanently at the Edinburgh court – but also gave rise to political antagonism between the two countries. Also, the introduction of the feudal system and the establishment of burghs, which quickly became centres of English speech, changed the structure of Scottish society. Until the 13C the majority of the Scots appear to have been Gaelic-speaking, but the use of English grew steadily – which made Scotland (with French at court and Latin added as a written prestige language) effectively a quadrilingual society, not counting the Scandinavian speakers on many of the isles and in the far north. When in the late 14C the House of Stewart emerged as the dynasty which was to rule Scotland for the next three centuries, the national language was clearly the northern form of English whose norms were based on the speech of the educated speakers at the court and the 'good towns' (as George Puttenham phrased it in 1589 for EModE, cf. Görlach 1991a:237) – just as London English provided the norms for England.

The political antagonism between the two kingdoms did not end close cultural links, something which is most clearly evident from the influence that English literature had on the makars (court poets) at Edinburgh (cf. 8.2). In fact, the sense of linguistic identity among the Scots seems to have been less well developed than the sense of political and religious distinctness. As a consequence, Scots never came to be cultivated as a full national language at the time when the replacement of Latin (and French) demanded such a medium. When James VI of Scotland became king of the United Kingdom in

1603, there was no consistent opposition to the takeover by written southern English – which had of course been current well before the union (cf. 9).

All these developments were more or less restricted to the Lowlands, the Celtic communities of the Highlands being largely outside the political nation right into the18C, although some attempts were made to 'civilize' Highlanders by the introduction of the 'proper' language and religion (see the *Statutes of Iona* of 1609 and the Education Act of 1616 demanding the establishment of parish schools, T20).

Scottish political independence was lost with the Union of the Parliaments in 1707, but economic recovery started from 1720 onwards, the two developments having conflicting results for the sense of Scottish identity. On the one hand, a nostalgic interest in past greatness documented itself in the re-editing of old poets, followed by the creation of a new tradition of the literary use of Scots by Allan Ramsay, Robert Fergusson, Robert Burns and, later on, Sir Walter Scott – none of whom ever intended to reinstate it as a full language. At the same time the leading intellectual role of Edinburgh as 'The Athens of the North' went together with the acceptance, by intellectuals and literati, of the spoken English of the south. Enlightenment thinkers like David Hume, William Robertson, Hugh Blair, Henry Mackenzie, Adam Fergusson, Adam Smith, and (in Aberdeen) James Beattie felt that their European mission as North Britons could only be expressed through a world language, and not a provincial idiom.

The 18C also saw the abortive attempts of the Stewart Pretenders to reclaim the British throne: the Jacobite Risings first in 1715 by James and then in 1745 by Charles Edward Stewart (Bonnie Prince Charlie). The defeat of the later rising led to the thorough conquest of the Highlands, which resulted in the destruction of its clan structures, its local economy and a drastic decline of the Gaelic language, which was to be replaced by school English (the Education Act 1872 completely eradicated the use of Gaelic from schools).

The historical developments sketched above are important also for defining periods of Scots: whereas its early history up to about 1375 is one of an English dialect, a following phase of growing divergence can be assumed until a norm came to be established by 1450, its (semi-)independence ending with the Union in 1603, or with its aftermath in 1707. From 1700 on, the variety is rightly called Modern Scots, a major watershed also recognized by the great dictionaries (cf. 7.2).

The periods can be correlated with the history of English as follows (cf. fig. 4, p.18). In addition, further subperiods can be delimited as follows: 1560-1603 saw a massive anglicization of the written language following the acceptance of the English Bible, and 1760-1832 the Scottish Enlightenment and widespread anglicization of the speech of the (urban) upper social ranks.

		North of the border	South of the border
		–1100	OE (Old Anglian)	OE (West Saxon)

			North of the border	**South of the border**
Older Scots		–1100	OE (Old Anglian)	OE (West Saxon)
	Early	1100 – 1375	N ME (pre-literary Scots)	Middle E.
		1375 – 1450	first texts characteristically Scots (Early literary Scots)	beginning re-establishment as a full language; literary peak in Chaucer etc.
	Middle	1450 – 1603	heyday of Scots poetry; beginning of Edinburgh norms after 1500	end of ME dialects as significant literary medium; standard E. established on London basis
		1603 – 1700	end of semi-independent Scots as a written norm; period of transition	establishment of E. as a national language for all registers/text types
Modern Scots		1700 – 1832	virtual end of remaining distinctness in Scottish documents; re-establishment of Scots for some types of literature; prescriptive correctness (according to E. norms) in writing	homogenization of written E.; Augustan English; prescriptive norms, cultivation of 'polite' style
		1832 – 1914	takeover of spoken English norms almost nationwide	foundations of homogeneous speech laid among the educated
		1914 –	same as in England	expansion of literacy, democratization of education, drastic reduction of dialects as consequences of mobility, compulsory education, cheap reading matter and modern communication

Fig. 4 Periods of English and Scots compared

1.6 Indigenous languages other than Scots and English

In the 15C, Andrew of Wyntoun in his *Original Cronikill* mentioned five languages once used in Scotland: "Bretis speech and Inglis syne,/ Pichtis, Scottis and Latyne" (McClure 1995d:45). If we take Scottis to refer to the Gaelic of the Scots from Ireland (McClure 1995d), then there is no mention of the differences between the two Anglic varieties, nor indeed is any reference made to Scandinavian Norn in Caithness and Sutherland. (Since Orkney and Shetland were not acquired before 1472, they did not form part of Scotland for Wyntoun). The situation was different for Harrison in 1587. In his chapter "Of the languages spoken in this iland", he mentions English, Cornish and Welsh (British) as indigenous in England, and

t13 even so manie are in Scotland, if you accompt the English speach for one ... wild Scots ... speake
good Irish which they call Gachtlet ... In the Iles of the Orchades ... & such coasts of Britaine as
doo abbut vpon the same, the Gottish or Danish speach is altogither in vse, and also in Shetland
(quoted from Görlach 1991a:235-6)

Scotland has, then, always been a multilingual society, though the proportion of Scotsmen competent in one language or the other has changed over time, and individual bilingualism has decreased – or the usefulness and communicative range of the individual language in question has. Modern census figures providing the basis of statistics, normally based on self-reports and subject to political evaluation, can be as misleading (the world over) as can be maps showing the proportion of speakers in individual regions – which tend not to take population density into account. Thus parts of the the maps of the Highlands and Islands in figure 5 suggest a much more important role of Gaelic in 20C Scotland than reflected in the absolute numbers of speakers.

Withers (1984) has also drawn attention to the fact that knowledge of Gaelic and bilingualism can mean very different things, depending on how much use is made of the minority language, on the proportion of its use in written or spoken speech acts, on its restrictions to or associations with specific topics, on the range of addressees it is used with and its degree of prestige or stigma. Also, what are the consequences of the fact that there have been times when Glasgow had more Gaelic speakers than the Highlands?

Ex 6 Summarize the objections against a naïve count of speakers of a minority language (following Withers 1984).

1.6.1 *Pictish*
(Price 1984:20-27, Jackson 1955)

Pictish is of minimal interest for present-day Scotland, even in a historical dimension. All attempts to identify the character of the language – documented (debatably) by a few incomprehensible short texts in Ogham script, loanwords in Gaelic, some placename elements (1.7.2) and personal names – have apparently failed. If Pictish represents indeed a pre-Celtic (pre-Indo-European) language, then it is tempting to connect it with Basque or Berber, but no such relationship has been established convincingly.

1.6.2 *British/Cymric*

Whereas Gaelic was largely imported from Ireland, the indigenous Celtic languages/dialects, especially in the southern parts, were closer to Welsh. Cymric may have survived in Galloway until the 12C but there is not enough evidence to be certain. Its influence on Scots (and N ME) is largely speculative (or concealed by Gaelic).

1.6.3 *Scandinavian*
(Barnes 1984)

Norse and Danish dialects were spoken in various parts of Scotland in different periods. The 10C Danelaw settlement did not affect the Lowlands directly, but only via the OE spoken by many of the later settlers. At the same time Scandinavian presence was dominant in Orkney and Shetland, Caithness and Sutherland, and the Hebrides. By 1500, Norn survived only in Orkney and Shetland, but the incorporation of the islands into the Scottish state in 1472 started a protracted language shift towards Scots with the ultimate death of Norn there, too. The fusion of two closely related Germanic languages (OE and Scandinavian) in 10C Anglia repeated itself in a way as two Germanic languages in Orkney and Shetland merged when their speakers shifted to the more prestigious Scots (before this itself came to be superseded by English). Barnes (1984:355) names five possible reasons for this shift in Shetland (Orkney had been infiltrated earlier, being much closer to the mainland):

1) Before the Reformation in 1560, Scots became the language of the economic and social local elite, the administration, the courts and the church – all this shows that it had higher prestige than Norn.
2) After 1560, Scots became the medium of religious discourse (using English Bibles, catechisms and psalters, possibly with Scots pronunciation).
3) Speakers of Scots from the Lowlands (especially Angus, Fife and the Lothians) migrated to the northern isles.
4) Trade with Lowland Scotland increased as connections with Norway became weaker.
5) Apparently, at least some Scots was taught in schools in the early phase.

The history of Norn is of special relevance for Scots because of the following facts:
1) Scots (and not English) was first adopted as a prestige language to replace the stigmatized vernacular Norn.
2) The specific merging of the two languages, a shift during which the distinction between the two must have broken down for many speakers resulted in enormous preponderance of Norn elements in the local Scots dialects (some 10,000 lexical items of Norn descent were collected in the late 19C by Jakobsen).
3) The notable preservation of Shetlandic Scots (as against ScE) has to do with the linguistic and geographical distance, but also with a strong sense of local identity largely based on ethnicity, the pride of descending from Scandinavians and being different from mainland Scots.

Ex 7 Contrast the connection between dialect and ethnic/regional identity in Shetland with attitudes elsewhere in Scotland.

1.6.4 *Gaelic*
(Withers 1984, MacKinnon 2001)

Gaelic is now Scotland's only surviving indigenous language outside the English-Scots continuum. It remained dominant even in the Lowlands until the 11C, was there supplanted by Scots by 1500, the Highland line forming a comparatively stable language boundary between Gaelic and Scots until 1746 (cf. fig. 5, which shows the expansion of Norman rule, and with it, of Scots, in the Middle Ages). The stability is explained by extreme cultural differences: the languages were mutually unintelligible; many Highlanders had remained Roman Catholic; and Highland territory was less fertile and was regarded as bleak and unattractive by Lowlanders (the love of the Highland landscape is a Romantic/Victorian innovation). The social structure, economy and culture of the Highlanders was regarded as strange to the extent that it was ignored or despised. That the Lowlanders felt superior to the 'uncivilized Highlands' is documented by a large number of texts. An early example is *The Flyting* between Dunbar and Kennedy (T4, ca. 1500), in which each poet takes the culture and the mother tongue of the other as a basis for his insults.

There were explicit attempts to 'civilize' the Celts from the late 16C on. James VI advised his son in 1599:

t14 Follow forth the course I have intended, in planting Colonies among them of answerable In-Lands
     subjects, that within short time may reforme and civilize the best inclined among them; rooting out
     or transporting the barbarous and stubborne sort, and planting ciuilitie in their roomes.
                                                              (*Basilicon Doron*, quoted from Price 1984:52)

The same James, now James I of England and Scotland, continued these plans ten years later when responsible for the *Statutes of Iona* (and the ensuing Education Act, T20).

However, if it had not been for the defeat of Bonnie Prince Charlie, the anglicization of the Highlands would have taken much longer. With the 'pacification' of the Highland Celts came the break-up of the clan structure and an end to the small farming communities, which culminated in the Clearances and large-scale emigration. The region has not recovered, and the Celtic language was doomed to continuous shrinkage, as the following maps show – with all the reservations mentioned above:

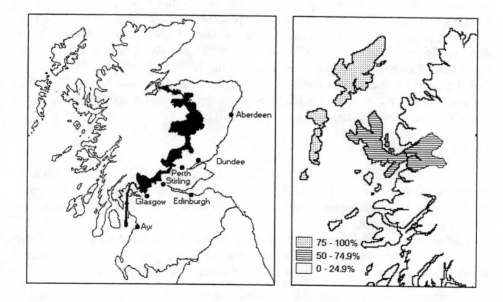

Losses of Gaelic 1698–1806   Percentage of population over 31 able to speak
                                                                                      Gaelic in 1981

Fig. 5 The decline of Scottish Gaelic (based on Withers 1984)

From Macpherson's fake 'translations' of the poems of *Ossian* in the 1760s, there has been a romantic glorification of Highland culture – but this came after the political threat had been broken and it had little to do with economic reality. Thus the new situation certainly did not stop the Highlanders' shift to English, which for many opened the opportunities of emigration or at least a job in Glasgow (compare the linguistic and social conditions in Ireland).

The history of Gaelic and its speech community is relevant for Scots mainly for two reasons:

1) After 1746 the stigmatized vernacular was replaced not by Scots (as it still was a hundred years earlier in Shetland), but by English, and the Highland Line was thus transformed from a language boundary to a dialect boundary.
2) The cultural distance between the two communities led to the exchange of only a very small number of loanwords; Gaelic has been affected more by English in the course of the last centuries than by the neighbouring Scots dialects (cf. 9.1.5).

Ex 8 Consider the likelihood of Gaelic achieving an increase in numbers of speakers and functions in present-day Scotland.

A specifically Scottish phenomenon is the large-scale 19C immigration of Gaelic speakers of the Highlands, and Irish and IrE speakers from Ireland particularly into Glasgow and Galloway (cf. Macafee 1994a:13). Although the Lowlanders and the immigrant Irish did not mix easily, some traits of IrE appear to have influenced the speech of Glasgow. It is, however, difficult to attribute these features clearly to Irish influence, since 're-imported' Ulster Scots is derived mainly from South-western dialects of Scots (Macafee 1994a:28). It is also difficult to distinguish how far IrE and not Highland English influenced the dialects of the Western areas in the 19C. Present-day Highland English enjoys considerable prestige, being more or less equivalent to ScE, but in the 19C, many of the Highlanders migrating into Glasgow had acquired it imperfectly as a second language.

1.6.5 *Other languages*

Scotland's close contacts with France, the Netherlands and the Baltic region led to some in-migration of foreigners in the 15-17C, but the numbers of speakers were too small, and their geographical dispersal too wide to allow them to hand on their languages to succeeding generations.

Scotland has never had large numbers of speakers of Yiddish, Romany, Shelta, Polari etc. which are more widely recorded for England in the 19C. This is what Hamish Henderson has to say on one of these marginal groups, the tinkers:

t15   the tinkers use a cover-language known as 'cant'. The cant of the tinker-gipsies of Galloway and southeast Scotland has quite a strong admixture of Romany in it, but north of the Forth-Clyde line the amount of recognizable Romany ... is hardly more than 15 per cent. The tinkers of the north and west, whose native language is Gaelic (or was, until very recently), have a cover-tongue of
   5   their own which resembles one of the secret languages of Ireland. Their name for it is 'Beurlacheard', or 'lingo of the cairds'   (in Daiches 1981:378).

Note, however, that a number of originally Gypsy words have spread into (SW, S) Scots and are thus recorded in recent dictionaries, such as *gaave* 'large village', *gadgie* 'man', *jowldie* 'money' and *manishee* 'woman'.

Recent immigration, too, from Asia, Africa and the Caribbean, has concentrated on urban England, in particular London and the Midlands. Still there are considerable numbers of speakers settled particularly in and around the industrial centres of Scotland who have none of the indigenous varieties as their first languages. Usually, they either speak English as a second or foreign language or learn ScE – not Scots or Gaelic.

1.7 *Place names*
(Nicolaisen 1976, 1977)

The value of the study of names for linguistics is limited (obviously excepting dialectology), but the evidence is highly relevant for the reconstruction of settlement patterns, conquests, and political, social and religious history. A convincing illustration of such uses is the map printed in Montgomery & Gregg (1997:574; cf. fig. 15), which combines the densities of Scottish-derived second names, Presbyterianism and the frequency of Scots dialect features in Ulster. For Scotland, river names and place names are often important evidence for extinct languages: names are likely to preserve such data, as amber encloses the proverbial insect.

Pictish: there are few elements which are uncontroversially Pictish and whose meaning is known (for example *pett* 'piece of land' as in *Pitlochry* and some 200 other places, *aber* 'river mouth' as in *Aberdeen*, where Q-Celtic has *inver* as in *Inverness*). Pictish names are concentrated in the NE where the Picts retained their independence to the 9C: *Buchan, Mearns* and *Moray* are also claimed to be of Pictish origin.

Cumbric names are frequent in Strathclyde and Lothian, where P-Celtic dialects were spoken and in Galloway where they may have survived into the 12C: compare *Glasgow* 'green hollow', *Linlithgow* 'lake in the moist hollow' and names containing *pen* 'head, end'.

Gaelic names are very common in the West, where the conquest of Scotland by the Irish of *Dal Riada* (the 'Scots' from Antrim) started in Argyll around 500; items like *bal-* 'town', *glen-* 'valley' and *kil-* 'church' often precede the other element specified by these names, as is common in Celtic languages, as opposed to the English order of elements in compound names: compare *Kilmarnock, Kilbride, Kilmartin, Balfour* and *Glencoe* with names like *Hamilton, Annandale,* and *Selkirk*.

Norse: Scandinavian-derived names dominate in Orkney and Shetland and are frequent in Sutherland and Caithness (all these county-names themselves are from Norse). In the Hebrides, Scandinavian names are often opaque since they have been adapted to Gaelic pronunciation, as they are in areas of mixed settlement (including Galloway).

Anglian: The existence of OE-derived names in the SE gives us important clues to the early settlement where names ending in *-ingham* and *-ington*, *-worth* and *-burgh* point to foundations of the 7-9C.

The variegated history of Scotland has left us with a remarkably large number of names which are hybrid, misunderstood (prompting folk-etymological re-interpretations), translated or discontinued (although renaming does not appear to have been as frequent as it was in the 9/10C Danelaw). In spite of all this blending, the two maps in figure 6 (showing concentrations of names of different origins) still capture much of the settlement history of Scotland. The first combines two maps from Nicolaisen (1976:95 and 102): it indicates on the one hand place-names, and thereby settlement areas, of the 'island' Scandinavians on the northern and western coast, ranging from Shetland to Argyll and Bute, with -*dalr* 'dale' as a second element. On the other hand, it shows 'Lake District' Scandinavian names on -*thveit* and -*kirk* in northern England and southern Scotland. Although the elements must have been available to both groups, they were predominantly used by one of them respectively, so that their distributions are neatly complementary. Figure 6a contains only selective evidence of Nicolaisen's research (1976), which yields a few sets of contrasting items such as West Coast -*stathr, -setr, -bólstathr, -dalr* as against Southern Scotland -*byr, -fell, -thveit, -kirk* (cf. further maps in Nicolaisen 1976).

A similar complementarity can be seen in figure 6b, which combines Anglian placenames in the SE and Gaelic names in the NW – although here the exclusive distribution of course depends on quite different factors, illustrating the first advance of Anglians northward in the 7C to 9C. The elements here mapped are *wīc, hām* and *worth* (Nicolaisen 1976:75; similar distributions are found with *ingtun, ingham, bōtl, bōthl+tun*, Nicolaisen, 1976:74). They are combined with Gaelic *baile* (Nicolaisen, 1976:137; cf. similar distributions of *achadh*, p.140, or with a stronger concentration in the west, of *cill*, p.142).

Ex 9 Can you detect a connection between placename evidence and the traditional classification of dialects of Scots (cf. fig. 6a, b)?

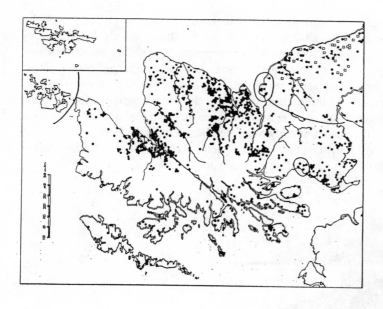

Early Anglian names (containg *wīc*, *hām* and *worth*) in former Bernicia, neatly complementary to Celtic placenames (here based on names containing *baile*, concentrating on the NE and SW)

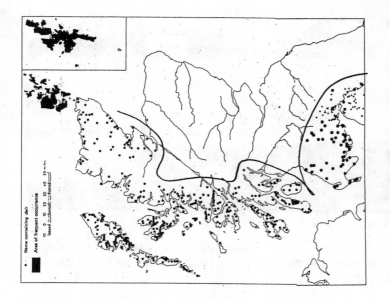

'Lake District' Scandinavian placenames (containing *-thveit* and *-kirk*) are confined to the SW of Scotland where they overlap with Celtic names – but not with 'island' Scandinavian names in the NW (evidence here based on names containing *-dalr*)

Fig. 6 Placenames and settlement history (maps combined from Nicolaisen 1976, 1977)

2 Varieties of Scots

2.1 Introduction

No language is completely homogeneous. Linguistic reality is characterized by variation. This is regulated by situation; within the resulting orderly heterogeneity individual users have to conform to pragmatic conventions. This ability constitutes their communicative competence. In monolingual societies this is regulated by a stylistic continuum of forms within the same language. However, most speech communities (including Scotland right into the present time) use different languages for different purposes. Although Scottish society has become more monolingual over the centuries, there is still a choice of language for many of its members, especially between Scots and English (and Gaelic and English on the Western Isles). A rough survey of this dynamic development can be broken up according to text types as follows:

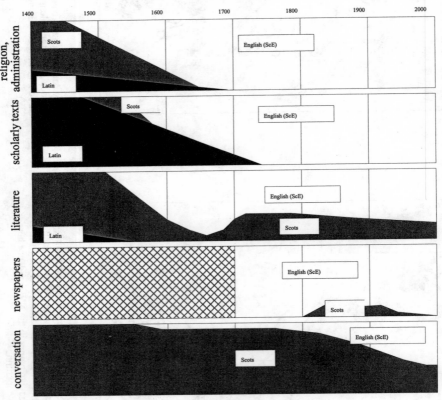

Fig. 7 Text types and language choices in the Lowlands 1400 – 2000

A comparison shows that Scots is much stronger in Scotland than English dialects in England, but that the reduction of its functions (i.e. replacement by ScE) follows the same tendency in principle.

Ex 10 Contrast the suggested distribution of languages in Scotland with the graph used to illustrate the situation in England (Fig. 8): what are the apparent similarities, and how are the differences to be explained?

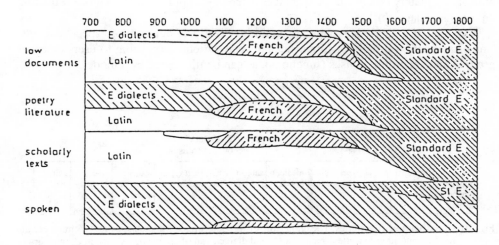

Fig. 8 Functional distribution of major languages in selected domains in England 700-1900 (quoted from Görlach 1992:738)

The following graph shows a similar survey for the Highlands:

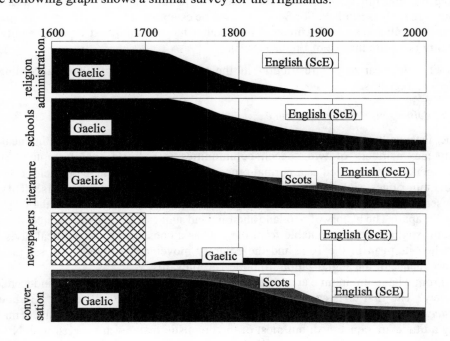

Fig. 9 Text types and language choices in the Highlands 1600-2000

The illustration combines the functional reduction of Gaelic with the ongoing regional erosion. Since the spread of English was largely effected through the schools, Scots is almost completely absent from the choices offered, except for border regions reflecting an early language shift.

Varieties of a single language are again idealizations, but on more specific levels. The classification usually distinguishes between varieties according to users (speaker groups) and according to uses (functions), as can be illustrated by a model:

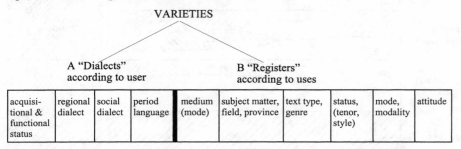

VARIETIES

A "Dialects" according to user				B "Registers" according to uses					
acquisi-tional & functional status	regional dialect	social dialect	period language	medium (mode)	subject matter, field, province	text type, genre	status, (tenor, style)	mode, modality	attitude

Fig. 10 Classification of varieties. The choice of A is predetermined for each speaker (within a certain range – but other varieties, such as a second dialect, can of course be *learnt*); in B, one variety of each category must be selected in accordance with situational appropriateness. A + B make up the individual *realization*; recurring (preferred) choices make up the *idiolect*. (Adapted from Görlach 1992:740).

Note that the full range of varieties illustrated in the graph is only found in a full language such as English. For Scots, it has to be established first whether the language is used at all for a certain function or whether the medium, text type, formality or intention require the use of English (ScE).

Ex 11   Summarize the restriction in the use of present-day Scots according to registers.

2.2   *Divergence and convergence*

The distance between two related systems is likely to increase when communication between members of two speech communities is reduced or interrupted. Such divergence is recognized as a normal process in dialectology where obstacles such as mountain ridges, rivers or political boundaries result in reduced intercourse. This, in consequence, reduces the necessity of linguistic accommodation and causes the varieties to drift apart. The history of Scotland and England suggests that the divergence of Scots (from Anglian) became notable from the 14C as a consequence of political division, reached its peak in the 16C, and the contrary movement, convergence, set in as a consequence of the anglicization from the 16C onwards.

From what point in time are we, then, entitled to speak of 'Scots' as an independent variety? The first texts commonly accepted as Scots date to the late 14C. Barbour's *Bruce* (T1) and the *Scottish Saints' Legends* are clearly Scottish as far as subject matter and attitude are concerned, but most of the linguistic features are shared with N ME. The separate character of Scots becomes more obvious in the 15C; this is the consequence of two related developments:

1) *convergence and divergence in*
2) *Scotland - look at Chaucers work for references, appendices*

n N England (where they slowly
d standard) as against Edinburgh
rd Scots).

dization makes northern features
elling, and in the lexis of certain
.
ivergence than we might expect.
e Spanish ambassador at the court
guage is as different from English
1995d:48).

d from and imitated Chaucer and
ge boundary, just like James I two
s's famous programmatic verdict
1513; cf. T6/1-17) that we get an
lage. The fact that Douglas makes
. Scottis' and 'Sudron' or 'Inglys'

as clear as he does may well be a consequence of his having lived in England from 1505 to 1509 – an experience that was quite uncommon for Scotsmen in his time (cf. McClure 1995d:51). Contacts involving the spoken level were rare (though there were, it is alleged, interpreters for Scots employed in the harbour of 16C London).

Other writers must have continued to feel that the great 'Inglis' poets continued to be part of the national heritage. When Bannatyne compiled his major collection of Scottish poetry in 1568, he included a Scotticized version of the song of Troilus from Chaucer (t16) and – apparently without even realizing the fact that the text was English – a few verses from Lydgate's "Temple of Glass" (t17, cf. MacQueen 1970).

GEOFFREY CHAUCER, *The song of Troylus* (t16)

Gife no luve is, o God quhat feill I so?
And gif luve is, quhat thing and quhiche is he?
Gife luve be gud, frome quhence cummys my wo?
Gife it be wicke, a wondir thinketh me
5 quham every turment and adversite
that cummeth of him, may to me savery think;
for ay thrust I the more that iche it drink.

And gif that at mine awin lust I brenne,
frome whence cummys my waling and my playnt?
10 Gife harme agree me, quhairto plene I thane?
I not, ne quhy unwery that I faint.
O quick deth! O sweit harme so queynt!
How may of thee in me be suche quantete,
bot gif that I consent that it so be?

15 And gif I consent, I wrongfully
complene, ywis. Thus possed to and fro
all steirles within a bot am I. (fol. 230ʳ)

JOHN LYDGATE (t17)

In to my hairt emprentit is so soir
hir schap, hir forme and eik hir seymlines,
hir port, hir cheir, hir gudnas mair and mair,
hir womanheid and eik hir gentilnes,
5 hir trewth, hir faith and also hir meiknes,
with all verteous, iche set in his degre;
thair is no lak bot onlie off pete.

Hir sad demenyng, of will nocht variable,
off louke benyng and rut of all plesans,
10 and exampillair to all that bene stable,
discreit, prudent, of wisdome sufficiens,
mirrour of wit, grund of gud governans,
a warld of bewty compasit in hir face,
quhois persant luk did throcht my hart race.

15 Quhat wondir is than thocht I be with dreid
inly supprysit for to askin grace
of hir that is a quene of womanheid? (fol. 230ᵛ)

t16-17 Poems by Chaucer and John Lydgate in the Bannatyne manuscript collection

Ex 12 Do any 'Sudron' features remain in the adaptation of the Chaucer and Lydgate texts in the Bannatyne MS (t16-17)?

The different character of Scots was sometimes seen in a positive light, when its greater purity and Germanic type was stressed, mainly between 1560 and 1630. One of the earliest English commentators was John Hart who stated in 1569:

t18 Some thinke Scottish speach more auncient Englishe than as we now speake here in England, yet
there is no liuing English man, so much affected to write his English as they doe Scottish, which
they write as they speake, and that in manye wordes, more neare the Latine, from whence both we
and they doe deriue them, as fruct for fruit, and fructfull for fruitfull, disponed for disposed or
5 distributed, humely for humbly, nummer for number, pulder for pouder, saluiour for sauiour, and
compt for account, and diuerse others, wherein we pronounce not those letters which they do, &
therfore write them not as reason is. Yet in others we do excéede with them, as the b in doubt, c
and h in aucthoritie, i in souldiour, o in people, s in baptisme, p in corps, and in condempned, and
certain like.   (*An Orthographie*, 1569: 18v-19r; quoted from Görlach 1991a: 57)

In their written forms the two languages ceased to diverge further from 1550 onwards, as a consequence of more and more English elements being taken over into all text types that were formerly available for Scots and of an increasing preference for shared items rather than specifically Scots ones. This internal borrowing may be seen as an acknowledgement of the 'superiority' of English – though English itself was suffering from an inferiority complex vis-à-vis Latin, at least until 1580.

However, occasional difficulties in understanding Scots texts were bound to arise. When Harrison based his "History of Scotland", written for Holinshed's Chronicles (1587, excerpts in Görlach 1991a:334-44), on Bellenden's Scots translation of Boethius' Latin version (T8), he admitted that it was sometimes difficult to understand his Scots source and that the Latin original provided valuable assistance:

t19 I haue chosen rather, onely with the losse of three or foure dayes to translate Hector out of the
Scottish (a tongue verie like vnto ours) than with more expense of time to diuise a newe, or follow
the Latin copie ... Hetherto I haue translated Hectors description of Scotland out of the Scottish
into the English toung, being not a little ayded therein by the Latine.
(1577, quoted from Görlach 1991a:21-2)

This partly explains why he sometimes made mistakes such as when he rendered "remembring þe weirdis gevin to him" as "The *woords* also of the three *weird* sisters, would not of his mind", thus giving rise to Shakespeare's *weird sisters* and the consequent misunderstanding of *weird* as an adjective meaning 'bizarre', rather than a noun meaning 'fate'.

From the English point of view, Scots was even more deficient in elegance and elaborateness than English. This was pointed out by Harrison in 1587:

t20 The Scottish english hath beene much broader and lesse pleasant in vtterance than ours, because
that nation hath not till of late indeuored to bring the same to any perfect order ... Howbeit in our
time the Scottish language endeuoreth to come neere, if not altogither to match our toong in
finenesse of phrase, and copie of words ...   (quoted from Görlach 1991a:235)

Views on the differences between English and Scots being, then, largely based on the written standard forms, it is obvious that

1) the restrictions of Scots in written and formal registers and its ultimate replacement by English in all written genres outside literature ended the divergence before a fully functional standard Scots was achieved in the 16C, and
2) the drifting apart of Scots dialects continued, and possibly even speeded up, since they were no longer 'roofed' (*überdacht*) by a cognate standard language.

When 16C diglossia was increasingly replaced by continua of Scots dialects and ScE as their end points, this must have resulted for many Scotsmen in a fusion of the two systems which were no longer kept apart except as stylistic markers depending on medium, formality and register. (In Aitken's tentative terms, dialect-switchers turned into style-drifters, 1979:86). A telling example is provided by W. Alexander who had to edit the (English and Scots) texts sent in to the *Aberdeen Free Press*. By the 19C, the ongoing anglicization apparently made it impossible for most writers to stick to 'pure varieties'; therefore the editor's dialect competence was required:

t21 My tongue runs freest i' the native Doric. An' so in place o' fine English, which was spoken by none but the gentry in my youth – though ye'll get it in ilka ane's mou now-a-days – we'se leave the Editor to dicht it up as weel's he can in the rael vernacular o' the Coonty.

(1870, quoted from Donaldson 1986:61)

Urban speakers suffered from similar uncertainties. Although Bell's depiction of Aunt Purdie's language in *Wee Macgreegor* (1901, T50) is a literary artefact, he appears to have captured the attitudes underlying genteel Kelvinside speech: her pronunciation and style is "dacent" and "rale genteel" – but she

t22 was inclined, alas! to look down on her homely relatives, and to regard their manners and speech as vulgar, with the sole result that her own manners were frequently affected, while her speech was sometimes a strange mixture. (1901/1977:32)

And yet there seem to be pragmatic rules which do not permit speakers to use all kinds of mixtures. Kay (1986:17) adduces a sentence in three varieties – Scots, his own usage (BK) and ScE – as follows:

t23 Scots: Afore I gaed ower the brig, the toon nock chappit hauf twa an thir lassies spierit gin I had got lousit shuiner nor I ettled.
    BK: Afore I went ower the brig, the toon nock chappit hauf twa an thir lassies asked if I had stopped work shuiner than I expected.
    ScE: Before I went over the bridge, the town clock struck half past two and these girls asked if I had stopped work sooner than expected.

Apparently, some linguistic items are more clearly marked as Scots than others and seem to induce the use of Scots forms in their environment. Some sentences, tentatively arranged on such a cline by McClure (p.c.), may illustrate acceptable and (*) unacceptable 'combinations':

t24 1) I'll not be going home till eleven o'clock tonight.
    2) A'll no be goin home till eleven o'clock tonight.
    3) A'll no be goin home tae eleven a'cloke the night.
    4) A'll no be gaun home tae aleevin a'cloke the night.
    5) A'll no be gaun hame tae aleevin a'cloke the nicht.
    6) *I'll not be going hame till eleven o'clock tonight.
    7) *I'll not be gaun hame tae aleevin a'cloke the nicht.

(quoted from Görlach 1991b:80, also cf. McClure 1995h:172)

Howe... ...stigation of this phenomenon
in he... ...only very weak implicational
tende... ...s – indeed, the only one she
notic... ...lid not vary freely; rather, the
choic... ...g Scots or English (Macafee
1994...

A... ...teristic of many written texts,
incl... ...tements on intentional mixture
was... ...-styled 'Scoto-Britaines' who
foll... ...)wns. His defence of the use of
Sco... ...sh structures (considered more
eleg... ...lat linguistic combination will
pro... ...f the kingdoms:

t25... ...inglish and Scottish Dialects; which
...oth nations. But I hope the gentle and
...me badge of mine owne countrie, by
...allie when I finde them propre, and

5 significant. And as for my owne country ..., ...t justly finde fault with me, if for the
more parte I vse the English phrase, as worthie to be preferred before our owne for the elegance
and perfection thereof. Yea I am perswaded that both countrie-men will take in good part the
mixture of their Dialects, the rather for that the bountiful providence of God doth invite them both
to a straiter union and conjunction as well in language, as in other respects.

(*Darius*, "To the Reader" (1603), quoted from Aitken 1979a:89)

In the 17C, Sir Robert Ayton (1569–1638) apparently considered the choice of languages, including varieties arranged on the Scots-English continuum, as correlated with styles and genres (cf. Jack 1997b:xv). Later on in the 17C, it becomes doubtful whether writers like William Drummond of Hawthornden and Sir Thomas Urquhart can be rightly claimed to use Scots at all (cf. 8.2.9). In the 18C, Robert Burns himself claimed to have sprinkled his English with Scots. And the 'folk ballads' traditionally associated with, and often originating from, Scotland, but sung all over Britain, were recorded in written form in a blend of Scots and English from the first collections onwards (cf. 8.3.5).

Ex 13 What were the linguistic consequences of the political border between Scotland and England (Glauser 1974, fig. 13)?

Ex 14 Compare the present-day continuum of English and Scots with the situation of standard and dialect in your native region.

2.3 *Language vs. dialect*

The status of Scots, then, is ambiguous: it may be seen as an independent language or as a dialect (of English); this uncertainty is due to the changes effected by the history of the speech community, in the course of the last 600 years in particular. Although all linguists realize how problematic the distinction between language and dialect is, the terms are widely used, and the concepts are important for the perceived identity of the speakers as well as for the attitudes of observers, and are therefore not to be lightly set aside. I propose to consider 'languageness' as a question of degree, the status of the variety depending on:

abstand – the greater the *distance* of a certain linguistic variety from a related one that is accepted as a (standard) language, the greater is the justification for classifying it as a language in its own right (rather than as a dialect);

ausbau – the greater the *homogeneity* of the variety and the degree to which it has achieved *linguistic norms* on the one hand, and the *range of functions* in written and spoken forms on the other, the greater is its claim to languageness; an attractive, if misleading, view would tend to attribute the predicate 'language' to a variety that has a published grammar and dictionary – and a translation of the New Testament;

attitude – speakers' attitudes can be even more important: if they wish to regard widely divergent varieties as dialects of one language (as in China), or minimally different ones as distinct languages (as recently in the case of Serbian and Croatian), the linguist cannot tell them they are wrong (though s/he might deplore the use of terms which purport to be objective and scientific to support tendentious cultural claims);

acquisition – incomplete language learning by entire groups of speakers can cause the vernacular to drift away from the initially intended aim so that new norms emerge: compare, for instance, the emergence of Romance languages and the birth of English-related pidgins and creoles.   (adapted from Görlach 1998c:2)

Ex 15   Which of the four criteria appear to be most important for a classification of present-day Scots? For Scots in the 16C?

2.3.1 *Abstand*

The distance between two language systems (*abstand*) is difficult to measure, but is manifest in the lack of mutual intelligibility or the frequency of misunderstanding. The desire to be understood leads to various kinds of accommodation, such as colonial levelling or loss of dialect (which is then normally replaced by a local accent) in speech and dilution of 'difficult' features in print. For written forms intelligibility can, of course, be secured by providing glosses (whether in the text, by way of footnotes, or in an appended glossary). How the situation is handled by individual authors depends on the intended readership. Therefore a simple count of words in a glosssary will not always provide a clear indication of the *abstand* of a Scots text in relation to English. For example, Annand's edition of Robert McLellan's *Linmill Stories* (1980, T90) has a minimalist glossary of only 144 items, insufficient by far for a reader unacquainted with Scots. In consequence, authors of Scots texts must pay careful attention to how 'dense' their Scots may be. (Often publishers object to densely non-standard versions, insisting on more reader-friendly dilution, i.e. approximation to standard forms).

Since linguistic competence, and the willingness to interpret deviant speech forms, is often socially determined and may vary from one person to another, 'density' and the degree of intelligibility are difficult to test empirically. There is, however, a feeling that the ability to understand 'dense' Scots particularly in writing is deteriorating, and that the high number of copies sold of Lorimer's *New Testament in Scots* (T69) may not be interpreted as indicating the numbers of *readers* of the book. However, such statements are mere hunches in the absence of properly conducted sociolinguistic investigations.

2.3.2 *Homogeneity*

Tendencies leading to homogeneity depend on the emergence of regional or national norms. An analysis of a corpus of early Scots texts shows that a diversification from N ME increased in the late 15C (Meurman-Solin 1997:21). However, this did not yet produce a homogeneous form of Scots:

t26   continued variation characterises the history of Scots. The degree of uniformity which can be
        recorded when statistical data are presented by grouping the texts in various ways is often
        considerably lower or absent when texts are looked at individually. Differences between texts can
        be at least partly explained with reference to extralinguistic factors which relate to textual history,
    5   the author, audience, subject matter or the social and communicative function of a text. As
        numerous fifteenth-, sixteenth- and seventeenth-century texts reflect a high degree of
        derivativeness, and as even more numerous texts are characterised by contextual styles which add
        to their inner heterogeneity, an attempt to classify them tends to be misleading in one way or
        another. The important role of text traditions, stylistic conventions in certain genres, and the
   10   intensity of innovative pressures in others, all result in multidirectional developments over time.
                                                                            (Meurman-Solin 1997:21)

Also, a new type of variation is introduced by the availability of English forms, first cultivated by the 15/16C makars and later by all authors. With the introduction of printing, the additional problem arises of relating authorial habits to printed representations. The consequences of this situation are that a continuum emerged in which 'pure' Scots dialects and pure EModE became the end points of a cline, but texts were increasingly mixed. The *DOST*, which covers the lexical data before 1700, therefore includes the entire evidence from pre-1600 texts and a selective range of material from 1600-1700, whereas the *SND* includes only items that are non-English in one way or another (cf. 7.2).

However, measuring 'anglicization' in the 15/16C is difficult. Individual items 'behave' differently from text to text: it is of course possible to follow up the decline in frequency of a specific Scots form and its supersedence by the corresponding English one. The situation is complicated by the fact that a great number of items on all linguistic levels are shared between English and Scots, so that 'anglicization' can also be achieved by avoiding marked Scotticisms (Scotland-specific features) and preferring a common item (cf. the concept of dialect levelling, as discussed in Trudgill 1986). Meurman-Solin rightly concludes:

t27   Addressee-oriented text types reflect a more intense need to appeal to a wider audience and
        therefore avoid possibly stigmatised linguistic features, preferring the shared or prestigious features
        of the majority variety.   (1997:21-2)

The fact that there are so many shared or cognate words in English and Scots means that Scots texts may appear more English than they are – or may be more Scots than they look (according to interpretation). The education system may have so preconditioned

Scots that naïve readers automatically assume something is English, and may even pronounce it as such (especially middle-class readers), unless the form of the word marks it as Scots. (F. Douglas, p.c.) . Questions such as whether the language of Knox (T12) is less Scots than that of James VI, and whether the king's language (and that in successive editions of the *Basilicon Doron*, T18) becomes more English over time may therefore only be answered from a perspective that takes St E as a gauge. Compare Murray's description of the difference of the English and Scottish reception of Burns's poems:

t28 And yet if a countryman of the poet were to recite these poems to a Southern audience, it is not too much to say that not more than three words in a hundred would be *heard* as the same as the English words with which they are identified in spelling. Hence the observation one so frequently hears from Englishmen – "I can understand Burns' poems quite well, when I read them; but I
5 cannot follow you when you read them." They read the words, spelled like their English equivalents, as English; and three-fourths to nine-tenths of the words being thus old friends, the context enables them to guess at the meaning of any new faces. Doubtless, an orthography so largely English renders Burns, or any other Scottish writer, more widely intelligible and enjoyable.
(Murray 1873:76)

A combination of an intentional avoidance of marked Scotticisms in lexis, morphology and syntax and the adoption of English spelling conventions for shared words also leads to McClure's characterisation of the language of Drummond, who "remained in the homeland, and he used as his medium a language which on the printed page is virtually indistinguishable from English" (1994:36).

Another objection to a quantitative measurement of Scots as against English elements lies in the fact that texts may easily be 'sprinkled' with Scottish characteristics in spelling and morphology to give a Scots veneer. (The term is Burns's who self-critically exaggerated his procedure of sprinkling English texts with Scots.) The use of such features tells us a great deal about attitudes, but little about linguistic structures.

These reservations mean that in order to define the status of Scots for every single period in its history the distance to its most closely related language, English, has to be analysed, the range of its text types determined (and how much use of Scots is made proportionally in each text type), the sources indicating speakers' attitudes collected and scrutinized, and the influences of speakers' other languages taken into account.

Since the sociolinguistic evaluation of a speech form depends on its changing cultural and functional importance, the fate of a minority language which comes to be dominated by a genetically related language of a greater degree of *ausbau* and higher prestige can easily be its dialectalization, or even its ultimate death. Such a development has happened to languages at all times – consider the fate of Oscan and Umbrian which became dialects of Latin in ancient Italy, and of Low German which has become a dialect of present-day German (2.9.1); Catalan, in contrast, resisted incorporation within Spanish (2.9.4).

2.3.3 *Scots as a first and as a second language*

Literary texts, but also jest-books and the like, are full of dialect specimens not representing the writers' native tongues. It is important for the linguist to recognize this fact since acquired dialects are even more prone to stereotyping than native ones: their representation can develop into downright gibberish. The history of written documents contains quite a few samples of imitated Scots, pseudo-Scots or mock Scots often introduced for comic effect.

A good example of this is the 16C tale about a boar's head, which was written by an Englishman; it illustrates the problems which could arise in oral communication between speakers of the two languages (encounters which must have been quite rare in the 16C). The misunderstanding is constructed around a few diverging pronunciations (especially the *bare : bore* difference) and lexical items – *Yule* being explained for the Southern reader:

t29 And he wente to London to haue a Bores head made. He dyd come to a Caruer (or a Joyner) saying
     in his mother tonge, I saye spek, kens thou meke me a Bare heade? Ye said the Caruer. Than sayd
     the skotyshman, mek me a bare head anenst Yowle, an thowse bus haue xx pence for thy hyre. I
     wyll doe it sayde the Caruer. On S. Andrewes daye before Chrystmas (the which is named Yowle
  5 in Scotland, and in England in the north) the skottish man did com to London for his Bores heade
     to set a a dore for a signe. I say speke said the skotish man, haste thou made me a Bare head? Yea
     said the Caruer. Then thowse a gewd fellow. The Caruer went and did bryng a mans head of wod
     that was bare and sayd, syr here is youre bare head. I say sayde the skotyshman, the mokyl deuill,
     is this a bare head? Ye said the caruer. I say sayd the Skotishman, I will haue a bare head, syk an
 10 head as doth follow a Sew that hath Gryces. Syr said the caruer, I can not tel what is a Sew, nor
     what is a Gryce. Whet h[o]rson, kenst thou not a sew that wil greet and grone, and her gryces wil
     run after her and cry a weke a weke. O said the Caruer, it is a pigge. Yea said the skotish man, let
     me haue his fathers head made in timber, and mek me a bird and set it on his skalps, and cause her
     to singe whip whir, whip whir. The caruer sayde, I can not cause her to singe whip whir. Whe
 15 horson sayde the skotish man gar her as she woulde singe whip whir. Here a man maye see that
     euerye man doth delight in his owne sences, or doth reioice in his fantasie.
                                            (quoted from Barber 1976:27-8, Görlach 1991a:21)

Shakespeare was much less sure of his linguistics when he created Captain Jamy in *Henry V* – this is at best an irregular mixture (cf. Blake 1981:86; much of the Scottishness, however, may have been left to the actor's pronunciation).

Although the Scots and their speech served as occasional butts of ridicule in the 18C, this was nothing compared to the derision levelled at the Irish and their brogue. When a new and very positive evaluation of Scots arose with the influence of Burns and Scott, their literary language was occasionally copied, but rarely by non-Scots: the Irish John Banim's adoration of Scots, however, went as far as using it in the dialogue of Irish peasants in *The Boyne Water* (1831). In the later 19C, Scots (as a dialect relatively easy to imitate in writing) was often used for humorous purposes in *Punch* (T47) – probably the texts were often written by non-Scotsmen. Nevertheless, it is remarkable that the great Victorian novelists of England, for all their use of dialects ranging from Wessex to Lancashire, do not appear to have touched Scotland and its language – with a few exceptions like the Irishman Bram Stoker in his *Dracula* (1897).

The momentum of the Scottish Literary Renaissance and its use of Scots in the 20C was obviously powerful enough to involve non-native speakers as well and turn the New Zealander Sydney Goodsir Smith into one of its outstanding representatives (cf. e.g. T54, 57). Lorimer himself, the celebrated translator of the *New Testament in Scots* (T69) was not a monolingual, native speaker of Scots, but like nearly all Scottish children of his class and generation, he grew up fully aware of the two codes.

David Purves, a Scots language activist who mainly deplores the continuous corruption of colloquial Scots, also points to the dangers of an artificial revivalist Scots written (rather than spoken) by well-wishers in Scotland:

t30 Against the background of continuing erosion of colloquial Scots, it is arguable whether a
   substantial proportion of recent writing, purporting to be in Scots, can be regarded as Scots at all.
   Much contemporary material contains few of the features which characterise the language, and
   appears to consist of attempts at back translation from English into personal notions of what Scots
 5 is.   (1997:4-5)

Complaints that other writers' Scots is not idiomatic but translated from English are in fact found from 1800 onwards, and a thorough search would no doubt discover many instances. Recent specimens are Young's characterization of Gibbon's "Lallanised Suddron, potent medium tho it is" (T56/77-8) and Horsbroch's of Telfer's "Suddron Scottified" (T73/17). There is the fear that the last generation of Scottish writers who grew up speaking Scots natively and are able to handle even 'Lallans' with unpretentious ease is ageing fast and in the course of the last twenty years has lost many notable members, among them J.K. Annand (1908–93), Robert McLellan (1907–90), Robert Garioch (1909–81), Alexander Scott (1920–89), Flora Garry (1800-99) and others. There will be, it is to be feared, no more *Linmill Stories* (T58) or *Dod and Davies* (T71).

A related problem is that of personal linguistic erosion effected by a long absence from Scotland. John Knox, who spent many years of his life in English and German exile, might have found it difficult to write idiomatic Scots, even if he had wanted to (cf. 8.2.3 and T12); and Robert Jamieson was aware of the dangers of mixing various chronolects when he translated his *Northern Antiquities* (1814), writing in Livonia, after many years of absence from his home country (Corbett 1999:116). On the other hand, some important Scots texts were written in exile (cf. Görlach 2001b): on the continent (Gau, 16C, T9), in Canada (Smith's *New Testament* about 1900, T69), in South Africa (some of Murray's poems, 19C, T48) and in Australia (Cameron's *Genesis*, 20C, T51). It is difficult to say how much the distance from Scotland has affected the writers' Scots.

2.3.4 *Ullans*

Very relevant questions of what the role of native speakers is in the language planning processes of code selection, codification, elaboration and implementation have in the past few years been raised in connection with Ulster Scots (cf. 2.8.1). The rural dialect which derives from the Ulster Plantation of 1610-25 and is spoken by some 100,000 (in varying degrees of broadness and frequency of use) in some northern counties of N Ireland and adjacent Donegal (fig. 15) was given political recognition as a minority language in the Good Friday Agreement of 1998 and the European Charter of Minority Languages (ratified by the Westminster Parliament in 2001). Code selection means in particular to decide whether the new standard form (conveniently named Ullans < Ulster Lallans) should retain the links with Scotland or be exclusively based on Ulster dialects (cf. Görlach 2000), which steps are necessary to provide it with a written norm and how to modernize it, especially its lexis, in order to make it a fully amenable standard language for the third millennium. First attempts at using Ullans for administration are less convincing – they provide a largely relexified English version with expressions that sound either artificial (in particular, where new calques are used in order to avoid anglicisms) or look deintellectualized, in an effort to avoid abstract terminology and replace it by a diction that is intended to sound colloquial (see Kirk's analysis, 2000, and T75).

It is too early to predict what will become of these modernizing revivalist attempts. The acceptability of Ullans for the native dialect speakers (who may well find that this is not 'their' language) will be crucial for the implementation. It is obvious that very strong political motivation must support the new written form if it is to survive, but this would add another divisive factor to a speech community already deeply split over other matters. Failing this support – and a correlation of language planning for Scotland (which does not seem to be forthcoming in spite of devolution) – the new language has no realistic chances to survive. (For further information on the complex problem see various contributions to the proceedings to the 2000 and 2001 Belfast conferences edited by Kirk & Ó Baoill, 2000, 2001a, 2001b).

2.4   *Written and spoken language*

For more than two centuries, Scots has been predominantly the medium of everyday informal speech. St E has become the language used for almost all written text types (except some literary ones, cf. Görlach 1998d). Formal instruction takes place only in English, and most writing – even of authors who use Scots in their fictional work – is in English.

The influence of St E is therefore likely to be stronger on written texts than on speech. Consequently, writing in Scots is a conscious process, influenced (to varying degrees) by St E, Scots models from the literary tradition and the spoken dialect of the individual writer. The reader (and researcher) has to keep in mind that written texts in Scots as a non-standard language underlie certain conditions: they will probably be more similar to St E than spoken utterances; they may follow structures of spoken Scots, but they may also preserve a number of archaic features, obsolete in Scots speech. These are severe restrictions for historical reconstruction: analysis of all but the most recent period of Scots must be based on written texts and our description concentrates, as mentioned above, on written texts throughout. (Cf. the restriction to certain text types, 2.7 below).

2.5   *Dialects of Scots*

Johnston's (1997b) very careful investigation of early Scottish regional varieties distinguishes Southern and East Mid (based on Anglian in the 'Old Frontierland'), North and West Mid, and burgh-borne dialects, but it is quite clear that much of his description remains speculative. With regard to Barbour who wrote in late 14C Aberdeen he states:

t31 It is possible that 14C Aberdonian was as yet not fully 'crystallised', in an early state where
people's speech says as much about where their parents come from as about the speech of the area
... It is perhaps more likely that the north-eastern traits were present in embryo in Barbour's time,
but (1) the innovations had not spread through the whole community or (2) there was already
5   sociolinguistic pressure to adopt Central Scots traits – or a combination of both   (1997b:61).

In the 16th century, regional varieties in Scotland came to be 'roofed' (*überdacht)* by an incipient Scots standard language, which was emerging as the norm based on the usage of the Edinburgh court. Any influence emanating from this centre would affect the central dialects first, and the peripheral ones later and in diluted form. The questions of how the individual dialects came to diverge, and how they have been converging for some time, is insufficiently documented and largely unexplored.

An anecdote told by Murray can serve to illustrate communication problems between speakers of different dialects of Scots in the 19C:

t32 Some "Wast-Cuintrie folk" were staying in the house at the same time, and in the morning I was
awakened by the shrill voice of a girl shouting behind my door, "Mither! mither! – the wain's
walkin'!" My instinctive impulse was to understand *wain* as *waggon,* and the sentence as,
"Mother! – the waggon's walking, or moving off!" when the voice of a child in an adjoining room
5   reminded me of *wean* – a word not in ordinary use in our dialect, but familiar enough in the
writings of Burns, where, however, I did not read *wain* but *ween,* or *weeän.* The sentence now
became, "Mother! – baby's walking!" Quite accidentally, I afterwards found out that what I had
heard as *walkin'* was *wauken* – awake – and that the information conveyed was neither "the
waggon is walking," nor "baby is taking its first toddle"; but "Mother! – baby is awake!" or as it
10   would have been in Teviotdale, "Muther! – the bairn's weäken!" I smiled to think how I had been
as completely tripped up by a simple sentence in a Scottish dialect, separated from my own only
by a ridge of hills, as if it had been French or German.   (Murray 1873:77)

The use of a specific dialect as a literary medium deserves separate treatment (ch. 8), but it may be useful to remember that the choice is both between degrees of density and between local dialect vs. a supraregional form of Scots. The Central Belt dialects achieved, from Ramsay onwards, some kind of 'standard' function in literary productions, due to the comparatively large numbers of speakers and to the model of major poets from the area (especially if we include the Ayrshire poet Burns). This is evident from the usage of some authors who were not natives of the region. Others, however, represented their local dialect with little compromise (cf. William Alexander's *Johnny Gibb of Gushetneuk,* T44). This latter tradition appears to be preferred in 20C writing – outside, at least, the 'Lallans' tradition.

2.5.1 *Modern dialects*

Dialectologists must decide how they identify 'a well-defined dialect'. Problems of this kind can, for instance, arise with the northeast, accepted as a unit by Mutschmann (1909), but seen rather as a cluster of individual dialects by Dieth:

t33   (The northeast) is too varied, linguistically, to yield to summary treatment ... The fisher dialects, then, are a study by themselves ... The City of Aberdeen should also be excluded from our area, belonging, as it does, together with Deeside   (1932:xvif.)

The new situation, after 1603, is that the dialects of modern Scots are no longer 'roofed'. This means a return to the ME situation in that there is no standard or normative court variety which speakers can accommodate to for formal registers or 'correctness' – unless they turn to St E (ScE), and that is what they have been doing for hundreds of years now. Therefore, the dialects they use may be interpreted in sociolinguistic terms as dialects of English – in spite of their distance and historicity.

Apart from that, the present-day distribution of Scots dialects largely reflects the settlements and the administrational expansion of Scots to 1625. As a consequence, the geographical boundaries have been comparatively stable: this applies to the Highland Line (which developed from a language boundary into a dialect boundary), the Scottish/English border (Glauser 1974) and, internally, the boundary between the Central and Northern regions close to Dundee.

The classification of dialects of Scots is usually made, in the tradition of 19C dialectologists like Ellis and Murray, on the basis of phonological criteria, with lexical distributions used to confirm the boundaries. The traditional mapping, often reprinted, is as follows (fig. 11, p. 41).

The geographical distribution of the dialects is generally described referring to counties, the administrative units abolished in 1975, because the *SND*'s research had been done on the basis of these divisions – and because 'perceptual dialectology' (Preston 1989) is likely to find that popular concepts of dialect boundaries will agree more with the traditional counties than with modern administrational units (cf. *CSD*, introduction p.xxxiv).

The degree of distance from the Central Belt was important for the preservation of dialect as a spoken medium in everyday communication. Although compulsory education in 1872 and the strongly prescriptive attitude of teachers made written English and its spoken use in formal registers available countrywide, NE 'Doric' resisted the pressures of English much better than the dialects of the Central Belt did– Aberdeenshire was more isolated, less densely populated and had a strong sense of local identity. Nevertheless, the erosion of broad dialect proceeded, especially as regards lexis (less so pronunciation).

Ex 16   Compile a list of distinctive features of individual dialects (using the parallel translations of Biblical passages, T69, and *Max and Moritz*, T71) in order to arrive at an estimate of their distance from the standard language.

Ex 17   What are the linguistic consequences if dialects are not 'roofed' (Kloss [2]1978)?

Fig. 11 The traditionally accepted major dialect divisions of Scots superimposed on a map showing the
pre-1975 county boundaries. Based on *CSD*.

2.5.2 *Dialectology*

Early attempts at collecting data from regional speech started in the 18C with glossaries and literary pieces in the form of 'dialogues' – but such publications were much rarer in Scotland than in England: apparently the standard language (ScE) had to become established first before writers would turn to rural dialects and discover their strange beauty. Also, 'dialect' was largely identified in Scotland with the literary diction of Ramsay, Burns and Scott, and this tradition stifled the interest in local varieties. As a consequence, there is nothing comparable with the rich tradition of local dialect glossaries of English. In Scotland, such lists were usually intended as aids for reading the classical poets (cf. 7.2).

The beginnings of Scottish dialectology were therefore bound up with the systematic investigation of dialects in Britain in the late 19C, which was prompted by a number of causes:

1) Adherents of the newly discovered discipline of historical-comparative linguistics saw in dialect data welcome samples of 'unadulterated' speech useful for reconstructing language history; also, the controversy about the neogrammarian principle that sound laws were inviolable demanded that it be tested on non-standard forms.

2) The new science of phonetics made the description of the most salient features of regional distinctions possible with greater precision than ever before.

3) The spread of St E, speeded up by social and geographical mobility and by the effects of compulsory education (1870/72), made observers aware of the fact that dialects were being eroded and that their own generation might be the last to witness dialects as full linguistic systems used by monolingual speakers (antiquarian interest).

The new wave of research, then, found its centre in the activities of the 'English Dialect Society' (EDS), founded in 1875 by Skeat with the explicit intention of producing a dialect dictionary to complement the newly begun collections for the *OED*. The *English Dialect Dictionary* (*EDD*) was published by J. Wright (1898-1906), including a dialect grammar in its sixth volume; the research was complemented by Ellis's enormous project of a historical analysis of regional pronunciation (1889). These activities included Scotland, and rightly so, since its dialects form a continuum with those of Northumberland and Lancashire. However, the documentation of Scots dialects was not quite as thorough as for England – consider the lexical data in Warrack (1911), which were drawn from the *EDD*.

Some of the best 19C and early 20C research was, however, made outside the EDS project; note in particular the investigations by J.A.H. Murray (1873; 2.4.3), J. Wilson (1915, 1923, 1926; 2.4.4, 2.4.5) and some Continental linguists such as Mutschmann (1909) and Dieth (1932) (2.4.6).

It was a great advantage that many researchers of the first generation like Murray and Wilson were excellent philologists, and that they described the dialects of their native villages (that is the speech forms that had been dominant in their own youth). Many of the principles applied were adopted from the EDS and the Continent.

Of course, scholars like Wilson were aware of the continuum of Scots and English which had replaced the former diglossia and had turned alternative options into stylistic choices corresponding to topic and formality – even in the rural area of Lower Strathearn:

t34 There is one serious difficulty which no doubt presents itself to all students of dialect in this
    country. The people from whose mouths it must be studied have almost all been taught to read and
    to speak standard English, and are mostly familiar with the language as employed in the Bible and
    other books or in the newspapers. Thus, sometimes consciously, sometimes unconsciously, they
  5 use in ordinary speech the English word or phrase which they have learned in place of the one
    peculiar to their mother-tongue, especially if the standard pronunciation is not very different from
    that of their own dialect. Similarly, in the same village, each of different men, or even the same
    man at different times, will alter the pronunciation, especially of vowel sounds, according to the
    state of his own feelings or his ideas of the intelligences or preference of the person he is
 10 addressing; and it is often difficult to decide which of the various pronunciations represents the
    true dialect of the locality. The safest plan in such circumstances seems to be to watch carefully the
    unthinking speech of the oldest residents, to note and compare their pronunciation, and to select
    that which is most unlike standard English, provided that it is frequently repeated, as probably
    representing the original speech of the people, the true dialect of the district.   (Wilson 1915:10)

When a new start was made on a British dialect survey after World War II, two projects were planned independently, an English one based in Leeds (the *Survey of English Dialects, SED*) and a Scottish one (the *Linguistic Survey of Scotland, LSS*), which was to include both Scots and Gaelic, in Edinburgh, fully described in the introductions to Mather & Speitel (*LAS*, 1975, 1977, 1986).

Ex 18   The Scottish and English projects both cover the northern counties of England.
            Compare the results with regard to a selected lexical item.

The distribution of items, mapped in the first two volumes of the *LAS* in particular, allows the user – after careful interpretation – to establish relations with settlement history, language contact, standard influences and geographical isolation. Thus, the maps serve as a valuable database for further research.

Fig. 12 (p. 44) reproduces two maps from the *LAS*, which records the Scots expressions for *the youngest of a brood*. It exhibits a large number of heteronyms, some Gaelic-derived items.

The most distinctive dialect area mapped by the *LAS* (as far as the lexicon is concerned) is usually the Northeast – but this is partly because Shetland usage was not comprehensively sampled.

In Scotland, there has not yet been any systematic investigation of speakers' perceived distinctions between dialects (perceptual dialectology, cf. Preston 1989) to establish how far the dialect areas or boundaries determined by traditional dialectological research coincide with popular views.

Ex 19   Check in how far isoglosses in the maps here reproduced agree with the dialect
            boundaries based on phonological differences (fig. 12).
Ex 20   How far do the characterisations of individual words given in the *LAS* and the
            CSD/SND match?

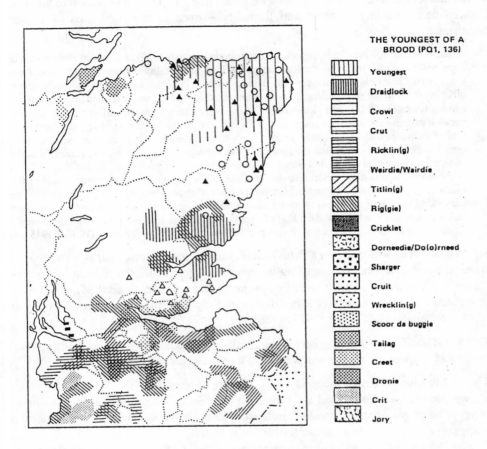

THE YOUNGEST OF A
BROOD (PQ1, 136)

Youngest
Draidlock
Crowl
Crut
Ricklin(g)
Weirdie/Wairdie
Titlin(g)
Rig(gie)
Cricklet
Dorneedie/Do(o)rneed
Sharger
Cruit
Wrecklin(g)
Scoor da buggie
Tailag
Creet
Dronie
Crit
Jory

Fig. 12 Map 65 from the *Linguistic Atlas of Scotland* (vol. 1) illustrating the distribution of Scots alternative expressions for *the youngest of a brood.*

From the earliest documented stages, the political border between Scotland and England cut right through a spoken dialect continuum. The linguistic differences found in the written texts are, then, a consequence of two standard languages becoming established on the basis of London and Edinburgh speech, and neighbouring dialects becoming 'roofed' by norms very far apart. Although this state lasted only for some 200-300 years, norms remained somewhat different after the Union of the Crowns, Scots occupying a middle norm between English and local dialects – which, among other things, delayed the erosion of old dialect characteristics north of the border.

These distinctions, often the result of features preserved in Scots rather than innovations, are present on all levels. For instance, Murray (1873) found that /x/ was retained in English dialects close to the border, but the phoneme is now restricted to Scots. Also, northern plurals like *een, shoen* are now considered 'Scottish' by

Northumbrians. The most conspicuous differences are, however, found in the vocabulary. Glauser (1974, 2000) combined geographical features of the three marches and their changeable political history with the linguistic evidence to show that the Border (the 'Lowland Line') coincides with clusters of isoglosses. The fact that both the English and the Scottish dialect surveys covered the region makes such statements even more valuable.

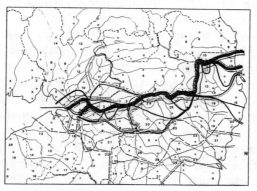

Fig. 13 Clusters of isoglosses in the Border area (from Glauser 1974:283).

In what follows four individual areas that are well researched and represent different regions as well as high degrees of dialect retention are sketched in order to provide a survey of problems and methods of the traditional dialectology of Scots.

2.5.3 *Individual studies I: the southern counties and the border*
(Murray 1873)

J.A.H. Murray spent the first 27 years of his life in Teviotdale. He wrote the classic account of *The Dialect of the Southern Counties of Scotland* (Murray 1873) before he went to London and Oxford to edit the *OED* and became one of the leading philologists of his time. The fact that he was a dialect speaker and a largely self-taught dialectologist was an excellent basis for writing the major study of a Scots dialect in the 19C. Although his approach was historical (as was to be expected in his time), the detail and descriptive adequacy of his analysis of Southern Scots phonology and morphology was rightly praised. It is sad to reflect that it did not spark off work for other dialects until Wilson's and Dieth's investigations more than forty years later – when much evidence had been lost and practically no monodialectal speakers were left. Murray's study does not of course include extensive discussions of the sociolinguistic conditions, but there are valuable incidental remarks on the diversity of Scots dialects (1873:77), test sentences to establish local dialect (79, 82) and a list of differences from Northern English (87).

Ex 21   Find out about the features and the status of Scots in the Borders in 20C, using for example the *LAS*, Wettstein 1942 and Glauser 1974.

2.5.4 *II: Ayrshire and Perthshire*
(Wilson 1923, Wilson 1915)

Ayrshire dialect had become prominent as the variety used by Robert Burns (even though John Galt's Ayrshire diction is more distinctly identifiable with the region than his, partly because of the different genres for which it was used). Features of this Western dialect have thus been added to the quasi-literary standard essentially based on Edinburgh. Therefore, two necessary warnings must be heeded by dialectologists, *viz.* that they have to take into account the selectiveness and 'polishing' of language used for literary purposes, and the later development of this 'Ayrshire Scots', which became more and more synthetic, if only because Fergusson, Scott and others came from other areas. Sir James Wilson gave a first comprehensive description of this dialect in 1923.

It was preceeded by Wilson's study of his native dialect of Dunning in Lower Strathearn close to Perth (1915), undertaken at a time when information from older speakers permitted him to recover the linguistic situation of the mid-19C. His very detailed account concentrating on the spoken dialect of villagers is a reliable description which avoids technicalities through the use of a readable transcription and which is not biased by a concern for historical data and the quest for a hypothetical 'pure' dialect. No claims are made regarding the currency of the features in local dialects elsewhere in Scotland – a disappointment for modern readers, for even impressionistic statements might have helped to put Wilson's findings into perspective. (His idiosyncratic spellings make it difficult to compare some of his data with the evidence included in modern dictionaries).

Ex 22   Compare this type of dialectological study with a newer approach to the investigation of Scots speech of Ayrshire in Macaulay (1991).

2.5.5 *III: Northeastern Scots*
(Mutschmann 1909, Dieth 1932)

The NE dialect, often referred to as 'Doric', or by one of its regional forms as 'Buchan', has been outstanding for its divergence from the better known Scots of the Central Belt, especially in pronunciation and lexis, and by its better retention of broad dialect, largely as a consequence of the isolation of the area. These facts have attracted a number of linguists, among whom Mutschmann (1909) and Dieth (1932) are possibly the most remarkable; sadly, only the first part of Dieth's research, his study of phonology, has been published to date.

However, in spite of the predominance of rural areas and small towns in Aberdeenshire and along the coast, NE Scots was not spared the attrition that affected other dialects. Dieth (1932), too, saw the erosion of local Scots; he summarized the situation for the 1920s in a much-quoted statement:

t35   The chief enemies of the dialect are, without a doubt, the press, the pulpit and above all the public school, that systematic suppression of anything with a local flavour. Time and again I was told by way of explanation: 'We're no longer allowed to say that'. The result is most deplorable; not because Standard English takes the place of good old *braid Scots* – from a utilitarian point of view

5 that would be an excellent thing, well worth the price – but because the effort almost invariably
ends in a compromise. The young folk have no sooner escaped the *dominie's* rod, than they slip
back, unconsciously, to their natural way of talking. The return, however, is not complete; the
effect of the teaching lingers on in their speech.   (Dieth 1932: xviif.)

He went on to complain: "Already it is late in the day, and the best chances (for a
description of NE Scots) have no doubt been missed" (1932:xx).

That the impact of St E (in its ScE form) must have affected NE Scots at an early
date is shown by the fact that only a minority of words have (or retain) the expected
Scots reflex of OE /a:/ as /e(:)/ in *gae, wae, hail, sair*) or the locally distinctive raised
/i:/ preceding /-n/ in *steen, aleen* etc. (found in Forfar, Kincardine, Aberdeen and the
Banffshire coast, Dieth 1932:17). In most words of both types, by contrast, /o:/ is
common in the dialect: "The spread of English [o:] is not recent: in some words [e:] has
been dead for generations, in others it can be remembered, in others again it is now
being encroached upon" (Dieth, 1932:20). A follow-up study of the conditions some 70
years after Dieth might show how far the losses of the old /e:, i:/ forms have proceeded.

Other typical pronunciation features of NE dialect include the retention of word-
initial /kn-/ and replacement of original /w/ by /v/ in initial clusters (as in /vriçt/ for
wright 'joiner') and between vowels: as in *blaavin* 'blowing'. Most notably, original
/hw-/ is realized as [f-] in a number of words, mostly form words of high frequency
(such as *faa/fa* 'who', *fat/fit* 'what', *faar/far* 'where', but also *foo* 'how'). In addition,
a few content words also have [f-]: *fup* 'whip', *futret* (white rat) 'weasel', etc. (Dieth
1932:17, 115-8). Murray (1873:79) quotes the following shibboleths to illustrate NE
Scots: *faa fuppit the feyte fulpie* ('who whipped the white whelpie'); *the vratch vras'lt
wi' the vrycht tyll hys vryst gat the vrang vranch* ('the wretch wrestled with the wright
till his wrist got a wrong wrench').

The Northeast has a long literary tradition, significant at least from the 19C, when
William Alexander for narrative prose (T44) and Charles Murray for poetry (T48)
created works once known and loved in most NE households, and of considerable
influence in other parts of Scotland. These traditions have continued to the present time
(Hewitt 1995); they include a large range of popular texts ranging from cartoons and
humorous snippets (such as Hardy 1985), popular drama and creative writing in school
competitions.

2.5.6 *IV: Shetland and Orkney*
(Robertson & Graham 1991)

The special position of the two island groups is explained by the fact that they became
part of Scotland as late as 1472, that Scandinavian Norn was the dominant language
until the 17C (1.6.3), and that due to the isolation from mainland Scotland a sense of
local identity, also expressed by linguistic separateness, is possibly stronger than
anywhere else in Scotland. This does not, however, mean that there is no erosion of
Scots dialects in the northern islands. Orkney, being much closer to the mainland than
Shetland, became affected by dialect attrition almost as early as other Scottish dialect
areas, and its speech-forms underwent similarly dramatic developments from the late

19C onwards, as a consequence of general education, changing lifestyles and increasing communication. Nevertheless, the population history and the geographical isolation of the islands have resulted in dialects which diverge from the common core of Scots more than any other. Research into the two varieties has been quite uneven to date; Shetlandic has received much more attention, whereas the description of Orkney is largely restricted to Lamb's (1988) and Flaws & Lamb's dictionaries (1996, cf. 7.2).

With respect to Shetland lexis, Graham (1979) documents drastic dialect erosion in the 20C: he found that of 720 Norn-derived words recorded in 1890, some 360 were then believed to be still in common use; of these Graham himself knew 109 in 1949, and a 21-year-old Shetlander in 1979 only 65 (1979:xix). To explain these losses it is important to remember that

t36 it is only since the 1950s that the Shetland speech and speaker has acquired a measure of respectability. The important post-war reports on education in Scotland emphasised 'the fundamental truth that education must be rooted in reality, finding its material and its starting point in the environment of the child' (Graham 1979: xix)

This development has, particularly in Shetland, also strengthened the acceptability and production of dialect in the schools. In the media, too, dialect is here more common than elsewhere. The local Radio Shetland has a fascinating range of speech-forms, extending from broad dialect to various degrees of standardness in ScE (Radio Orkney displays some of the same).

Despite drastic losses, many dialect words not shared with other Scots varieties survive in Orkney and Shetland; thus they are often excluded by one-volume Scots dictionaries. These items relate to everyday life, but also to technical terms of seafaring and shipbuilding, crofting and weaving or types of wind. Compare for the latter category in both Orkney and Shetland dialect: *bat* 'slight gust', *flan* 'sudden squall', *gouster* 'strong gusty wind', *guff* 'strong puff'; and for Shetlandic only: *laar* 'light wind, diffused', *pirr* 'light wind in patches' and *vaelensi* 'strong gale' (Graham 1979: xviii). As regards pronunciation, most features are shared with mainland Scots, but note for instance [ʏ] in *göd* 'good', *shö* 'she', and [d] for [ð], [t] for [θ] in *midder* 'mother' and *tank* 'thank', and (only in Shetland) [ʃ] for [ʧ] in *shair* 'chair'. In grammar, informal *du, dine, dee* 'thou, thine, thee' were common until recently (and are still found in Shetlandic), and verbs (not only those of motion) characteristically form their perfect with 'be' rather than 'have'.

The small island community has produced a noteworthy literature in Shetlandic dialect; among the better known authors of the present century are John Graham (T64), William Tait (T59) and 'Vagaland' (T.A. Robertson), cf. Graham & Robertson's anthology (1964).

Ex 23 Try to identify specifically Shetlandic features in T59, 64, 69f and 71d.

2.6   *Sociolectal variation*

The rise of urban populations in the 19C meant that by 1900 urban speakers of Scots had come to outnumber those in the rural and more provincial regions – and they certainly were more noticeable in many respects. In the general stigmatisation of urban speech everywhere in Western Europe, where broad varieties became widely associated with poverty and lack of education, Glaswegian was no exception. McNaught comments:

t37   Nine tenth of so-called modern Scots is a concrete of vulgarized, imperfect English, in which are
       sparsely embedded more or less corrupt forms of the 'lovely words' with which Burns wove his
       'verbal magic'   (1901:27, quoted from Pollner 1985a:64)

The list of such comments is endless – cf. McAllister's almost forty years later:

t38   It is, however, a mark of many forms of the degenerated dialect found in the speech of large cities
       and also of some of the county areas that the carelessness of articulation has led to a lengthening
       of the vowels which can only be described as slovenly drawling.
                                                                          (1938:129, quoted from Pollner 1985a:66)

Conservative dialectologists like Murison even saw the existence of Glaswegian as one of the major factors responsible for the death of 'proper' Scots:

t39   one may question how far it is Scots at all and not merely a kind of broken English. This is
       especially true of the speech of the industrial areas, where the influence of Highland and Anglo-
       Irish dialect, the new vocabulary of industrialism imported from England, the general currency of
       standard and sub-standard and slang English, particularly in the social strata of the towns, have all
    5 combined to attenuate and even obliterate Scots   (1977:56, quoted from Pollner 1985a:75)

Sociolinguistic research in Scotland is quite a recent discipline, and the results of the research have scratched the surface only – concentrating on the Central Belt, where urban speech is most widespread (and traditional dialect most drastically eroded), and where therefore correlations with social-class parameters are most fruitful.

2.6.1 *Methods of description*
         (Hudson [2]1996:144–202)

Quantitative sociolinguistics investigates the correlation of linguistic features with social categories by way of determining countable linguistic units (variants) which are diagnostic of social distinctions, i.e. which reflect social stratification in verbal behaviour. While hypotheses may be guided by the experience gained from investigations elsewhere, linguistic and social variables have to be determined separately for each speech community: relevant linguistic items differ from one language or culture to another, as do the concepts of social class or status and the relevance of parameters such as age, sex, education, religious denomination, ethnic provenance and income. Sociolinguistic description assumes the existence of (orderly) heterogeneity, rather than homogeneity, to be the normal state of linguistic reality. Therefore the appropriate method is quantificational, calculating the probability of the occurrence of individual variants as reflecting social stratification within the speech community.

The hypothesis that social variables correlate with linguistic features applies as a general principle to present-day Scots and its earlier stages as much as to most other languages. The actual social determinants and linguistic choices, however, obviously depend on the specific society and historical context. The special sociolinguistic characteristic of Scots is the fact that intended norms of correctness and appriateness are not always well-defined and that at least some uses of the vernacular cannot be equated with features like 'uneducated' or 'lower-class', but may represent deliberate middle-class choices; this is particularly true of written uses, which may be expressions of nationalism and markers of cultural identity, not usually found in monolingual societies. Moreover, the local English norm (usually modern ScE) in itself deviates from St EngE, which – especially when pronounced with an RP accent – is now regarded as affected by the Scots (to a certain extent, this may have been the case throughout the process of anglicization, cf. T55). We must also take additional variables into account: even though a contrast between 16C Protestants and Roman Catholics is probably not consistently reflected in attitudes towards specific uses or the broadness of Scots in written communication, some influence of religious affiliation on the linguistic selection cannot be excluded.

Scotland is, then, an especially promising area for sociolinguistic investigation since we can expect the coexistence of broad (traditional) dialect, urban speech, ScE and possibly St E with 'Southern' norms in grammar and 'Southernized' pronunciation. Hanley stated in relation to his childhood in Glasgow:

t40 We ourselves grew up trilingual. We spoke the King's English without any difficulty at school, a
     decent grammatical informal Scots in the house, and gutter-Glasgow in the streets
                                                          (1958, quoted from Macaulay 1977:4)

To summarize: what makes Scotland possibly a unique field for sociolinguistic investigation is that different kinds of prestige relate to different linguistic norms as expressing local or national identity in a more complex way than in most regions in, say, England. Regarding the attraction of such a sociolinguistic laboratory, the number of scholarly studies has been relatively small, so no comprehensive judgment of the situation is possible.

2.6.2 *Glasgow*
         (Macaulay 1977, Macafee 1983a, 1994a)

Sociolinguistic investigations have concentrated on Glasgow and Edinburgh and some smaller towns in the Central Belt. The following account chooses Glasgow as an example, because it has been studied in greatest detail, employing a variety of methods.[1]

---

[1]For studies based on Edinburgh cf. Chirrey (1999), Reid (1978) and Romaine (1979) and the summary in Jones (2002). Stimulating insights can be gained by listening to the CD, and reading the transcriptions, in Robinson & Crawford (2001). The authors chose speakers from the four major urban centres, Glasgow, Edinburgh, Dundee and Aberdeen, "to offer guidance to actors working on Scottish accents" (2001:9).

The history of Glasgow provides a promising background for sociolinguistic hypotheses (cf. Macafee 1983a). It was the fastest-growing British city in the 18C, competing with Edinburgh in wealth derived from industry and trade. In the 19C, the city was the first and major centre of industrialization (cotton, later coal and iron; shipbuilding from 1870 on). Its demand for workers made Glasgow the destination of large numbers of Irish and Highland immigrants, who were often forced out of their home areas by famine and clearances, and other economic reasons. This made the city more polyglot (and more Roman Catholic) than any other in Britain; and it had more second-language speakers of English or Scots than any other Lowland community. The complexity of the sociolinguistic situation is underpinned by the fact that Glasgow also had a native W Scots dialect, and that anglicization of the spoken forms had set in from the 18C Enlightenment onwards. In the early 20C, with a notable decline in wealth, Glasgow became notorious for poverty and social problems. It was only from the redevelopment from the 1950s onwards that things began to change, and even in the more prosperous period after 1945: "Glasgow has a national reputation for slums, social deprivation, unemployment and violence" (Macaulay 1977:16).

The first major sociolinguistic investigation of Glasgow by Macaulay (cf. Macaulay 1976 & 1977) was partly modelled on the classic Labovian research pattern. On the basis of interviews with a stratified sample of 48 informants, Macaulay correlated five phonological variables with four social criteria he assumed to influence speech: sex, age, social class and religion. In contrast to Labov's studies there was no attempt to isolate contextual styles – all of Macaulay's data represent formal interview style. By means of a further series of interviews with teachers and employers, Macaulay investigated attitudes towards linguistic variation and change and the importance attached to the 'quality' of speech of pupils and employees (extensive quotations from the informants' reactions constitute a most important feature of his study).

The results of the 'community survey' show that variable use is consistently stratified according to age, sex and social class, but religion does not influence speech significanctly (also cf. Macaulay 1978). The study also documents a high degree of linguistic awareness by speakers of overt norms. In particular, the most stigmatized feature of urban speech, the glottal stop, was almost consistently avoided when informants were asked to read out word-lists, but was dominant in all other situations among the 10-and 15-year-olds (regardless of sex), and was rare only among adult women (1977:53). This linguistic awareness was even more clearly evident when attitudes to speech varieties were elicited. There are obvious educational implications – complicated by the fact that accent tolerance may be insincere, and may add to the linguistic insecurity of the less well educated (1977:132). (For further interpretation of Macaulay's data, not only from Glasgow but also from a later study in Ayr, cf. Macaulay 1997). A follow-up study of the attitudinal section of Macaulay's work (Menzies 1991 in Easterhouse, Glasgow) supports his findings, although speakers tended to view their speech form in a slightly less negative way than twenty years before. Moreover, the study revealed that even very brief discussions of topics such as the historical differences between Scots and English, the status of Scots and Glasgow dialect, the difference between slang and dialect and the concept of code-switching, resulted in a significant change of attitudes towards the informants' own variety and suggests ways in which linguistic insecurity may be diminished.

Macafee (1994a) carried out a different type of sociolinguistic investigation of Glasgow dialect: her emphasis is on standardisation and urban dialect erosion in working-class speech aiming at a sociological understanding of the speech community. She found that the use of dialect words is receding – knowledge of dialect words, however, is not. New dialect words are created and used. Attitudes to new dialect words differ from those to old items: especially among the older generations old words are regarded as 'good old Scots', whereas new words are rejected as slang; the younger generations see old words as old-fashioned. (Pollner found similar age-grading in his study of dialect words in Livingston, 1985c). Attitudes are, therefore, not necessarily class related, that is, the use of dialect words does not evoke strong associations of class distinctions. These results are in clear contrast to Macaulay's findings for the use of phonological variables.

2.6.3 Gender and language

Among the many social correlates of linguistic variation, sex/gender has received particular attention in recent years. However, there is still no comprehensive account of how gender relates to attitudes towards, and usage of, Scots and ScE. Traditionally, NORMs (= non-mobile older rural males) are taken to be the best informants for non-standard lexis and pronunciation, because they are regarded as being less norm-conscious than women, and thought to be more guided by covert prestige, which prescribes the use of the vernacular.

By contrast, stereotypical expectations of female speech associate them with close-to-standard, even with RP accents and hypercorrections – a phenomenon which has given us in the Scottish context the terms 'Morningside' and 'Kelvinside'. These middle-class districts in Edinburgh and Glasgow led the anglicization in the 18C/19C, with women in particular cultivating (as it was perceived) a hypercorrect, affected 'refained eccent' of English. (It is insufficiently known whether this originated in girls' private schools, as claimed by Johnston (1985), and how widespread it once was outside the two districts.) The attitudes behind such behaviour are of course well-known and near-universal (for literary illustrations of the accent see T50 and the 1940s McFlannel novels by Helen W. Pryde). Romaine (1982b) has shown that a stronger orientation towards the perceived official standard in female speakers started quite early on among Edinburgh schoolchildren, when it was noticeable at the age of six to eight.

The role of women in language change has been seen as a paradox (Labov 2001): they tend to conform with overt norms – but they are leaders of innovation where there are no fixed rules. While Labov states that this is true for pronunciation in Philadelphia, Macafee (1994a) shows that girls also may be innovators with respect to the introduction of individual lexical dialect items.

2.6.4 *Historical sociolinguistics*

How far sociolinguistic insights can be applied to historical conditions obviously depends on the quantity and quality of linguistic and social data available on early speech communities. Individual topics can be researched with more or less expectation of satisfactory results, as in test cases like the following:

1) the social correlation of language choice in a multilingual situation in a 14C burgh like Aberdeen;

2) the relationship of linguistic variation and social class (of senders and addressees) in informal texts not meant for publication, such as early Scottish letters;

3) the degree of anglicization found in 16C texts as depending on education, social rank, political persuasion and religious affiliation;

4) anglicization of speech as a process depending on age, social class, residence (metropolitan vs. urban vs. rural) and political persuasion or national attitude in informal texts from late 18C urban Scotland;

5) the impact of compulsory education on attitudes towards St E, ScE and local dialect in the late 19C, etc.

As modern conditions show, the sociolinguistic setup of Scottish speech communities is more complex than, for instance, that in most parts of England, and since available research data on historical Scottish communities are less dense than in England, any description must remain patchier for Scotland.

Two major studies of 16C Scots show the limitations of sociolinguistic transfers to historical conditions. Romaine (1982a) examines one linguistic variable (relativization techniques) in a corpus of Middle Scots texts of various text types sampled from the period c.1530-50 in the Central Scots area. Romaine sees the social relevance of anglicization, but largely disregards the sociological aspects in not taking the author/addressee relationship of the selected texts fully into account. Moreover, the period chosen may be too late to trace anglicization of this particular feature in written Scots, and she considers the historical situation insufficiently by not analysing the EModE input that greatly modified the Scottish system in the field she describes (cf. Macafee 1983b). The fact that some of her textual material is translated from Latin is not accounted for either.

By contrast, Devitt's (1989) study of the processes of standardisation examines five morpho-syntactic variables (relative clause marker, preterite inflection, indefinite article, negative particle and present participle) in various text types sampled from the larger period of 1520-1659 (cf. fig. 14). Devitt considers the sociolinguistic conditions of authors and recipients more carefully, defines the text types she studies more precisely, and bases her analysis on a greater number of linguistic variables than Romaine.

Another major problem of applying sociolinguistic methods to historical Scots texts is the fact that the available corpus is not only restricted to written data but also clearly focused on literary uses from the time of Ramsay onwards. The individual writer's decision to use Scots at all and in what form is largely determined by factors which cannot be fully explained by traditional sociolinguistic parameters.

Therefore, from the 18C onwards, sociolinguistic investigations must always consider both ScE and Scots. Fortunately, the sources concerning the process of the anglicization of Scottish speech in the 18C are comparatively rich. They include, in particular,

a) statements of grammarians, usually voicing prescriptive concerns for the correct uses of English, complemented by incidental remarks about contemporary attitudes towards Scots (and its various forms) and the incoming English; and

b) written texts in which linguistic variation, hypercorrection and remaining interferences from Scots document the language shift to ScE.

Of course, even in a richly documented period such as that of 18C urban Scotland, large gaps remain which do not permit us to apply modern sociolinguistic methods to describe and explain the shift – no matter how much we might wish to use insights gained by, for instance, Labov's analysis of the effects of an incoming new norm in New York in the 1960s (cf. 4.3).

2.6.5 *Sociolectal variation in creative writing*

Sociolinguistic data on a different level are found where socially determined speech is made functional in creative writing. The history of Scottish literature seems to provide particularly frequent instances in which the social function of Scots is used as a means of characterization (cf. McClure 1995a). Consider, in addition to the detailed evidence that can be gathered from texts written by Sir Walter Scott and John Galt, for instance:

1) the ironic view of the anglicization in Robert McLellan's *Flouers o Edinburgh* (T55);
2) the contrast of Aunt Purdie's 'refained' speech and Wee Macgreegor's lower-class diction (and behaviour) in Bell's *Wee Macgreegor* (T50);
3) Docherty's linguistic accommodation in the urban setting of early 20C Kilmarnock (alias 'Graithnock'), Ayrshire, in William McIlvanney's novel (T62).

The list could easily be continued.

One way of indicating that characters in literary texts belong to the 'lower classes' is the use of modified spellings that do not represent deviant pronunciation. The method, which involves a great deal of eye dialect, was frequently used in 19C EngE, but is much rarer in Scottish texts. Donaldson adduces the 1875 "burlesque *Address to Katts*", whose neo-classical facade masks a gleeful deconstruction of the imperial pretensions of high English literature by means of what is intended to appear as a Scots of the most demotic kind:

t41 Dicend ye 15. hevinly graces and mewsis 9.
     give words that brethe – and Burnin' thocht to Shine,
     Inspire my Mus – ye Anshint Gods o' greese,
     & ayd a sun to Write A Mr Peese
   5 on Katts. Thebease fo'k Keeps in their hooses –
     for the ekspress purpise of catchin' Their moosis
     ye Bruts – sume of you ar Black & sum o' ye White   (1875, quoted from Donaldson 1986:60)

A close look shows, however, that there is little 'demotic Scots' here – but mainly an accumulation of 'incorrect' spellings in a largely English text, some of them representing Scots pronunciations.

2.7   Registers, styles and text types
(Devitt 1989, Görlach 1998d)

The functional distribution of Latin, French, Scots and English has been in a dynamic balance over the centuries (cf. 2.1); after 1500, the choice in the Lowlands was almost entirely reduced to Scots and English. From then on, English began to gain ground over Scots.The trend meant a two-fold reduction of Scots which involves more complex issues than the mere process of anglicization: first, the number of text types for which Scots was acceptable decreased, and did so dramatically after 1603 (with a revival in certain types of literature from the 18C onwards, cf. Jack 1998). Secondly, the density of Scots features also diminished, that is, even texts considered, and intended as, Scots were likely to contain fewer and fewer diagnostic variants, authors preferring English elements or those shared by the two languages (the proportion was further increased by the adoption of English spelling conventions).

Devitt's (1989) statistical analyses of the anglicization processes between 1520 and 1659 support the obvious assumption that criteria such as 'formality' and 'degree of removal from ordinary and domestic life' explain some of the developments, but she also shows that the early introduction of biblical English and conservative/nationalistic tendencies in public records played an important part, too (fig. 14, p. 56). Devitt analyses five textual categories: religious treatises, official correspondence, private records, personal correspondence and public records. She therefore captures only a small selection of the possible uses of written language in the period. Although she rightly concentrates on these five broad types (which exhibit an especially great amount of variation and change), it will have to be tested how far the genres and the selection of texts in each of them are representative. The graphs abstracted from her data (1989:56-8) show bewildering zigzags which point to excessive instability, choices being largely determined by individual preferences. A few consistent facts provide a starting point for further research: why are religious treatises so overwhelmingly Scots between 1540 and 1559 and then lead the anglicization process? Is the influence of the English Bible the only possible explanation for this? And why do personal correspondence and (less consistently) private records have their peaks of Scottishness between 1560 and 1579?

In a survey of text types in the history of Scots (Görlach 1998d) I tried to capture a greater variety of genres in which Scots can be found and to cover a longer period. The descriptions can here be summarized as follows:

Scholarly prose: there were only few Scots texts in the 16C, doubtless because the switchover from Latin to the vernacular (after 1580 in England) was too late for Scots to be employed on a large scale, and fewer texts still after 1603, in the period immediately before the tradition came to an end in the 17C.

Grammar books and metalinguistic reflexion: from the beginning (cf. Hume 1617, T21) authors described the *English* language, taking in bits of Scots only for comparative (remedial) purposes; the first grammars of Scots that deserve this designation originated in the phase of scientific dialectology (Murray 1873), but then they described individual spoken dialects. (The variety used for exposition might be in

A Textual History of Scots

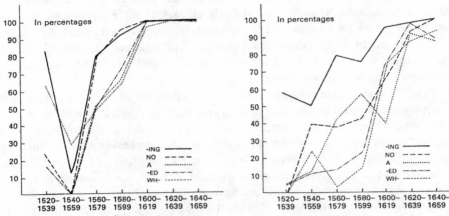

Figure 4.1 Anglicization in religious treatises

Figure 4.2 Anglicization in official correspondence

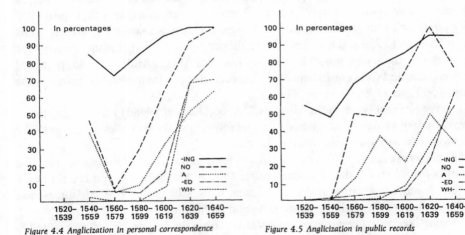

Figure 4.4 Anglicization in personal correspondence

Figure 4.5 Anglicization in public records

Fig. 14 The increase of English variants in four linguistic variables (from Devitt 1989)

diluted Scots, as Hume's was in 1617). Modern reflexions on the forms and functions of Scots that are written in the variety are largely determined by language-planning concerns, such as Young's "Thochts anent Lallans prose" (1947, T56) – and there was a continuous trickle of such texts in the *Scotsman* well into the 1980s. These attempts can be seen to culminate in the collection of papers "Our ain leid?" (McClure *et al.* 1981, T63-4). More recently, Alasdair Allan's M.A. dissertation on Scots orthography written in Scots throughout (summarized, also in Scots, in Allan 1995), as well as his PhD thesis (Allan 1998), broke new ground in reclaiming for the language the domain of linguistic exposition – but this *tour de force* has not found many imitators to date (cf. Horsbroch 2000, T73 and a few contributions in Kirk & O'Baoill 2001b). The use of English for expository prose on the subject is much more common: Sydney Goodsir Smith's reply to Young in his "In defence of Lallans" (1949, T57), and Billy Kay's realistic decision to use ScE with Scots admixtures, in his book *Scots: The Mither Tongue* (1986, ³1993) are typical of the genre (cf. 1.1.3).

Administrative texts: a substantial number of formal texts survives from the chancery and burghs in the 16C, exhibiting various degrees of Scots spelling and morphology. A contrastive analysis with EModE texts would be needed to show how far the distinctness of Scots documents is also found in lexis and syntax. The 17C saw a rapid increase of English elements, but burgh records were less consistently affected than other text types. Scots features were apparently supported by tradition and the formulaic character of the texts. Nevertheless, the Scottishness of texts like the Education Act of 1616 (T20) – explicitly giving order to spread the use of *English* in the Highlands – and the *Dundonald School Regulations* (ca. 1640, cf. Görlach 1991a:387-9) is surprising.

Religious texts: the modest start of a tradition of the use of Scots in Murdoch Nisbet's unprinted translation of the *New Testament* of c.1520, and in the tracts around 1540-60 seems to have been smothered by the acceptance of the English Geneva Bible in the Reformation (also cf. Knox 8.2.3 and T14). The fact that the Bible – the only book in many households – was in English whereas all spoken uses were Scots, greatly contributed to establishing the diglossia which existed right into the 20C. All written religious text types were affected by anglicization from 1560 to the present day, whether they were treatises and other forms of expository prose, printed catechisms and church hymns or smaller forms like gravestone inscriptions (specimens in Scots are extremely rare, and likely to be facetious).

These statements do not apply to *spoken* Scots in the religious context. Most probably, sermons were preached, and hymns sung, in Scots – its broadness accommodated to the specific community, reflecting their competence in, and emotional adherence to, the 'language of the heart'. However, we cannot be sure about the original oral performance of texts which are extant in written English form only. We also have to consider that the respectability demanded of religious language may well have led to a more anglicized register in speech which greatly differed from other, more colloquial uses, and which necessitated code-switches when topics were changed. However, any reconstruction of the restricted survival of Scots in the religious domain must rely on patchy evidence, including the language used in biblical translation and on literary representations (cf. 8.1.2 and Tulloch 1989).

Formal speech: the few indications of the survival of Scots in secular registers after 1603 come from secondary sources. Sir Walter Scott's description of educated Scots in the *Chronicles of the Canongate* indicates that formal spoken Scots was replaced by English in educated Edinburgh society from 1750 on:

t42 Scotch was a language which we have heard spoken by the learnd and the wise & witty & the accomplishd and which had not a trace of vulgarity in it but on the contrary sounded rather graceful and genteel. You remember how well Mrs Murray Keith – the late Lady Dumfries – my poor mother & other ladies of that day spoke their native language – it was different from the
   5 English as the Venetian is from the Tuscan dialect of Italy but it never occurred to any one that the Scottish any more than the Venetian was more vulgar than those who spoke the purer and more classical – But that is all gone and the remembrance will be drownd with us the elders of this existing generation   (*Letters*, VII:83)

Compare Lockhart's comment on the same period, taking up Scott's description:

t43 The poet's aunt spoke her native language pure and undiluted, but without the slightest tincture of that vulgarity which now seems almost unavoidable in the oral use of a dialect so long banished from Courts, and which has not been avoided by any modern writer who has ventured to introduce it, with the exception of Scott, and I may add, speaking generally, of Burns. Lady Raeburn, as she
   5 was universally styled, may be numbered with those friends of early days whom her nephew has alluded to in one of his prefaces as preserving what we might fancy to have been the old Scotch of Holyrood.   (*Life*, I:75, both texts quoted from Tulloch 1980:172)

Whereas Scottish lexis (with the exception of ScE terms relating to regional features in education, the law and administration) had been replaced early on, markedly Scots pronunciations were avoided only after 1750 in formal educated urban speech. (Contrast, to a certain extent, statements like A. Scot's, quoted in Jones 1995:13).

Informal language, letters: while private correspondence shows a fair number of Scottish features well into the 18C (Devitt 1989), such letters are not written in what might be called 'pure' or 'broad' Scots. After 1700, specimens remain rare. Burns's only example is a playful exercise written to his good friend William Nicol (T34). Obviously, sociolinguistic conventions did not permit the use of Scots in this text type. Accordingly, Scott appears to have violated such norms and expectations when he made his character Jeanie write letters in Scots in *The Heart of Midlothian* (1818, but the plot is set in 1736, a relevant fact if we wish to consider the linguistic 'realism' employed in the novel; cf. T37, and for a similarly unmotivated use, T46/30-8). Even today, the few letters in Scots or using Scots elements are either playful or state a (political) point (cf. T70) – with a few exceptions. Recently, I was pleased to receive a couple of e-mails in Scots from D. Horsbroch which illustrates that the auld leid can of course be adapted to modern media (although such attempts are still rare):

t44 Manfred ma frein, fit lyke cheil?,
      A'm writin efter a favour aff ye. A'm ettlin tae pit thegither a screid o seminars for the session 2002-2003 here at the Institute in Aiberdeen, on the Scots leid. A wes wunnerin whither ye wad gree tae gie the first ane on the Germanic backgrun tae Scots? A'v been forritsome an pit yer name
   5 doun on ma plan (see the eik tae this email), but, o course, the'r naethin set in stane til A hear back whither fowk is willin tae tak pairt or no!!!The Institute wad pey yer air flicht,taxis, ludgin, an aw that, sae ye wadna be oot o poutch. Oniewey, cuid ye lat me ken whither ye wad be for gien a seminar? Leuk forrit tae hearin fae ye. Fairfaw, Dauvit (...)

Manfred, ma frein,

10   Monie thank for yer swip repone; A'll speir at Derrick anent the Erasmus exchynge an get back tae
ye aboot it. But ye wad be itherwise free for 18 October? Fairfaw, Dauvit

However, the number of colleagues that are likely to do this is quite limited – A. Allan,
B. Kay and D. Horsbroch, and the use of Scots for such informal communication is an
expression of strong attachment to the language: these three are the only people known
to me who, when addressed in English, make a point answering in Scots – at least they
did to me.

Journalism (cf. 9.5.1): the range of texts written in Scots remained surprisingly wide
in the 19C, including a great variety of forms ranging from reports on international
affairs to chatty local items, from letters to the editor (T41-2) to advertising, and from
literary pieces to advice and instruction. Donaldson (1986, 1989) has documented the
upsurge of newspaper uses of Scots, mainly selecting his texts from provincial
publications which mushroomed after 1850, when cheap paper and printing methods
had become available. However, the decline of such experiments was predictable with
the loss of Scots as the dominant form of everyday speech, though it was less drastic
with informal uses as in gossip columns and cartoons. Humorous texts in particular have
always been a stronghold of Scots – but jokes printed in Scots are comparatively rare
(anti-Scots jokes tend to be in English, and there does not seem to be a tradition of anti-
English jokes told in Scots). Most specimens of humorous Scots also appear to be
spoken; this is shown by their presence on radio and TV. Perhaps the best known
tradition of humorous Scots is, however, not based on St Scots or rural dialect, but on
Glaswegian, which relies on racy idiomatic expressions, linguistic and other stereotypes
and (if such texts reach print in collected editions) phonetic spelling (cf. Mackie 1979).
The Aberdeen *Press and Journal*, catering for the NE dialect area, where the use of
Scots is stronger and better preserved than on the rest of the mainland, carries a weekly
column in Scots discussing various topics, whereas most other regional and the national
papers restrict their more serious use of Scots to debates on the language itself
(particularly in the letters to the editor).

Literary texts: narrative prose and poetry have remained the major stronghold of
Scots (cf. the detailed discussion in ch. 8). The most conspicuous problem here is the
increasing distance that exists between dense forms of literary Scots and sociolinguistic
reality. This means that today authors either write for small numbers of readers (who
tend to be middle-class and often academic literati), or have to employ a thin, colloquial,
urban kind of Scots.

The use of early Scots extends to minor text types; these include everyday genres
such as medical recipes, like the ones printed and discussed by Hargreaves (1981). As
with other such collections, the items tend to be copied from various sources. Therefore
it is impossible to establish the author's spelling conventions or his NE dialect with any
degree of certainty. The spelling used does, however, appear to be representative of its
time (1605).

Although the limited evidence is far from conclusive for more wideranging
interpretations, it seems remarkable how much less Scots the manuscript household

books and the printed cooking recipes of the 18C are (see the specimens printed in Görlach 2001a: 349-52). This at least suggests a conspicuous dilution of Scots in such texts in the intervening one hundred years.

Ex 24   Discuss the interrelationship of formality and audience with regard to the acceptability of Scots in the history of the language.

2.8   *Scots outside Scotland*

There is no comprehensive investigation of the linguistic impact of Scots outside Scotland. Ulster alone is covered in satisfactory quantity and quality (cf. the references in Montgomery & Gregg 1997). Otherwise, some work has been devoted to the Scottish literary and cultural influence (for the US cf. Hook 1999, Montgomery 2001), or settlement history (for Australia cf. Jupp 1988:759-90), and there are a few studies dealing with the survival of Scots or its influence on English in individual countries outside Great Britain.

1700 marks a watershed for the 'export' of Scots. In the (early) 17C, Scots was still the unrivalled language that was spread to new territories, when Scotland expanded its borders and settled new places:

1) The Education Act of 1616 (T20) ruled that landowners in the Highlands send their sons to be taught English in the South, but the linguistic form of the document makes it more likely that the language actually used was *Scots*.
2) In Shetland and Orkney, Norn was first replaced by Scots in the 16/17C (cf. 1.6.3), which was then the desirable prestige language for the islanders to adopt, before English in turn ousted Scots.
3) The Ulster Plantations of 1610-25 (cf. 2.9.2) established a strong Scots-speaking community outside Scotland (though separated by a short distance which made interchange and linguistic reinforcement possible).

Later developments, such as the massive emigration of Lowlands Scots to various parts of the British colonies, carried Scottish culture around the globe. This large-scale emigration came at a time when St E was the unquestioned (written) norm. Although Scots varieties were not as stigmatized as IrE, broad dialect was not easily tolerated – and thus Scots and salient features of ScE were given up even where the concentration of Scottish settlers would have made the (diluted) survival of their speech likely (cf. New Zealand etc. 2.7.4).

A particularly relevant statement comes from the Rev. John Witherspoon. He was born near Edinburgh in 1722, received a classical education and became a Presbyterian minister. His upper-middle-class education included all the Enlightenment attitudes towards Scots. When he was invited to become president of the College of New Jersey (later Princeton University) in 1766 he carried these evaluations across the Atlantic. His criticism (published in various essays in *The Pennsylvania Journal* in 1781, see Mathews 1931:13-30) is as harsh on the new varieties he met in New England as it was on the ones back home, and thus his opinion is as important for the slow emergence of American linguistic independence as it is for the non-survival of Scottish speech overseas:

t45 Scotland, or the northern part of Great-Britain, was once a separate independent kingdom, though,
except in the Highlands, the people spoke the same language as in England; the inhabitants of the
Lowlands, in both countries, having been originally the same. It is justly observed by Dr.
Robertson, in his History of Scotland, that had they continued separate kingdoms so that there
5 should have been a court and parliament at Edinburgh, to serve as a standard, the small differences
in dialect and even in pronounciation would not have been considered as defects, and there would
have been no more opprobrium attending the use of them in speech or writing, than there was in
the use of the different dialects of the ancient Grecian republics. But by the removal of the court
to London, and especially by the union of the two kingdoms, the Scottish manner of speaking,
10 came to be considered as provincial barbarism; which, therefore, all scholars are now at the utmost
pains to avoid. It is very probable that the reverse of this, or rather its counter part, will happen in
America. Being entirely separated from Britain, we shall find some centre or standard of our own,
and not be subject to the inhabitants of that island, either in receiving new ways of speaking or
rejecting the old. (1781, quoted from Mathews 1931:17)

He explains the status of Americanisms with regard to the attitudes towards the
vernacular he experienced in Scotland:

t46 The first class [of expressions] I call Americanisms, by which I understand an use of phrases or
terms, or a construction of sentences, even among persons of rank and education, different from
the use of the same terms or phrases, or the construction of similar sentences in Great-Britain. It
does not follow, from a man's using these, that he is ignorant, or his discourse upon the whole
5 inelegant; nay, it does not follow in every case, that the terms or phrases used are worse in
themselves, but merely that they are of American and not of English growth. The word
Americanism, which I have coined for the purpose, is exactly similar in its formation and
signification to the word Scotticism. By the word Scotticism is understood any term or phrase, and
indeed any thing either in construction, pronounciation or accentuation, that is peculiar to North-
10 Britain. There are many instances in which the Scotch way is as good, and some in which every
person who has the least taste as to the propriety or purity of a language in general, must confess
that it is better than that of England, yet speakers and writers must conform to custom.
(1781, quoted from Mathews 1931:17)

Ex 25 Are there other parallels between the attitudinal history of AmE and Scots
apart from the ones pointed out by Witherspoon?

With the scarcity of linguistic Scottish relics in mind, it may come as a surprise that the
literary uses of Scots overseas have been considerable. The most substantial
contribution comes, of course, from Ulster, where the community of Ulster Scots always
felt as a part of the larger Scots area. But there are also substantial corpora of literary
texts written in Scots in the United States and later South Africa, Australia and New
Zealand, mostly by Scottish expatriates.

2.8.1 *Northern Ireland*
(Montgomery & Gregg 1997, Kirk and O'Baoill 2000, 2001a,b)

The massive settlement of Ulster by English (some 20,000) and Lowland Scots (some
100,000) in the early 17C (1610-25), established a belt of stable Scots-speaking
communities especially along the coast from Antrim to Donegal, although the native
Celtic speakers were still in the majority in the region (cf. fig. 15). Until the 19C there
was little dialect erosion, mainly because differences in religious persuasion prevented
extended contacts between the Presbyterian Scots-speaking communities and the native

Catholics (cf. the match of Scottish surnames, Presbyterianism and Ulster-Scots dialect in fig. 15), whereas contacts were maintained strongly with mainland Scotland across the short sea crossing.

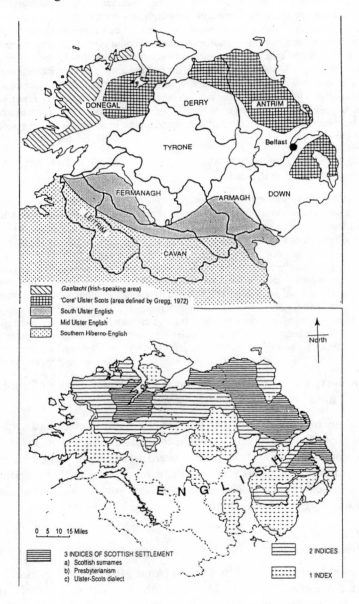

Fig. 15 The correlation of dialect, names and religious affiliation in Ulster (from Montgomery & Gregg 1997:578, 580)

Complaints about dialect erosion start in the second half of the 19C, as in Alexander Knox's comment about County Down:

t47　The Scottish idiom is most observable in the baronies of Ards and Castlereagh and their confines, although extending as far as Hillsborough and Dromore. Until recently it was spoken as broadly as in Ayr or Wigtownshire, but it is gradually dying out, although innumerable words imported from Scotland are in daily use in the northern part of the county.

(1875, quoted from Montgomery & Gregg 1997:576)

The (relative) isolation may have caused certain archaic features to survive, although the following statement from 1814 is likely to be exaggerated:

t48　The Dissenters speak broad Scotch and are in the habit of using terms and expressions long obsolete, even in Scotland, and which are only to be found in the glossary annexed to the bishop of Dunkeld's (i.e. G. Douglas') translation of Virgil.

(quoted from Montgomery & Gregg 1997:582)

In the 20C, Ulster has seen the expected decline of dialects (including Scots) so common elsewhere. Since Scots is particularly distinctive, and strongly connected with rural lifestyles, the erosion is here particularly conspicuous – although Gregg's (1972) prediction of language death within the next generations has turned out to be premature. The fact that Ulster Scots has recently been recognized as a minority language by the European Bureau of Lesser Used Languages (2.3.4) is, however, not likely to guarantee its survival, or even revival, in spite of language activism as expressed in works like Robinson (1997). Still, it is the best researched variety of Scots outside Scotland (cf. the section on Ulster in Macafee's online bibliography of studies in Scots) and the only one with a scholarly dictionary of its own (Macafee 1996).

A particular stronghold of Scots in Ulster was and is its use in dialect poetry. Many 17C documents are in unmistakable Scots, and there is a large corpus of 19C prose texts, mainly tales and humorous pieces in newspapers and small booklets, which is exemplarily documented in Montgomery & Gregg (1997:593-604). Most prominent, however, is the work of 19C Ulster Scots poets, who wrote in the style of Burns (some also earlier or contemporary). Their language, thus, appears to be stereotypical Scots, but Robinson (1997) describes the situation as follows:

t49　The only type of Ulster-Scots literature which is reasonably well-known today is the poetry of 200 years ago. However, these poems often seem like imitation Scots because of the frequent use of words such as *sic* ('such'), *gif* ('if'), and *unco* ('very'). Although most people would instantly recognize these as Scots words, they are not used in Ulster-Scots speech today. Many people
5　assume that, therefore, they were used only by Burns imitators as a literary device, and were not part of the poets' everyday speech. Yet, these same weaver poets always protested that the language they used was their own native tongue – and were often offended by suggestions that it was artificial Scotch.

(Robinson 1997:11)

Ex 26　Summarize the factors that made Scots in Ulster diverge from dialects in mainland Scotland.

Ex 27　Sketch the importance of political factors for the modern status of Ulster Scots (Görlach 2000)

2.8.2 *North America (the United States, Canada and Caribbean)*

United States : The Scots formed a major portion of 19C immigrants, but 'braid Scots' has not survived in any part of the country. Detailed research on the vernacular in areas of Scots/Irish settlements such as the Appalachians (Montgomery 1989, 2001) has shown that even in relative isolation unambiguously Scottish features in pronunciation, morphology and lexis are few. Accommodation to the local norms appears to have been the rule amongst Scottish immigrants, whether Gaelic- or Scots-speaking. Nationwide, relatively few terms for Scottish realia (*bannock, lobbered milk* etc.) are in evidence. A preliminary examination of the first two published and indexed volumes of the *Dictionary of American Regional English* (entries for letters A to H), however, shows that dialect words of Scots origin form a not insignificant group within the corpus: 365 of the 21,000 forms indexed are marked as *Scots*, as compared to 241 from German, 178 from French and 51 from Dutch (Hamilton 1998:108).

The United States can serve as an illustration of how literary Scots continued to be influential in a (post-)colonial society. Hook summarizes the data on the huge popularity of Ramsay, Burns, Scott and Hogg, in the 18/19C as documented by the large number of American editions of their works (in the days before copyright). This was apparently in spite of the linguistic divergence:

t50   There is little evidence that Burns's vernacular was any barrier to American appreciation, though
      it is true that anthologies tended to reprint some of his more popular English language poems.
                                                                                (Hook 1999:109)

In addition, there was a great deal of Scots literature written in the country:

t51   Between 1790 and 1820 there was quite a vogue for the writing of poems in the Scottish
      vernacular, mainly of course in imitation of Burns, in America. Produced mainly in New England,
      New Jersey, and Pennsylvania, most of this verse is of course of little or no literary value, but the
      fact that it could be written at all is of some interest. It suggests sustained interest in Burns and
  5   perhaps other Scottish vernacular poets; and it certainly implies the existence of an American
      audience to some degree receptive towards Scottish vernacular poetry.   (Hook 1999:109)

The popularity of Scots writings apparently extended to more everyday forms of literature: it is well known that the so-called *Kailyard* authors in the 1890s (cf. T46) and texts like *Wee Macgreegor* (1901, T50) sold very well in America and the colonies – and not only to emigrant Scots.

Canada: While the influence of IrE on local or regional Englishes is well-researched, the importance of Scots and ScE is not. No Scots dialect appears to have survived the first generation of emigrant speakers or so, and even the impact of ScE appears to be quite limited. No lexical items that connect present-day dialect words with Scottish immigration are found in the *Survey of Canadian English*, and the possible influence of Scottish pronunciation on the shibboleth of spoken CanE, the 'Canadian Raising', is unclear. The fact that the diphthongs in words like *nice* and *house*, i.e. preceding voiceless consonants, have 'Scottish' qualities (but not the ones in *wise* and *crowd*) may point to a Scottish input which was re-ordered in a specifically Canadian allo-phonic distribution (Trudgill 1986:153-61; but also cf. a different interpretation in Britain & Trudgill 1999).

The Caribbean: Most dialect features were melted down in Caribbean creoles so that etymologies of many present-day items are at best conjectural. However, if there is evidence of any regional input at all, it is from SW English rather than Scots. Although Scottish emigration to the Caribbean was considerable (even Burns almost took this fateful decision), the Scottish linguistic input appears to be almost totally lost.

2.8.3 *Australia*
(Tulloch 1997b, 1997c, Cardell & Cumming 1992/93, Jupp 1988:759-90)

Although the proportion of Scottish immigrants was not particularly large (ranging between 10% and 20% according to region) and Scots dialects have not survived in any place, the original impact of the Scots has been considerable, especially in the areas of early concentrations of Scottish settlers in Victoria from the 1820s onwards, many of them working-class assisted emigrants (the proportion of Scots among the *convicts* was minimal; cf. Jupp 1988). Apart from its dominant influence in the Presbyterian Churches, a certain amount of linguistic heritage remains:

t52　For those familiar with the Scottish accent, it is the most easily distinguished characteristic of the Scot in Australia, often being heavy and difficult to lose but generally being well-accepted among non-Scots. The use of many Scottish words and phrases by the popular press in articles concerning Scots and Scottish activities also suggests that many Australian readers are familiar with
　　5　expressions such as bonnie, bairn, canny, lassie, blether and sassenach. (Bain in Jupp 1988:788)

The Scots literary tradition in Australia is even stronger than in the United States (Tulloch 1997c). Again, it was mainly the models provided by Burns and Scott that sparked off a remarkable literature. With respect to prose, Tulloch points to Catherine Helen Spence's novel *Clara Morison* (1854) which contains very dense dialogues in St literary Scots (making little allowance for regional variation):

t53　"How do you think you will like the colony?" asked Clara of the woman.
　　"There's a hantle bonnie trees, and the grass is braw and green, but oh, sirs! we're gaun a lang way frae the sea. We wunna hae a fish frae ae year's end to anither, I'm thinking."
　　"I suppose your husband went to the fishing at home?" said Clara.
　　5　"Aye, and to the whale fishing in the season, – and I minded the hairst, and had the corn tight under thack and rape, or ever he cam hame. There's a hantle left to the women-folk our way, ye ken."
　　"Is your husband used to mind sheep?" Clara asked.
　　"Ooo aye! we had nae less than five sheep of our ain, and a cow forbye; and I span a' the woo' in
　10　the winter nichts, and braw stockings an flannen coats I made o't; but the gudeman is a canny man as weel."
　　　　　　　　　　　　　　　　　　　　　　　　(Spence 1854, quoted from Tulloch 1997c:320)

Even Joseph Furphy, though not a Scotsman himself, has a character speak broad Scots in *Such is Life* (1903, Tulloch 1997c:322). The most remarkable product with respect to linguistic detail (though not necessarily literary merit) is perhaps John Service's *The Life and Recollections of Doctor Duguid of Kilwinning* (1887), a novel entirely written in Scots. Tulloch points to the linguistic paradoxon involved (*not* just that the text was written in the Antipodes):

t54　The difficulty... is that, although Service has created a Scots-speaking narrator, Duguid is not speaking but writing. ...To write Scots in circumstances where all literate people in Scotland would expect English requires a new style of language, but...Service's narrative reads as typical English novelistic narrative of the time with an overlay of Scots vocabulary　　　　(Tulloch 1997c:323)

He also quotes a passage for illustration:

t55 Sanny Duguid, a second cousin of my grandfather's, whyles, when he got fou', used indeed to
    descant on the family pedigree, and said he had heard his father tell that we came with King Haco
    from Denmark. In fact, he went so far as to say that ance in Paisley, he had seen a very ancient
    print of our coat-of-arms, with the motto, so far as he could mind it, of "Oukum wankum sane
   5 podavia". "I'm no' a vera guid Latin scholar", quo' Sanny, "but the general meanin' o't, I believe,
    is 'Strong in the strength o' the Lord'".
       It was always my private opinion that Sanny lee'd like a mill-shillin'; and now that I have
    learned the Latin tongue myself, I feel sure of it. Hoosever, we'll let that flee stick to the wa', and
    I would merely make the observe here in passing, that for some hundreds of years back, as it would
  10 appear from the books of the kirk-Session, my forbears have been sma' bits o' tradesmen, cottars,
    feuars, blacksmiths, and siclike, in the west kintra, and chiefly aboot the toon and parish of
    Kilwinning itself.   (Service 1887, quoted from Tulloch 1997c:323)

With this strong literary tradition in mind, the fact that even biblical translations into
Scots were undertaken in Australia, does not come as a surprise. This includes the first
translation into Scots of *Genesis* by H.P. Cameron (T51), who emigrated to Australia ca.
1896, translated à Kempis' *Imitation of Christ* and completed and published the *Genesis*
in the year of his death, 1921.

t56 Cameron was conscious of the strangeness of working on a translation into Scots "i' the Australian
    'bush'", but he claimed that "still-and-on e'en mids the eldritch yowling o' the dingo, the rowtin
    o' nowte, the maein o' fe, and the schrill crawin' o' the 'rooster', he hes hard athin his saul and
    abune them a' the 'saft, couthie' müsick o' the Doric"
                                             (Prefatory Note, quoted from Tulloch 1989:65-5)

In poetry, the model set by Burns was an obvious one; however, as Tulloch argues
(1997c:324) the choice of Scots is difficult to justify. When the *auld leid* is used, it is
usually mixed with English (as it is indeed in Burns). Joan Torrance's "The Mother's
Wish", included in her collection of poems, *Twixt Heather and Wattle* (published in
Sydney, 1904), is a characteristic specimen, continuing in a way the *Whistle-Binkie*
tradition of the 19C (cf. 8.5.2):

t57 Aye, laddie, 'tis oor ain auld hoose,   I little kent that summer nicht
    Sair tears bedim mine een,   Thy heaven was sae near,
    As looking roun' the wa's I see   15 That death's pale messenger was nigh
    The changes that ha'e been.   To claim thy mither dear.

  5 Your gran'sire laid the mossy stanes,   His cauld han' touched her bonny brow,
    An' this wee but an' ben   It made her bright een dim,
    Was added when his winsome lass   Wi' failing breath she whispered low –
    Was coming hame – ye ken? ...   20 'A minister mak' him'.

    An' hoo her face wad lighten up   'Bring him up fitted for the wark
  10 When ye cried 'Fayther's hame',   'Oor Maister bid us dae,
    Or held your hands across the burn   'Mebbe that I can ken his coorse
    His sweetie bag to claim. ...   'From whaur I'm ga'ing tae'.

                                            (Torrance 1904, quoted from Tulloch 1997c:325)

Most of the Scotticisms were "boringly predictable [but they had] at least the advantage
of being well known to Australian readers" (Tulloch 1997c:326).

2.8.4 *New Zealand*
(Bauer 1997, Bartlett 1992)

As the placenames clearly show, the South Island was largely settled by emigrants from Scotland; however, the Scots do not appear to have formed the majority in any of the major towns, and their proportion was further reduced when the mid-19C goldrush washed more people into the country. Although popular belief has it that Scottish characteristics are strong in the area, a close analysis shows very few retentions; even features such as postvocalic /r/ cannot be unambiguously attributed to the Scottish inheritance. The lexical evidence (Bauer 1997:269-70) looks more impressive, but is negligible when compared with the entire vocabulary.

Ex 28   Summarize the reasons why the influence of Scots and ScE was less permanent in Australia and New Zealand than might have been expected.

2.9   *Sociohistorical parallels with the Scots/English situation in Europe*

New languages can emerge by splitting off from existing ones, when the *abstand* suggests independence and attitudes of speakers demand it: Lëtzebuergsch and Macedonian are 20C illustrations. On the other hand, linguistic independence can be lost, by language shift or merger with a related variety – or the process of language formation may not come to completion. The case of a smaller language being dialectalized by the more powerful, prestigious or expressive neighbour is not unique, as a sketch of various European cases can show.

2.9.1 *Low German*
(Görlach 1985b, 1991b)

The closest parallel with the history of Scots is found in Low German, which is still spoken by some 6 to 10 million speakers in Northern Germany; the major similarities between the two varieties are:
1) a former status as a largely standardized language of wider communication (Low German even had an international function as the language of the Hansa) in the 15-17C;
2) a takeover by the more prestigious 'southern' language, first in the towns, and in formal/administrational registers;
3) the loss of the domains of education and religion in the 16-18C;
4) a limited survival in poetry and literary prose;
5) attempted, but largely ineffective moves at revival in the 20C, the failure of which has largely reduced the language to the spoken, informal medium of older speakers in rural districts.

From a certain stage in the history of Low German, speakers came to identify their native language as a dialect of German, or as an informal, colloquial or even incorrect form of the standard language. The stable diglossia which existed for several centuries has now largely given way to monodialectalism, i.e. the use of modified standard German spoken with various degrees of local accents.

2.9.2 *Frisian*

The case of Frisian is of particular relevance for Scots, not just because of the close genetic relationship with English, forming so to speak a missing link between (Low) German and English/Scots. The coexistence of two closely related languages in the Netherlands (Dutch and Frisian) has led to many types of interference and the emergence of a unique type of Town Frisian; also attitudes and language loyalty or revivalist moves offer interesting comparisons with Scots. In the special case of North Frisian, even four genetically related languages coexist in a complex polyglossia (Frisian, split up into various dialects, and Danish dialect, Low German and Standard German). The situation is in some ways similar to Shetland: as Norn was pushed out by Scots which in turn was replaced by English, so Frisian succumbed to Low German in the 14C to 19C in many localities, which is now ceding to Standard German.[2]

2.9.3 *Occitan (Provençal, Gascon etc.)*

Unlike Scots and Low German, the varieties of the langue d'oc show great distance to French which came to dominate them from the 16C onwards; they are in fact much closer to Catalan and Italian. The restriction of the functional range of Occitan, especially after the French Revolution, and the social stigma attracted to the 'patois' are very much like the consequences sketched for Scots and Low German: the development has led to a conspicuous erosion of Occitan dialects. How early the parallels with Scots were seen is attested by an author in 1678:

> t58 You know I came to *England* the last time upon no other account, but to learn the language, and
> promised to keep correspondence with you upon this condition, that you would make remarks
> upon my Letters, and faithfully Admonish me of all the Scoticisms, or all the Words, and Phrases
> that are not current *English* therein. I confess I have a great Veneration for our own and the
> 5 Northern *English* Languages, upon the account of the Anglo-Saxon, to which they are so nearly
> ally'd; but yet... am as ambitious to write modern *English*, as any Gascon, or Provencal can be to
> write the modern French.(*Ravillac Redivivus*, London 1678:77, quoted from Aitken 1979a:94-5)

2.9.4 *Catalan*

By contrast, Catalan survived the danger of being swallowed up by Spanish. From equal status with Spanish in the 16C it came to be reduced in functions and prestige, but became the accepted language of a prosperous industrial region including its capital Barcelona in the 19C. Although many educated speakers considered it inferior to Spanish, Catalan never lost the stronghold of the major towns, and thus was not reduced to a rural patois. With so many native speakers in a region of great economic strength and a strong feeling of regional identity, the present-day expansion of its functions (after the language became official in 1975) was not a question of revival, but of successful corpus planning and attitudinal change, which has now firmly established Catalan in domains such as education and the mass media.

---

[2]Comprehensive information in Frisian is now available in Munske (2001); for the lessons that the Low German and Frisian experience can teach see the parallels for Scots and Ullans pointed out in Görlach (2001b).

3   *Writing and spelling*

All data from before 1900 exist only in written form; this must be carefully interpreted, if we wish to gain insights into the linguistic structure and arrive at valid dialectal, sociolinguistic and historical conclusions. The need for reconstruction is also the reason, why in this book writing and spelling are treated before describing the phonology of Scots.

The most important level of graphematic analysis for (historical) linguistics is clearly the analysis of the writing system itself, i.e. its distinctive features and their distribution (cf. Görlach 1991a:42). Minimal pairs on the graphic level (such as *mous* : *hous*) help to establish the graphemes, i.e. the distinctive units of the written form. Units that do not contrast may be in free variation, that is, their choice is unpredictable (including personal preferences and idiosyncrasies) or they may be complementary: early printed texts can have a regular complementary distribution of *v* vs. *u* and *s* vs. in word-initial as opposed to central or final position, or *r* as the regular form of the grapheme <r> unless preceded by a letter which is curved to the right, such as *b h o p w*. Consider the spellings *hauand* 'having', ſ*levv* 'slew', *vter* 'utter', ſ*uccedit* 'succeeded', *foʒ* 'for' in the facsimile of c1540 (fig. 17). Non-contrasting allographs are subsumed under one grapheme.

It is obvious that the coexistence of Scots and English in written form from the beginning (and of Latin in the early period) complicates the analysis: the spelling norms that writers had in mind are often uncertain, and in most cases they may not have had any, wavering between conventions taken from English books and renderings of more local practices which may reflect Scots pronunciations to a greater or lesser degree. Differences in graphemes help localize texts, but only to a limited extent (cf. 3.3). If variability was the rule in EModE before conventions became stable around 1700, then the coexistence of two largely unsettled systems in late 16C Scotland allowed for even greater variation.

Ex 29   State the specific problems that arise with spelling conventions in societies using two related languages, such as Scots and English.

3.1   *Handwriting*
         (Simpson 1977)

Medieval styles of writing, in England as well as Scotland, can be distinguished by forms and functions as book hands, charter hands and court hands. The first, mainly employed for volumes used in churches and monasteries, was largely replaced by bookprinting – as is also illustrated by the continuity of the letter forms of Gothic bookhands into Black Letter (Gothic) typefaces. Court hands are characterized by their cursive forms, which allow ease and speed in writing; these scripts, originally used in court and government administration, developed into the everyday handwriting of notaries, secretaries and the few private people who were able to write. The typical secretary cursive hand of the 16C may have been imported into Scotland from France; it seems to have been taken up slightly later than in England:

t59   French scripts penetrated so far in government administration that in the reign of Mary some of the
      records of the Scottish parliament itself were written in French hands, presumably by French
      clerks.   (Simpson 1977)

After 1603, the conventions of writing largely merged, that is, Scotland took over
English conventions, especially with the adoption of italic hands (which had been
occasionally used before, as illustrated in James VI's handwriting, cf. the facsimile in
Görlach 1991a:44).

   Original texts can be holographs (i.e. written by the author) or – more likely in early
periods in which writing was a rare accomplishment and scribes were required to
multiply texts – copied by scribes. At any rate, early documents are now usually
encountered in edited form (unless given in facsimile, cf. Simpson 1977). The editor has
to identify the original letter forms, transliterate them into modern equivalents, expand
abbreviations, and (where necessary) emend the text to make it intelligible. Many recent
editions also have modern conventions introduced with regard to capitalization,
punctuation and uses of <i, j>, <u, v, w> (replacing earlier allographic distribution or
free variation). As a consequence of their regularization/modernization, the value of
such editions for linguistic analysis is, therefore, restricted.

   Late 15C conventions are here illustrated by a facsimile of a passage from the Bodley
manuscript, fig 16.

Ex 30   How far can choices of spelling variants be explained by the fact that a specific
             text c1500 is handwritten rather than printed?

3.2   *Printed texts*

Printed texts are much easier to read and to analyse than manuscripts because the
graphic units (letters) are invariable and separated from each other – the steps leading
towards graphematic analysis are therefore greatly reduced. The currency of printed
materials also makes them easy to imitate, and printed texts tend to have more prestige
than handwritten ones. It is of great significance for the cultural history of Scotland that
the local production of books was very modest compared with the output of
London/Westminster, and that most of the books printed in Edinburgh after 1560 were
not in Scots (cf. 1.4). It is insufficiently understood to date in how far specifically
Scottish conventions in spelling and punctuation were established or whether practice
was determined by the adoption of the conventions of London printers from 1500
onwards (cf. Aitken 1971).

Ex 31   How far can we be sure that the spelling of a printed text (such as James VI's
             T18) reflects the author's intentions?

Heigh in the hevynnis figure circulere
The rody sterres twynklyt as the fyre;
And in Aquary Cinthia the clere
Rynsid hir tressis like the goldin wyre,
5 That late tofore in faire and fresche atyre
Through Capricorn heved hir hornis bright.
North northward approchit the myd-nyght.

Quhen as I lay in bed allone waking,
New partit out of slepe alyte tofore,
10 Fell me to mynd of mony diuerse thing,
Off this and that, can I nought say quharefore
Bot slepe for craft in erth myght I no more;
For Quhiche as tho coude I no better wyle
Bot toke a boke to rede apon a quhile.

15 Off quhiche the name is clepit properly
Boece, efter him that was the compiloure,
Schewing the counsele of philosophye,
Compilit by that noble senatoure
Off Rome, quhilom that was the warldis floure,
20 And from estate by fortune for a quhile
Forjugit was to pouert in exile.

And there to here this worthy lord and clerk,
His metir suete full of moralitee,
His flourit pen, so fair he set awerk,
25 Descryving first of his prosperitee
And out of that his infelicitee,
And than how he in his poleyt report
In philosophy can him to confort!

Fig. 16 Facsimile of the beginning of James I's *Kingis Quair* from Bodley MS Selden B.24 (copied in Edinburgh ca. 1490)

(t60)

☞ ¶Hovv Makbeth slevv his lordis for the proffet of thair landis and gud-dis.Hovv he biggit the castell of Dun-synnane,and slevv Makduffis vvife and
5 his barnis.Of the orisoun maid to Mal-colme Cammore be Makduf. Ca. vi.

NA thyng succedit happely to Makbeth efter the slauchter of Banquho.for plk man began to
10 feir his life,and durst nocht compeir quhare Makbeth was.Thus follo-wit plk day mair displeseir.for qu-hen this tyrane persauit plk man ha uand hym in dreid,he began to dreid
15 plk man in that sampn maner,& be pat way he grew maist odius to his subdittis ay slaing his noblis,or ellz confiscand pair guddis be bane cau sis.At last quhen he had gottin gret
20 proffet be slauchter & proscription of his noblis,he began to put his han-dis mair pertly in thair blud.for he thocht the proffet sa sweit p come to hym be slaucht of his noblis,that he
25 mycht not desist thairfra.for he had doubil proffet be p at way.First thay war slane p he dred · And secoundly he gat thair guddis to sustene ane gard of armit men to defend hym fra
30 iniure of pam p he suspeckit.forthir p he micht inuade p peppl with mair tyranp,he biggit ane strang castel in ye hicht of Dunsynnane,ane hyll in Gowrp.x.milis fra Perth.pis castel
35 was biggit wt infinit expensis.for for na stuf micht be cariit to p sampn but gret difficulte.And zit he ceissit not fra pe bigging pairof,bot causit al the Thanis of plk schire to big pe
40 said castel pair cours about.At last it fel to Makduf thane of ffif to big his pt of p said castel,And becaus he durst not cu to pis werk,in auenture p king put handis in hym as he did
45 afore in othir noblis of ye realme,he

send craftismen with al prouision,& comandit pame to do sa i his absence, p pe king micht haue na occasion to be mouit aganis hym.Sone efter
50 Makbeth come to besp his castell,& becaus he fand notMakduf present at the werk,he said. pis man wyl not obep my chargis,quhill he be riddin with ane mollet brydpl.Nochtheles
55 I sall gar hym draw lik ane auir in ane cart.fra thens he mycht neuir se makduf wt pacience,othir becaus he thocht his power ouir gret.Or el lis becaus it wes schawin be the pro
60 phecy of pe foresaid wichis,pat mak duf suld inuaid hym with displeseir. And (as oft occurris)quhare onp prince takis suspitioun,ane smal of-fence is occasion of gret iniuris.fi-
65 nalie he had slane Makduf be sum slycht,wer nocht ane wiche,in quho he had gret confidence said,To put hym out of all feir.pat he suld neuir be slane with man pat wes borne of
70 wife,nor vincust,quhill the wod of Birnane wer cu to pe castell of Dun synnane.Makbeth hauand gret co-fidence in thir wourdis,set alyde all feir of deith.And traistit fermely pat
75 he mycht do quhat he plesit but onp punition eftir following.for be p ta pphecy he beleuit it wes vnpossible to vincus hym.And be pe tothir,vn-possible to sla hym.Bot pir fals illu-
80 sionis of pe deuil brocht hym to vter cofusion,& gart him rage in Ithand slaucht of his subdittis but onp feir of his lyfe.At last Makduf disparit of his lyfe,tuk purpos to pas in In
85 gland,p he mycht bring Malcolme Camore in scotland to resist the tyrá ny of Makbeth.And zit the sampn was not deuisit sa secretly,bot Mak beth gat knawlage thairof.for all
90 kingis (as the prouerbe sapis)hes scharp sycht & lang eiris.pis Mak-

Fig. 17 16C Scottish printing: a section from Book XII of Bellenden's *Chronicle*, fol. 175ᵛ–176ʳ (repasted), illustrating italic and black letter fonts (special characters or combinations in italic: <vv>, < ʃ ~ s>; in black letter: < ʃ~Ꝣ >, <r ꝛ >, <v ~ u>, <ʒ>, <y> ~ [i, j, θ, ð]) (printed by T. Davidson in Edinburgh c1540, STC 3203)   (t61)

3.3 Spelling: the historical development
3.3.1 Conventions before 1450

As even a cursory look at early Scottish texts shows, the spelling conventions in the first period largely agree with those of Northern ME. This means that

a) individual writing systems are used in restricted geographical areas; conventions are determined by regional scriptoria, but they also depend on the spelling of the original to be copied;

b) spelling is not consistent; there are not even fixed spellings for each word within any one text;

c) as in other forms of ME, the renderings combine native (OE-derived) and Romance traditions, but the principle followed is largely phonemic. The differences between northern and southern texts therefore mainly result from the implied pronunciation in cases where the dialects diverge (as in the development of OE /a:/, cf. English *stone* vs. Scots *stane/steen*);

d) features that later developed into markers of Scottishness (cf. 3.3.2) are too sporadic to be regarded as characteristically Scots, yet. Moreover, "all the spelling features which count as diagnostic in Scottish orthography were already found in Northern English texts, and earlier than the examples in Scotland" (Kniezsa 1997:33).

3.3.2 Scottish conventions stabilized, 1450-1700
(Kniezsa 1997)

Concurrent with developments in England, the functions of the vernacular expanded in Scotland in the 15C to include official administrational texts, a fact which necessarily resulted in greater homogeneity at least in the registers affected (which were then taken as norms by other writers and for other text types). Many of the conventions in Scottish texts are shared with manuscripts or prints from England, including most rules of allography, and the use of abbreviations (cf. *ā* = *an* etc., *t'* = *ter*, *yᵗ* = *that* in Simpson 1977). But the following spelling conventions have by this time developed into characteristics that permit us to identify a text as originating from Scotland:

1) free variation of <u, v, w> for both /u(:)/ and /v/ and for the second element in /oʊ, aʊ/, although allographic distribution of word-initial <v> and medial and final <u> (as in EModE *vnto, haue*) is occasionally found;

2) <u>, <uCe>, <ui>, <uiCe> for developments from OE /o:/ (spelt <o(o)> in ME);

3) <i, y> added to <a>, <e>, <o> and <u> to indicate vowel length;

4) among the consonant graphemes, <þ> (later replaced by <th>) and <ß> (= <ss>) probably lasted longer than in ME; <ȝ> (to be replaced by <y, ch>) was sometimes rendered by <z> because of its similarity in shape (surviving in names like *Menzies*), and <þ> by <y> in abbreviated forms *yᵉ, yᵗ* etc. (as in EModE);

5) specifically Scottish consonant combinations include <quh> for /xw/ (EModE <wh>), <sch> for /ʃ/, <ch> for /x/ (in EModE represented by <gh>) and sometimes <ȝh, yh> initially for /j/.

Other features concern preferences in individual items (*bot, cum* vs. English *but, come*) or reflect Scots pronunciations rather than spelling conventions (*amang, sic, ony, mekil, ane*) and are therefore discussed in 4.2.

It is not quite clear to what extent conventions in manuscript texts (which had to give priority to easily legible forms) were changed by the advent of printing. In medieval manuscripts , <y> and <o>, for instance, were preferred in certain consonant environments to <i> and <u> in order to increase legibility, which was no longer necessary in print. The same is true for the use of capital forms especially of <A, J, R>, which were often employed in manuscripts to assist the reader. On the other hand, the use of abbreviations was drastically reduced in printed texts.

Ex 32   Analyse the grapheme system of fig. 16 and 17. Is the inventory employed the same as in EModE (for both type faces), and are the allographic distributions for <u>, <s> and <r> identical, and consistently used? What is the status of <y>?

Ex 33   Discuss the usefulness of 15/16C Scottish spelling for rendering phonological distinctions.

3.3.3 *Modern Scots spelling and spelling reforms*

Modern spelling conventions cannot be seen as independent of English (i.e. solely reflecting Scots pronunciation). After 1700, and especially in the 20C, spelling has a clear identificational function, highlighting Scots-spelt words as non-English. An author may disregard this contrastive aspect and use English spelling rules to indicate Scots pronunciations, and also employ St E spellings for shared words, possibly relying on readers to supply properly Scots pronunciations when texts are read aloud – end rhymes being (often) the key –, or even rely exclusively on Scottish rhythms throughout without modification of spellings.

Where Scottishness is indicated, it serves to reflect phonological divergence in cognate words. That English spelling conventions are the underlying pattern is of course justified by the fact that all readers from the 16C on learnt the craft by reading *English* texts. However, this practice brings with it a number of problems, such as:

1) the various ambiguities of the English spelling system with regard to phoneme/ grapheme correspondences;
2) uncertainty on the part of the reader as to whether a text written according to St E orthography is meant to be English or Scots;
3) deviations from English spelling (including the use of apostrophes where sounds would be expected in English but do not exist in Scots) make Scots look like non-standard, uneducated varieties of English – instead of establishing an independent norm;
4) transfer of inconsistencies and silent letters from the English spelling system for easier legibility and to stress the shared element;
5) by contrast, the rejection of individual English spellings or conventions for the sole purpose of being different.

All through the history of Scots, then, the spelling of individual authors exhibits a wide range of variability, choices depending on the phoneme structure of the dialect used, accommodation to either English norms or whatever was conceived as a Scottish standard, and morphological and etymological considerations, with certain idiosyncrasies added. As a consequence, the identification of individual lexemes can be difficult, and even the use of a comprehensive dictionary will not always solve all difficulties of understanding.

The absence of an orthographical norm also means that the massive influence of spelling on English pronunciation, which is so conspicuous especially from Johnson (1755) onwards, is lacking in Scots – with the exception of a few personal and place names (such as *Auchinleck*, formerly ['aflɛk]), whose pronunciations have changed towards forms more predictable from the spellings. Others, however, keep their pronunciations – at least in certain circumstances: *Dalziel* is still [di:'el], *Kirkcaldy* is [kɪr'kɔdɪ], *Menzies* – unless referring to the bookshop chain – is often [mɪŋɪs] and *Garioch* is still [girɪ] as a place name, but [garɪɔx] in the poet's name.

Ex 34 Find out alternatives for the pronunciations of the names quoted and of *Ruthwell, Milngavie* and *Culzean* (check for instance Jones *et al.* [15]1997, Bollard *et al.* [2]1997).

In contrast to EModE, there was no substantial discussion of what spelling reform measures would be necessary as a first step towards providing Scots with a homogeneous norm. The absence of such arguments before the 20C is even more significant since such language planning would have both distanced Scots from English in a way that left no doubt about its being a separate language, and provided an opportunity of basing the spelling on a close relation with the phonological system of the most prestigious contemporary form of (East Central) Scots. The sociolinguistic conditions, however, were such that relevant proposals would have had little chance of being implemented. As a consequence, Elphinston's unique suggestion was apparently never followed up:

t62 Scotland reannimated to' prezerv her illustrious fammilies at least in dheir names; lerns widh justice to' ballance dhe buties and blemmishes ov her wonce melodious and expressive, dho now passing, dialect. Finding it here howevver braught into' a system, she now can (hwat she nevver cood before) discrimminate her won from dhe Inglish diccion; az dhe Poartugueze or Cattalan, from dhe Castillian; dhat so dhe Scotch may be reggularly and effectually trezzured.

(1786:273, quoted from Rohlfing 1984:17)

Considering the negative reactions to the author's proposals for a reform of English spelling (collected by Rohlfing 1984:35-7), it is easy to see that a reform could not succeed in a society that was striving to be fully literate in English. Thus, the wealth of information on EModE pronunciation that may be gathered from treatises on and suggestions for spelling reform is missing for Scots of that period.

What we do get is information on the pronunciation of 18C ScE, as in the text by Alexander Scot, who used a largely phonetic system to indicate contemporary pronunciation of educated ScE (discussed by Jones 1993 and here quoted from Jones 1995:13):

t63 Oy haiv massalf tnoan dip-lairned professours oaf fowr destengueshed oonavarsetays, caupable oaf
     coamoonicatten airts aund sheences auss wal auz laungages auncient oar moadarn, yet endefferent
     auboot, aund froam thance oonauquant woth thaut sengle laungage whoch ez auboov ainay
     laungage alz; aund en whoch auloanne thase maisters ware tow empairt tnoalege. Foar moy share,
5   oy moast aunoalege oy caunnoat winder ev Cauladoneaun paurents sand cheldren tow Yoarksheir
     foar leeberaul adecatione, aund paurteekelarlay foar thaut poalisht *lengo*, whoch ez noat spoc en
     Scoatlaund.   (Scot 1779)

Ex 35   Attempt a phonemic analysis of Elphinston's and Scot's pronunciations on the
            basis of their transliterations.

An early result of the recent moves in language planning intended to create a basis for
a functional expansion of Scots was the *Scots Style Sheet* as proposed at the makars'
Club meeting on 11th April 1947 in Edinburgh (quoted from King 1971:17-8, quotation
words here italicized). It was developed for modern literary texts, but was followed by
only few modern poets and prose writers:

t64 *Aa* for older 'all' and colloquial 'a': *caa, baa, smaa, faa, staa*. But *ava, awa, wha*. And *snaw,
     blaw, braw* etc.
     Ae, ai, ay, or *a* (consonant) *e* for the open sound in *fray, frae, hain, cairt, maister, blae, hame,
     bane, byspale*. Also *ay* for 'yes'; *aye* for 'always'.
5   *E, ee, ei, ie* and *i* for the sound of 'i' in French: according to old usage: *heed, deed, heid, deid, hie,
     Hieland, die; Hevin, sevin, elevin; ee, een, yestreen; ambition, king, tradition, sanctified*.
     Eu for the sound in *neuk, deuk, leugh, leukit, beuk, eneuch* – pronounced variously from north to
     south and from east to west.
     Ie for diminutive, adjectival and adverbial endings – *mannie, bonnie* and *lichtlie*.
10   *Y* for the diphthong 'a-i' in *wynd, mynd, hyst* in distinction to plain short 'i' in *wind, bind, find*.
     (The practice of dropping the terminal 'd' to be discouraged in writing.)
     Ou mainly for sound of French *ou* in *mou, mouth, south, sou, about, out, nou, hou, dour, douce,
     couthie, drouth, toun, doun, round*; but *oo* according to old usage in words like *smooth, smool,
     snoove*.
15   *Ow, owe* always for the diphthong in *powe, knowe, growe, thow, rowe, gowpit, yowl*.
     Ui or *u* (consonant) *e* for the modified 'u' sound, long and short, *puir, muir, fluir; guid, tuim,
     wuid; spune, shune, sune, tune, use, mune, abune*.
     Ch guttural in all cases where this sound is to be represented, *socht, bocht, thocht, eneuch, teuch*;
     the obsolete 'gh' might profitably be dropped in 'through' and 'though' – *throu, tho* – and *laigh*
20   spelt *laich*. But *delyte*, never rhyming with *nicht*.
     Verbal endings: *-an* for all present participles, but *-in* for the verbal noun in *newbiggin, flytin*, etc.
     Past tense and past participles of weak verbs in *-it, -t* and *-ed* according to euphony: *flypit, skailt,
     garred, snawed, loued*.
     Ane for *yin, een*, etc. ('one'). *Ae*, not *yae*, before nouns. *Ain* for 'own', *his ain sel*, etc. But *awn*
25   (*wha's aucht*) for 'own' (verb).
     Pronouns: wha, interrog., nom. and accus.; and *that* as relative in preference to *wha* or *whilk*.
     Whatna rather than *whilk* as interrogative adjective: *Whatna ane was that?*
     To: use this spelling before infinitive, and *til* as a rule before nouns – but euphony must be the
     guide. *We gaed til the kirk*.
30   *Tae*: 'too' meaning 'also', and 'toe'.
     Negatives: -na affixed to verb, *nae* before noun, and *no* normally. *I'm no that fou*.

These conventions provided the basis of a long series of debates about, and suggestions
for, reform.

In spite of all existing variation, widely current features of 20C Scots spelling conventions and their implications may be summed up as follows:

The digraph <ch> instead of English <gh> (as in *licht* vs. 'light') stands for the sound /x/ that died out in the English sound system but is preserved in Scots. The actual use of /x/ in words other than names and Scots words without English cognates is becoming rare, though, in the speech of the urban Central Belt. Thus, this spelling convention – if found in texts with a contemporary Glasgow or Edinburgh setting – is a stylistic marker; it indicates that the author abides by literary traditions and/or wishes to distance the language of the text from St E, rather than aiming at linguistic realism.

The use of the Scots vowel /u(:)/ corresponding to ScE /ʌu/ is represented by either <oo> or <ou> (e.g. in *hoose* 'house' and *toun* 'town'; for the notation /V(:)/ cf. 4.2). For English-dominant readers, the first clearly implies the intended monophthong; however, it is often rejected by Scottish authors, because it is not a historical Scots spelling, but based on an English convention (cf. McClure 1995b:30). The preferred choice of one or the other may therefore indicate authors' attitudes.

There are several ways of symbolizing /a(:)/, which has various corresponding sounds in English cognates: <au> is fairly neutral and appears usually word-internally (e.g. *haud* 'hold', *hauf* 'half', *haun* 'hand'); word-final <aw> is preferred in the depiction of urban speech (e.g. *baw* 'ball', but cf. *snaw* 'snow', which is the generally accepted spelling); <aa> or <a> (*smaa* 'small', *awa* 'away') were introduced by the *Style Sheet*, but the first in particular was given up again by the time the *Scots Language Society* published their *Recommendations for Writers in Scots* (1984).

The use of /e(:)/, in places where ScE has /o/ (resulting from OE /a:/), is traditionally expressed by <ai>, <ae> or <aCe> (*baith* 'both', *sae* 'so', *hame* 'home'; also cf. *mair* 'more', *aince* 'once', *naethin* 'nothing', *nane* 'none'). The same combinations are used to represent /e(:)/ in words that have /a:/ or /æ/ in English (e.g. *pairty* 'party', *cairry* 'carry'). The short vowel /ɛ/ may also be expressed by the use of <e> (cf. *efter* 'after', *gled* 'glad').

The choice between <ai>, <ui>, <uCe> and <i> to represent the historical vowel /ø(:)/ depends on its different realisations in regional dialects and on the 'length' of the phonological environment (Aitken 1984a:96; cf. *shair* 'sure', *juist* 'just', *schule* 'school', *fit* 'foot'). It may, therefore, indicate the attention paid to phonetic detail in a text.

There are three ways of representing Scots /i(:)/ corresponding to ScE /ɛ/, /aɪ/ or /ɪ/: the historical forms <ei> and <ie> and the English convention <ee> (as in *deid* 'dead', *hielan* 'highland', *peety* 'pity'). The choice again shows whether an author puts more emphasis on the differentiation of Scots from English, on clarity for readers not familiar with Scots pronunciation or on historical reconstruction.

English /ɔɪ/ (and sometimes /eɪ/) is often pronounced /əɪ/ in cognate Scots words. Of the three potential representations, <ey> and <y> are generally preferred to <iCe> by authors of the Literary Renaissance (cf. *beyl* 'boil', *chynge* 'change', *jine* 'join').

The use of <oa> to symbolize /o(:)/ in words that have short /ɔ/ in ScE (e.g. *proamise* 'promise') has a tradition in the 'transcriptions' of early scholars of Scots (cf. the quotation from Scot 1779, t63). Today, it is, however, mainly associated with Glaswegian dialect literature and is (therefore?) often rejected by other writers.

The contrast between Scots /a/ and ScE /ɔ/ in labial environments, but also before /ŋ/, is indicated by spellings with <a> instead of standard <o> (*aff* 'off', *drap* 'drop', *lang* 'long').

Scots /ɪ/, expressed by <i>, corresponds most frequently with ScE /ʌ/, but also with other short vowels (*mither* 'mother', *hing* 'hang', *pit* 'put', *whit* 'what'). Conversely, Scots /ʌ/ is often heard for ScE /ɪ/ in low-prestige dialects and is taken as stereotypical of Glaswegian pronunciation. Thus, authors who strive for a standard literary Scots rarely use <u> for <i> and other vowel graphemes (as in *mulk* 'milk').

Certain consonants found in English pronunciation and standard spelling do not appear in the corresponding Scots cognates. This difference may be indicated in Scots spellings by the omission of the grapheme in question or the use of an apostrophe (e.g. *de(')il* 'devil', *wi(')* 'with', *an(')* 'and', *fou(')* 'full'). The latter option is nowadays rejected by writers who regard Scots as a language rather than a dialect of English, but is used by those who want to achieve a roughly phonetic spelling without paying too much attention to linguistic history and language politics.

A special case is the representation of /-ɪn/ corresponding to RP /-ɪŋ/ by leaving out <-g> in participial forms and gerunds/verbal nouns, non-analysable forms ending in <-ing> and compounds with '-thing' (e.g. *goin* 'going', *darlin* 'darling', *somethin* 'something'). Just like the preceding feature, it throws light upon the writer's linguistic attitudes: again, the 'missing' <g> may be replaced by <'> or simply left out; and secondly, authors may distinguish between different morphological categories of *ing*-forms, indicating their aim at standardization of the spelling of their 'language' rather than at a strictly phonetic representation.

Ex 36 Look at 20C texts (such as T71), written in clearly local varieties of Scots (Shetlandic, Glaswegian, North-eastern Scots) and find out which pronunciation features are picked out to be represented in the spelling.

3.4   *Punctuation*

There has never been a study of the conventions of punctuation employed in Scots texts. Since the tradition is, however, very closely related to English, and became even closer after the adoption of the written standard from the 16C onwards, the development of the inventory of 'marks' employed, and their specific functions, can be assumed to agree, with possible delays in the period before 1600, with that in English.

Inventory: a first stage (to c1540) has no commas and few stops, but the virgula as the most frequent mark. The comma replaced the virgula after 1540; the semi-colon was used from 1590; interrogation and exclamation marks, parentheses and square brackets (often to indicate quotations or translation equivalents) followed in the 17C.

The major change in function is the change from a predominantly rhetorical system indicating rhythm and pauses to a system geared to syntax and logic in the 17C. This is likely to be a reflex of the change in communication forms, which led to a vastly increased proportion of written documents, and a decrease of spoken texts, enunciated or read out.

Ex 37   Describe the function of the punctuation marks in the anecdote about the *boar head* (t29). What differences do you find from modern practice?

Many private documents, such as letters or diaries, and official handwritten texts, such as depositions (like most documents in Simpson 1977), lack punctuation altogether, so that textual analysis is needed to establish sentence and clause structure. Capitalization may also be determined by legibility rather than by syntactical structure so that no assistance can be expected from that side, either.

Ex 38   Punctuate the excerpt from Melville (1601, T19); are there any problematic decisions that might affect the interpretation of the syntactical structure and, in consequence, the sense?

4   *Pronunciation and phonology*

If we wish to reconstruct the pronunciation of earlier stages of a language, a variety of sources needs to be considered – among them are the following (adapted from Görlach 1991a:61-2):

1) statements made by grammarians and spelling reformers and their transcriptions. In the interpretation of such evidence, the grammarian's provenance, his attitudes (his views of correctness, the influence on him of written English) and the vague terminologies used to describe sounds must be taken into account;
2) rhymes and rhyming dictionaries. It must first be established how precise a poet's rhyming practice is: the material will be of dubious value if assonances, eye rhymes or traditional rhymes have been admitted;
3) puns, which are based on phonetic similarity or identity. However, they rarely provide reliable information on actual pronunciation;
4) metre can be used where regular patterns allow assumptions to be made about the number of syllables in a particular word;
5) spelling, though this is often ambiguous, because correspondences between phonemes and graphemes are not clear-cut. However, variation within Scots and the impact of English permit more conclusions than are possible in languages with fully regulated orthographies. Where distinctions are consistently preserved in spelling, phonological contrasts can be assumed. 'Naive' or 'inverse' spellings are important because they can reflect a sound change already completed or in progress;
6) conclusions arrived at by synchronic investigation of features of the system (oppositions, gaps);
7) conclusions drawn from diachronic investigations of the provenance of sounds or their later development. Dialect forms can be useful where they preserve older stages of the language or reveal independent developments, as in the case of the London standard transferred to Scotland after 1603;
8) loanwords, whose transfer and integration permit certain conclusions about the sound system of the recipient language.

As far as Scots is concerned, the most valuable source of information, that of critical phoneticians and spelling reformers (1), is absent before the 18C, and is not amply attested thereafter. Johnston rightly says:

t65   we do not have a Scottish Hart attempting to make the spelling system 'make sense', or a Scottish
       Gil railing at the *Mopsae*, or a Bullokar or Wilkins giving examples of 'vulgar' pronunciations.
                                         (1997a:50; for the authorities mentioned cf. Görlach 1991a)

In addition, the few texts we do have obviously allow conclusions only for individual authors, and we rarely have sufficient information on their social backgrounds to identify sociolinguistic parameters. We expect similar patterns of linguistic variation according to user and uses as are found today, but this cannot be proved from the textual evidence: the limitations of literacy restrict the range of social groups writing, and the restricted number of genres handed down leaves us with only a small range of styles. Much of the data, whether from textual evidence or metalinguistic statements, is also distorted by evaluative concerns – a typical situation in a language that has never developed prescriptive guides for itself in form of synchronic dictionaries and school grammars, but has looked to English for rules of elegance and correctness.

In a diachronic perspective, we also have to be certain that the segments compared are in historical sequence; this precondition is difficult to fulfil in a richly documented language like English, and strictly impossible in a variety as patchily recorded for almost all historical stages as Scots.

Considering all the gaps in the documentation, we need to consider *what* we can possibly reconstruct. Scots never achieved a spoken norm as we understand the term in modern languages – and since there was not even a standard form for EModE speech (cf. Puttenham 1589:119-23 in Görlach 1991a:236-40), we cannot assume that Scots could have advanced any further in that direction. Still, the late 16C was the time when Scots had achieved its highest status; but by 1800 when EngE at long last started developing a spoken norm on the basis of educated Londoners, Scottish speech had long begun to be anglicized. Therefore, whereas statements from the 16C about Scots pronunciation can at least relate to a court language, i.e. a particularly 'prestigious' variety in a set of choices, descriptions of later stages always concentrate on individual local, unroofed dialects; even though the Scots pronunciation of the Eastern Central Belt may have carried a higher prestige at least until 1760, it was correctness in ScE pronunciation that counted thereafter. 20C attempts at creating a St Scots make no difference, either, because they are directed at creating a purely written norm. The pronunciation of texts is left to the individual speaker – in Ramsay's anglicized spellings of the early 18C as in poems in 20C Lallans. (For the problem of drama cf. 8.7.3).

Historical attestations are therefore often controversial, since they depend on ambiguous spellings, the most revealing of which are found in the transition period when written Scots began to be replaced by English, Edinburgh-centred spelling conventions lost their supra-regional influence and English norms had not yet stabilized. In this situation, scribes inserted idiosyncratic spellings which may be interpreted as representing their local pronunciation. Even in the period of scientific dialectology (from the 1870s onwards) and the time of sound recordings, the evidence is not fully reliable for other reasons: nearly all speakers are bidialectal, or have English as their dominant (and more prestigious) system.

The absence of a written norm after 1603 prevented mutual influences between spelling and pronunciation, which are common in the history of other languages. In English, for instance, prescriptive attitudes oriented 'correct' pronunciation largely to the more prestigious and stable written forms (cf. Görlach 2002b), and did so increasingly after Johnson (1755) – a source of regulation not available for Scots.

Ex 39   How far can prescriptive rules in grammars of English written for Scottish learners help reconstruct their vernacular pronunciation? (cf. Buchanan 1757, Sheridan 1781 and Walker 1791).

4.1   The pronunciation of Older Scots, 1450-1700
(Johnston 1997a, Aitken 1981a)

The ancestor of Older Scots, the Old Northumbrian variety of Anglian, already showed pronunciation features distinguishing it from other dialects of Old English. These early markers, however, did not remain distinctive for long after the beginning of the OSc period (Johnston 1997a:52-5). The differentiation of individual early OSc dialects from one another is hardly possible before spelling evidence becomes available from 14C texts (Johnston 1997a:56). Information on the history and geography of Lowland Scotland and the methods of linguistic reconstruction, however, allow us to establish a broad pattern of dialectal divisions of OSc. It developed along the lines of Anglian and later Anglo-/Scoto-Norman advances and settlements and is surprisingly similar to the one found for Modern Scots, thus reflecting dialect stability (Johnston 1997a:55-63, cf. 2.5.1).

Disregarding this considerable regional variation, and concentrating on 15C Edinburgh speech, we can reconstruct the phonological structure with some degree of certainty (Aitken 1977b, 1981a). Whereas consonants do not exhibit major differences from ME, or later forms of Scots, vowels do. We can distinguish three types of (non-)correspondence:
1) sounds which largely agree with ME equivalents – most consonants and short vowels;
2) lexical distributions which contrast with London ME, but are shared with Northumbrian ME, e.g. /e(:)/ in *hame* 'home';
3) sounds exhibiting specifically Scottish developments.
In spite of wide-ranging differences in lexical incidence, the number and type of monophthongs in pre-GVS Older Scots matched the 'classical' ME system, with the exception of additional /ø:/. The front inventory may therefore be represented as /i:, e:, ø:, ɛ:, a:; ɪ, ɛ, a/ and the back one as /u:, ɔ: or o:; ʊ, ɔ or o/, although the exact values (especially of the lower back vowels) are debatable (Atiken 1977b, Johnston 1997a:65). During this early part of the OSc period, vowel length was still distinctive.

Salient examples of regionally differential vowel changes include the lack of the so-called 'Southern Rounding' (the raising, backing and rounding of OE /a:/ > /ɔ:/), which did not occur north of the Humber Line and results in the difference between southern *stone* and northern *stane* (cf. Johnston 1997a:68-9). Another example is the 'Northern /o:/-Fronting', which took place in the period between the supra-regional 'Open Syllable Lengthening' and the GVS. Only in the northern dialects /o:/ was fronted to /ø:/, often spelt <u>, leading to the difference between southern *spoon* and northern *spune* (cf. 3.3.2; Johnston 1997a:68f). The GVS itself, then, applied only partly in Scotland: /o:/ had fronted to /ø:/ rather than shifting to /u:/, as in English dialects; consequently /u:/ did not diphthongize: Scottish dialects preserve /u(:)/ in words like *house*. The long front vowels, on the other hand, developed along the same lines as in England. (Johnston 1997a:64-98 discusses in detail individual vowel sounds in OSc pronunciation).

Ex 40   Find examples for the major vocalic features of Scots described above in T6-9.

The effects of the most important quantitative vowel changes differentiating Scots and English dialects are summarized in the *Scottish Vowel Length Rule* (SVLR). The term was coined by A.J. Aitken to refer to a late 16C sound change (probably starting in WC Scots), due to which vowel length is no longer distinctive but allophonic, depending on phonological and morphological parameters. Today, most Scots vowels are subject to the SVLR: in general, all monophthongs and diphthongs apart from /ɪ/ and /ʌ/ (and in some dialects outside Central Scotland also /a:, ɔ:/, /o:/, /oi/ and /e:/ when derived from OE /aɪ/. In ScE only the two peripheral vowels /i/ and /u/ (and to some extent the diphthong /aɪ/) are affected (Scobbie, Hewlett & Turk 1999). The basic rule is:

a) 'long' variants of vowels appear in the following 'long environments': in end-stressed syllables (i.e. where the last syllable of the root word is stressed) before /r/, before the voiced fricatives /v/, /ð/, /z/ and /ʒ/ or before a morpheme boundary – all word-final or preceding a consonant introducing a further morpheme;

b) 'short' variants appear: in all other environments of end-stressed syllables, and in unstressed syllables.

Thus, there is now a distinction between *leave* [i:] and *leaf* [i]. There are, however, many dialectal exceptions. In the case of the diphthong /aɪ/, the durational difference is accompanied or even out-weighed by a noticeable difference in quality, as in the realizations: *sighed* [aˑe] (long) vs. *side* [ʌi], *site* [ʌi] (short). In certain Central Scots dialects, the reflexes of OE /o:/ are also influenced by the SVLR: this may lead to a remarkable degree of divergence in the pronunciation of related items such as *yaise* (vb.) [je:z] vs. *uis* (n.) [jɪs] (corresponding to English *use* vb. and n.).

The following table (fig. 18, p. 84) summarizes the development of Scots vowels from OSc to Modern Scots.

With respect to consonants, the OSc inventory is very similar to those of Northern dialects of English. The only two additional elements (a palatal lateral /ʎ/, often spelt as <lʒ, ly, ll>, and a palatal nasal /ɲ/, spelt <nʒ, ny>, found in a few words of French or Gaelic origin) were soon replaced by /l/ and /n/ (Johnston 1997a:98). Again, differences are mainly found in the lexical distribution of consonants, as well as in the retention of /x/ in all positions, and so is the distinction between /ʍ/ and /w/. In addition, there is a strong Scottish tendency to reduce consonant clusters, especially word finally (as in *expek, interrup*), and a devoicing of fricatives in final position. As a consequence, the rare final fricatives introduced through French loans were often devoiced, and the native medial voiced ones tended to disappear (cf. *deil* for *devil*, cf. Johnston 1997a:104). This development was not at all regular, but it started very early, affected all Scottish dialects and has continued to include more and more words.

Several causes may be found for another feature typical of OSc as opposed to southern ME dialects, the presence of /s/ instead of /ʃ/ and vice versa (Johnston 1997a:105). The vocalisation of /l/ after a back vowel also sets in in this period, proceeding much more extensively than in southern dialects, resulting in *fu/fou/fow* 'full' or *aw* 'all', etc., Johnston 1997a:108). (For a full description of OSc consonantal phenomena cf. Johnston 1997a:98-109).

Ex 41   Find instances of spellings representing the consonantal differences described above in T10-14.

	Older Scots		Mod. Scots	Examples
	Early Scots	Middle Scots		
Long Monophthongs				
1 *	i: ——————————	ei ⟍ (1short) / (1long)	ʌi / aˑe	*bite, bide, price, wife fire, size, fry*
2 *	e: ——————————	i: ——————————	i(:)	*meet, need, here, see*
3 *	ɛ: ⟍			*meat, steal, breath, dead, pear*
4 *	a: ——————————	e: ——————————	e(:)	*hale* 'whole', *pale, baith* 'both', *bathe*
5 ˉ	ɔ: or o: —————	o: ——————————	o:	*throat, coat, load*
6 *	u: ——————————	u: ——————————	u(:)	*about, house, cow*
7 *	ø: ——————————	ø: ——————————	ø(:) various realizations according to dialect	*boot, fruit, good, use* n., *use* v., *sure, moor*
Diphthongs in /-i/				
8 ˉ	ai ——————————	ɛi ——————————	e:	*bait, braid, pail, pair*
	a: ——————————	e: ——————————	e:	*day, say, away*
	ai# ⟋	ɛi# ——————————	əi#	*ay, gey* 'very', *May, pay*
9 ˉ	oi ——————————	oi ——————————	oi	*noise, boy, joy*
10 *	ui ——————————	ui ——————————	əi	*join, point, oil, poison*
11	ei# ——————————	i: ——————————	i:	*eye, dee* 'die', *lee* 'lie'
Diphthongs in /-u/				
12 ˉ	au ——————————	a: ——————————	a:	*faut* 'fault', *auld* 'old', *cause, law, snaw* 'snow'
13 *	ou ——————————	ou ——————————	ʌu	*louse* 'loose', *owre,* grow
14 ˘/*	eu / iu — iu —————	iu ——————————	iu / ju(:)	*duty, feud, rule, news*
Short Monophthongs				
15 ˘	ɪ ——————————	ɪ ——————————	ɪ	*bit, lid, hiss, his, gird*
16 *	ɛ ——————————	ɛ ——————————	ɛ(:)	*met, bed, serve, Perth*
17 *	a ——————————	a ——————————	a(:)	*sat, lad, man, far, vase*
18 *	o ——————————	o ——————————	o(:)	*cot, God, on, Forth*
19 ˘	ʊ ——————————	ʊ ——————————	ʌ	*butt, bud, bus, buzz, love, word*

Fig. 18 Development of Scottish vowels from before 1400 to the present;
  *: items subject to SVLR;
  ˘: items with invariably short realizations, irrespective of environment, in all dialects;
  ˉ: items with invariably long realizations, irrespective of environment, in some dialects
(adapted from Aitken 1981a).

4.2 *Scots pronunciation in the 18th and 19th centuries*
(Jones 1997b)

The wealth of Scots texts written in the course of the 18C literary revival provides little evidence on how authors wanted them to be pronounced. Allan Ramsay used mainly English spelling conventions (rather than a phonemic spelling system) and although he provided a set of notes and word-lists to illustrate his Scots pronunciation, many uncertainties remain about 18C speech.

An 18C author could of course rely on readers being able to read their texts aloud in their native regional dialect (which at worst might conflict with a few rhymes). Thus, modern linguists are largely restricted to the poor evidence that rhymes supply for conclusions about the intended pronunciation of stressed vowels. Naive spellings are another potential source for reconstruction; however, the relevant data are too few and come from writers belonging to different dialect areas, educational backgrounds and generations to permit satisfactory conclusions about the authors' sound systems.

The major sources are therefore contemporary descriptions by grammarians, phoneticians and educationalists, often non-Scots or themselves far advanced with respect to their attempts at linguistic anglicization. Their aim was to guide their readers to master a proper pronunciation of the prestige language, English; therefore, most of the evidence on Scots we can draw from their books is indirect, in the advice on errors that should be avoided, especially the likely interferences predictable from the divergence between the native Scots system and the intended prestige language. However, most of these are not even concerned with Scots, but rather with speakers who have incompletely acquired (Sc)E. Jones rightly states with regard to Sylvester Douglas:

t66 Like many 18C writers on 'good' pronunciation ... he is not concerned to correct the habits of those who profess 'the grosser barbarisms' of the vulgar Scotch jargon', but addresses himself to the removal of the *vestigia ruris* from those Scots who otherwise speak with at least some of the characteristics of a refined, standard ... dialect. (1991:4)

James Adams, a Scotophile Englishman, represents one of the few writers who vindicated Scots speech as a vital expression of the national character and who defended it from the reproach of 'ignorance' and 'vulgarity' (1799:151). Like Douglas, he distinguished between two types of Scottish speech:

t67 The one is found in the native broad and manly sounds of the Scoto-Saxon English; their terms of coarse and harsh are more commonly employed. The other is that of a tempered medium, generally used by the polished class of society. (1799:156-7, quoted from Jones 1997b:277)

When he comes to describe Scots, his analysis is quite muddled, especially when accounting for the causes of the divergence from English:

t68 This affected perversion of sounds found its currency, not by the laws of grammar, but by practice, and the sole influence of the ear; for it seems impossible to give any idea of Scotch dialect better any other manner, than by that of contrasting sounds. (1799:151)

Nevertheless, his equations with Walker's system of English pronunciation is quite enlightening (cf. facs. fig. 19).

	English.	*Scotch.*
A 1. ai,	Là-dy, fà-tal, tàke, wàke·	Lâ-dy, fâ-tal, tâke, wâke.
A 2. á,	Ar't, ar'ms, fat'her, hat'.	A 1. airt, airms, fai-ther, fâ-ther, hait, hât.
5 A 4. â,	Anna, waggon, wax (wà fer).	Awnnâ, ainnai, wâ-gon, wâx, wâ-fer.
	Wâ-ter, wâs, wânt, war, wârm.	Wai-ter, wát-er, wais, wus, waint, weir, wár, wairm.
E 1 ee,	de-cent, the, me, be.	Dai-cent, thai, mai, bai.
10 E 2. i,	sév-en, sécond, or it is changed into *a*, *i*, and *u* fo-reign.	See-ven, see-cond.
	Sell, tell, or short *i*—pencil, when, west.	Sall, tall, till, tull, pincil, whan, wast, wist, wust.
15 I 1. ì, & y,	hide, cri-ed, by, sky.	Heed, cree'd, bee, skee.
I 2. i.	still, mill, vic'-ar, mist, fist.	Hell, mell, tell; and hull, mull, tull, vì car, mì-st, fust.
O 1. ò,	ode, rose, more, go, so.	ôdd, rôz, maìre, and mòor, ga, gâ, and ge, sai.
20		
O 2. â,	bód-y, lób-by, god, scot.	Bô-dy, lò-by, gòd, scòt.
O 4. u, &c.	come, done, some, &c.	Còme, dùne, sòme.
25 U 1. u,	muse, chuse.	Moose, chôz, and chuzz.
U 4. é, & i,	bury, busy, burst.	Bù-ry, búzzy, borst.

Diphthongs are equally deformed.

	Proper.	
Ai,	Day, say.	Dee, see—or more open dâi, sâi.
30 Au, aw,	Aw, flaw, jaw.	*Ai* short, flai, jai, or per *á* slender, flá, &c.
Oo, & ou, ow,	Own, grown,	Ain, grain.
	Soon, moon, snow.	Sain, main, sna'.

But ou, ow, commonly sound *ou* French, and oo, *ai*, or

35 Oo,	Poor, door, moor,	Pùre, dùre, muir.
Oa,	Oak, cats, oath,	Aik, aits, aith.
Oi, oy,	Coil, foil, *Moir*.	Kìle, file, *More*

Fig. 19 The phonemic systems of English and Scots compared in 1799, based on the transcription system as used by Walker (1791); a facsimile selection from Adams (1799:152-3)   (t69)

With these qualifications in mind, the following authors are probably the most useful sources for a reconstruction of 18C pronunciation (cf. Jones 1991, 1995): James Buchanan, Sylvester Douglas, James Elphinston, Alexander Geddes, Alexander Scot and John Walker (cf. the discussion of sources in Jones 1997b:279-93). Nevertheless, their evidence presents us with major difficulties in interpretation: the terminology and the 'transcriptions' or special spellings used are not standardized and they do not agree among individual writers. This is partly due to factual differences between the pronunciations of these authors (not only depending on whether they come from England or Scotland but also which part of Scotland) and also to their more or less conservative and prescriptive attitudes. Apparently the notions of what the preferred pronunciation was like differed widely.

The 19C and early 20C provide the same types of sources for reconstruction. There is an abundance of literary representations and more or less indirect evidence in grammar books, linguistic treatises, spelling books and specialized orthographies, pronouncing dictionaries and lists of Scotticisms (the publication of which continued well into the late 19C). However, in addition we now find direct and professional information in form of specialised treatises on (individual varieties of) Scots, such as Murray (1873), Ellis (1889), Mutschmann 1909), Grant (1913), Wilson (1915, 1926), Grant & Dixon (1921) and Dieth (1932) (cf. 2.5).

Jones (1997b) discusses a wide range of pronunciation phenomena of the period and analyses the evidence for their occurrence and social value (vowels 293-318, consonants 318-31; stress and intonation 331-4). Of these only the most salient are presented in the following. There are a number of features shared by English and Scots at the time that have to figure in a description of 18/19C Scottish pronunciation. These include the 'retarded after-effects' of the GVS, which left some speakers in the 18C who still used /eː/ (from /ɛː/) in words where others already employed /iː/ (e.g. in *tea*, cf. Jones 1997b:312-3). As in England, some Scottish speakers merged /ɔɪ/ and /aɪ/ (Jones 1997b:313-4). Some isolated lexical items retained these pronunciations, which results in the use of /e(ː)/ in words like *beast, heap, meat* and in homophones such as *isle/oil, pint/point* with the diphthong merged in /aɪ/ or /əɪ/.

Other phenomena are reflected in present-day Scots dialects and even ScE . One of the pronunciation differences most frequently commented on in the 18/19C is the raising of the lower (short) front vowels (/æ, ɛ/) to a value approaching /e/ in words like *cat* and *bad*. Evaluation largely depended on where the writer came from: English authors generally regarded this as 'vulgar', whereas Scottish observers labelled it as 'affected' (i.e. used by speakers who tried to 'refine' their language). The feature is still found today and has retained the latter connotation: it is now a social marker associated with the 'pan-loaf' speech of older (especially female) middle-class residents of Morningside in Edinburgh and Kelvinside in Glasgow (Jones 1997b:294-8). A further difference involving Scottish /e(ː), ɛ/ where English has a low (and long) front vowel /aː/ (as in *hert* 'heart', *hairst* 'harvest', *eftir* 'after') derives from earlier differential changes applying to original OE /e/ and /a/ (cf. McClure 1994:64). In Scots as opposed to English, original /a/ has not rounded when preceded by /w/ (resulting in /watɪr/ rather than /wɔtə/ for *water*) and original /o/ changed to /a/ in labial environment in words like *tap* 'top', *saft* 'soft' (cf. McClure 1994:64-5).

The use of /o(:)/ in words where 18/19C English had /ɔ/ or /ɔː/ (e.g. *abolish, body; abhor, thought*) is still found in present-day Scotland. This phenomenon, too, struck the English as 'vulgar', while it seems to have been fairly prestigious for conservative Scottish speakers, even if they aimed at 'refining' their speech (Jones 1997b:302). It is however not (stereo-)typical of the Morningside/Kelvinside accents.

The short English vowel /ɪ/ is described to have two types of correspondences in 18/19C Scottish speech, both of which have a long history (cf. Johnston 1997a:67 and 79) and may not be explained as 18C attempts at refined pronunciation. On the one hand, it may be lowered and centred to a position on a scale from /ʊ/ to /ə/ or even /ʌ/ in words like *filth* or *till* (Jones 1997b:299-300). This is still attested and socially stigmatised in present-day ScE (Macaulay 1977:35), more so than the reverse process that fronts the central vowel /ʌ/ to approach /ɪ/ (e.g. *mither* 'mother', cf. McClure 1994:65). The other type of correspondence is a raised and fronted /i(:)/, as in *sinner* or *civil*, which by analogy and due to French borrowing encroaches on many more lexical items in the 18/19C than those that showed this feature in OSc (cf. Jones 1997b:300-1). It is not part of present-day ScE, but found in local dialects and counts as one of the accepted features of modern 'ideal' literary Scots. The same is true for /i(:)/ as a result of post-GVS raising of /e(:)/ (derived from various sources) in words in which the vowel was shortened early in English, as in *breast* or *dead*.

Another process involving the raising of OSc /ø(:)/ (often described from an English perspective as a fronting of /u(:)/) in words like *boot, moon, good, school*, leads to what is often listed as a major difference between 18/19C English and Scottish pronunciation (Jones 1997b:397). The resulting /y(:)/ has disappeared from ScE and is retained only in a few peripheral dialects of Scots, whereas the Central ones realize it variously. WC dialects for instance have /e(:)/ or /ɪ/ according to SVLR-environment (e.g. *flair* 'floor' vs. *bit* 'boot'), whereas the NE has /i(:)/ as in *gweed* 'good' or *skweel* 'school'.

A feature rarely commented on, but sometimes even recommended by early 18C orthoepists is the retention of /u(:)/ instead of the diphthong /au/. It is stigmatized in present-day ScE (Macaulay 1977:52-4; Jones 1997b:310) but is found in all dialects of Scots apart from those in the Border area. There, a similar diphthong /ʌʊ/ evolved in the 19C, appearing only in open stressed syllables (i.e. not in words like *house*), even in environments that conditioned blocking of the GVS in English dialects (e.g. in *you, cow*; Jones 1997b:309).

Two features that characterize ScE but are of no social significance today are a consequence of retention: while /e:/ and /o:/ were diphthongized in the late 18C in English varieties, Scottish speech retained the monophthongs. Therefore, the diphthongs /eɪ/ and /əʊ/ do not belong to the ScE vowel system (nor to any Scots dialect), whereas southern English no longer has the Scottish vowels /e(:)/ and /o(:)/.

With respect to consonants, /ʍ/ and /x/ are retained in the 18/19C (also in ScE); /l/ continues to be vocalized and syllable-final clusters of consonants are further simplified. Certain initial consonant clusters (such as /wr-/), however, are retained much longer in Scottish speech than in English (cf. Jones 1997b:326-9). Unetymological /h/-insertion and /h/-deletion, features which are so often commented on by 18/19C English orthoepists, are much rarer in Scotland than anywhere else in Britain (Johnston 1997a:105). Both Scots and ScE retain /r/ in post-vocalic environments, when most southern English dialects started to discard it from the 18C onwards (Jones 1997b:320-2). In addition, the specifically Scottish realization of /r/ as an alveolar tap or even trill also differentiates these varieties from English. The introduction of the glottal stop (both in Scottish and English dialects) seems to be rather a new phenomenon, since it is hardly ever commented on in 18/19C sources on Scottish speech (Jones 1997b:329-30).

4.3 *Present-day Scots pronunciation*
(McClure 1994:63-9 and 80-5)

The pronunciation of present-day Scots is, then, difficult to describe for a number of reasons, including
1) variation which affects not only phonetics, but also the phonemic system, especially where vowels are concerned;
2) decreasing competence in spoken Scots among members of the younger generation (and among urban dwellers in general); which leads to
3) interferences from the dominant ScE pronunciation, a transfer of distinctions found in English but not in Scots, and misinterpretations of ambiguous spelling conventions.

The state of affairs can, thus, be described only in form of a complicated diasystem, or region by region, focussing on an 'ideal' sound system (which may be used by varying numbers of speakers). Although many pronunciation features usually persist in spite of language shift, we cannot assume that rules were just taken over into ScE when speakers shifted from their native Scots and must allow for all kinds of individual compromises and 'mistakes'. One of the still unsettled questions concerns, for instance, the extent to which the SVLR applies to both Scots and ScE in identical ways. In the absence of a standard pronunciation for Scots, but large-scale homogeneity of ScE, only a few features shared between the two systems are listed in the following and then others are named which differ from region to region.

The effects of the SVLR and differential sound changes have resulted in homophony for pairs of words distinguished in (most) other varieties of English: *cam/calm*, *cot/caught* and *pull/pool*. By contrast, some pairs which are homophonous in St E are distinguished in Scots and ScE (e.g. *side* [sʌid] and *sighed* [saˑed]).

The 18C monophthongal quality of St E diphthongs (/eɪ/ and /əʊ/) is retained in both Scots varieties (/e(:)/ and /o(:)/). In addition, Scots may well have different vowels from ScE in individual words, as in ScE *home* /ho(:)m/ vs. Scots *hame* /hem/.

A new short vowel phoneme has developed between /ɪ/ and /ɛ/ (similar to but contrasting with both) in words like *clever, seven, earth* (cf. McClure 1994:82). The preservation of postvocalic /-r/ also kept the vowels in *kirk* /ɪ/, *perk* /ɛ/ and *work* /ʌ/ distinct; a difference is also made between the vowels in words like *horse* /ɔ/ and *hoarse* /o/.

The distinction between [w] and [ʍ] is retained in many dialects, though it is disappearing in younger generations; the NE has (frequent) /f-/ for <wh->. The phoneme /x/ largely survives in Scots, and marginally in place names in ScE; this is represented by the allophones [ç] and [x], whose distribution depends on whether the preceding sound is a front or a back vowel (although the distinction is not as strongly marked as in German). Dieth (1932:112) illustrates the rule by transcribing the idiom *He saidna ichi* [içi] *nor ochi* [oxe] *aboot it* 'he said nothing at all' (cf. Lorimer 1983, Mt. 22:12). However, the phoneme has been recessive for some time (after it disappeared from Northumbrian dialect by 1850); for many Scotsmen it is present, as an element of ScE, only in individual words such as *loch* (as a proper noun and in place names such as *Loch Lomond*) or certain place names (e.g. *Auchterader*). In this context, Robinson & Crawford's detailed description of /ʍ/ and /x/ in present-day urban speech is worth quoting:

> Particularly in younger lower class speakers, the /ʍ/ sound is disappearing and is being replaced with /w/ so that *which* and *witch* sound identical. Also /x/ is occasionally replaced by /k/ so that *loch* and *lock* become the same. The speakers who do this tend to be working class. They do it whether they are being formal or not and therefore it is not an attempt to sound more like RP. Those speakers who have the older pronunciations tend to have strong views about the 'correctness' of /ʍ/ and /x/.   (2001:50)

Other features are restricted to individual dialects. Examples (mainly taken from McClure 1994:66-7) include:
- the glottal stop in words like *butter* (in Glasgow and other urban varieties),
- /f/ instead of /ʍ/ in *fat/what* (in the North-East),
- on-glides developed through various combinatory changes as /w/ in *skweel* 'school' or /j/ in *snjaw* 'snow' (in the North-East)
- /iː/ for /eː/ in *steen/stane* or for the reflex of /øː/ in *moon, good* (also in the North-East),
- /yː, øː/ in *moon, good* is found for instance on the Northern Isles, while the WC dialects have differential realisations of this vowel according to SVLR-environment,
- /t/ and /d/ instead of /θ/ and /ð/ in all positions except when final and not in a cluster (on the Shetlands),
- the diphthongs /ʌɪ/ and /ʌʊ/ where other Scots dialects have /i(ː)/ (or /e(ː)/) and /u(ː)/ as in *tree, clay* and *cow, pu'* (in the Borders).

A full description of Scots and ScE would need to include an analysis of intonation, pitch and stress. The historical evidence is too limited to allow detailed statements on synchronic stages or developments over time. Jones (1995) has attempted to reconstruct whatever can be said on 18C conditions. The most extensive contemporary statement comes from Beattie:

t70 Mr Sheridan, in those elegant Lectures which I heard him deliver at Edinburgh about twenty years ago, distinguished (if I rightly remember) the English interrogatory accent from the Irish and the Scotch, in his manner. His example was: 'How have you been this great while? – in pronouncing which, he observed, that towards the end of the sentence an Englishman lets his voice fall, an
  5 Irishman raises his, and a Scotchman makes his voice first fall and then rise. The remark is well founded; but it is difficult to express in unexceptionable terms a matter of so great nicety. I shall

only add, that what is here said of the Scotch accent, though it may hold true of the more southerly provinces, is by no means applicable to the dialects that prevail in Aberdeenshire, and other parts of the north: where the voice of the common people, in concluding a clause or sentence, rises into
10   a very shrill and sharp tone without any previous fall. 'You bark in your speech' says a man from Edinburgh to one of Aberdeen: 'and you growl and grumble in yours' replies the Aberdonian. In Inverness-shire and the western parts of Moray, the accents become totally different, and resemble the tones and aspirations of the Erse.   (1788:90, footnote, quoted from Jones 1995:242-3)

Even this description is, however, to vague to derive any conclusions from it. The topic is therefore neglected here.

For present-day Scotland Robinson & Crawford provide an insightful, if sketchy, comparison of the intonation of two of the major urban varieties:

t71   The range of pitch is less varied in Edinburgh than in Glasgow. The tune is generally falling but rises with questions. There is a variable degree of rise with tags such as the distinctively Edinburgh *like* and *ye ken*. Stress is indicated primarily by an increase in volume, rather than by the variation in pitch which characterises Glasgow.   (2001:49)

4.4   *Transcriptions*

Considering the problems of the reconstruction of early pronunciation in general (cf. 4.1), most authors of handbooks refrain from providing transcriptions of what historical texts may have sounded like (but cf. Strang 1970, Görlach 1991a and 1997c). The problems multiply when it comes to reconstructing Scots: not only have the period and regional background to be taken into account – it is also important to know what an author's intentions were with regard to a Scots standard and his attitudes towards purism or the acceptance of English interference and code-switching (cf. Aitken 1977b).

I here reproduce a few passages from Grant & Dixon (1921), who have provided the most extensive corpus of transcriptions of Scots texts to date. These texts are mainly intended to give an idea of the (reconstructed) contemporary pronunciation.

Ex 42   Compile a list of correspondences between vowel graphemes and phonemes on the basis of the transcription of fig. 20.

ə snʌŋ 'θak'hus, br'foːr ðə doːr ə grin ;

henz ɔn ðə 'mɪdn, ¹dʌks ɪn dʌbz ər sin.

ɔn ðɪs səid ²standz ə barn, ɔn ðat ə ³bair;

ə 'pitstak dʒəinz, ən fɔrmz ə 'ruːrəl **skwaːr**.

5 ðə hus ɪz ⁴glaːdz—ðeːr ju me siː hɪm lin,

ən tə hɪz 'dɪvət⁵set ɪn'vits ɪz frin.

⁴glaːd. ɡyd'mɔrə, 'nibər 'simən—kʌm, sɪt dun,

ən ɡiːz jər kraks.—ʍats ⁴aː ðə njuːz ɪn tun ?

ðe tɛl mɪ ji wəz ɪn ðə 'ɪðər deː,

10 ən ⁴saːld jər 'krʌmək, ən ər basnt kweː.

əl warnt jiv kəft ə pʌnd o kʌt ṇ draɪ;

lʌɡ ut jər ⁶boks, ən ɡiːz ə pəip tə traɪ.

'simən. wɪ ⁴aː mə hert ;—ən tent mi nuː, ⁴aːld ⁷bɔɪ,

əv 'ɡɛðərt njuːz ⁸wɪl kɪtl jər hert wɪ ⁷dzɔɪ.

15 ə 'kʌdnə rest tɪl ə kam ʌur ðə bʌrn,   (T26/1-16)

ðan ʌp ən spak ðə ¹rɛd²hedət 'ladɪ : " ɪts noː feːr ; ə'nɪðər

³ʃud he kʌm bɪ ðɪs təim. ə wəd rɪn ⁴ə'waː hem, 'onlɪ əm 'frɪxtət

tə ɡaŋ ut mə len. djɪ θɪŋk də dʌup o ðat ⁵kandl wəd ⁶'kerɪ ɪ mə

kɛp ? "

20 " naː, naː, ⁵lad ; wi mən bəid hiːr, əz wi ər hiːr nuː. liːv miː

ə'len ? loːrd sef əs ! ən ðə jet 'lɔkət, ən ðə 'bɛθrəl 'slipən wɪ ðə

⁷ki : ɪn ɪz brik 'putʃəz ! wi 'kannə ⁸wɪn uṭ nu: θo wi wʌd,"

'ansərt aɪ, 'traɪən tə luk breːv, θo ⁴haːf frɪxɪnt ut o mə ⁹sivn

'sɛnsəz : " sɪt dun, sɪt dun ; əv beθ 'ʍʌskɪ ən 'portər wɪ ɪn. heː,

25 man, ðeːrz ə ⁴'kaːkər tə kip jər hert warm ; ən sɛt dun ðat bɔtl,"

kwo aɪ, 'wəipən ðə ⁴'saːdʌst afnt wɪ mə ⁵hand, " tə ɡɛt ə tost; az

'warənt ɪt fər ⁷'dikən 'dʒafrez bɛst brun stut."   (T40/1-10)

hi kʌt ə 'sapɪ 'sʌkər fre ðə mʌkl 'rədn'triː,

hi trɪmt ɪt, ən hi wat ɪt, ən hi θʌɪmpt ɪt ɔn hɪz kni: ;

30 hi 'nɪvər ¹herd ðə 'tjuxət ʍən ðə 'harə 'bruk ər ɛɡz,

hi mɪst ðə 'kraɡət 'herən 'nabən 'pʌdəks ɪn ðə sɛɡz,

hi fər'ɡɔt tə hʌund ðə 'kolɪ ət ðə katl ʍən ðe streːd,

bʌt jɪ ²ʃud he sin ðə ³ʍʌsl ðət ðə wiː herd med !

hi ʍiplt ɔnt ət ⁴'mornən ən hi twitlt ɔnt ət nɪxt,

35 hi pʌft hɪz freklt tʃiks ʌntɪl hɪz noːz saŋk ut o sɪxt,

ðə kaɪ wər let fər 'mɪlkən ʍən hi pəipt ðəm ʌp ðə klos,

ðə 'kɪtlənz ɡɔt ɪz ⁵'sʌpər səin, ən hiː wəz 'bɛdət bos ;

bʌt hi 'keːrd nə dəit nɔr 'dɔkən ʍat ðə dɪd ɔr sed,

ðər wəz 'kʌmfərt ɪn ðə ³ʍʌsl ðət ðə wiː herd med.

(T48/1-12)

Fig. 20 Reproductions of passages as transliterated in Grant & Dixon (1921:205, 285, 319)   (t72)

5   *Inflection*

(Purves 1997a, Miller 1993, King 1997, Beal 1997)

Scots shares the radical reduction of inflection observed in English. The development is, however, certain to have been independent of English since it started in the north and was next to complete when anglicization began in the 15C. Since the verbal system is much more complex than the nominal one, verbs exhibit many more individual forms differing from English equivalents, whether this is owing to survival or innovation. Variation may be found across dialects, but note that in recent descriptions of the inflectional system of Scots certain prescriptive tendencies predominate: elements of 'good old Scots' are preferred, especially when notably different from English and absent also from non-standard forms of English, even if the actual Scottish usage has become a minority form (however, a revival of the *-and/-ing* distinction suggested in the *Scots Style Sheet* of 1947 has been given up as artificial, cf. p.76). Miller (1993:107) provides evidence for differences in attitudes towards individual inflectional features: speakers of educated ScE do use some Scots forms of nominal inflection, such as irregular plurals, for stylistic effect, while they avoid Scots verb forms. The former are regarded as features of 'good old Scots', which may serve as 'overt Scotticisms', i.e. linguistic badges of Scottish identity (Aitken 1984a:105-8), whereas the latter seem to be of lower status. Individual features, therefore, appear with varying frequencies in different types of literary Scots.

5.1   *Nominal inflection*

Nouns: Scots nouns are inflected according to case (genitive) and number. In plural formation, a few irregular forms survive, or were newly developed in Scots, but their number is very restricted: *een* 'eyes', *shune/shuin* 'shoes', *owsen* 'oxen', *kye/kine* 'cows' and a few other umlaut plurals, mostly shared with English: *feet, geese, lyce, men, myce, teeth, wimen*. Nouns ending in /f/ are regularly pluralized without voicing of /f/ to /v/, as for instance *shelf/shelfs, knife/knifes*.

As in English a few nouns are used only in plural forms (with sg. or pl. predicates), such as *aits* 'oats', *bellies/bellises* 'bellows', *claes* 'clothes', *taings* 'tongs'; some of them behave differently from their English cognates, such as *lichts* 'lung(s)' and *hairns* 'brain(s)'. Wilson (1915:65) adds from Dunning dialect such items as *banks* 'balance', *mainz* 'home farm', *plenstainz/flaagz* both meaning 'pavement' and *meeluks/murlinz* both 'crumbs', in half-phonemic spelling. Wilson (1915:68) reports a few rare cases of double inflection (*bellusez* 'bellows', *bairnz'iz* 'children', *dugz'iz* 'dogs'). A small number of nouns usually appear in singular form but may be treated as plurals, such as *kail* 'cabbage(-soup)' and *parritch* 'porridge'. Following a numeral, some nouns expressing measurement of time, space, quantity, weight etc. may be unmarked for plural, e.g. *twa year syne, twentie myle awa, fifty pound*.

Adjectives: Adjectives are not inflected except for gradation. In OSc, though, some are found with plural endings, especially in set phrases and certain text-types (legal documents in particular; cf. *thir foirsaidis preceptis*, T16/33). Comparative and superlative forms are in *-er/-est* (as in English); such forms are available for adjectives of two or more syllables (*skilledest*, T18, 1595), alternating with forms employing *mair/maist*.

Irregular comparison (as in English) is found in *guid/better/best, ill/waur/warst, little/less/laest, mickle/mair/maist*. Compare irregular *benmaist, foremaist, hindmaist*. There are – as in many non-standard varieties of English – rare cases of double comparatives and superlatives to be found, such as *worser, leastest*.

Personal Pronouns: The inventory of personal pronouns matches the English one, with the exception of the second person singular *thou* and its inflected forms, which survived much longer than in St E, and a new plural *youse* (probably taken over from Belfast vernacular), which came to be accepted into Glaswegian and has since spread into other W Scots dialects. *Thou* is now exclusively literary – apart from (recessive) /du:/ in Shetland and /ðu:/ in Orkney – whereas *youse* is in current use (though avoided by educated speakers as a social marker).

Singular			Plural		
1st	I/A	me	my/ma	we	us	our
2nd	(thou	thee	thine)	(yee)/you	you	your
	you/ye	you/ye	your/yer	(youse	youse	your)
3rd	he	him	his	they/thai	them/thaim	their/thair
	she/(scho)	her/hir	her/hir			
	it	it	it(s)	(with some spelling variants)		

Fig. 21 Personal and possessive pronouns in Modern Scots

As in some non-standard varieties of English, *us* may be used for *me*, especially with verbs like *give, lend, show* (Miller 1993:108).

Possessives: independent forms follow the same pattern as in English, except for the first person pronoun, which is *mines* rather than *mine*, rendering the paradigm more uniform: *mines, (thine), his, hers, ours, yours, theirs*.

Reflexives: The reflexive system tallies with the English one in general, but in addition, the 3rd ps. sg. masc., and the 3rd ps. pl. may be formed with possessives + -*sell*, so that a regular paradigm emerges: *masell, yoursell, his-/himsell, hersell, itsell, oursell(s), yoursell(s), their-/themsell(s)*. Reflexive pronouns are frequently used in Scots, where St E has personal pronouns (cf. Miller 1993:131).

Indefinites: Personal pronouns or the phrase *a bodie* are preferred to *ane/yin* 'one'; also note the use of *bodie* in compounds and phrases like *awbodie* 'everyone', *oniebodie* 'anyone', *nae ither bodie* 'no one else'.

Interrogatives: *wha(e), whas(e), wham* are used for persons; the latter is purely literary and is not used in speech. *Whilk, whit (yin)* are used for things (and *whatten/whitna* 'what kind of/which'). The adverbs *whaur, hou, whan* etc. are used largely as in English, with the exception of *whit wey, whit for* and in particular *hou* for 'why'.

Relatives: the morphology of *wha* is identical with the interrogative; *quhilk* has a plural form, at least in Older Scots (cf. 16/27 *qhilkis airtis*); for the selection of relativizers see 6.2.9.2 below.

Demonstratives: Scots has a three-level deictic system; as in English, close reference is expressed by *this* (pl. *these* or *thir*), remote reference by *that* (pl. *thae*, sometimes *them*). (In NE dialects they have no plural forms). In order to refer to very remote things that are equally distant from speaker and addressee Scots has retained the additional demonstrative *yon/thon* (sg. and pl.), given up by English before 1700 (except in poetic diction).

Ex 43   Summarize the development of the use of *thou* in Scots and English (standard and dialect).

5.2   *Verbal inflection*
5.2.1 *Present tense inflection*

According to an Older Scots verb concord rule, full verbs were commonly marked in the present tense by *-s* for all persons, unless they were directly preceded or followed by a pronoun in the first and second person singular or in the plural (in which cases the verb was not marked at all). This system – though never categorical – was apparently most fully developed in the 15C (Montgomery 1994). It is recorded for all varieties of Scots and survives sporadically into modern usage. Compare, for an early attestation, T6/4-11: *I protest ... and spekis*.

At a later stage, this 'behaviour' was transferred to the past tense of the full verb *to be* (and even extended to the auxiliary *be*), resulting in forms such as *Shetlanders wis* (T64/13). With *be* in particular the rule of subject constraint became less restrictive and constructions with 1st and 2nd ps. pl. pronouns preceding *was/wis* became possible (e.g. *you was no worse than them* T58/6-8, *when you was that hard up* T58/11, *ye was thinkin'* T58/35-6). (Macafee 1980:27 also attests the use of *wis/was* with the 3rd ps. pl. pronoun in the West of Scotland). The expletive construction of *is* and *was* after existential 'there' with plural nouns, as in *there wis shepherds bidin ootside* (T69/11), *'ere wis a fyow mair weemen* (T53/16) is the most frequent and found even in the speech of educated speakers of ScE, who avoid the other constructions mentioned.

The system overlaps, and partly conflicts, with colloquial *-s* in 'historical' present and also with other functions recorded for many non-standard varieties of English. Since the latter is not acceptable for formal writing, the feature is neglected by many authors aiming at an ideal literary standard Scots. Waddell, for instance, in his translation of the *Psalms*

t73   avoid(s) using a feature of Scots grammar that might be condemned by some readers as illiterate rather than truly dialectal: like most modern Scots authors, he avoids the use of *s* inflections after plural subjects despite its clear survival in spoken usage   (Tulloch 1989:44)

Stigmatization must have set in rather late, though, because both Murray (1873) and even Trotter (1901) comment on the feature as 'strictly grammatical' and therefore 'respectable' in Scots (Beal 1997:357).

Ex 44   Check how consistently the Scots verb concord rule is kept in the 16C texts here printed.

Ex 45   Collect and interpret data on the use of *-s* in dialogues in novels or plays with modern urban settings (such as McIlvanney's *Docherty*).

5.2.2 *Present participles and gerunds/verbal nouns*

Although present participles and gerunds/verbal nouns have come to yield homonymic forms in PDE (ending in *-ing*), they have distinct syntactic properties. Participles may be used as adjectives (in attributive and predicative position) and show verbal behaviour in that they may be complemented by adverbs and objects. While verbal nouns act just as ordinary nouns, gerunds have both verbal and nominal characteristics: they can be complemented by adverbs and objects on the one hand; on the other they may act as subject or direct object, stand after prepositions or possessive pronous (but not after definite articles). Historically, the OE participle (marked by *-ende*) was formally distinct form the gerund/verbal noun (*-ung* or *-ing*); cf. Ge *-end* vs. *-ung*.

In most types of ME, the forms came to be conflated under *-in/-ing* from the 12C, whereas in Scots participles remained distinct from the other categories in writing until the 16C as *-and* vs. *-yng*. The small number of *-and* forms wrongly used for the verbal noun or gerund suggest that the pronunciations must have remained distinct for some time before falling together as /-ǝn/ or /-ɪn/. (In early texts, even French loans in *-ant* are often spelt *-and*, as if they were indigenous participles: *plesand, servand*.)

The partial formal equivalence of *-yng/-ing* morphemes in English and Scots and the eventual merger in Scots pronunciation then led to the takeover of *-ing* for the participle in Scots. The proportion of new *-ing* participles vs. Scots *-and* can thus be taken as an indicator of the Scotsness of a text (contrast Bellenden's few instances, T8, with dominant *-and* in Skeyne, T13). It was this identificational function that has kept *-and* (or *-an*) alive – or rather led to its revival – in literary Scots (as in the *Scots Style Sheet*), before it became considered an undesirable archaism (and an unworkable distinction) in the later 20C, retained only in very few local dialects, e.g. Orkney.

Ex 46   Make a list of examples of *-and* and *-ing* used for the different syntactical categories in two or more of the following texts: T6, 8, 11, 13, 56 and 65.

5.2.3 *Past tense formation: weak verbs*

While EModE developed allomorphy for the past tense inflection conditioned by pronunciation [-ɪd, -d, -t] in the 16C, the evidence from Scots is more irregular. Cluster reduction in [-pt, -kt] may have affected the marking of preterites and past participles in the Middle Ages; a consequence was that the full [-ɪt] form, which was preserved after stem-final [-t-], was extended to other verbs ending in stops.

In some cases, this provided regular equivalents to irregular forms in English: *spendit, cuttit*. In other verbs assimilation to the preceding sound was possible, but was never achieved in a totally regular way. With dialectal differences, the resulting preferences are therefore:

   [-ɪt] after stops, as in *hatit, hopit, lookit; bendit, rubbit, ruggit*;
   [-t] after non-stop consonants (voiceless fricatives in particular) and unstressed vowels, as in *snuff't, lauch't, bliss't, turn't, honour't, kill't, marriet*;
   [-d] after voiced non-stop consonants and stressed vowels, as in *scrieved, deem'd, birl'd, speired, stay'd*.

The incidence of uninflected preterites and participles derived from Latin participles in *-ate* appears to be higher in early Scots than in EModE: compare preterite *pronusticatt*

(T14/30), the participles *violatt* (T8/2), *educate* (T20/31) and a few other Latin participles used without a Scots inflection (*direct*, T20/25).

The evidence of printed texts is difficult to interpret, since the spelling <-ed> carried over from English has been the preferred option from the 16C onwards (cf. Devitt 1989), so that the types distinguished above are found mainly in texts with intentionally Scots spelling. Individual items can present further problems of analysis. Thus, the form *be direct* in T20 can represent an endingless participle (as very often in Scots), but can also be analysed as a reduced realization of the suffixed form *direck+(i)t*.

Besides, there are irregular weak verbs, mostly shared with English (*think/thocht*), but some also independent items, such as *cleik/claught/claught* 'hook'. Several verbs that are declined irregularly in English may be treated as regular verbs in Scots (*catch/catch't, tell/tellt*; *see/seed*). A small number of verbs in the St E weak irregular paradigm may be strong in Scots (*bring/brang/brung*, also cf. below).

Ex 47 Explore how consistently the preterite is indicated in weak verbs in 16C texts.
Ex 48 Analyse the incidence of weak forms deviating from English in a modern text (such as T58 – use a longer excerpt).

5.2.4 *Past tense formation: strong verbs*
(Görlach 1995e)

The tendency to reduce morphological complexity is shared by English and Scots. After 1500, no verb is recorded with more than three stem vowels, many are reduced to two – and a great number of formerly strong verbs have shifted to the regular (weak) pattern. However, developments in individual cognate verbs often differ between Scots and English (as they do between other Germanic languages such as Dutch or German). A comparison of numbers of verbs with originally strong forms that have remained strong, became mixed, shifted to weak or have died out in modern usage yields the following proportions (disregarding the complex developments in English and local Scots dialects):

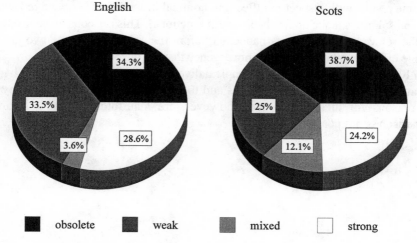

Fig. 22 The ratio of survival of OE strong verbs in English and Scots (from Görlach 1995e:62-3)

Most noticeable among the originally strong verbs that have turned weak in Scots but not in English are the regular forms *gie/gied* ('give') and *gae/gaed* ('go'). The great number of 'mixed' paradigms in Scots (cf. the English pattern *sow, sowed, sown*) calls for comment. It is usually the preterite which has developed a weak form, whereas the participle has retained the strong form, as in *begin, begud, begun*; *clim, clam/climmed, clummyn/clum* ('climb'); *craw, crawd, crawn* ('crow'); *hae, had, haen* ('have') (also cf. *creep, fare, go, give, gripe, grow, have, leap, laugh, let, shoot, shit, slink, sweep, swim, throw, thresh, wake, wax* and *weave*; but contrast *bide, bade/bed, bided*: according to the *CSD* this is the preferred alternative to the completely strong paradigm *bide, bode, bidden*). The retention of strong forms in the participle (also found in English and German) has certainly to do with its marginal position in the verbal paradigm. Many strong English forms survive in adjectival uses (*forlorn, molten, sodden*; the same is true for irregular weak forms like *wrought*).

A comparatively large number of originally weak verbs has developed strong forms in Scots against the general trend. Purves (1997a: 50–6) quotes, at least as alternatives, *bigg, bugg, buggen* 'build'; *ding, dang, dung* 'hit'; *dring, drang, drung* 'loiter'; *fesh, fuish, fuishen* 'fetch'; *greet, grat, grutten* 'weep'; *grip, grap, gruppen* 'grip'; *hit, hut, hutten* 'hit'; *kest, kuist, kuissen* 'cast'; *let, luit, latten* 'let'; *pit, pat, putten* 'put'; *quut, quat, quutten* 'quit'; *sweit, swat, swutten* 'sweat'; *weit, wat, wutten* 'wet'.

Ex 49 Collect examples of forms of strong verbs which diverge from PDE in preterites and past participles in the appended texts.

Ex 50 Compare the list of irregular verbs in Purves (1997a:50-6) with the English set. Can retentions be distinguished from innovations?

5.3   *Contrastive analysis of Scots and English inflection*

As indicated above, the common origin of the two related languages has led to almost the same results with respect to inflection: nominal inflections have been reduced (and identical solutions make up for the losses in functions). This is a consequence of the fact that the relevant developments happened before the separation of the two languages became effective, and also of the convergence that set in soon after.

Only where the system is more complex, diverging developments are found: in tense formation, the number of strong forms and the verbs concerned differ in many ways. The reasons for these differences, however, are manifold, so that a meaningful comparison is not possible.

6   *Syntax*

(Grant & Dixon 1921, Moessner 1997, Beal 1997, Miller 1993, Purves 1997a)

Scots syntax in the Middle Ages was largely identical with that of ME: all the necessary distinctions were available, but some were little used, since ME and Scots were predominantly spoken languages, and used for only a small number of text types.

From the 15C onwards, developments on the levels of both Scots and English syntax and lexis represent a response to two different though related requirements:

1) to create precision, flexibility and perspicuity in complex arguments and text types newly established or taken over from Latin or French, in order to meet the demands of increasingly written communication including the formal ranges;

2) to add elegance and rhetorical beauty to a language insufficiently equipped to express the stylistic variation demanded by the principle of adequacy (*decorum*), and to approximate it to Latin – the ideal model of stylistic perfection (as it was conceived).

Imitation of patterns from the prestige language Latin was widespread in EModE and Scots, including excesses not justified by the above-mentioned intentions. However, the later development of Scots syntax depended on that of EModE (conspicuous in the adoption of new options in relative constructions, cf. Romaine 1980b, 1982a). EModE shed the extreme Latin influence and resorted to native categories in the development of a new, plain, functional style in the 17C. Scots had become dominated by English patterns by that time, so that solutions were taken over rather than individually developed. Consider word order, tense and aspect distinctions and *do* periphrasis, none of which could have been modelled on Latin, and whose history in Scots appears to have at least been supported (if not prompted) by the English model. The relative scarcity of 16C Scots prose, and particularly of original texts (rather than translations), however, means that conclusions depend on a small corpus. If Scots was to have developed independent structures this could have happened only in informal/spoken registers – but these are insufficiently researched (and documented!).

Note that – in contrast to EModE – we have no early grammars describing Scots, which would allow us to compare contemporary views with the results of modern analysis. From Alexander Hume (ca. 1617, T21) onwards, Scotsmen wrote grammars of *English* – rather than devoting analytic attention to their mother-tongue – till at least Murray's pioneering work in 1873.

The following description will be data-based, but not supported by quantification drawn from text corpora: to date, these are not available in sufficient number (and certainly not in tagged form) to make such attempts fully convincing (cf. Moessner's critical remarks on the Helsinki Corpus, 1997). My description will be structuralist, as derived from the surviving texts; however, it will include a contrastive element (summarized in 6.1.3 and 4) because it is not clear how much of 16C syntax was

1) modelled on Latin structures (not only in translated texts); educated Scotsmen, who learnt their grammar and rhetoric in Latin-medium schools exhibit a great range of both deliberate and unintentional transfer. (It can even be argued that they may have had, to a certain extent, a fused syntax containing elements of Scots and Latin), or

2) imitating English – in so far as the two systems were still distinct (as written media) for the individual author or copyist.

Comparison with English is also useful because the structural elaboration of the two languages was determined by the same functional needs. Moreover, differences between the two systems point to features that might be affected by anglicization of Scots in due course. Note that with statements on syntax it is particularly important to specify whether they are based on poetry or prose, and to indicate the stylistic level of the text.

Even with these cautions, we must remember that our linguistic knowledge depends on surviving texts, and what we describe is at best adequate to account for the structures we find. However, we cannot hope to reconstruct the syntactic competence of a 16C Scotsman, fluent in Latin, English and Scots, and explain the use he made of the structures of these languages in a specific context. Acceptability in particular is very difficult to reconstruct: there are, for instance, cases of mixed constructions, and it is impossible for a modern grammarian to assess how acceptable these were – or whether they would have been classified as mistakes by contemporary readers (cf. Bellenden's *skarslie **had** his inymyß **cassin** ... and **cumand***, Görlach 1991a:338/106-7.)

6.1   *The influence of Latin and English*

Greater syntactic expressiveness and precision in both Scots and EModE were achieved by various means discussed in greater detail below. They may be summarized as an increase in

1) sentence length,
2) sentence depth (that is, the number of subordinate clauses, and their relation on various levels),
3) conjunctions and prepositions,
4) non-finite clauses (infinitives, participles and gerunds),
5) coherence within texts, established by means of logical-syntactic connections and better organized structures (on the pattern of rules adopted from classical rhetoric).

With respect to most of these strategies the influence of Latin certainly raised the frequency of their use in Scots and EModE, but Latin impact cannot be claimed to be responsible for individual instances. The Latinity of a text can, thus, only be assessed with reference to transferred features not shared by Latin and Scots/EModE, and interpreted having an eye on the text type. Additional evidence (as from the strategies mentioned above) then needs to be called in to support the interpretation.

As noted above, there is in the history of Scots no break corresponding to the one in English syntax in mid 17C, when EModE came to shed its dependence on Latin in some text types and started developing its own English categories: by that time, Scots had been largely fossilized and was no longer independently adapted to new syntactic requirements of formal writing.

It is difficult to postulate Latin influence on individual syntactic features in Scots texts, but it is even more problematic to prove the model function of English syntax. However, in some cases it is unlikely that an independent development of the two systems led to identical results. In these we assume English influence, as in the following structures (detailed below, but cf. Beal 1997:370):

1) the development of the relative-clause system;
2) functionalization of *do* in questions and sentences negated with *not*.

Other cases are, however, much more doubtful. Is the development of progressive aspect in Scots independent (may the development in Scots even predate the emergence of the functional distinction in EModE)? Did fixed word order develop in Scots independently of EModE, or was the pattern copied? (So-called 'inversion' was largely a matter of idiosyncratic choice in EModE until 1650). Did the contrast of past vs. present perfect arise in Scots independently of EModE? A plausible hypothesis might be to assume that English-influenced developments would spread into ScE first and only later into Scots – unless register- and style-specific differences made such transfers unlikely. However, much of this is speculation at the present stage of research which permits statements on EModE with some qualification, but not on Scots, and less so, for contrastive analyses (cf. relative clauses below).

6.2 Features of Scots syntax

(Beal 1997; Macafee 1980, 1992-3; McClure 1994; Miller 1993; Moessner 1997, Purves 1997a)

Scots and English agree in many aspects of syntax, but there are a number of characteristic differences. In the following some of the most striking of these will be pointed out.

6.2.1 Determiners

The use of articles in contemporary Scots sometimes reflects older usage (as suggested by ME conventions or parallels in German) or represents Scottish innovations. The definite article is preferred instead of possessive pronouns or zero for instance with institutions (*the kirk, the skuil*), diseases (*the cauld, the rheumatics*), parts of the body (*the heid*), members of the family (*the wife*), days and seasons (*the Setterday, the simmer*), occupations (*the jynerie*), languages (*the Laitin*), fields of learning (*the Chemistrie*) or in fixed combinations with various periods of time (*the day* 'today', *the nicht* 'tonight', *the morn* 'tomorrow', *the streen* 'yesterday', *the year* 'this year', *the noo* 'now'). *The* is also regularly used preceding *baith/both* and *maist/most*. The possessive personal pronoun is often found with names of meals (*my breakfast, your tea*) and certain other nouns where English has another determiner or zero (cf. Beal 1997:363, Miller 1993:129).

6.2.2 Premodification

In the early period, Scots shared certain types of premodification with EModE which are lost or have become very rare in PDE and present-day Scots (examples partly taken from Moessner 1997:118-20):
1) 'split genitive': *þe nobillis childeryn of France* (cf. EModE 'the Archbishop's grace of York', Shakespeare),
2) 'possessive dative': *that gud his grace, this present Dutches hir body* (cf. EModE 'Sejanus his Fall', Ben Jonson),
3) pre- and postmodifying adjectives combined: *ane gud knycht and hardy*.
In present-day Scots there is an exceptional range of quantifiers which may be used as premodifiers of nouns (i.e. without the preposition 'of'), as in *a (wee) drap tea, a bit bread, a morsil bacon, a wheen poets*, etc. (cf. Purves 1997a:8-9).

With premodifying nouns, the question of whether the combinations should be described as compounds rather than as nominal phrases is sometimes difficult to decide (as it is in English). If we accept them as compounds, then the freedom of forming such compounds appears to be greater than in English (and more like German). Purves adduces *breik backside, muck midden, table heid* (1997a:9) and Wilson (1915:69) has *swein-saim* 'hog's lard'.

6.2.3 *Prepositions, adverbial particles and conjunctions*

Although prepositions and adverbial particles might well be treated under 'lexis', they are traditionally dealt with in chapters on syntax because they are more notable for their syntactic functions than for their often indistinct lexical meanings.

Most Scots prepositions and adverbial particles largely agree in form and use with their English cognates, while a few others differ in either or both. According to their form, three categories may be distinguished:

1) words almost equivalent to English such as: *aboot, at, by, efter, for, o(f), on, oot, ower, wi(th)*;
2) words with obvious formal cognates in English: *abune* 'above', *athout* 'without', *intil* 'into', *till* 'to', and the set of words which in English have *be-* rather than *a-*, like *ablo* 'below', *afore, ahint, aneath, aside, atween/atweesh, ayont*;
3) words lacking a formal equivalent in English: *anent* 'concerning', *athort* 'across', *atour* 'across, over, out of, above, beyond, etc.', *ben* 'into', *forby* 'besides', *forgain* 'opposite to', *fornent* 'in front of', *gin* 'by' (time), *inower* 'within', *outby (of)* 'without', *outwith* 'outside' and *syne* 'ago'.

Also compare the large number of intensifiers (commonly adverbs of degree used without *-ly*, thus retaining earlier English usage): *awfu, byordinar, clean, fair, fell, fou, gey, maist, rael, unco* (Purves 1997: 34) and other modifiers, such as *aiblins* 'perhaps', *mebbie(s)* 'maybe', *middlin* 'fairly', *whiles* 'sometimes'.

Many of the words in categories 1) and 2) agree with their English cognates in meaning and usage, too. Some, however, have developed (or retained) additional senses and thus may be used in other kinds of constructions. The preposition *oot*, for instance, may be selected where English has 'out of' (*oot the windi*), *on* for 'about' (*the lad ye was thinkin' on*), *intil* for 'in' (*there wis nae room for them intil the inn* T71b/10). Some verbs shared by English and Scots take differing prepositions, e.g. *to wait on someone* ('wait for'), *to be/get married on someone* ('married to'), *to ask at someone* ('ask someone'), *to shout on someone* ('shout at') .

Some of the words in categories 2) and 3) are obsolescent today (such as *atour*), whereas others have become 'overt Scotticisms' which makes it possible for them to occur in ScE contexts (*outwith*). A few also occur in northern English dialects.

The same is true for conjunctions. Most of them are similar in form and function to their English cognates (e.g. *but, that, acause* 'because', etc.), but some have no close relative in English (*gin* 'if', *binna* 'unless, except', etc.; *an(d)* 'if' is EModE, but now obsolete). Some behave as in English, others do not (e.g. *nor*, which is used as a conjunction of comparison, like 'than').

6.2.4 *Word order*

Fixed word order was established in EModE and early Scots; this was clearly a late accommodation to make up for the loss of case inflections in ME, but it is incompletely known how far the developments in the two varieties were independent of each other, or whether there was any influence of English on Scots, and how this influence progressed. SVO patterns obviously increased in Scots and English in the course of the 15-17C and became virtually obligatory in 17C prose; though inversion is found in both varieties after sentence-initial negative adverbs: *scarslie had his inymyß cassin* (Bellenden, see quote above) .

The structure of the noun phrase is shared by Scots and English: genitives precede the head, prepositional phrases and expanded participles follow it (rarely if unexpanded). In contrast to English, the fixed sequence of indirect and direct object may, however, in Scots also apply if the indirect object is a noun rather than a pronoun: *Gie him it – Gie the bairn it* (Purves 1997:13).

Fixed word order made the sequence Obj.-V-Subj. unusual and, thus, the use of impersonal verbs rare as in EModE (my examples are from Older Scots):

> *So me behufyt quhilum* (T6/15); *it becummis euerie one .. to be* (T13/3); *it hes plesit God* (T13/9), *suth thyngis þat ar likand/Tyll mannys heryng ar plesand* (T1/9-10.)

6.2.5 *Negation*

The system of Scots negation is an area of grammar that remains more distinct from English than most other features. This is partly a consequence of the incomplete adoption of *do*-support of negated sentences in the 17C. Today, negation in Scots is, then, possible

1) by the enclitic particle: common with auxiliary verbs and modals (*dinna* 'don't', *canna* 'can't') and sporadically, especially in literary texts, retained with a small number of high-frequency full verbs (*kenna* 'don't know'); the form of the particle varies: *-na*, the earliest form, is preferred in ideal literary Scots, *-nae* seems to be stylistically neutral, though today related to Western and South-western dialects, whereas *-ny/-ni* is associated with urban speech in the Central Belt;
2) by the independent particle *no* (today in Southern and Central) or *nae* (in Northern dialects); in Older Scots usually *na*. A former alternative, *nocht* (e.g. T1/92), is now obsolete, though sometimes used in literature to create an archaic style. Another – modern – one is emphatic *nutt*, which is used in negative response to a positive statement (Macafee 1980:5). In Older Scots the independent particle did not need *do* support with full verbs; this construction only survives in rare usages in some Southern dialects and in certain types of imperatives (Macafee 1980:8).

While both may be found in variation with the English form *not*, the English enclitic particle *-n't* is largely avoided, even by speakers of ScE (tag questions being the exception to the rule; Miller 1989:14).

The attachment of the enclitic particle may modify the form of some of the operator verbs: negated *dae* becomes *dinna* 'don't', *will* may become *winna*, *s(h)all* > *sanna*, *hae* > *hinna*.

Apart from the forms of the negative particles, their relative distribution in declarative clauses and questions is characteristic of Scots and also ScE: at least in the Central Belt the isolated form seems to be used much more frequently than in (other varieties of) English (Miller & Brown 1982:14). Disregarding local variation, Scots usage may be summarised as follows:

In negative statements, it is more common, if possible, to attach the contracted operator to the subject and use independent *no/nae*, than to contract the negative particle and attach it to the operator (Macafee 1980:5; cf. the deviant uses of *isna*, *urnae* (T68/70) and of *havena*). On the other hand, *-na(e)* is preferred if the operator may not be contracted and attached to the preceding noun or pronoun (e.g. for phonotactic reasons; Miller 1989:14). In these cases independent *no/nae* only appears, if it does not refer to the operator but to its complement (cf. Macafee 1980:7). In negative statements there is, thus, a tendency not to use operator and negative particle in isolation simultaneously (Brown & Millar 1978:161). Emphatic sentences are the exception: there the independent particle may appear along with a full operator, but then it usually takes the emphatic form *nutt/not* (Brown & Millar 1978:161).

While these preferences are only a matter of degree, the use of contracted 'will' with *no/nae* in negative statements is in itself a marked feature of Scots syntax (*he'll no come* rather than English *he won't come*). St E employs the constructions *won't* or *will not* instead. Aitken (1984a:106) describes this usage as a *covert Scotticism*. The Scottish alternative with enclitic negative particle (forms such as *he winna(e)* or *wilna(e) come*) seems to be current in NE Scots and in literary language (cf. e.g. T55/60).

In negative questions, again independent *no/nae* is preferred (Miller & Brown 1982:13). This entails a difference in word order: Scots usually has {(interrogative pronoun +) operator + subject + *no/nae*} as opposed to St E {(interrogative pronoun +) operator + *-n't* + subject} (e.g. *is he no going? whit way is he no going?* vs. *isn't he coming? why isn't he coming?*) .

McClure (1994:73) states that these preferences probably represent a recent development, negative questions introduced by *dinna* ... (rather than *dae* + pronoun + *no/nae*...) being frequent in 19C literature. Again there are dialectal differences, with the NE showing less distinctive preference for subject-operator cliticisation than other areas.

As noted above, Scottish speakers often use *-n't* (as opposed to *-na(e)*) in tag questions of the form {operator + *-n't* + pronoun}, the most common one in St E (e.g. ..., *isn't he?*). However, there are two other constructions specifically Scots (McClure 1994:73, Macafee 1980:22): One inverts the word order, so that it parallels the 'normal' negative question (e.g. ..., *is he no?*). The other – newer – variant, which is often associated with urban speech, involves double negation and may be formalised as {operator + *-n't* + pronoun + *no/nae*}; here the first negative particle must be contracted, generally in the form of *-n't* (..., *isn't he no?*, but cf. *wullen we na?*).

In negative imperatives, the isolated form *no/nae* only appears in the rare cases of co-ordinated clauses where *do*-support is absent (cf. Purves 1997a:27f.: *Mynd an no be late for the skuil!*). Forms like **do no...!* or **dae no...!* do not seem to be in use. While *dinna* is the dominant choice, the enclitic negative particle is also obligatory in the absence of *do*-support, e.g. *waitna till du's grown aald* (T59/13), *Be-na gliff'd* (T69a/13) and *latna ma naitur hinner me* (T72/35).

Scots, as several non-standard varieties of English, also has multiple negation, a construction eradicated from St E by prescriptive grammarians in the 18C. This explains why this traditional construction is avoided in some approaches to creating a standard literary Scots (but cf. T69b/14). A special type of double negative, in which the two instances are not mutually reinforcing, but rather cancelling one another out, is occasionally found (cf. Brown & Millar 1980:106). This is the type of sentence in which the independent negative particle does not take the operator as its scope and may therefore appear in the form *no/nae*, as noted above.

Negation is also possible by means of the particle *never* without *do*-support (again a feature shared with many non-standard varieties of English; Miller 1989:15). This non-emphatic function of *never*, which may "apply to single events, [...] and to specific stretches of time" (Miller 1989:15) is particularly clear in sentences in the simple past (Miller & Brown 1982:15, cf. T48/3). This usage seems to be a fairly new development (possibly imported from N IrE, cf. Beal 1997:372). It is common in present-day Scots, and even ScE speech (Miller 1993:115).

Ex 51   Check the above statements in a larger corpus of modern Scots prose (a novel or play of your choice).

6.2.6 *Tense, aspect and mood*

Reference to future time in Scots may be indicated by the auxiliary *will* (or formal *sal*, which is restricted to written usage today), but its use is not obligatory to the same extent as it is in English (and has been from the 18C). This is partly a result of Scots lacking formal registers typically influenced by prescriptive correctness. Of the further options in English to refer to the (immediate) future, *going to*, *be + -ing* and *be about to*, the latter seems to be rare in Scots (though it does appear, e.g. T63/2). The other expressions are common constructions in Scots: the first usually appears in the form *gaun tae* or *gonnae* and the second implies immediate intention (McClure, p.c.).

In Older Scots, as in EModE, forms such as *wrait* / *hes written* / *dyd write* / *wes writand* were stylistic options for the description of a past event well into the 17C. They then came to be distinguished by taking over specific grammatical functions, marking off perfective and progressive aspect from the simple past. Again, English influence on Scots is difficult to assess; the data fail to reveal how much of the similar modern results can be ascribed to syntactical borrowing and how much to independent development by functional selection. The only thing that is perfectly clear is that Latin had no influence since it has no equivalent categories that could have served as models.

Note that in both Older Scots and EModE the past participle of verbs of motion was expanded alternatively by *have* and *be* (e.g. T12/6). In Insular Scots the perfect of any verb may still be formed with the auxiliary *be*, and this is also possible for a small group of verbs in general Scots (Macafee 1980:29 gives *start, come* as examples).

The form *be + present participle* is quite common in some 16C texts (cf. T8/30, T12/1, T14/10). This indicates that the use of this construction need not be an instance of anglicization – though its later interpretation as an expression of a 'progressive' aspect may well have been influenced by the developments in EModE. However, since its grammaticalization as the progressive marker in English happened late in the 17C/18C, it cannot have influenced formal written Scots.

Today, the Scots use of the progressive *V+ing* largely agrees with English, but note that the range of verbs that take the construction is larger in Scots. A number of verbs designating mental activities can occur in the progressive for which it would be ungrammatical in St E, e.g. *dout, forget, hear, jalouse, ken, like, mean, mynd, remember, think* and *want* (e.g. T62/68-9). Some other restrictions on the use of the progressive form in St E do not seem to be valid in Scots, either (cf. Beal 1997:373, Miller 1993:121-2), so that it occurs much more frequently than in English. This broader application of the progressive in Scots, which was described as "very common" in the late 18th century (Beal 1997:372) and still is, could be seen as an innovation in Scots, due to the late grammaticalization of the feature in St E (cf. Beal 1997:373). It may, however, also be interpreted as evidence for the separate, parallel development of the phenomenon in Scots and English.

Ex 52   Can you find cases where tense and aspect in older Scottish texts do not agree with modern English expectations?

Towards the end of the Older Scots period, synthetic forms of the subjunctive mood were gradually replaced by combinations of *wald* + infinitive (as in EModE, where *should/would* were increasingly used). Only *-s*-less forms of the 3rd ps. sg. pres. of full verbs indicate subjunctive functions: *howbeit it become me rather* (T13/14) as opposed to indicative mood: *it becummis* (T13/3).

Subjunctive forms of *be* and *have* in main clauses remained more frequent until the 18C: *sic interpryses had bene nothing profitable* 'would have been' (T13/15); *the crown war searchit and gottin againe* 'would be' (T14/16). Further examples of the subjunctive are found in later texts especially in subclauses: *I'll be in Dumfries the morn gif the beast be to the fore* (T34/33); *Diel hae me in da warld be na just gaen gyte!* (T41/1). From the 18C subjunctives are found in a negated construction, too: a separate form *binna* is used to express the negative present subjunctive: *gin the weather binna a' the waur* (T42/12), *For whaur is trewth to be fun gin it binna i' the Bible?* (T51/6).

In older texts, irrealis is sometimes found to be expressed in perfective infinitives, a construction absent from EModE and impossible in PDE as well as in modern Scots and ScE: *it become me rather (quha hes bestouit all my Zouthe in the Sculis) to had vrytin the samin in Latine* 'to have written' (but he did not) (T13/14-5).

6.2.7 Modal verbs

The inventory of Older Scots modal auxiliaries includes *aucht/aw* 'ought'; *behove; can, couth/c(o)ud; da(u)r, durst; ma(u)n/mone* 'must'; *may, mycht/mocht; sall, suld; usit to; will, wa(l)d; dow* 'be able, may', *dought* 'could'; *mote* 'may, might, must'; *note* 'need'; *tha(i)r* 'need' (with several spelling variants) of which at least the last three have become obsolete. Most of them have parallel forms in northern ME and there is little difference in usage of the shared items (for exceptions see McClure 1994:56). Past-tense forms, however, more consistently expressed pastness (or reflected tense sequence according to Latin rules) than they do today. By the 17C, the list is completed by *must/most* and *need* (which may, from the late 18C, take *not(e)/nott(en)* as its past and past participle form in NE Scots).

The inventory of modals in Modern Scots is, then, similar to that of English, though some differ in form and *maun* is not found in English. Nevertheless, there are remarkable differences in usage, which determine what modalities can be distinguished in the two systems. A few modals have become rare in present-day Scots. *Behove* 'is/was obliged to', which used to occur in a great variety of forms (e.g. *bude*), is, for instance, extremely rare. The same is true for *dow* and *dought*, which convey an archaic flavour. *Da(u)r* and *durst* seem to underly the same stylistic restriction in Scots as in English. *Shall* is not found in spoken Scottish, and is accordingly used very rarely in contemporary writing in Scots. McClure summarizes this change:

t74 The loss of *sall* from contemporary speech is fairly recent. Literary attestations of both the full form and the reduced *'se /z/*, used with personal pronouns, are common until the beginning of the present century; the reduced form may still be heard in conservative speech.   (1994:71)

Miller and Brown (1982:11) go even further in their claim that *shall* is today completely missing from both the Scots and the ScE modal system. The same development is described for *may* ("*might* is regarded as separate from *may*" Miller 1982:11); non-epistemic usage of *must* and *ought to* is now also restricted to formal written language.

In the absence of *may* in contemporary Scottish speech, 'permission' is expressed by means of *can* or – more frequently – *be allowed to* (Aitken 1984a:106, Miller & Brown 1982:8). A further alternative is a construction with *get + V-ing* (Miller 1993:117). *Might* rarely implies 'possibility', but usually has epistemic meanings (Miller & Brown 1982:8). 'Possibility' is most commonly expressed through the adverb *maybe* (*perhaps* is extremely rare).

In Scottish usage, *must* is restricted to its epistemic meaning, referring to 'conclusion' and 'probability'. It does not usually imply 'obligation' or 'necessity'; *have to, have got to* or *are to* occur instead (Aitken 1984a:107 and Macafee 1980:30). *Need to* may also have the same meaning: "'Need' is no less strong than 'must' or 'have to'" (Miller & Brown 1982:10) – a usage which is very rare in St E. Alternatively, the Scots modal *maun* is used (for both meanings). Accordingly, negated *must* does not – as in St E – necessarily express 'prohibition', but may have epistemic meanings (Miller 1993:119). On the other hand, Scots may negate *have to* in order to signify 'prohibition'. Where *must* indeed expresses 'obligation', specific emphasis is put on the necessity of the action (Miller & Brown 1982:8). According to Miller & Brown (1982:10), *ought to* is today absent from the spoken system, "*should* being the lexeme primarily associated with moral duty".

A few modals, especially *can*, also occur in constructions such as *he wull niver can unnerstaun* (cf. Miller & Brown 1982:12f., Miller 1993:119f.). Double modals, though not attested in Older Scots (Moessner 1997:113), are not a very new phenomenon; their use, however, appears to have increased in the 20th century, especially in urban Scots (McClure 1994:72-3, Brown & Miller 1982:12, Miller 1993:119f.).

Ex 53   Summarize differences in the modals in present-day Scots and English.

6.2.8 *Functions of 'do'*

The question of how Scots came to share the uses of *do*-support with English is still largely unsolved. "The periphrastic auxiliary *do*, which is always followed by the bare infinitive, is absent from the early texts. It begins to appear in the sixteenth century in affirmative statements" (Moessner 1997:115). *Do* as auxiliary in questions and negative statements is rare in Older Scots. The verb obviously represented a stylistic choice in 16C Scots (as in EModE) serving functions of rhythm, word order patterns, emphasis and the extension of the verbal group (e.g. T5/9, T11/30); in many cases, the particular reasons for its use are, however, unclear. Meurman-Solin (1993c) is the only study of the question to date, but her data do not suffice to establish whether *do* in 17C Scots is an imported feature, an independent development, or a fusion of the two. There seems to be a somewhat more frequent non-use of *do* in colloquial Scots than in English (a feature which has not been systematically investigated, but found in questions, negative statements and imperatives, e.g. *what think ye o' the joy in the Father's Hoose?* T46/36, or *latna ma gleg knife see*, T72/42). If this is so, it could reflect the incomplete takeover of the pattern transmitted through written English, especially in the form of prescriptive grammar. McClure (1994:72) agrees; he sees here "a much greater degree of conservatism than in southern English" well into the 19C, whereas "contemporary Scots follows general English usage".

A notable feature uniquely recorded in Scots (which points to its being an old indigenous usage) is the use of *done* in middle position between auxiliary and participle – such uses do not seem to be found in EModE at all: *He hes done petuously devour* T5/49; *his bukis had done compyle* 'had compiled' T11/91. Apparently, the construction was often used in conditional sentences.

6.2.9 *Complex sentences*

When Scots had to acquire syntactic precision for expressing abstract ideas and creating scholarly texts in the 16C, the use of complex sentences (consisting of at least one main and one subordinate clause) increased. Their construction was notably influenced by Latin (and English). However, the cultivation of syntactic sophistication seems not to have led to the excesses of Ciceronian prose like Bullokar's (1580, in Görlach 1991a:225-6) or Lyly's experimental emulation of Latin (*Kunstprosa* replete with rhetorical ornament, in his *Euphues* of 1578), so that there was no need of a Scottish Bacon (cf. Görlach 1991a:T15) to point out the dangers of such beautification. Scholarly writing such as Skeyne's (1568, T13) comes closest to the complexity of many EModE texts of the 16C.

Complex sentences are peculiar to expository texts, especially scholarly treatises, legal discussions and the like. They are found, in the 16C, in texts like Bellenden's (T8) and Skeyne's (T13), but are much less prominent in, for instance, biblical translation or James VI's *Basilicon Doron* (T18, which has structural affinities with other types of instruction). The number of clauses per sentence and their interdependence are important characteristics, but so is the ratio between

1) adverbial and relative clauses, and
2) clauses containing finite verbs and those with non-finite forms (infinitives, participles, gerunds) only.

The relative frequency of non-finite forms is also a characteristic distinction between original prose and texts translated from Latin. However, with the fluency in Latin achieved by 16C scholars, and the model character of the prestige language, the difference between translated and orginal texts is often smaller than might be expected.

6.2.9.1 *Adverbial clauses*
(Häcker 1999)

Older Scots has the full range of adverbial subordinators introducing resultative, purpositive, concessive, comparative, adversative, temporal, conditional, causal, modal and local clauses. Such clauses alternate with adverbial phrases or, very frequently in early prose and especially in texts translated from Latin, with participial constructions (cf. T8, T13). The Scots subordinators largely agree with EModE, though some diverge in form (such as *sen* 'since') or function (e.g. *quhill* 'until'). A few adverbs, however, do not have a corresponding form in English (e.g. *gin* 'if, whether', *an(d)* 'if, although'), and there are rare cases in which Scots develops new subordinators, independent of English, as late as the 19C, such as *binna* 'unless' or *beis* 'compared with'.

Today, according to Häcker (1999), Scots and St E show the same repertoire of adverbial clause patterns, i.e. both varieties allow the construction of finite adverbial clauses, of verbless, infinitive and other non-finite structures. There are some differences between the two varieties in their inventories of adverbial subordinators, but the most significant differences seem to concern the semantic range of individual items, and the frequencies of specific semantic relationships expressed through adverbial clauses. The latter may partly be explained by the differences in the ranges of text types covered by Scots and English.

6.2.9.2 *Relative clauses*

The Scots relative system has been greatly affected by the English pattern in the 16C (Romaine 1980b, 1982a); this has left a great range of choices which can now express stylistic, regional, social or personal distinctions. The original relative markers, used in Scots from the beginning, are:

that and *at* (both uninfl.): the two parallel forms may derive from different origins (*at* apparently borrowed from Old Norse, *that* a native element), but this difference is no longer perceptible; they are used to refer to both inanimate and animate nouns (human or not) in both restrictive and non-restrictive relative clauses; the form *at* is now archaic or purist in writing, except in the North, but represents the common pronunciation in colloquial speech all over Lowland Scotland;

Ø: relative clauses may also be constructed without explicit relative marker, Ø taking on both object or (more rarely) subject functions (as in *I've gather'd News will kittle your Mind with Joy* T26/15).

The following additional options are found in Middle Scots, but are considered never to have been integrated into the spoken language: they are rare, compared to *that*, and only found in formal texts (Caldwell 1974).

quhilk and its plural form *quhilkis* (both occasionally preceded by *the*): this northern form of the interrogative pronoun slowly encroaches upon native *that* in the function of a relative marker in Middle Scots, as *which* does in ME – a major difference being that *which* was never inflected (Romaine 1982a:70-1).

quha: this equivalent of English *who* is first found – infrequently – from the mid 16C (Moessner 1997:144), and is only used to refer to animate antecedents. The inflected forms *quhais/quhois* and *quham/quhome* precede *quha* as a relative pronoun. While *quhais/quhois* is extremely rare (possessive relatives being infrequent on the whole), *quham/quhome* was better established where the relative depended on a preposition (Romaine 1982a:72).

Apart from these relative pronouns, relative adverbs (such as *quhar, quhen, quharfor*, etc.) were also used to introduce relative clauses.

While the *quh*-options remain comparatively rare, a shift in their spellings takes place as a result of the anglicization of Scots (cf. Devitt 1989). From the mid 16C, *which* (always uninflected) begins to replace *quhilk*, etc. (sometimes via a mixed form *quhich(e)*). By the mid 17C the change-over is largely complete, the last isolated instances of *quhilk* are found in the 18C. The hybrid form *whilk* is retained up to the present time as a literary option. A similar shift is observable towards *who, whose* and *whom* (the mixed forms *wha(e), whase* and *wham* sometimes appear in literary Scots).

There has been a great deal of diachronic change, on top of regional diversity. Today, *wh*- pronouns in Scots speech (as opposed to writing) are still extremely rare. *That* and Ø are preferred in all types of relative constructions. McClure (1994:74), however, surmises that *wh*- pronouns were more common in writing and even in formal speech in the 18/19C than they are now. Still, though Murray's criticism (repeatedly expressed in the 20C, e.g. by Purves 1997a:14) of Burns's verse "Scots! *wha hae* wi Wallace bled!" as a quasi-Scottish version of a more authentic "Scots *(th)at haes*" is not just, it holds true with respect to normal colloquial Scots usage.

The general non-standard use of *what* as a relative pronoun in attributive function seems to be a new feature, sometimes found in the WC region (cf. *glaur = muck what is in a puddle after the puddle goes away* T62/57).

Ex 54   What is the proportion of relative pronouns in the excerpts of Bellenden (T8) and Skeyne (T13) and can distinctions be found according to the nature of the antecedents and restrictiveness?

6.3   *Text syntax and rhetoric*

Scots was as much affected as English by the challenge of expressive, well-ordered, prestigious Latin when it came to replace the language in the fields of scholarly texts and some literary genres in the 15/16C. Rhetoric, the discipline of good usage (grammar being the field of correctness) was one of the three constituent parts of the *trivium* in medieval universities, carried on into 16C grammar schools. However, while we have dozens of Renaissance treatises on rhetoric and 'poesie' in English, there is hardly anything in Scots. Conclusions about how the precepts were followed in good writing must therefore be based on the Scots texts themselves, and since translations have to be excluded (because they largely exhibit the rhetorical structures of their sources), there is little to base our analysis on, especially since after 1560 so much may have been transmitted through English.

It is thus likely that the evident impact of rhetorical concepts on the writing of 16C Scots was based on Latin manuals (less frequently, on English works which became frequent only after 1550). Many authors aware of the limited potential of their vernacular stressed the inadequacy of their style, as Douglas did in his *Eneados* (T6), or Skeyne in his treatise against the pestilence (T13). Much of this is of course stereotypical, and therefore in itself represents a rhetorical 'figure', *viz.* the topos of modesty. The attitude is possibly best expressed by Bellenden who claimed rhetorical incompetence for his translation, but then produced a stylistically very adequate text:

t75 Thairfor sayid Marcus Cicero, 'He that is ignorant of sik thingis as bene done afoir his tyme, for lak of experience, is bot ane barn.' For thir reassonis, maist nobill Prince, I, that bene þi native and humyll servitour sen thi first infance, be impulsioun of luff and vehement affeccioun quhilk I bere vnto the samyn has translatit 'The History of Scotland' sen þe first begynning þerof in wlgair
5   langage; and þocht the charge was importabill throw tedious laboure and feire of this huge volume, quhilk has impeschitt my febill ingyne, havand na crafty witt nor pregnant eloquence to decoir the samyn, ȝite I am constranit for schort tyme to bring this my translacioun to licht, nakit of perfeccioun and rethory, siklike as implvme birdis to flicht.

(1531, quoted from Corbett 1999:50)

Still, he was critical of contemporary writers who overdid their rhetorical embellishments by 'improving' their sources:

t76 new authoris ...be þare crafty eloquence traistis to vincuss [vanquish] the rude language of anciant authoris.

(1531, quoted from Corbett 1999:53)

The author of the *Complaint of Scotland* goes even further in his criticism of such linguistic behaviour:

t77 Nou heir i exort al philosophouris, historigraphours & oratours of our scottis natione to support & til excuse my barbir agrest termis for i thocht it nocht necessair, til hef fardit ande lardit this tracteit vitht exquisite termis, quhilkis ar nocht daly vsit, bot rather i hef vsit domestic scottis langage, maist intelligibil for the vlgare pepil. ther hes bene diuerse translatours ande compilaris in ald
5   tymys, that tuke grite pleseir to contrafait ther vlgare langage, mixand ther purposis, vitht oncoutht exquisite termis, dreuyn, or rather to say mair formaly, reuyn, fra lating, ande sum of them tuke pleiseir to gar ane vord of ther purpose, to be ful of sillabis half ane myle of lyntht, as ther was ane callit hermes, quhilk pat in his verkis, thir lang tailit vordis, conturbabuntur, constantinopolitani, innumerabilibus solicitudinibus ther vas ane vthir that vrit in his verkis, guadet honorificabili-
10 tudinitatibus, al sic termis procedis of fantastiknes and glorius consaitis.

(1549, quoted from Stewart 1979:13)

The only theoretical text in Scots that deals with related questions, James VI's *Reulis* of 1584 (T16), is on poetics, particularly metrics, explicitly excluding rhetoric since "... they are figures of Rhetorique and Dialectique, quhilkis airtis I professe nocht."

7   Lexis

7.1   General problems of description

The lexis of an individual language may be structured by way of various parameters according to which they can be collected and arranged in reference works, such as
1)   alphabetical order (the common dictionary; reverse and rhyming dictionaries);
2)   spelling and pronunciation (spellers and dictionaries of pronunciation);
3)   regional distinctions (dialect dictionaries; glossaries);
4)   sociolinguistic patternings (esp. dictionaries of solecisms compiled for corrective purposes; dictionaries of slang);
5)   technical language of the trades (dictionaries of science, economy or other fields; largely also included in encyclopedias);
6)   the lexis of a specific era (period dictionaries);
7)   the vocabulary of individual authors (glossaries appended to *Works*; author dictionaries; concordances);
8)   the origin and the history of words (etymological or historical dictionaries);
9)   semantic and encyclopedic fields (thesauruses);
10)   collocations (dictionaries of idioms and collocations);
11)   names and facts (onomasticons; encyclopedias);
12)   frequencies (frequency dictionaries);
13)   first occurrences (chronological dictionaries).

Not all of these dictionaries are available for even the major European languages. A comparison with English shows that Scots is lacking most of these; data collection has not even started for many of such research tools. A particular problem with Scots lexis is, of course, that so many items are shared with English and have been from the very beginning (so that it is impossible to define them as either English or Scots), and so many others have been taken over in the course of anglicization from the 15C onwards (cf. internal borrowing 7.3.1; 9).

7.1.1 Archaism and innovation

Lexical change affected Scots as a system (partly) separated from English in various ways. Whereas innovation will be dealt with under the headings of loanwords, word-formation and change of meaning, the use of archaisms is a special feature of the variety. This is to be expected for two reasons:
1) The comparatively peripheral position of the speech community leads one to assume that innovations spreading from London would reach ScE only in a somewhat diluted form, and Scots possibly not at all. The old assumption that dialects are repositories for early lexis may be even more true for an isolated minority language.
2) The fact that Scots is so bound up with the literary tradition and the occasional deliberate imitation of old authors is likely to support the survival (which may in some cases be a revival) of archaic lexical items.

In order to test this hypothesis, the lexical evidence from dictionaries was quantified in Görlach (1987). The 100 words taken from the *CSD* (all apparently obsolete in English) were evenly spread by a competent informant among the categories 'not known / obsolete / known from literature / frequent in literature / common in Scots / also found in ScE' – his assistance was necessary because usage labels in modern dictionaries are partly contradictory. The test clearly indicated that 'survivals' were largely words remembered from the works of Burns and Scott. The conclusion can, then, only be that the alleged retention of greater numbers of old words in Scots does not apply to modern spoken usage, and that higher figures are determined by occurrences in older literary texts, and imitations of these.

There are other indications of lexical loss in everyday Scots progressing quite rapidly: When S.G. Smith in 1948 (T57) defended his use of Scots against the charge of its being archaic, he claimed that words like *antrin, smittel, waukrife, begrutten* and *wancanny* could be heard in the streets of Edinburgh. Can they today? How far is Lorimer's translation of the *New Testament* actually understood, when the text is used in the kirk? Another case in point is Annand's edition of McLellan's *Linmill Stories* (1990, T58), which has an extremely short glossary. Annand relies (optimistically?) on the intended readership to know many Scots words without this help. The tales were first broadcast on the radio, which imposed even greater demands on the listeners' comprehension, since glossing was impossible, though, admittedly, to Scots speakers (and many Scottish residents), Scots is more familiar to the ear than to the eye. The rapid loss of dialect lexis is also confirmed by Macafee (1994b) and Pollner (1985c).

7.1.2 *The mixed language*

In the 16C the two languages, for all their overlaps, were largely distinct in their vocabularies. This can be seen in 'translations' such as Harrison's of Bellenden (T8) and the anglicized versions of James VI's *Basilicon Doron* (T18), in which items like the following were replaced by English equivalents:

> *wrangwis* 'unrighteous', *gudeserr* 'grandfather', *biggit* 'builded', *traisting* 'trusting', *barnis* 'children', *put him to þe horne* 'proclaimed him traitour', *fretis* 'prophesie', *schorne* 'ripped'; *soldatis* 'souldiers', *hardiment* 'hardiness', *Spagnoll* 'Spaniard'

However, *ualkeryfe* (in the excerpt from the *Basilicon* in Görlach 1991a:310), which would have been incomprehensible for Englishmen, was adapted in spelling only, and many Scots words in Bellenden's text were not translated either (*weirdis, foulʒeit, landwert, subdittis, compere*).

Ex 55 Are the lexical differences listed due to survival or independent development in Scots (borrowing or word-formation)?

Even if we classify an individual text as 'Scots' we cannot overlook the fact that the language is heterogeneous – in spelling, morphology, syntax and lexis. That this applies even to the lexis of one of the protagonists of the use of Scots in literature, Robert Burns, is evident from all of his poems (unless they are completely in English); compare the following synopsis of the origins of selected Scots words in his works drawn from a modern glossary:

Old English (but obs. in St E)	Old Norse	Celtic	French etc.	unknown/ uncertain
barm yeast	*big* build	*airt* quarter,	*callan(t)* lad	*aizle* hot cinder
biel protection,	*biggin* building	direction; to	*corbie* raven	*blypes* peelings
shelter, cover	*blae* blue,	guide	*douce* grave,	*brogue* trick,
bouk body, carcase	livid, bitter	*bogles*	sober, gentle	hoax
buirdly stalwart,	*brae* hill,	hobgoblins,	*dour* harsh,	*clavers* idle
stately	hillside, high	ghost, spectre	severe,	talk
cushat wood-pigeon	ground by a	*brats* rags	unyielding	*cuif/coof* fool,
daurk day's work	river	*caird* tinker	*fawsont*	clown
dree endure, suffer,	*cleckin* a brood	*bannock* cake of	respectable,	*crowdie* oat-
put up with	*doup* backside	oatmeal	seemly	meal mixed
ferlie wonder, marvel	*dowff* dull,	*clachan* village	*feat* spruce,	with water
fey doomed	melancholy	*cranreuch* hoar-	trim	*gilpey* young
fiel softly, cosily	*drouk* drench,	frost	*feck* valve,	gitl
fiere companion,	soak	*crummock* stick	return,	*glaiket*
comrade	*flinders*	with crooked	advantage	careless,
fyle defile, foul	fragments,	head	*grozet*	foolish
gleede live coal,	smithereens	*drummock* oat-	gooseberry	*gowan* daisy
glowing fire	*fyke* trouble,	meal + water	*grunzie* snout	*hallion* idler,
greet weep, cry	fuss	mixed	*kimmer*	rascal
haffets the temples	*gar* cause,	*ieroe* great-	cummer,	*hurdies*
ho(a)st cough	make,	grandchild	married	buttocks,
kythe discover, make	compel	*ingle* fire	woman,	backside
known	*gear*	burning on a	gossip	*hyte* crazed,
lave the rest,	possessions,	hearth	*mailen* piece of	daft
remainder	money,	*kelpie* water-	arable land	*lug* ear
lift heavens, sky	property	spirit, water	held on lease	*lum* chimney
loof palm of hand	*gowk* cuckoo;	demon in the	*stank* pool of	*paukie/-y*
mirk darkness	fool, dolt	shape of a	standing	cunning,
mool earth, clod	*loup* leap,	horse	water	crafty
quean young woman	jump	*linn* waterfall		*raploch* coarse,
rede counsel, advice	*lowe* flame	*lough* lake, loch		homely
reek smoke	*nieve* fist	*spleuchan*		*rowth*
souter shoemaker	*nowt(e)* cattle,	tobacco-pouch		abundance,
spier enquire	oxen	*tocher* dowry		plenty
teen vexation,	*quey* young			*skouth* scope,
chagrin	cow			liberty
thairm intestine	*snock* to snuff			*spunk* spark
thole suffer, endure	*starn* star			*stoure* dust,
toom empty	*swarf* swoon			battle, tumult,
warlock wizard	*tow* rope			storm
wight strong, stout	*wale* choice			*swither* state of
yule Christmas				agitation

Fig. 23   18C literary Scots: the provenance of a selection of Burns's vocabulary (adapted from the glossary in James Kinsley, ed. 1968. *The Poems and Songs of Robert Burns*. Oxford).

Any compiler of a dictionary of PDE has to decide how much of ScE and Scots should be included. Pollner (1994) has shown that the number of Scottish items in 17/18C English dictionaries was very small, and though the coverage has been conspicuously improved, Aitken (1987) holds that ScE is still largely underrepresented. He checked a list of 324 Scottish items in various dictionaries and showed that only Chambers (published in Edinburgh!) and Webster's *Third* (which has many more entries than the others) registered a large proportion.

Since Aitken's list contains many items which should perhaps not be included even by liberal editors of English dictionaries, I repeated the test with a small selection of items (also using different dictionaries, and more modern editions):

		Wyld	*SOED*	Chambers	Cassell	Collins	Longman	Webster	
Covert Scotticisms	*ashet* 'serving-plate'	–	N	Sc	Sc+	Sc+	Sc+	–	5
	carry-out 'take-away'	–	Ø	–	–	Sc	Sc+	Ø	4
	coup 'rubbish tip'	–	Sc	Sc	–	Sc	–	–	3
	swither 'hesitate'	–	Ø	Sc	Sc	Sc	Sc	Br	6
Overt Scotticisms	*ben* 'into the house'	Sc	Sc+	Sc	Sc	Sc	Sc	Sc	7
	couthy 'congenial'	–	Sc	Sc	Sc	Sc	Sc	Sc	6
	darg 'job of work'	–	Sc+	Sc	Sc	Sc+	Sc+	–	5
	dreich 'dreary'	–	Ø	Sc	Sc	Sc	Sc	Sc	6
	dwam 'stupor'	–	–	Sc	Sc+	Sc	–	–	3
	fushionless 'spiritless'	–	–	Sc	–	–	–	–	1
	kenspeckle 'conspicuous'	–	Sc+	Sc+	Sc	Sc	Sc	Sc	6
	slaister 'mess'	–	Sc+	Sc	Sc	Sc+	Sc	–	5
Cultural Scotticisms	*tack* 'lease'	–	Sc+	Sc	–	Sc	–	–	3
	teind 'tithe'	Sc	Sc+	Sc	Sc	Sc+	–	–	5
	dominie 'schoolmaster'	Sc	Sc	Sc	Sc	Sc	Sc	Sc	7
	tawse 'leather punishment strap'	Sc	Sc	Sc	Sc	Sc	Sc	Br	7
Burnsisms	*aiblins* 'perhaps'	–	Sc+	–	Sc+	–	Sc	Sc	4
	airt 'direction'	–	Sc+	Sc	Sc	Sc	Sc	Sc	6
	clachan 'village'	Sc	Sc+	Sc	Ø	Sc+	Sc+	Sc+	7
	collieshangie 'uproar'	–	Sc	Sc	–	–	Sc	Sc	4
	tapsalteerie 'upside down'	–	Sc	Sc	Sc	Sc	–	Sc	5
	thairm 'bowel'	–	Ø	Sc	–	–	–	–	2
	threap 'argument'	–	Sc+	Sc+	Sc+	Sc+	–	Sc	5
	tocher 'dowry'	–	Sc+	Sc	Sc	Sc	Sc	Sc	6
	N = 24	5	22	22	18	20	16	15	118

Fig. 24 Scots and ScE items in general dictionaries of English.
  The categories and selected words are taken from Aitken (1987). The notations are to be interpreted as follows: –: not registered; labels used in the dictionaries: Sc = Scottish, Sc+ = Scottish and elsewhere, Ø = unmarked, N = northern, Br = British. Dictionaries used for the analysis: H.C. Wyld, *The Universal English Dictionary* (n.d.), *The New Shorter Oxford English Dictionary* (1993), *Chambers English Dictionary* (1988), *Cassell Concise English Dictionary* (1989), *Collins English Dictionary* (1991), *Longman Dictionary of the English Language* (1991) and *Webster's New Collegiate Dictionary* (1977). Note that in recent editions the number of Scots words (and IrE items) has been somewhat increased, as the comparison of *SOED* [1]1933 with [2]1993 shows. For a similar study of Irishisms cf. Görlach (1995d).

Ex 56 Can you trace the OE etymons of the words listed in fig. 24?

Ex 57 Do dictionaries give any information about the etymology of words here listed as 'unknown'?

Ex 58 Test whether the items in fig. 25 are included in dictionaries not used in the test., and compare more recent editions.

7.1.3 *Style and register*

The lexis of Scots is characterized by the range of functions the language has had over time. In the period when it acted as a full national language, it provided an almost complete range of choices according to medium, topics, text types, modes and styles – as far as the respective domains had been acquired for Scots. But at the time of the great expansion of EModE (after 1550) the impact of English on Scots was so great that its own expansion, especially in formal registers, was slowing down and finally came to a halt. There were stylistic choices according to formality and demanded by the principle of decorum, but they were limited to fewer cases than in contemporary EModE; Agutter (1988b:15-6) quotes the following specimens for 15C Scots:

style	'face'	'dog'	'go'
high	*visage*	*hound*	*pas*
neutral	*face*	*dog*	*ga*
low	*gane*	*tyke*	*gang*

Fig. 25 Stylistic grading in Scots

For a poet in particular, it would be vital to have the necessary copiousness of speech (Douglas's "fowth of langage" T8/19) to respond to the demands of rhetorical appropriateness.

A prose writer like Skeyne stresses the fact that the "benevolent readar" does not need "greit eruditioun nor eloquence" and he should not expect, in a piece of technical prose, "poleit or affectionat termis" (T13/12-3). In a similar way, Lyndsay justifies the translation of Latin texts in the spirit of Tyndale and Luther for "Colȝearis, Cairtaris, & to Cukis" (T11/12) – no doubt referring also to the need to avoid Latinate diction. This was usual in religious texts, which, it was often claimed, need to be true, but not ornate.

The wide range of literary genres of 15/16C Scots has left us with an unusually dense documentation of colloquial and 'low' Scots, as found in comic, burlesque and vituperative poems such as the flytings (e.g. T4), a specifically Scottish text type (a contest between poets in mutual abuse). In due course, the formal uses of the language were largely replaced by English. Consequently, the *Scots Thesaurus* (Macleod *et al.* 1990) has an impressively full selection for words designating emotions, social behaviour and character traits on the one hand, and (often obsolescent) terms from agriculture, botany and fauna – the niches which were unaffected by the impact of English, and are only now in the process of being lost as a consequence of environmental change and a general erosion of dialect lexis.

7.1.4 *Regional lexis*

The situation that Scots has been in for the past four hundred years at least has caused the fragmentation of the lexis into vocabularies with often small regional extension. Academic dictionaries of Scots teem with labels indicating geographical restrictions. The diversity is strengthened by the fact that most words refer to rural occupations, local features of dress, meals, plants and animals and belong to informal and humorous diction. Such parts of the vocabulary tend not to be standardized even in modern national languages. What we find is, then, a second level of heteronymy in which 'village words' coexist for more or less isolated speech communities.

Typical specimens were elicited in dialectological research (*LAS* = Mather & Speitel, 1975, 1977, 1986). Thus, an insect can be a 'centipede' – in the Central Belt and in places just west of the Highland Line, both regions showing the most massive influence of St E – or can be called *Jennie hundred feet/many feet/hundred legs*, *Mag(gie) mony feet*, *forty feeted/footed/legged Jennie*, or, without a personal name, a *forty feeter*, *hundred legs* or *thousand taes*, or plain *granny*. In many cases, one of several regional variants has achieved something like standard status – most often because of its use in literature, which is why it is frequently the Ayrshire or Lothian heteronym.

There is no statistical analysis of how independent individual Scottish dialects are of general Scots, i.e. the ratio of pan-Scots items and local/regional words has not been quantified (and it would be difficult to find a convincing method for such a comparison). The special status of regional lexis can be owing to local conditions favouring
a) the retention of items formerly more widespread;
b) loanwords (from, say, Celtic or Scandinavian);
c) innovation based on native resources, in particular through word-formation and semantic change.
Even though reliable figures are lacking, it is quite obvious that the NE (as a consequence of relative isolation for centuries and comparatively late anglicization) and Orkney & Shetland (because of isolation and the extensive Scandinavian substratum), but also the Borders and the Southwest stand out against regions which were more thoroughly affected by English influences and urbanization, especially in the Central Belt. The regional labels in the *CSD* clearly illustrate this distribution – although Norn-derived items restricted to Caithness and the Northern Isles are not included, in order not to swell the numbers of entries inordinately.

A small-scale comparison between the lexis of four parallel translations of *Max and Moritz* (Görlach 1986, cf. T71) – though far from conclusive – is still suggestive. The number of glosses regarded as necessary for non-Scottish readers for the 418 lines of the poem are as follows: Glaswegian (47), Lallans (153), Northeastern (238) and Shetlandic (171). Although the authors were guided by different principles regarding the distance of their lexis from English and general Scots (as against the desire to be comprehensible), the status of the impoverished traditional Scots element in Glaswegian is particularly apparent.

Another comparison of translations of the "Christmas story" (T69) into Smith's mainstream Scots, Lorimer's more experimental version, Annand's Central Belt one, Garry's NE dialect and Graham's Shetlandic yields the following lexical differences:

Smith	Lorimer	Annand	Garry	Graham
betrothed	haund fastit	(guidwife)	promise't	contractit ta mairry
mither-to-be	boukin	big-boukit	expeckin	gyaan ta cry
son	bairn	laddie-bairn	loonie	peerie boy
row't	swealed	happit	rowe't	rowed
barrie-coat	barrie	swaddlins	happin-claes	hap
manger	heck	manger	haik	stall
kintra	pairt	airt	country-side	(neebrid)
flocks	hirsel	hirsels	flocks	flocks
glintit	shined	skinkelt	bleezt	(in a glöd)
sair	uncolie	gey	fair	braaly
gliff'd	frichtit	feart	terrifiet	faerd
tidins	blytheness	wittins	news	news
a' at ance	in a gliff	suddent	on a suddenty	–
thrang	thrang	menyie	crowd	gadderi
thing	unco	ferlie	unco thing	fairlies
anent	anent	anent	aboot	aboot
ferlied	ferliet	ferlied	marvell't	stranged

Fig. 26 Lexical differences in five Scots translations of the "Christmas story", T69.

Ex 59 Which of the items listed in Fig. 26 are marked as regionally restricted in Robinson 1985?

7.1.5 *Occupational jargon*

Regional lexis often survives in the special jargon of the trades. Many of these terms are strictly in oral use. In a tradition so dominated by literature as modern Scots is, they thus have little chance of being written down. However, such words are special targets of dialect research (in particular where this investigation combines with the documentation of material culture in a *Wörter-und-Sachen* approach). Unsurprisingly, the amount of data listed in the *Scots Thesaurus* (Macleod *et al.* 1990) under the headings of 'farming', 'fishing' and 'trades' is particularly impressive. However, the objects designated by these words are especially subject to technological change, which makes this type of lexis even more endangered than Scots vocabulary generally is as a consequence of dialect erosion. The number of headwords marked as obsolete (†) or described as now restricted to a small, peripheral area is therefore particularly high.

　The loss of Scots words is evidenced on a more popular level, too. Some time ago, the *baxter, brewster, chapman, cottar, (horse-)couper, dominie, dorbie, flesher, soutar, theeker, webster* and the *wricht* might have been among the most important people in the community. But now many of the Scots designations have been replaced by English words (and/or the occupations have disappeared).

Such obsolescence is also found – as in many European cultures – in the field of currency, weights and measures: You no longer buy a *drap* of something for a *bodle*, or a *mutchkin* of whisky for a *wheen bawbees*. Consider the following sequences arranged from smaller to larger units:

Money:	*penny, bodle, plack, bawbee, shilling, merk, pound*
Weights:	*drap, ounce, pound, stone*
Capacity (liquid):	*gill, mutchkin, chopin, pint, gallon*
– (dry):	*lippie/forpet, peck, firlot, boll, chalder*
Yarn measures:	*cut, heere, heid, hank/hesp, spinle.*

Group-related language, though not normally classified as jargon, is also very richly documented for Scottish law, the kirk and education. Text types like statutes yield a large amount of data, as T20 does: *Forsamekle, heiranent*, and the duplications so typical of legal style (many representing Scotticised English terms – as indeed the whole document impresses us as an English text with a Scottish veneer). In the later tradition after 1700, relevant lexical items are often derived from Latin and form part of ScE rather than Scots. Thus, they do not strictly belong to the topics here discussed. The extent of the special lexis of the Scottish legal system may be illustrated for instance by *probation, probationer, probative, process, procurator (fiscal), procuratory, procure, production, professional examination, propone, prorogate* and *protestation* – all found on a single page in a Scots dictionary. (For Scott's use of legal diction cf. Tulloch 1980:238-40).

Ex 60 Is the obsolescence of *baxter* and the other items quoted above a consequence of the disappearance of the trades designated or of the takeover of the English term?

7.1.6 *Slang*

There is no dictionary or comprehensive monograph devoted to Scottish slang (as there are for BrE, AmE and AusE), and since the existing dictionaries of Scots concentrate on 'respectable' vocabulary, often preferring printed sources, the documentation of Scottish slang is poor. It is a feature of social groups like the army, the universities and particularly the lower classes in the major conurbations; this means that slang is concentrated in the urban vernacular, where it contributes to the widespread stigmatization of it as 'gutter Scots'.

Rhyming slang is of particular interest since it has not spread around the world as extensively as other forms of slang have, and it appears to have taken root and produced new items only in AusE/NZE as far as overseas varieties are concerned. In Scotland, it is concentrated in Glasgow and Edinburgh, both as regards imports from London and homegrown expressions. This vocabulary has never been systematically collected; not being considered 'proper' Scots, it is not normally included in the recent dictionaries of Scots – with a few exceptions in the *Scots School Dictionary* (Macleod & Cairns 1996), which includes the more frequent items.

Munro says: "A fair amount of rhyming slang is in everyday use in Glasgow. A great deal of this is, of course, not exclusive to this part of the world..." (1985:81). He then goes on to list items which, to the best of his knowledge *are* found only in Glaswegian. The list includes items like

corned beef 'deef' (i.e. 'deaf') > *corny*
gone an dunnit 'bunnit'
hoosie Frazer ('House of Fraser' = a big department store chain) 'razor' > *hoosie*
radio rental 'mental' (i.e. 'crazy')
wine grape 'Pape' (i.e. 'Roman Catholic')
winners and losers 'trousers'   (1985:81-2)

Macafee (1994a:66) – discussing *tisharoon* (or *tishy, macaroon* etc.) 'hauf a croon' (2s6d.) – reminds us that "there is a stereotypical identification of rhyming slang with the English, which several people mentioned", but the local origin of the term is proved by the fact that the word "as a rhyme, only works in Scots and Northern English." Her list of 111 specimens recorded from Glasgow speakers in the late 1980s (excluding items imported from London) represents the largest collection of Scottish rhyming slang so far (1994a:153-60), but Macafee freely admits that it "merely scratches the surface" (1994a:153). Note that many examples relate to quite recent events and persons, and many presuppose Glasgow words and pronunciations. The English character of rhyming slang is supported by the fact that the pattern may be a comparatively recent import – Iseabail Macleod (p.c.) did not find any specimens clearly dated before 1930.

7.1.7 *Purism*

Various languages have been purged of 'unnecessary' foreign words, word-watchers usually being guided by nationalistic considerations and the fear that a sizeable part of the indigenous lexis might be replaced by foreign intruders. In the case of Scots, purists stress the distance from English by choosing exclusively Scots equivalents where available and, possibly, coining new words to increase these choices. They also stigmatize urban varieties of Scots as 'corrupt', because of their mixed character.

Germanic languages like German or Norwegian have often served as models in attempts at creating Scots calques for Latinate words. McClure quotes Douglas Young's concoctions *light-bumbazit* for 'dazzled', *keethanlie* for 'apparently', *ice-flume* for 'glacier', *flownrie* for 'fragile', *owreset* for 'translate', and *thraipfu* for 'famous' (1980:28). None of these (or innovations like *yearhunner* for 'century' suggested elsewhere) have been successful – the rejection of such nativizations has in fact a long history in English (consider the failure of 16C *flesh-string* for *muscle*, or 19C *folkwain* for *omnibus*). Obviously, the more promising alternative is the revival of older Scots words from its rich literature and the competent collections of the two great Scottish dictionaries. Such tendencies have recently been revived in the attempt to create a written standard for Ulster Scots (see the discussion in Kirk 2000).

Ex 61 Summarize the reasons for Scottish purism and contrast them with those given for other European languages.

7.1.8 *Idioms*

Much of the richness of Scots lexis rests in the wealth of proverbial, pithy sayings and idiomatic expressions. Graham (1977:19-28) lists the following: *atween the wind and the waa* 'in dire poverty', *auld claes and parritch* 'routine', *a dreipin roast* 'a good source of income', *to gae doun the brae* 'to deteriorate in health or circumstances', *a peeled egg* 'a piece of good luck', *kaim ane's hair backwards* 'annoy one' and *saut somebody's brose* 'get one's revenge on someone'.

7.2   The lexicography of Scots
(Aitken 1990, Macleod 1998)

7.2.1 General Scots

The 70,000 Scots words collected for the period after 1700 in the *Scottish National Dictionary* (*SND*) and some 20,000 in the *Dictionary of the Older Scottish Tongue* (*DOST*, about to be completed) for the time before 1700 testify to the enormous wealth of Scots lexis, which is much more differentiated than that of any English dialect.

Lexicography in Scotland started, as in England, in the form of glossaries appended to editions of literary works. When in the 18C Thomas Ruddiman and Allan Ramsay re-published writings of classical authors from an independent Scotland, they were aware of the fact that the intelligibility of texts written 200-300 years earlier would be very restricted without the help of glosses. Ruddiman's 1710 edition of Douglas's *Aeneid* (1513) – lexically one of the richest texts of its period – consequently contained "A Glossary or Alphabetical Explanation of the hard and difficult Words" (80 pages, comprising some 3,000 entries).

Ramsay provided such helps to accompany his own *Poems* (1721), too: "A Glossary or Explanation of the Scots Words us'd by the Author, which are rarely or never found in the modern English Writings" (16 pages, some 900 entries). Here, the glosses were meant to elucidate contemporary texts – an indication that Ramsay's poetical Scots was beginning to drift away from spoken usage, although it has to be kept in mind that he hoped to reach a pan-British audience that could not be expected to know Scots. Such glossaries were also added to the works of other authors, as for instance to the second edition of Burns's *Poems, Chiefly in the Scottish Dialect* ([2]1787). This was intended for an Edinburgh audience and far more extensive than the one in the original Kilmarnock edition that aimed at a local readership.

By contrast, lists of Scotticisms served a different purpose; these were intended as educational self-helps for people who wanted to rid their speech, and particularly their writings, of all traces of Scots interference. The tradition started with Hume (1752, some 80 entries, T30), and continued through Beattie ([2]1787, some 500 entries, T31), Mackie (1881, some 400 entries) and many others.

By the 18C it had become clear that Scots should not be included in English dictionaries. Only few Scottish words were recorded by Johnson (1755) – who encouraged Boswell, as the latter reported in his *Life of Johnson*:

t78 He advised me to complete a Dictionary of words peculiar to Scotland, of which I showed him a
     specimen. "Sir", said he, "Ray has made a collection of north country words. By collecting those
     of your country, you will do a useful thing towards the history of the language." He bade me also
     go on with collections which I was making upon the antiquities of Scotland. "Make a large book
  5 – a folio." Boswell: "But of what use will it be, Sir?" Johnson: "Never mind the use: do it."
                                                                              (Boswell, 19 Oct. 1769)

Basker (1993) points out that a large proportion of the few Scots words that made it into
Johnson's dictionary have subsequently entered St E. This may be due to the fact that
the abridged editions retained these entries but cut the warning labels marking them as
Scottish usage.

     After a few abortive projects, Jamieson's monumental *Etymological Dictionary*
(1808) was the first ever compiled exclusively for Scots, and it was a great achievement:

t79 (It) was the first in Britain to substantiate its definitions with accurately referenced quotations from
     original texts; more often than not these are placed in chronological order: so Jamieson can claim
     to be the first ever completed dictionary on historical principles of any variety of English.
                                                                                  (Aitken 1990:1984)

What was especially remarkable about the project was the popular support it received;
it did so at a time when the ultimate takeover of spoken English as the respectable
prestige language had brought Scots to a low in public esteem – regardless of its
expansion as a literary medium. It "struck a cord of patriotism among the Scots and
stimulated many new offers of help, financial and philological" (Aitken 1990:1984).
Jamieson's "Dissertation on the Origin of the Scottish Language", prefixed to his
Dictionary, starts with a nationalistic, self-confident tone, presenting the erroneous
theory of the derivation of Scots from Gothic and its independence of English:

t80 It is an opinion, which has been pretty generally received, and perhaps almost taken for granted,
     that the language spoken in the Lowlands of Scotland is merely a corrupt dialect of the English, or
     at least of the Anglo-Saxon. Those who have adopted this idea, have assigned, some one era, some
     another, for the introduction of this language from the South; each preferring that which seemed
  5 to have the most plausible claim, without entertaining a single doubt as to the solidity of the
     hypothesis which rendered it necessary to fix such an era. Having long adhered to this hypothesis,
     without any particular investigation, it is probable that I might never have thought of calling it in
     question, had I not heard it positively asserted, by a learned foreigner, that we had not received our
     language from the English; that there were many words in the mouths of the vulgar in Scotland,
 10 which had never passed through the channel of the Anglo-Saxon, or been spoken in England,
     although still used in the languages of the North of Europe; that the Scottish was not to be viewed
     as a daughter of the Anglo-Saxon, but, as in common with the latter, derived from the ancient
     Gothic; and that, while we had to regret the want of authentic records, an accurate and extensive
     investigation of the language of our country might throw considerable light on her ancient history,
 15 particularly as to the origin of her first inhabitants.   (1808, Introduction)

Two more volumes, which included more recent evidence and were based on some 1200
written works, appeared in 1825, and a much expanded edition (by Longmuir &
Donaldson) in 1879-82; abridgements of 1818 and 1840-1 made the essential data
accessible to larger numbers of readers, and there were several plagiarized versions.

     In England, there had been a large number of local glossaries compiled by amateur
lexicographers, a tradition that started with Ray (1674) and continued into the late 19C,

when such collections were important sources for Wright's *English Dialect Dictionary* (*EDD*, 1898-1906). By contrast, Scotland had comparatively few such efforts. Accordingly, *SND* (vol. X) lists comparatively few glossaries among their sources. Nearly all those mentioned were intended "to promote the understanding of the most celebrated Scotch authors" rather than to record local or regional dialects.

Alexander Warrack's one-volume *Chambers' Scots Dialect Dictionary* (1911) proved highly successful, but (being based on the *EDD*) it did not provide full coverage, although it has some 60,000 entries (the figure is increased by many duplications of words listed under different forms). Therefore, two large new historical dictionaries were conceived by Craigie and Grant in the early 20C. The *DOST* (of which nine volumes, A - Sch, have been published so far) is to cover all texts up to 1700 and to record the complete vocabulary used in Scotland up to that time (it includes all pre-1600 words, but is selective on the period 1600-1700). The *SND* registers specifically Scots words and meanings after 1700 (complete in 10 volumes 1931-76). Aitken's enthusiastic appraisal of the two is worth quoting:

t81 They include many words missing from all previous dictionaries and, from their very much more copious supply of examples, identify and display details of meaning, collocation, formal history, chronology and regional and stylistic distribution previously unknowable, and withal offer not a few improvements in etymology also. (Aitken 1990:1985)

More recently, there has been a remarkable revival in interest in smaller dictionaries of Scots. Publication started with the *Concise Scots Dictionary* (*CSD*, Robinson 1985) – an updated distillation of the two major dictionaries – followed by a *Pocket Scots Dictionary* (1988), *The Scots Thesaurus* (Macleod *et al.* 1990) and a *Concise English-Scots Dictionary* (Macleod & Cairns 1993), which now permits users to improve their active command of Scots rather than use the book only as a help for understanding texts. This development culminates in *The Scots School Dictionary* (Macleod & Cairns 1996) which is the first two-way bilingual one and is explicitly directed toward active competence in the neglected language, containing a "basic vocabulary, as well as some more literary words likely to be met in stories and poems – notes on how to get the most out of your dictionary – grammar notes and verb lists – spelling guidance – help with pronunciation – a brief history of the Scots language – accompanying activities booklet" (1996: blurb). In 1998, this was complemented by an electronic version, the *Electronic Scots School Dictionary*, which also includes a grammar guide (the *Grammar Broonie*, Rennie *et al.* 1999), interactive word games and other features.

For a language lacking a supraregional norm, lexicographical decisions are particularly difficult to take: how much stylistic, semantic, collocational and regional differentiation is needed to guarantee that a user, unassisted by sufficient native-speaker competence, picks the right word from a sequence of items which would look like synonyms? Are words not listed identical in English and Scots, and therefore omitted? Are shared items included only if their Scottishness can at least be indicated in spelling?

Ex 62 Restate the problems of modern Scots lexicography using introductions to recent dictionaries.

7.2.2 *Dialects of Scots*

As was remarked above, in the 19C there were fewer glossaries documenting local dialects of Scots than of English. The last decades of the 20C, however, saw a great increase in such works. Still, large dialect areas of the country remain insufficiently covered. Kynoch (1996), a glossary to the works of authors who wrote in NE 'Doric' dialect, is not intended as a full dictionary of the regional variety. With Buchan & Toulmin (1989) and Wilson (1993/95) and publications like Fenton (1959) the area is well represented. Marwick (1929, ²1992), Lamb (1988) and Flaws & Lamb (1996) for Orkney, Jakobsen (1921, ²1928), Graham (1979, ⁴1999) for Shetland and Geddes ([1978]) and Sutherland (²1996) for Caithness provide lexical accounts of the northern and island dialects – complementing the *CSD* and other general Scots dictionaries. Fife (Kerr [1979]), Galloway (MacTaggart 1824, Riach 1988), Roxburghshire (Watson 1923) and the East Neuk (Murray 1982) also have individual publications, and Glasgow is catching up with several glossaries in a humorous vein.

However, in these collections antiquarian interest tends to predominate – readers are not sufficiently informed about which words are obsolete, obsolescent or current (and which are shared for instance between Shetland, Orkney and Caithness, and which with general Scots). With Macafee (1996) Ulster Scots is the only variety of Scots that has received a comprehensive dictionary firmly based on scholarly principles (the book includes data from a large number of dialect glossaries) – complemented by Fenton (²2000) whose collection is largely based on his individual competence

7.3 *Loanwords*

Language contact with various languages has been a major cause of linguistic change in the history of Scots. These contacts (in spoken and written form) have affected all levels, ranging from spelling, pronunciation, syntax and text types to lexis – possibly the most obvious field of such influences. As in the history of English – for which the history of loanwords is much better documented – Scots borrowed words mainly from Latin and French, as stated in Gavin Douglas' famous lines (T8/15-17).

The preponderance of these two source languages is easily explained by their range of functions and high prestige. In addition, Scots had *Sudron* to borrow from – whether as a source of Germanic words, or as a mediator for others (including Latin and French). Other languages have had much less impact, as a consequence of less continuous contacts and/or the lower prestige of the languages concerned (which would have made borrowings appear as undesirable interferences).

In principle, two major motivations for borrowing (and the full integration of loanwords into the receiving language) can be distinguished:
1) filling up lexical gaps – frequently in the extension of the vernacular into new registers (such as scientific Scots in the 16C);
2) rhetorical improvement and increase in expressiveness – often a consequence of cultivating a literary language and formal styles.

Since motivations can be mixed and are hardly ever reconstructable, the reasons for adopting individual items are frequently opaque.

The composite nature of the vocabulary of Scots was well known to early observers – who of course gave only impressionistic evaluations of the state of affairs. One of the most explicit statements comes from Geddes:

t82 On analysing the Scoto-Saxon dialect, I find it composed; First, and chiefly, of pure Saxon; Secondly, of Saxonized Celtic, whether Welsh, Pictish, or Erse; Thirdly, of Saxonized Norman or old French; Fourthly, of more modern French Scotticized; Fifthly, of Danish, Dutch, and Flemish, occasionally incorporated; Sixthly, of words borrowed from the learned dead languages. It must
5 not however be supposed, that all these are blended together in the same proportion in every Scottish provincial dialect. The Welsh words are principally to be found in the more southern provinces, the Pictish and Erse in the more northern; the Danish, Dutch, and Flemish all along the eastern coast, especially in the trading towns and fishing villages: terms relative to the arts, politeness, and luxury, are mostly French; and Greek and Latin words are rarely to be found but in
10 authors. (1792:415-6, quoted from Jones 1995:16)

The only quantitative analysis of the provenance of Scots lexis so far is that reported by Macafee (1997a:190). Basing her statements on 2,5 % of the entries of the then published material of *DOST*, she found the following proportions of word origins of Early Scots:

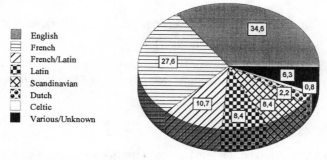

English
French
French/Latin
Latin
Scandinavian
Dutch
Celtic
Various/Unknown

34,6
27,6
6,3
0,8
10,7
2,2
8,4
8,4

Fig. 27 Word origins in pre-1700 Scots

In spite of the restrictions of the data base, the findings largely correspond with those for EModE (and even for PDE). However, the Latin/Greek element is much smaller in Scots, which indicates its incomplete *ausbau* in the 16C, and its fossilization thereafter, in the scientific and formal registers – only partly compensated by borrowing from French.

For the time after 1700, the share of newly adopted French/Latin words is likely to have dropped significantly in Scots, the relevant lexis now being borrowed into ScE. It is no coincidence that the *Concise English-Scots Dictionary* (Macleod & Cairns 1993) has predominantly polysyllabic English headwords followed by Germanic or etymologically indeterminate Scots glosses.

A special problem of Scots – not clearly shown in the figures – is the great number of words of uncertain etymology. Entries in dictionaries have a remarkably high incidence of 'etym. unknown', 'perhaps from....', 'perhaps onomat.' and of forms which have been changed to such an extent that the etymologies are effectively disguised (blends, folk-etymological accommodations and the like).

7.3.1 *Gaelic*
   (McClure 1995e)

Although one might well expect that the limited intake of Celtic words in English (from OE times to PDE) contrasts with a more thorough infusion of Gaelic in Scots, the findings are not so drastically different. True enough, McClure found more than 600 words of Celtic origin in the *SND*, but this figure represents only 0.8% of the total Scots lexis recorded there (to which the presence of a much larger vocabulary not restricted to Scots, but shared with English, must be added). Moreover, the Gaelic words fall into various categories, most of which are of restricted currency (cf. McClure 1995e:81-2):
1) words of the common core (few);
2) words designating Scottish cultural items (and as such also part of IntE: *claymore, kilt, loch, pibroch, slogan, sporran*);
3) words found in the classical authors (especially Burns and Scott), and thus known to a wider community, but marked as literary or archaic: *ingle, oe, sonsie*;
4) words restricted to dialects, especially those in the vicinity of (former) Gaelic-speaking areas and largely unknown to the common Scottish speaker (*bledoch* 'buttermilk');
5) words now archaic, outside 3) (if they ever were part of Scots proper), such as words uniquely attested in Jamieson's *Dictionary* of 1808.

Ex 63 Summarize the reasons why loanwords from Celtic languages are rare in the individual varieties of English in Britain. Does the case of Scotland differ from, say, Wales?

7.3.2 *Scandinavian*

Words borrowed from Scandinavian languages come from various sources which can be roughly grouped under three headings:
1) words deriving from the Danelaw occupation of the 9/10C, which created a bilingual community in the English Midlands leaving many traces in the local dialects. Migrations carried these influences into London English (mainly attested from texts later than Chaucer) – and through Bernicia into the Anglian-speaking parts of early Scotland, strengthened by massive immigration in the 12/13C. This accounts for many words
   a) shared with St E (*skill, sky* , etc.);
   b) shared with N English dialects (*big* 'build', *gar* 'cause', *hoast* 'cough', *nieve* 'fist', *wale* 'choose', etc.);
   c) words uniquely attested (or solely surviving) in Scots (*ettle* 'plan', *sark* 'shirt').
   Only b) and c) words are relevant for our discussion, and b) only because they rose to 'standard' status in Scots, whereas they remained dialectal in England;
2) words deriving from the settlements of Scandinavians in Scotland. These words are mostly dialectal, being restricted to the areas dominated by Scandinavians until the end of the Middle Ages: Caithness, Orkney and especially Shetland. Few of these were accepted into General Scots;

3) words borrowed for modern cultural items; these (like *lemming, ski*) are shared with English and are largely international.

Ex 64 Try to correlate settlement history and the evidence of placenames with the data from Scandinavian loanwords.

7.3.3 *Dutch*

Medieval and Renaissance contacts with Dutch (and Low German) were extensive, particularly in trade and fishing (including settlements for instance on the Fife coast). Although the lexical impact of this contact is sometimes rated quite high, it is in fact restricted to a few words in General Scots (*pinkie* 'little finger', *dub* 'puddle', *cuit* 'ankle' and *howff* 'haunt') and many more in the special jargon of fishing.

Ex 65 Is the local concentration of the Dutch loanwords evident from labels in dictionaries and from their distribution indicated in dialect atlases?

7.3.4 *Latin*

Latin was a major source for Scots mainly in the period to 1400 and in the subsequent period of the formation of a national tradition in various text types ranging from poetry to administration, science and chronicles and religion to law. Although it continued to be of eminent importance as the language of scholarship in 15/16C Scotland, the influence on the vernacular appears to have been slightly less than on contemporary English. If this impression is correct, it could be explained by the fact that its use in Scots aureate diction was confined to the language of the makars, as a poetic device largely modelled on its use found in Chaucer and Lydgate. Unsurprisingly, then, Latinisms are most frequent in prologues which are rhetorically 'ornate' and in rhyme where they serve practical needs (especially those ending in *-able, -ance, -ate, -ence, -ern, -(i)on,* etc.), and they concentrate in special fields like 'astronomy' (*ascendent, capricorne, celestial, coniunctioun, mappamound, zodiac,* etc.) – as they would in English. The types of prose genres that contained most Latinisms in EModE were restricted in 16C Scots (in particular scientific, medical, theological and philosophical writings and chronicles, many of these translations) and the numbers of Scots works in each type were quite small compared with the contemporary EModE output. This imbalance increased after 1603, so that only legal terms – which still have a strikingly high percentage of items in Scottish law – exhibit a notable Latin component (but then these texts are not in Scots, but in ScE). As other languages which stopped expanding their uses into scholarly, technological and formal registers (e.g. Low German) because they took over these text types wholesale from another language, so did Scots when adopting English for these purposes.

In periods when the borrowing process was independent of English, there was a chance not only of different words being taken over, but also different forms being adopted: compare *to conquess* in Bellenden corresponding with *conquer* in Harrison's EModE translation and further *promit* 'promise' and words in *-ar* where English has *-ary* as in *dictionar, notar, ord(i)nar* and *secretar.*

Ex 66 What are the differences from, and what the similarities with, the impact of Latin on English and Scots in the 16C?

7.3.5 *French*

Two types of lexis are of particular interest here. There are many loanwords from French shared with early English but which survived only in Scots (*ashet* 'plate' < *assiette*, *disjune* 'breakfast' < *dejeuner*, *stank* 'pool' < *estanque*) and another group which was independently borrowed. This procedure was to be expected in the age of the *Auld Alliance* continuing to 1560, although the number of such borrowings was apparently smaller than might be assumed (*corbie* 'raven', *dour* 'sullen', *fash* 'trouble'). In other cases, both English and Scots borrowed the same item, but in conspicuously different forms (such as *fruct*/'fruit', *disponed*/'disposed', cf. John Hart's comparison 1569, t18).

Although the basis for their statements was impressionistic, there seems to have been some agreement among linguists around 1600 that northern English (which for many would have included Scots) was purer and more Germanic than the southern standard – and these statements were based on the smaller number of loanwords from Latin and French.

The French contribution to Scots has not yet been systematically analysed, nor has it been compared with the French element in English. Thus, we cannot evaluate the statement found in an article in the *Weekly Magazine* (18, 1772), which points out the large number of loans, often "mutilated or corrupted in pronunciation", adducing *servet* 'towel', *rouser* 'watering-pot', *chosser* 'chaffing-dish', *to fash* 'trouble', *orlich* (*orlage*) 'dial-plate' and *cannel* 'cinnamon' and another "five hundred instances of the kind (might be) mention(ed)" (quoted from Jones 1995:255).

Ex 67 Has the *Auld Alliance* (to 1560) had a notable influence on the spread of French loanwords into Scots (cf. Murray 1873:58)?

7.4   Word-formation

The patterns according to which new words can be coined in Scots are identical with the ones in English. As in English, the 'traditional' word-formational patterns of compounding and derivation predominate in the early phases, whereas 'irregular' ones, such as back-formations and coinages not based on morphological structure (e.g. blends, clippings, acronyms) are more widely attested in more recent times. Onomatopoeic and phonaesthetic formations are frequent in all periods, but insufficiently attested as they are often created *ad hoc* and more frequently used in informal, spoken registers.

There has been no comprehensive study of Scots word-formation (and certainly not one comparable with Marchand ²1969 as regards quantity and quality), so our remarks must be considered provisional until a full study is available. As a consequence, statements on the frequency and acceptability of individual types (such as the impression that zero derivation and synthetic compounds are less frequent in Scots) must be based on selective dictionary evidence, e.g. data from the *CSD*. This is, however, incomplete in so far as it includes only 'proper' Scots and is selective when it comes to listing transparent derivations and compounds. A full study of Scots word-formation might also help to answer a very important question which is relevant for all *halbsprachen*: how far does the existence of an English item block the production of a Scots word, that is, how far does the coexistence of the two varieties work like a unitary system as far as new coinages go? (Compare, as an explanation for the decline of derivation in ME, the easy availability of the French loanwords when it came to filling lexical gaps).

Sound changes can lead to loss of motivation. This has happened to the Scots word *fouth* 'copiousness' (from *full+th*, involving a non-productive derivational suffix) and, among former compounds, to *haffet* 'sidelock' (from *half-hēafod*).

The special freedom of poets in coining new words is well illustrated by Douglas Young. McClure quotes from his works innovations such as *sainless* 'incurable', *trullerie* 'foolishness', *untwynable* 'inseparable', *thraipfu* 'renowned', *owerset* 'translate', *yearhunner* 'century', *ferly-potency* 'magic power' and *fuddrie-leams* 'lightning-flashes (2000:119-20).

Ex 68 Check whether dictionaries (e.g. Robinson 1985) help you with understanding Young's coinages. Are the words listed, or at least the word elements which make the individual items intelligible?

7.4.1 *Compounding*

The structure of a determinans followed by the determinatum dominates in Scots compounding as it does in English; this means that compounds belong to the part of speech of the second element, and semantically they tend to be its hyponyms. Two nouns are freely combined; it is not always possible to distinguish between a compound and a loose syntactic combination (a decision mainly dependent on stress): consider *barlie-bree*, ~ *fever*, ~*pickle*; *bed-evil*, ~*mat*, ~*pan*, ~*plaid*; *belly-brace*, ~*thraw*, ~*timber*; *burgh-* (11 items in *CSD*). A similar productivity is found in combinations of adj./adverb + noun, as in *back-* (35 combinations listed), *black-* (37) or *blue-* (11).

Note that compounds make up a substantial share in loan translations, such as those suggested from purist motives like *yearhunner* ('century', modelled on German *Jahrhundert*). For combinations of two nouns which are possibly better described as syntactical units cf. 6.2 above.

Ex 69 Summarize criteria for distinguishing between compounds and syntactical units of Adj/N + N including an analysis based on letter **B-** in the *CSD*.

7.4.2 *Suffixation*

The principles of suffixation are the same as in English, and most Scots derivations are formally inconspicuous. Occasionally a different suffix is selected, as in Scots *gentlemanny* or *idlety*, *hatesome* or *fousome* (both 'filthy' and 'filling'). Sometimes, the form of the derivational basis differs, as in *wrangeously* 'wrongly'. Only a selection of Scots patterns is discussed below.

Diminutive formations are rare in EngE, but hypocoristic *-ie* is widespread in Scots (also in AusE). The derivations are largely informal, which explains why they are more widely attested in dialect (especially in the NE and the North) than in St Scots: *bairnie, batchie* 'baker', *beastie*. Compare *-ock/-ach* which occur in similar functions (*boorach/boorock, bittie/bittock*), occasionally combined as in *lassie/lassock/lassockie, wifie/wifock/wifokie* or *pawkie* 'mitten' (possibly from *paw+ock+ie*). A (related?) suffix serves to derive names for persons characterized by the quality of the base: *daftie, deafie, dummie* etc. (Wilson 1915:59).

Other suffixes change the subclass of nouns. An example of a suffix of this type, which differs in form from English, is *-heid*, as in *bairnheid* 'childhood'. The *-ster* suffix deriving agent nouns seems to be better preserved in Scots than in English: *baxter* 'baker', *brewster, webster*.

In the derivation of adjectives, the suffix *-ie/-y* predominates, as *-y* does in EngE (cf. the Scots derivations *gentie, ill-willie, thochtie*). Individual choices may again differ from English: *bairnlie* 'childish'. Scots alternatives to *-ie* are for instance *-sum* (*gledsum, lichtsum, lithesum, loosum* 'lovely', *skunnersum, ugsum*) and *-rif* (unproductive; *cauldrif, waukrif*); *-fu* ('full'; *mensefu, awfu, wearifu*) and *-lik* (*bonnielik, daftlik, wycelik*) can be added more freely to various bases than in English, including adjectives, and *-sell* can mean 'covered with' *floursell, snawsell*. The de-adjectival verbal suffix *-en*, which is shared with English, seems to be more productive in Scots (e.g. *barken* 'encrust', *blaiken* 'become pale').

As in English, the type most frequent in modern Scots is zero derivation, notably the pattern producing new verbs from nouns. Zero derivation seems to operate mostly on monomorphemic nouns (cf. *cairn* 'heap of stones' > 'to heap', *clart* 'mud' > 'to dirty', *cleuk* 'claw' > 'to scratch'). As in non-standard varieties of English, many adjectives may be used as adverbs without additional *-ly*, as in *drive slow, cum here quick*.

7.4.3 Synthetic compounds

The pattern, which combines compounding and derivation, is not particularly frequent except in combinations of N/Adj + N + *-it*, a type also found in English *-ed* (*hauf-wuttit, humfie-backit, ill-hertit, ker-haundit, lang-chafted, ~-craigit, ~-drachtit, ~-luggit, ~-nebbit, ~-shankit*). Otherwise, the type is most productive in the formation of two types of new substantives, *viz.* agent nouns in *-er*, including names of tools (*horse-couper, ~hirer, ~setter*) as well as in action nouns in *-ing* (*handfasting, ~makin, ~shaking*), even if the number of such coinages appears to be smaller than in English.

7.4.4 Prefix formations

The number of prefixed words listed in the *CSD* is impressively large; this applies to separable prefixes (*in-, out-, ower-*) and unseparable ones (*be-, for-, mis-, umbe-, up-*) in both verbs and nouns. It is, however, not quite clear how much this difference from English is a consequence of large-scale survival of earlier words from periods when the patterns were still productive, or owing to formations in Scots after the two languages split apart. The category includes a few slightly exceptional types, as in the 'deprecatory prefix' or 'intensifier' *car-* (from Gaelic?) as in *carmudgel* 'to bash' or *carnaptious* 'irritable' – a group which includes a few words of obscure etymology.

Ex 70 Which of the prefix formations listed above can be shown to represent survivals of OE/ME patterns, and how many of the respective items entered in dictionaries are obsolete?

7.4.5 *'Irregular' types*

Many patterns which have become productive in modern phases of European languages are largely absent from Scots which stopped (or slowed down) expanding its formal written lexis from the 18C onwards except for a few purist innovations not generally accepted). Therefore, the number of instances of backformations and acronyms is limited in Scots.

By contrast, some patterns associated with informal usage are widely attested – blends, reduplication, phonaesthetic formations; evaluation is, however difficult because the etymology of most of these words is highly speculative, uncertain or totally obscure. Compare the entries for such words as *argie-bargie, catterbatter, cattiewurrie, collieshangie, gaberlunzie, heeliegoleerie, hingum-thringum, ramgunshoch, ramiegeister, sculduddery, scurryvaig, tappietourie* or *wallydraigle* in the *CSD*. (Some of the enigmatic words could of course be owing to attempts to make phonetic 'sense' of opaque Gaelic words or blending two lexemes; the number of multiple etymologies appears to be comparatively high; cf. 7.3.1).

Ex 71 Discuss the hypothesis that the great number of 'irregular' forms has to do with the informal nature of the texts they are used in.

7.5 *Lexical semantics*
(Görlach 1997:119-26)

A linguistic sign is defined as the combination of a form (spoken or written) and a content; the two are in an arbitrary (non-transparent) and conventional relationship, that is, the meaning is agreed on by the speech community. The following relations between meanings or contents of different words can be defined:

Monosemy: the content of a sign consists of one meaning;

Polysemy: the content is composed of various sememes overlapping in at least one component;

Homonymy: the content is composed of various meanings which do not have a single semantic component in common;

Synonymy: two signs have identical semantic structure;

Antonymy: two signs represent complementary, gradable or relational opposites.

For situations in which more than one language is in use in a speech community, in particular for the diglossia of complementary functions of two genetically related languages (as in Scots and English), two further categories are necessary in addition to the four above:

Heteronymy: two signs have identical semantic structure, but they are not synonyms because they belong to two different varieties. (Compare the concept of 'translation equivalent' where two non-related languages are involved). The items are seen as equivalent in meaning and the choice depends on whether the speaker determines to use Scots or English, such as *pinkie* vs. *little finger*, or *dominie* vs. *schoolmaster*.

Tautonymy: two signs have identical form, but different contents. They are not homonyms because they belong to two varieties. (Compare the concept of 'faux amis' normally used in translation studies). For instance, the *CSD* lists two Scots homonyms *loan*: the word can mean 'roadway' or, from another source, 'provisions for a campaign'; the English tautonym *loan* 'lending' is of course not included.

Semantic relations are much more complex than distinctions on the phonological level (though similar methods are used in the analysis of the underlying structure). They are further complicated in a situation as in Scotland where the coexistence of Scots and English, and the conspicuous variation along the diachronic and stylistic dimensions, create more ambiguity and dangers of misunderstanding than elsewhere.

Meaning is determined by the syntagmatic and paradigmatic relations of a sign. Words are used in texts, and the sum of their potential uses (including the author's intentions and readers' expectations) makes up their collocational range. Instances of polysemy and homonymy are also disambiguated by the selection of words combined with the word in question. On the other hand, paradigmatic classes (characterized by exchange relations) and minimal semantic distinctions may be established by contrasting words of similar content.

A componential analysis of Scots words for domestic animals and human beings can be compared with the description of English terms (in Görlach 1997c:122). The field offers itself for a model interpretation because most of the components also serve as referential distinctions (which become semantic through their linguistically distinctive function). Moreover, the agricultural terms are likely to differ from English – the problem being that many are local rather than 'general' Scots. In the tables below items which are shared with English (though often varying in form) are printed in capitals, Scots words without English cognates are italicized. The data are gathered from the *CSD*, the *Scots Thesaurus* and the *CESD*:

generic	+male	+female	+young
MAN	*carle*	WUMMAN	*bairn/wean*
nowt	BULL	COO	CAUF
CHICKEN, *hen*	COCK	HEN	*chookie*
HORSE	*staig*	MEAR	COWT, *naig*
SHEEP	*tuip*	YOWE	LAMB
SWINE	*gaut*	SOO	*grice*
DUG	DUG	BICK	WHALP

Fig. 28 Semantic features distinguishing items within the lexical fields of domestic animals and human beings

A stemma, or tree model, for the item 'cow', which incorporates additional distinctions, may look as follows:

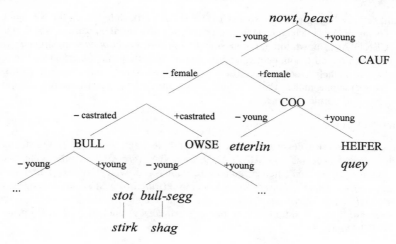

Fig. 29 The semantic structure of the field 'cow'

Components included in the stemma are age, sex, and characteristics such as 'being castrated', 'having calved', a further component could be 'type of horns' (as in *crommie* 'with crooked horns', *doddie, moylie*).

Full definitions of some items are needed to specify their meaning:

beast	'a cow, any bovine animal',
bull-segg	'a bull castrated when fully grown',
eean	'one-year-old horse or cow'
etterlin	'two-year-old cow or heifer in calf'
shag	'ox castrated incompletely or when fully grown'.

Further distinctions are locally made according to colour and uses of cows. With pigs, various terms are known for the 'smallest of a litter', with horses special words for those used in racing and tournaments, or old and useless animals. Note that the joke in the anecdote about the *boar head* (t29, above), which works on the understanding of words for members of the semantic field 'pig' (*bare, sew, gryce*), would be impossible today, the cognate of *boar* having died out in Scots in the 17C.

The minimal distinctions offered for the glosses in *CESD* help to point to semantic/referential distinctions in a few other fields. For 'basket' the differences are apparently based on encyclopedic specifications:

t83 **basket** (*esp for meal, potatoes*) skep; (*esp for bread*) maun; (*shallow, scoop-shaped, eg for fish*) scull; (*round, for fish-bait etc*) murlin NE; (*round, for fish, eggs*) rip; (*deep, eg for peat, fish*) creel; (*for seed*) happer; (*straw, for seed, meal*) ruskie; (*of strips of wood*) spail basket; (*deep, carried on back*) creel.

By contrast, the translations offered for English 'child' are mainly semantically distinguished (with geographical restrictions added):

t84 **child** *see also* **boy, girl**; bairn, wean CENTRAL, chiel(d), chile NE, chillie NE, sproot, get *often contemptuous*; bilch *comtemptuous*; (*small: see also* **toddler**) bairnie, wee thing, littlin N, E CENTRAL, smowt, tottie, totum, smool, eeshan N, getlin *often contemptuous*; (*affectionate term*) cuttie, bird, doo, poutie, lambie, trootie, taid NE, posie; (*mischievous: see also* **rascal**)

5   tike, smatche(r)t, sorra, wick, dirt *contemptuous*; (*precocious*) nacket; (*restless*) stourie; (*petted*) sookie, mither's bairn, minnie's bairn, mammie-keekie; (*wheedling*) flairdie SW; (*bad-tempered*) girnie-gib, blastie.

Compare for verbs, the entry 'eat':

t85 **eat** *see also* **ate, sup, devour, munch, crunch, nibble**: 1 aet, corn. 2 (*quickly*) snap (up); (*heartily*) lay yer lugs intae, tak awa SHETLAND, ORKNEY; (*greedily*) lay intae, guts, rive, haam NE: '*jist haamin intil im*', hunch, gulch NE, pootch NE, worry NE; scaff SHETLAND, heck, gorb(le); (*of animals, down to the roots*) rump. 3 (*without appetite*) pewl amang yer food, chawl,

5   smurl; (*with the mouth nearly closed*) mimp; (*furtively*) smacher; (*of people or animals*) smurl. 4 (*messily*) slaiger, slitter, slaister; (*messily and noisily*) slubber, slabber, slorp, sloch, slorach; (*noisily*) slork.

The semantics of adjectives tends to be difficult to describe because their distribution is largely defined by collocations, and frequently their modifying meaning becomes intelligible only in combination with the noun they accompany (cf. the meanings of adverbs in relation to the verbs they modify). An example in which paradigmatic and syntagmatic factors combine is provided by the entry 'dry':

t86 **dry** *adjective* (*of weather*) drouthie; (*withering*) bask; (*of wind*) druchtie NE, hard NE; (*parched, shrivelled*) gizzen; (*dry and brittle*) freuch NE; (*of wood etc*) funseless CAITHNESS; (*of touch, taste*) hask; (*stale*) haskie; (*of soil*) hirstie; (*thoroughly, of clothes etc*) hert-dry NE, horn-dry, threid-dry, (*sun-dried*) rizzered.

The analysis of word fields in Scots is subject to grievous limitations. They are a consequence of its being a semi-language; this means that

1) the lexis stopped expanding (or expanded only incompletely) after it came to be the L(ow) variety in a diglossic situation, at least after 1603; this fate is shared by varieties like Low German, and by dialects of European languages in general;

2) the L(ow) part of the linguistic spectrum of the speech community predominates in lexicography, whether Scots-English (the *SND*, *CSD*), English-Scots (the *CESD*) or in the *Scots Thesaurus* (in addition, the specifically Scottish vocabulary items of ScE are also recorded).

Such incomplete data do not even permit for Scots a comprehensive discussion of 'easy' semantic fields like 'vehicles'. Since we lack concordances of most works written in Scots, we cannot check how exactly such fields are divided up into Scots vs. ScE elements. We can only assume, in the absence of relevant entries in the *CESD* that the Scots words for *motorcar, railway* and *bicycle* are – *motorcar, railway* and *bicycle*.

Ex 72 Analyse the semantic relations in the field of 'relatives' and arrange them in form of a grid (as above) using the items *guidman, guidwife, minnie, luckie,* *gudesir, tittie, brither, eme, auntie, grandsher, guid-mither, nevoy, brither-dochter, guid-dochter, oe, get, loon, dochter, bairn, ieroe, granbairn* (mainly from Grant & Dixon 1921:81-3; some terms are now obsolete).

Ex 73 Establish the distinctive features of the field 'swine' and form a stemma (*gaut, gilt, grice, gussie, shott, soo*).

Ex 74 Do the specifications for the Scots equivalents provided as glosses for *child, boy, girl* in English-Scots dictionaries permit a regional, social, stylistic and semantic/connotative differentiation?

7.6   *Semantic change*

The arbitrary relationship between form and content makes change of meaning possible – if the speech community agrees on the new conventions. Reasons for such change can be (1) extralinguistic and (2) intralinguistic:

(1a)   Changes in the material culture usually change the meaning of individual words and may entail new distinctions in the semantic field concerned.

(1b)   Changes in the knowledge of things can change the meaning, as happened to words designating the concepts 'animal, mammal, fish, bird, plant', etc.

(2)   Intralinguistically, the need for unambiguous reference leads to specification. This is often achieved by differentiating formerly synonymous words or by borrowing specific vocabulary from other languages, thereby opening the way for semantic specification of the existing more general native words.

Changes can result from semantic transfers, the most productive but least predictable process. In metaphors we need a *tertium comparationis*, i.e. a feature shared by the old content and the new concept to which it is applied. This overlap is used for an extension of meaning which is first *ad hoc* and contextual, but can be accepted by the speech community and thus become permanent; finally the metaphorical connection can be entirely lost. Metonymy is not based on semantic relations but on extralinguistic coincidences, such as 'part for whole', 'material for product', 'cause for effect'; since the connection is culture-bound and often based on specific situations, the origins of metonymic extensions are easily lost.

An analysis of semantic change can be based:

1) on the number of meanings in the content of a sign: the increase of meanings (e.g. through metaphoric transfer) is semantic extension; by contrast, the reduction (the loss of meanings, often replaced by more specific designations) is semantic narrowing;

2) on the number of semantic components making up one meaning: an increase (i.e. the addition of a specific feature) narrows the range of applicability, that is specification; the reduction of features (by neutralization of formerly distinctive components) widens the range of applications, that is generalization.

The specific Scottish situation has meant that the adaptation to changing functions was thoroughly influenced by Latin first, and then overwhelmingly by English, which filled all the formal registers and served as a pattern of correctness also for word meanings where Scots words were identified with their English equivalents (unless the English term was borrowed).

There has never been a comprehensive study of semantic change in Scots. The examples discussed so far are only a small selection which is not based on a systematic and large-scale investigation; this might well start with faux amis which suggest a change in one of the two varieties – which can mean that Scots innovated or remained closer to the original meaning, as to be expected in a marginal community. However, the coexistence of the two related languages over five hundred years has led to the equation of a huge number of lexical items which is certain to have caused numerous semantic loans, often of a very subtle nature, which can be established only by very careful historical analysis – investigations which appear to be entirely lacking.

The process of such equations is easy to illustrate from the relexification of Scots by English which led speakers to replace one item by another. This is probably still going on to a certain extent. It is exercised by the eponymous hero of McIlvanney's novel *Docherty*, who – punished by his teacher for the use of the sentence "Ah fell an' bumped ma heid in the sheuch, sur" – starts writing up a list of such assumed correspondences: *sheuch – gutter, speugh – sparrow, lum – chimny, brace – mantalpiece, bine – tub, spicket – tap*, including items which obviously lack a proper equivalent as in *glaur – muck what is in a puddle after the puddle goes away* (T62:47-65).

Ex 75 The semantic field of 'human settlement' is still somewhat different from English – which means that individual members have different meanings – which can be the result of different changes: consider *ferm, fermtoon, toon, veelage, clachan, burgh.* and compare your analysis with the stemma in Görlach (1997c:125).

8   *Literary Scots*

8.1   *Literary language*

8.1.1   *Introduction*

The language used for a literary work is determined by a large number of factors; these include:

1) decorum – the principle that genre, subject matter and linguistic features chosen must be correlated, i.e. the style must be appropriate. In the earlier stages the correlation was prescribed by (handbooks of) rhetoric;

2) imitation (tradition, intertextuality, genre conventions) – an author will normally follow a pattern set by earlier writers, preferably in his own language (otherwise imitation will be across language boundaries – not only in cases of straightforward translation);

3) the author's linguistic competence and that of the intended audience;

4) specific intentions of the individual author.

Conclusions about poetic diction can be based either on an empirical analysis of relevant literary works or on theoretical statements, in prefaces or treatises on poetics (whether separate books or included in handbooks of rhetoric). The latter option does not exist for Scots, because such rhetorical manuals are totally absent (6.7.1), and only one text on poetics survives from 16C Scots – James VI's *Reulis and Cautelis* (T16), which is surrounded by a spate of contemporary English essays reprinted in the collection by Smith (1904). It is a pity that, of the subdisciplines of poetics, James treats only metrical problems (and the correlation of topics and verse types) at length, but does not include a discussion of lexis appropriate for the poet – nor a 'sociolinguistic' survey like the one provided by Puttenham for English in 1589 (cf. Görlach 1991a: T11).

The situation in Scotland was complicated from the very beginning of the literary tradition by the close co-existence of English and Scots, but only for a few bilingual writers, like James I, this allowed for a choice of either language. To borrow spellings, pronunciations, and morphological, syntactic and lexical elements from English was, however, common and not considered illegitimate cross-breeding. Rather (except for affected displays) it was regarded as acceptable, assisting in

1) the filling of lexical gaps;

2) rhetorical heightening of the language, where it lacked copiousness (*fowth of langage*, Douglas, T6) and elegance (a function similar to that of borrowings from Latin);

3) the intentional following in the footsteps of an English author (for the early writers especially in the Chaucer/Lydgate tradition, cf. Fox 1966).

It was only later that the use of Scots as opposed to English (or the density of Scots features employed) began to involve an element of a political statement, and was so understood by part of the audience. From the 18th-century Vernacular Renaissance, starting with Ramsay, authors had a choice between Scots and English, which to a certain extent was ideologically motivated.

It would be shortsighted to overlook the great importance that publishers had on the linguistic choices of authors from the 17th century onwards. One particularly caustic statement is found in a review in *Blackwood's Magazine* 117 (1875:634-5) where

t87   George Macdonald is castigated for adopting a regional standard for his Scots-speaking characters:
      'Why will Mr Macdonald make all his characters, almost without exception, talk such painfully
      broad Scotch? Scotch to the fingertips, and loving dearly our vernacular, we yet feel it necessary
      to protest against the Aberdeen-awa' dialect ... which bewilders even ourselves now and then, and
  5   which must be almost impossible to an Englishman. So many beautiful thoughts, tender, and
      delicate, and true, must be obscured to the reader by this obstinate purism, that we feel angry,
      disappointed, and impatient at the author's perseverance in this mistaken way ... It is poor art, and
      not truth at all, to insist upon this desperate accuracy. Sir Walter's Scotch was never like this.'
                                                                        (quoted from Donaldson 1986:170)

The question of whether a poet is allowed to create a 'synthetic' Scots, combining the
lexis of various diachronic layers and different dialects, has been discussed with
particular reference to MacDiarmid's practice in the 1920s (cf. 8.6). However, the
method is not new but frequently documented in English literary language, as in
Spenser's bucolic diction which combines classical allusions, northern dialect and
Chaucerian loans – a practice which provoked Ben Jonson's criticism that "Spenser, in
affecting the ancients, writ no language". It is no surprise that Allan Ramsay, who
looked back to the great period of Scottish literature of the makars, frequently employed
archaisms – as indicated by William Hamilton in his address to Ramsay, 1719:

t88   Wha bourds wi' thee had need be wary.
      And lear wi' skill thy thrust to parry,
      When thou consults thy dictionary.
          Of ancient words.
  5   Which come from thy poetic quarry
          As sharp as swords.

8.1.2 *Biblical translation as an example of stylistic appropriateness in Scots*

Biblical translation can serve to illustrate the question of whether an individual text type
requires specific language, and what kind. In the early 16C, Murdoch Nisbet was not
yet confronted with a stylistic choice, since Scots was the language accepted for all
purposes. Later translators had to make a deliberate decision as to which type of Scots
to use. In 1871, P.H. Waddell claimed in the introduction to his translation to have
employed authentic spoken, though somewhat archaic, rural dialect:

t89   The bulk of the language, both in terms and phraseology, is such as was in daily use by all well-
      educated peasants and country gentlemen for the last generation...With such language the
      Translator was familiar in his youth, as many of his readers must also have been
                                                                        (quoted from Tulloch 1989:40)

W.W. Smith (cf. T69a) in 1901 found that the literary tradition left no choice as to the
appropriate form of Scots:

t90   With respect to the style: whoever now writes in Scotch must necessarily conform to the dialect of
      Burns. The Translator is a Borderer; but in many respects he departs from Border usages, in order
      to conform to Burns – whose influence has made the 'Ayrshire' the classical dialect of the
      Lowland Scotch   (quoted from Tulloch 1989:54-5)

Whatever style is selected for biblical translation must seem awkward: if the formality of the text was to be rendered, the choice would, in the absence of a St Scots, have to be English rather than Scots. Waddell (1871) appears to justify his diction by pointing to the *well-educated peasants* (for stylistic acceptability) and the language of his *youth* (for archaic features as expected in biblical language).

By contrast, W.L. Lorimer (1983, cf. T69b) developed an alternative by creating a 'synthetic' diction (again including archaisms) – and justifying colloquial components by the fact that

t91 Jesus spakna Standard Aramaic – for ordnar oniegate – but guid ('braid') Galilee, an the N.T. isna
      written in Standard Greek, as the Kirk Faithers alloued   (1983:469)

He adopted different styles for the individual gospels of the New Testament – a strategy not usually found in Bible translations, showing the versatility of Lorimer's Scots – and commented on his choice:

t92 I have deliberately refrained from writing in a uniform 'standard' Scots. On the contrary, I have
      made differences between different writers.

By the 1990s, Jamie Stuart was able to use "the language of the people", i.e. "the distinctive and vivid vernacular of Glasgow" for the Gospel (1992), after an earlier successful experiment with "colloquial and modern Scots, but one rooted in the traditions of the past" (1985). He also adapted Old Testament tales mostly into Glaswegian, but trying to incorporate "the various dialects spoken in Scotland" (1993). (Quotations are taken from the prefaces of the respective publications.)

Bible translations also served as records of authentic regional dialect, irrespective of the genre and its stylistic requirements, as for Prince Louis Lucien Bonaparte, who found:

t93 The only corrupters of dialects... are the *literary men* who 'improve nature', by writing them, not
      as they *are*, but according to their notions of what they *ought to be*
                                                          (Murray 1873:75n, quoted from Tulloch 1989:19)

– or for Murray, who, intent on dialectological authenticity, criticised the idealization of the Scots of Riddell's translation of *Matthew* in 1859:

t94 It is an attempted *restoration*, and not the Scotch of any particular time or district... Thus, though
      interesting, the work has not to posterity the scientific value that would attach to the rendering of
      any passage into the precise spoken language.   (quoted from Tulloch 1989: 48).

8.1.3 *Literature in Scots: regional distribution*

A map illustrating the geographical provenance of major Scottish writers shows how dominant the Central Belt (and adjoining Fife and Angus) has been for centuries; it has to be noted that not all authors who came from 'the provinces' not all wrote in their local dialect.

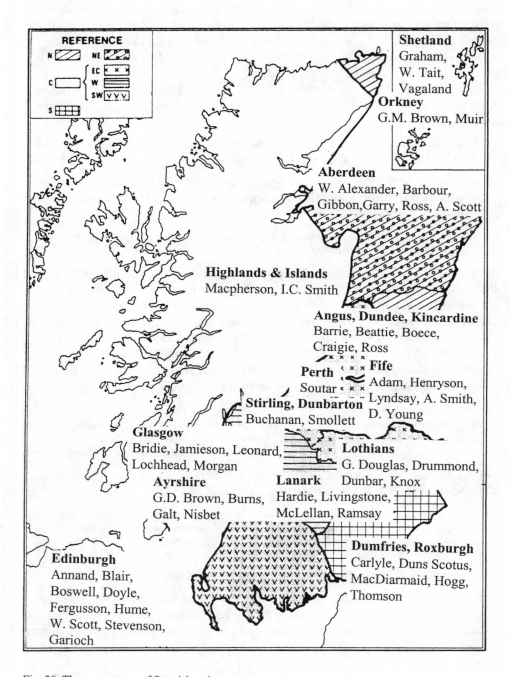

Fig. 30 The provenance of Scottish writers

8.2 *Literary Scots before 1603*
8.2.1 *The beginnings*
   (Aitken 1983)

Early Scots poetry impresses us through the variety of genres employed, each having a specific style – as required by decorum. The wide range of forms and contents is best illustrated by 16C anthologies compiled by educated Scotsmen with literary interests, especially the Bannatyne MS (1568), the Maitland Folio (1580) and the Maitland Quarto (1586), which contain devotional, moral, political, amatory and other forms, written by various authors including the major Scottish makars. Aitken (1983) distinguishes several branches, specifying the linguistic/stylistic choices made by authors writing in the individual genres. He suggests the following categorization:

1) *plain narrative verse* (T1) – fairly plain vernacular language, unpoetic in vocabulary and unelaborate in syntax, except for some of the diction of poetic synonyms shared with alliterative verse and very occasional passages of heightened rhetoric and elevated diction in some courtly, hortatory or didactic prologues and digressions;

2) *alliterative verse* (*Howlat, Rauf Coilȝear*) – plain vernacular language laced with elements of poetic diction from a repertory of words and formulae characteristic of medieval English and Scottish alliterative verse;

3) *elaborate narrative verse* (*Aeneid*, T6) – lexically more wide-ranging, syntactically, rhetorically, and, in many cases, metrically more elaborate than the simple narrative verse;

4) *instructive and hortatory verse* – secular, religious, social or moral, more overtly and straightforwardly didactic than courtly allegory;

5) a wide variety of stanza forms characterising reflectively *personal poems* (e.g. T5).

(3), (4), (5) largely do without the stereotyped diction of the simple and alliterative narrative modes, and relatively sparsely draw on the staple vocabulary of low life (8).

6) *Courtly verse in the grand manner* (fig. 16) – elaborate dream-allegories more or less saturated with classical, as well as (rather more incidentally and cursorily) scriptural allusion; somewhat simpler love-allegories and dream-visions and 'debates'; grandiose panegyrics and laments; set pieces prefaced or appended to, or introduced into, works mainly in the narrative and didactic modes – allusions to classical authors, innumerable catalogues, *descriptiones loci amoeni*, clichés of descriptive detail in the equally recurrent formulae, praise of earlier masters of rhetoric or poetry, various rhetorical techniques.

7) *Low-life verse* (the closest example would be the *Flyting* of Dunbar and Kennedy, T4) lies at an opposite pole from courtly verse – burlesque, comic and vituperative poems, flytings, lampoons, and parodies. In their language and diction they are the most distinctively Scottish.

8) *Verse of denunciation, protestation and petition* (T11) for reform or reward.

9) *Realistic nature verse* – virtually free of clichés (cf. 6), simple narrative verse, unpretentious vocabulary adapted to their subject matter.

(adapted, with drastic abridgement, from Aitken 1983: 19-25).

As Aitken's categories demonstrate, genres were not well-defined for early Scots authors (as they were not for ME writers, either), and most texts are in fact conglomerates if categorized according to modern parameters of form and content.

A further problem regarding the description of early Scots texts is their potential anglicization in the versions of the surviving manuscripts – not only in the particularly serious case of the *Kingis Quair* (T3, see below). Aitken suggests that "the different types of anglicised forms are distributed through the Anglo-Scots canon along an 'implicational scale'" (1983:27), listing the words most commonly found in English spelling, especially the "*o* for *a* feature" (1983:28) as in *home* for *hame*. The intentions of authors and copyists would have been immediately apparent to contemporary readers, whereas for modern ones it is very difficult to identify them in the spellings, inflections and lexical items as generally 'Southern' or 'Chaucerian allusions' and then interpret their functions for the text under examination.

The Scottishness of the first two substantial texts in Scots from the late 14C – Barbour's *Bruce* (T1) and the *Scottish legends* – is undoubted on the basis of their contents. Their language shows, however, little difference in lexis from texts from N ME, and the few more or less consistent spelling conventions that can be defined as Scots may, in the case of the *Bruce*, be a consequence of the more than one hundred years that lie between the composition and the date of the only surviving manuscript. Significant differentiation from N ME only starts with the Scottish makars.

8.2.2 *The makars*

James I (1394-1437) is the early centre of the group of poets formerly sometimes referred to as the 'Scottish Chaucerians'. James's debt to Chaucer in his *Kingis Quair* (fig. 16) is not surprising, if we take into account the fact that he spent his formative years in England, and composed the poem during his stay there or shortly after his return. We might even hesitate to decide whether it forms part of English or of Scots literature – especially if we interpret the Scots features in the text (whose earliest surviving copy dates from the late 15C) as scribal Scotticizations, performed to make it conform with period style and national considerations. Lewis states James's debt to Chaucer, but rightly adds:

t95   But even in the *King's Quair*, and still more in Henryson, new elements begin to appear. The most
      obvious of these is what critics call aureation, that is, the use of polysyllabic coinages from Latin
      (*celsitude, jocundity, lachrymable*, &c.) as an ornament to style.   (1954:75)

Since genre-specific concepts of decorum led James I when composing his poem, a comparison with the linguistic features present in his holograph letter of 30 Nov. 1412 (Edinburgh Nat. MSS Scot. No. LXII) is interesting, but not conclusive for the ascription nor helpful for a reconstruction of the language of the *Kingis Quair*:

t96   Jamis throu the grace of god . kynge of . Scottis . Til all that this lettre heris or seis sendis gretynge
      . wit ʒe that we haue grauntit & be this *presentis* lettres grauntis . a speciall confirmaci*on* in the
      mast forme til oure traiste and wele belofit Cosyng *schir* willm of douglas of Drumlangrig of all
      the landis that he is possessit and chartrit of with-in the kynᵍdome of Scotlande that is for-to say
  5   the landis of drumlangrig of hawyke & of Selkirke the-whilk*is* char*tris* & possiouns . be this *lettre*

we conferme . and wil for the mare sekernes this oure confirmacioune . be formabilli efter the
fourme of our chaunssellur & the tenor of his . chartris selit with oure grete sele in tyme to come
in witnes of the-whilkis this presentis lettres we wrate with oure propre hande vnde the Signet vsit
in selyng of oure lettres as now at Croidoune the last dai of Nouember the ȝere of oure lorde . I^{mmo}
10   . cccco . xij°   (transcribed by I.K. Williamson)

Robert Henryson (ca. 1420-90), "the schoolmaster of Dunfermline", is one of the most
important of the makars. His poetry ranges from a kind of sequel to Chaucer's *Troilus*
(*The Testament of Cresseid*, T3) to the lighter adaptation of the *Morall Fabillis of
Esope*. The range of genres and styles is impressive, and his poetry is possibly the most
intellectual of the period, characterized by inventive language, much of it (as in Dunbar)
aureate – in a creative misunderstanding of the Chaucer-Lydgate rhetorical tradition.

William Dunbar (ca. 1460-1520) has somewhat overshadowed Henryson's fame,
certainly in the 20C, when MacDiarmid's slogan "Back to Dunbar" was a programmatic
call to return to the period when Scots was a full language. Dunbar is prominent for his
wide range of topics, and of a great variety of genres and styles which includes very
colloquial diction or even obscene slang. By contrast, the "sprinkling (of his) verse with
newfangled and obtrusive Latinate words" peaks in his *Ballat of Our Lady*, in his
attempt to "refine, purify and gild their native tongue" (Fox 1966:181-2). It is a
characteristic of the times that we know very little about the lives of Henryson and
Dunbar so that we are forced to draw conclusions about their language exclusively from
their poetry.

The alleged newness claimed for James and Henryson is, however, much less
spectacular if we see the Chaucerian tradition transmitted to the makars through
Lydgate, since he (and his contemparies) had already stressed the 'rhetorical' perfection
of Chaucer's language; cf. T6, T11 and Ellenberger (1977) for an analysis of the
Latinate element.

Ex 76   Summarize the controversy about how many of the Scots features in the *Kingis
        Quair* may be owing to later Scotticization (Craigie 1939, McDiarmid 1973).

The intellectual climate of the late 15C Edinburgh court of James IV provided the ideal
ground for a flourishing literature which most critics see as superior to that of
contemporary England. "James himself has been pronounced illiterate by Buchanan, but
the humanist probably only means that his Latin was not Ciceronian. In reality the king
was something of an intellectual, 'weill lernit in the art of medicine' and proficient in
several languages which included not only Latin but even 'the speech of the savages
who live in some parts of Scotland and the islands'" (Lewis 1957: 67).

True to the ancient and Renaissance concept of *imitatio*, the court poets, then, looked
to Chaucer, "the founder of our fair language" (as Lydgate put it). Fox aptly
summarizes:

t97 They considered him to be, in a very essential sense, the father of modern English poetry, the man
     who purified, regularised, and clarified English, and so made it possible for highly civilised and
     highly wrought poetry to be written in the vernacular ... Like the Augustans, the Scots took very
     seriously the traditional doctrine that poetry is thought dressed in beautiful language and
  5   rhetorically ornamented.   (1966: 169, 171)

Note that most of these poets wrote in what they still referred to as *Inglis*; they apparently did not see a language boundary between themselves and Chaucer.

Looking back on the intellectual and poetical climate at the court of James IV, the period has been claimed to be the (first, Scots) golden age of Scotland – a second (English) golden age to follow three hundred years later during the Scottish (mainly Edinburgh and Aberdeen) Enlightenment, 1760–1832.

Ex 77   Compare aureation in a poem of Dunbar (e.g. T5) with that in one of Lydgate's (e.g. t17).

The great achievement of Gavin Douglas was that he created a poetic language adequate for the first translation of the *Aeneid* in Britain (England followed c1540, when Surrey translated the epic into EModE, borrowing freely from Douglas; for textual comparisons cf. Görlach 1991a:288). Douglas's diction did not, however, imitate precisely the high style of his source, and demanded by the rules of classical rhetoric. Realizing that Scots was at times "scant" and "imperfite" (T6/17 and in line 64; similar formulas are also frequently found in contemporary EModE writers), he did his best to equal Virgil in rhetorical "cullour" (T6/20), expression of the "sentens" (T6/21) and in conforming with metrical and rhyming needs, but still making his translation "braid and plane" (T6/9), so that it could be understood by less educated readers; of course, there is also the inevitable aureation, in imitation of both Chaucer and Virgil. Douglas's prologues (from which T6 is taken) are especially important for his reflections on literature and language – programmatic statements which can be compared with his practice.

Scottish prose as a literary, narrative medium developed later than in England: there is no Scottish Malory or Elyot. One reason for this was that verse lingered on in Scotland until later as a literary form for chronicles, romances and legends, the other that 'respectable' prose was more frequently in Latin than it was in England (but cf. Jack 1981). Also there was no Scottish Caxton (or his successors Pynson and de Worde) to flood the market with reasonably priced books of unassuming prose. This time gap resulted in an earlier stylistic expansion of EModE, which appears to have stimulated and stifled the development of Scots prose at the same time. These facts give great importance to Bellenden's *Chronicles of Scotland* of 1531 (T8), which (though of course a translation commissioned by James V and not always structurally independent of the Latin source) provides a forceful example of most of the virtues demanded of literary prose by contemporary rhetoricians: complex and yet transparent sentence structures, a highly differentiated vocabulary expressing both precision of reference and copiousness (Douglas' *fowth of langage*, T6/19) with an impressive proportion of words not shared with, or borrowed from, English (cf. Jumpertz-Schwab 1998) – and of course a great deal of attraction provided through the national subject matter (increased, for a modern reader, where Shakespeare's version of *Macbeth* can be compared). The degree of linguistic independence from English of the Scots text confronted Harrison with problems, and much of his 'translation' into EModE reads, in fact, more flabby and occasionally unnecessarily ornate. Little is known about Bellenden – whether he really came from the NE (Moray?) cannot be judged from any regional peculiarities of his language, neither in his *Chronicles of Scotland* nor in his *Livy's History of Rome*.

Ex 78   Compare the text of Bellenden in T8 and the excerpt of the facsimile, fig. 17, for differences in spelling and lexis.

The best contemporary criticism of the Chaucerian poetic tradition in Scotland is found in the works of Sir David Lyndsay (c1490–1555). In his long poem *The Testament and Complaynt of Our Soverane Lordis Papyngo* (1530, published 1538) aureation is connected with the famous names and specific genres, and contrasted with other, more popular traditions. The poet, educated at Haddington (Lothian) or Cupar (Fife), was at the courts of James IV and James V; his fame mainly rests on the only surviving 16C drama in Scots, *Ane Pleasant Satyre of the Thrie Estaits*, first produced in 1540, and the *Papyngo*, both of which contain serious criticism of the church. Royle summarizes the author's personal beliefs as "a reformer by inclination, but as far as is known, a Catholic by persuasion, Lyndsay was an early supporter of John Knox" (1983:184). This Protestant attitude is clearly behind the fervent appeal in his *Exclamatioun to the Redar* (in *The Monarch*, T11) to have all religious texts translated into the "vulgair toung" (T11/3) to make them accessible to "Colȝearis, Cairtaris & to Cukis" (T11/12), a remark which calls to mind Tyndale's aims. Lyndsay, however, did not insist in having other types of writing (as in philosophy, astronomy or poetry) in the vernacular (T11/50-6), but restricts his demand to "bukis necessare for our faith" (T11/57-9). That is, he did not claim equality for the vernacular, as Mulcaster did for English in 1582 (cf. Görlach 1991a:231). However, he does not specify what exactly "our toung vulgare" refers to. It is thus at least likely that he would have accepted the English Geneva Bible, adopted for the Scottish Reformation five years after his death, as being in the "maternall language".

Ex 79   Contrast Lyndsay's attitude towards technical prose in the vernacular with Skeyne's (T13).

8.2.3 *Knox and the Reformation*

As regards the influence of religious diction on 16C Scots (cf. 2.7), the dominant figure of John Knox makes him a representative for attitudes, linguistic behaviour and for the impact that an individual can have on the development of his native culture and language. Jack (1997a:253-4) points to two factors that are partly responsible for the anglicized character of some of Knox's writing. "As most printing was done in London or abroad, this further destabilized all modes of written Middle Scots", and "when the reformer appears to anglicise in the Geneva edition of *The First Blast* ..., it is quite possible that some or all of the changes are made in the printing house" (253).

Equally important is that the choice of a more English or more Scots variety was determined by text type and decorum. In a letter Knox stated "I wryte to ȝou my mynd in Latin, for I am nocht acquyntit with ȝour Southeron", and Scots "now is not the same as *the auld plane Scottis* which his mother had taught him" (254). Jack goes on to say:

t98 Decorously and pragmatically, Knox wished to convey religious truths in the high style to as many
    people as possible. Anglicised Scots is the appropriate choice on either logic.[...] Equally
    consistent is his more regular employment of Scots forms in his unprinted sermons, where no
    audience other than Scots is contemplated [...] The changing nature of spoken Scots, the issue of
  5 textual transmission, the authors upbringing and decorous propriety are all relevant.(1997a:254)

Ex 80   Collect Scottish features in Knox's *History* (T14).

8.2.4 *James VI and I*

King James VI of Scotland and I of England (1566-1625) created a new centre of cultural activity in Edinburgh, a group of poets and musicians, called the 'Castilian band'. Crowned after the abdication of Mary in 1567 at the age of one, he was under the strong influence of the humanist scholar George Buchanan (his tutor from 1570 to 1578, cf. T15). When analysing James's idiolect, we are in the fortunate position of having a great range of text types, including a few holographs, at our disposal; moreover, these stretch over a long period and permit us to see changes of linguistic options, perhaps reflecting the author's developing attitudes. In addition, there are statements by the king on style and language, which is exceptional in 16C Scotland.

The following texts by James give us particular insights into his use of, and attitudes towards, Scots:

1) The *Essayes of a Prentise in the Divine Art of Poesie* (1585), often quoted as *Reulis and Cautelis* (T16), is the major theoretical treatise on poetics extant in 16C Scots.

2) The *Basilicon Doron* (MS 1599, printed in Edinburgh in 1599 and 1603 and in London in 1616, T18) shows the king, at a stage when Scots was increasingly eroded by English, as a proponent of the use of the national *leid*, thus providing a model for his son and his subjects. However, with Elizabeth ageing and without an heir, the union of 1603 was in sight, and he was ready, as early as 1599, to stress the unity of religion and language (T18). The stages in which the text survives provide us with the most persuasive and easily analysable evidence of how anglicization proceeded by a gradual deletion of the Scots features, which are so prominent in the manuscript version, on the levels of spelling, morphology and lexis.

3) James's private correspondence with Elizabeth, though of course written by his secretaries, is important as evidence of Scottish features in official, external functions (cf. T17). There is evidence that Elizabeth knew Scots (Horsbroch 1999), but James used a form of EModE – sprinkled with Scottish features (almost exclusively in spelling) – which may be interpreted as convergence on her linguistic variety intended as a signal of kingly courtesy.

4) His *Counterblaste to Tobacco* (1604) is programmatically English, avoiding all remnants of his Scots vernacular, which was proposed as a language worthy to be cultivated only a few years before in the *Basilicon Doron*. Published anonymously, the work was acknowledged only in the 1616 edition of his collected works. The accommodation to London English is not only obvious in spelling, morphology and lexis but also in less easily monitored features – Meurman-Solin (1993a) found the text remarkable for its high incidence of 'empty' *do*, no doubt reflecting EModE rather than Scots conventions.

Ex 81   Analyse the adaptations of James' manuscript text of the *Basilicon Doron* by later printers (T18, Görlach 1991a:310-2, and if available, the STS edition).

8.3   *Literary Scots between 1603 and 1707*

The language of William Drummond of Hawthornden (1585-1649) is remarkable for the author's use of EModE throughout his extensive poetical work – at least in the printed works, where he showed himself a forerunner of 18C Edinburgh anglicizers: "In his published works Drummond attempted to erase Scotticisms, but occasionally examples survived his vigilance ..." (MacDonald, quoted by Corbett 1999:77).

Drummond spent almost all his life in Scotland, but – having written a few poems in Scots – after 1603 he decided against Scots as a medium for both his poetry (Petrarchan sonnets and satirical verse) and his prose. His choice of English includes even archaic *-eth* as a verbal inflection, which was long obsolete outside biblical language. Whatever Scottishness there is in his poetry is then in contents and attitudes; the claim that it can also be detected in the rhythm or that it comes to the surface when read out with a Scottish accent, is questionable in the light of the poet's deliberate decision to use written standard English. The same is true for other writers of the period, such as William Alexander, Earl of Stirling (cf. *The Monarchicke Tragedies* (1607) or his cycle of sonnets, *Aurora*).

Thomas Urquhart (1611–60), who is mainly known for his translation of Rabelais, has possibly a still lesser claim to being classified as a writer of Scots. As Corbett points out (1991: 88-92), he referred to his native speech as "English" or "the Saxon tongue", and his rendering of *Pantagruel* is in English throughout, with the exception of a sentence of gibberish and a significant passage from Chapter VI in which Scots renders the original's Limousin dialect to provide a butt of provinciality. Corbett interprets this as

t99 signal(ling) the beginning of a new trend in the use of Scots in translation, and it is an early
   example of a narrative strategy later exploited in Scottish novels by Walter Scott, John Galt,
   Robert Louis Stevenson and countless others. As the standardisation process was arrested in Scots,
   the very non-standard nature of the medium allows it to carry meanings that a deracinated standard
5   variety cannot.   (Corbett 1999:92-3)

Archibald Pitcairne uses Scots in his satirical comedy *The Assembly* (T24) – one of the very few 17C Scottish stage-plays handed down at all – for a similar effect.

A very moderate output of literature in what is more easily to be termed as Scots in this period may however be found in collections of Scottish proverbs (T22).

8.4   *Literary language between 1707 and the death of Sir Walter Scott (1832)*
8.4.1 *Introduction*

The rediscovery of Anglo-Saxon as a language attesting to the ancient provenience of English by the 'Saxonists' from 1620 onwards also drew attention to Scots, widely considered purer Germanic than contemporary English. In this context, as F.W. Freeman claims,

t100 Scottish songs and ballads too enjoyed a vogue in England chiefly through the plays and song
   collections of Mrs Behn, Tom D'Urfey, and Playford. Long before Ramsay, these song
   collectors and composers invented the myth of a pastoral Scotland, full of unlettered Jockys and
   Maggys, who spoke a pure poetic tongue.   (Corbett 1999)

However much these fashions may have prepared the ground, all commentators agree that there is an immediate connection between Scotland's final loss of political power by the dissolution of the Edinburgh parliament and the strengthened interest in the country's glorious cultural past. To rediscover, and to republish with the addition of glossaries, the works of 15/16C poets such as William Dunbar and Gavin Douglas was widely seen as an act of reestablishing national identity at least in the literary sphere. However, when poets chose to use the *auld leid* actively, they did not intend to reinstate it into the full functions of a national language covering all written uses and text types, but mostly restricted themselves to poetry. It is easy to overlook that even in this domain their active use of Scots did not include all genres. Their writing, in general, fitted into an English Augustan framework of decorum, which left niches for Scots mainly in the informal branches of 'low' style, such as satirical poems, bucolics and ephemeral pieces; even in the few cases of translations of classical authors these genre restrictions were generally observed. Programmatically, Fergusson in the *Farmer's Ingle* not only described a country scene, but started off with the following invocation: "Begin, my Muse, and chant in hamely strain". Burns, imitating him in *The Cotter's Saturday Night* addressed Robert Aiken with the words: "To you I sing, in simple Scottish lays, The lowly train in life's sequestered scene."

The 'revival' should therefore not blind us to the fact that even the protagonists of the use of Scots, such as Ramsay, Fergusson, Burns and others, also wrote English poems on Augustan models, and where they used Scots, it was often diluted or mixed with English, whether code-switches were motivated by genre distinctions or not. They also eschewed peripheral or clearly local dialects of Scots in favour of a General Scots – or at least their publishers did. A typical example is Scott's *The Antiquary*, which "is laid in or near the town of Arbroath, E. Forfarshire. The language, however, is Mid-Scottish and ... gives little evidence of local peculiarities" (Grant & Dixon 1921:232). This appears, however, to be largely the effect of editorial interference with Scott's manuscripts, which has been found to be particularly significant with respect to dialect matters. Scott's original publishers were responsible for several cases where a passage which he had written in a marked local dialect were ironed out into 'standard' Lothian Scots (McClure, p.c.).

Other authors, such as James Thomson (1700-48), chose to write exclusively in English, and Dunbartonshire-born Tobias Smollett (admittedly before Scott had established a tradition for Scots dialogues in novels) included only few traces of Scots in the speech of his main characters, even if they were Scotsmen, such as Lesmahago in *Humphrey Clinker* in 1771 (cf. Blake 1981:120).

Ex 82   Correlate the 'revival' of Scots poetry with political developments 1700-1750.

8.4.2 *Allan Ramsay*

The importance of Allan Ramsay (1684-1758) for the history of Scots can hardly be overvalued. McClure rightly claims:

t101   he provided a focus for the circumambient revival of interest in Scottish letters, and by his
       prolific output and strongly emphasised individual personality he exerted a fundamental
       influence on their subsequent course. In particular, the use which he made of the Scots tongue
       played a major part in determining not only the use of it made by his successors but also the
   5   attitudes to the language and its possible range of functions.   (1995: 161)

His admiration of older Scottish poets (which gave him the nickname 'Gavin Douglas' in the Easy Club) provided a boost to national identity at a ·time when political independence was finally lost; but his active use of Scots has not gone without criticism. In particular, he

1) used English spelling conventions (especially the apostrophe) for words shared with English to indicate Scots pronunciation, or even employed StE spellings, leaving proper Scots pronunciations to the individual readers and their fluency and regional differences;

2) used a cline of Scots and English, in which the varieties are correlated with genres, reserving the broader, more vernacular forms to the 'Standard Habbie' (a term coined by Ramsay for a type of six-line stanza, invented in the mid 17C by Robert Sempill for his poem *The Life and Death of Habbie Simpson, the Piper of Kilbarchan*), which is mainly used for comic and satiric poems;

3) used a somewhat synthetic Scots enriched with old words which he had encountered in old authors, e.g. in Gavin Douglas, whose works Ramsay had edited and glossed (cf. 8.1.1 above)

However, "he was never a systematic writer nor one with a clearly defined theoretical approach to language" (McClure 1995g: 162), and (intentionally or not) he contributed to the understanding of Scots as an 'anti-language' which excellently fitted into some niches of the prevalent literary framework, and (especially through the use of English spelling conventions) remained largely intelligible to non-Scottish audiences. McClure, pointing out that only one of the poems in heroic couplets is in (thin) Scots, notes: "that Ramsay did not experiment more extensively with this Scots Augustan register is greatly to be regretted" (1995g:162). But he did not, and thus failed to establish a tradition. Whether a fuller revival of Scots as a literary medium (or even as a language of local administration, education etc.) would have been feasible in the 1720s is open to doubt, but the attempt was not made – which left little choice for poets like Burns but to follow in Ramsay's footsteps. On the positive side, it can be said that Ramsay's policy established 18C Scottish writing as a part of English literature – in a way that Dunbar's work is not (just like that of Low German authors like Klaus Groth and Fritz Reuter, who can never be part of a German national literature).

Ex 83   Analyse the proportion of unambiguously Scots spelling features in three of Ramsay's texts (T28–30).

8.4.3 *Robert Fergusson and Robert Burns*

Robert Fergusson (1750-74), after leaving the university of St Andrews without a degree and working as a clerk in his native Edinburgh, started writing poetry in English modelled on Gray and Shenstone, but from 1772 turned to Scots, leaving 33 poems in Scots (and some 50 in English). Using the Standard Habbie verse form, he dealt with urban society in vigorous Scots – with far fewer compromises towards English than Ramsay before him and Burns after him. Widening the thematic scope and occasionally also using his competence of the Aberdeen dialect (inherited from his parents, who moved to Edinburgh before he was born), his language shows a broad stylistic range. It remains, however, doubtful whether we can therefore regard him as a forerunner of 20C synthesizers of 'Plastic Scots' as Corbett (1999:106) suggests. His influence on Burns was considerable – and it was through Burns (who freely admitted his debt to him) that Fergusson's poems came to be known to a wider readership after his early death, which deprived 18C Scotland of possibly its finest poet, but certainly one who handled the native language with exceptional skill.

Robert Burns (1759-96) spent a somewhat turbulent youth in Ayrshire, working in various positions; he started writing poetry in English and Scots from 1783 on. The publication of his *Poems, Chiefly in the Scottish Dialect* at Kilmarnock in 1786 was an immediate success and attracted the praise of the Edinburgh literati: Henry Mackenzie (1786) discovered in him the "heaven-taught ploughman" – an epithet which was in line with contemporary taste, though greatly misleading considering how learned and well-read Burns really was (cf. Low 1974:1-11). An Edinburgh edition, with a greatly extended glossary, followed in early 1787. The favorable reception at a time when the intellectuals of Edinburgh had almost completed the process of anglicization does not come as a surprise: they could here praise, in anticipation of Romanticism, a Scottish genius, allegedly uneducated – overlooking the strong Augustan element in many of his concepts and his diction.

The styles of the two poets can be contrasted convincingly by comparing Fergusson's *The Farmer's Ingle* and Burns's treatment of a similar topic which was obviously stimulated by it, *The Cotter's Saturday Night*. This brings out the uncompromising use of Scots in Fergusson and the heavy dependence of Burns on Augustan diction. Burns is much more original in his love songs and in narratives like *Tam o' Shanter* – and there he also uses Scots more consistently. With all the accommodation to English literature and an anglicized Scottish readership, it is worthy of note that the knowledge of Scots had become so eroded (at least in Edinburgh) that Henry Mackenzie could deplore the fact that an appropriate evaluation of Burns's genius was made impossible due to the linguistic difficulties of his poems:

t102   One bar, indeed, his birth and education have opposed to his fame, the language in which most
       of his poems are written. Even in Scotland, the provincial dialect which Ramsay and he have
       used is now read with a difficulty which greatly damps the pleasure of the reader; in England it
       cannot be read at all without such a constant reference to a glossary as nearly to destroy that
5   pleasure.   (1786)

The poetic and linguistic impact of Burns's work was immense. He was imitated by Scottish poets in Scotland and Ulster (and by English dialect poets like Edwin Waugh in Lancashire) and his diction created something like a standard for literary Scots. This was admitted by the *Kailyard* writers (8.5.3) and by biblical translators like Smith in 1901 (cf. 9.1.1), and it formed the butt of MacDiarmid's criticism. Finally, the special status of words kept alive through the literary influence of his poetry is evident from the category 'Burnsisms' used by Aitken (1987, cf. 7.1.3). For the literary world, and for the anglophone cultures in particular, Burns has long been established as the national bard of Scotland, and his diction identified with 'Scots'.

After Burns, there were modest attempts of using local dialects rather than mainstream general Scots, but such attempts became important only from the middle of the 19C onwards (cf. 8.5.2).

Ex 84   Compare the opening stanzas of Burns's *The Cotter's Saturday Night* with his English 'sources' (such as Shenstone) and with Fergusson's *The Farmer's Ingle* to illustrate what Burns may have meant by 'sprinkling' his poems with Scots.

8.4.4 *Sir Walter Scott*
(Tulloch 1980)

The impact of Sir Walter Scott (1771-1832) on world literature is of course far more extensive than that exerted by his use of the vernacular, and yet this specific aspect assigns to him a prominent place in a treatment of the history of Scots. There were at least two models for Scott's use of the language: Maria Edgeworth had employed IrE dialect in some of her novels from 1800 on, and Scott was ready to acknowledge his intellectual debt to her (in his postscript to *Waverley*, cf. the quotation in Tulloch 1980:167); secondly, Burns's use of Scots in his poems had made the vernacular acceptable as a poetic medium throughout Britain. Scott's biographer Lockhart noted his remark:

t103   Burns, by his poetry, had already attracted universal attention to every thing Scottish, and I confess I couldn't see why I should not be able to keep the flame alive, merely because I wrote Scotch in prose, and he in rhyme.   (*Life*, III, 297, quoted from Tulloch 1980:168)

The fact that Scots was a living language throughout the country and becoming restricted in oral use only in educated urban circles gave Scott an ideal position to use his excellent linguistic competence for convincing representations of the speech of his characters, especially those who belonged to the 18C or to the lower classes, for both of whom the use of Scots was sociohistorically plausible. Among Scott's many novels the following therefore provide the richest data on the *auld leid*: the action of *Rob Roy* takes place in 1715, of *The Heart of Midlothian* in 1736-7 and 1750, of *Waverley* in 1745-6 and of *Guy Mannering*, *Redgauntlet* and *The Antiquary* in the late 18C. Only in *St Ronan's Well* has Scott attempted to describe the contemporary society of 1823:

t104   [Scott used] Scots only for those who, given their social class, would still be speaking it: daft Davie Gellatley in *Waverley*, the gipsies and Dandie Dinmont in *Guy Mannering*, the Headriggs in *Old Mortality*, Edie Ochiltree and the fisher-folk of Musselcrag in *The Antiquary*, Andrew Fairservice in *Rob Roy*, the Deanses in *The Heart of Midlothian*, Meg Dodds, the innkeeper in
5   *St Ronan's Well*, and so on.   (Murison 1981:192)

Ex 85   What do the characters mentioned by Murison have in common, apart from
their use of Scots?

Summarizing Scott's achievement, Tulloch is, however, certainly correct in saying: "By
limiting Scots to dialogue, Scott restricted its range – dialogue is for example more
informal than narrative and tends to deal more with the everyday than with the
universal" (1980: 181).

    The fact that Scott used various period languages in English and Scots has made him
the author with the largest vocabulary attested in his work; that he was so widely read
by Englishmen and Americans has meant that he introduced more Scots words into
English vocabulary than any other author, even more than Burns. Many of these are no
longer felt to be either Scots or literary, their meaning often having changed quite
notably. When the major edition of his novels appeared, an appended glossary still
included definitions for *awesome, glamour, grewsom, uncanny* and *slogan*; also
compare *forbear, raid* and *scantly* which were imported into St E from Scott (Tulloch
1980: 233-4).

Ex 86   Did Scott take diachronic aspects into account when depicting the language of
James VI/I in *The Monastery* and *The Abbot*, both set in 16C Scotland?

8.4.5 *James Hogg and John Galt*

The importance of James Hogg (1770-1835) and John Galt (1779-1839), whose main
prose writings coincided with (and were stimulated by) Scott, lies in the fact that they
attempted to employ Scots outside dialogue, and that both used Scots with reference to
their contemporary society, where Scott had introduced it for plots dated some 60–100
years before the time of writing, thus making the choice of broad Scots
sociolinguistically plausible. A survey of the three authors' main prose works published
between 1814 and 1824 may be helpful:

	Scott	Hogg	Galt
1814	*Waverley*		
1815	*Guy Mannering*		
1816	*Old Mortality, Antiquary*		
1817			
1818	*Rob Roy, Heart of Midlothian*	*Brownie of Bodsbeck*	
1819			
1820	*Legend of Montrose, Bride of Lammermuir*		*Ayrshire Legatees*
1821			*Annals of the Parish*
1822		*Three Perils of Man*	*The Provost*
1823			*Entail, Ringan Gilhaize*
1824	*Redgauntlet, St Ronan's Well*	*Private Memoirs and Confessions of a Justified Sinner*	

Fig. 31 Major novels written by Scott, Hogg and Galt, 1814-24

James Hogg (1770-1835), the 'Ettrick Shepherd', was a poet and novelist, whose life was determined by his meeting Scott, for whose collection he contributed ballads collected by himself and his mother. In 1818 he turned to prose, which culminated in *The Private Memoirs and Confessions of a Justified Sinner* (1824), one of the great novels of his time. Linguistically, the choice of somewhat diluted Scots, which is however carried through the entire text, illustrates an advance over Scott, whose denser Scots is restricted to dialogue.

Galt's great achievement is the almost photographic depiction of the society of Scottish villages and small towns in the early 19C. This makes his documentation of Scots and English in his novels (such as *Annals of the Parish*, 1821, and *The Provost*, 1822) of immediate sociolinguistic relevance. McClure, when analysing the works, concluded:

t105 Galt throughout *Annals of the Parish* and *The Provost* uses a language in which Scots forms appear with continuously varying frequency; and this demonstrates not only the capacity of his characters for expressing themselves vividly in Scots, but shifting of registers which was, and still is, an inherent feature of Lowland speech. The notably inconsistent language of his memoir-
5   novels has been adversely criticised: the charge was brought against *The Provost* on its first appearance that its language was "not Scotch, because the words are English, – and not English, because the forms of speech are Scottish"   (1995:130)

Galt's solution was, then, to expand the use of Scots into the narrative, but disguise it so to speak by using English spelling and by concentrating on shared vocabulary (which would be pronounced in a Scottish way by Scotsmen). Tulloch's analysis is worth quoting extensively:

t106 ... he does use quite a lot of Scots vocabulary but he virtually never uses Scots spelling of words which also appear in English. A novel like *The Provost* has a strong element of distinctively Scots vocabulary. Nevertheless, despite Crockett's claim that "Galt spares no pains to introduce every old and recondite Scots word he knows" and that "his books are, indeed, a Larger
5   Catechism of the Scottish language, in so far as they are by no means written for those of weaker understanding" [...], Galt is clearly concerned for his English reader and places some limits on his use of those Scots words which are not shared with English. The use of English spelling and limited purely Scots vocabulary creates a narrative language which presents few problems for English readers.   (1985:164)

Galt defended his procedure in the 'postscript' of *Ringan Gilhaize* (1823):

t107 It does not seem to be, as yet, very generally understood by the critics in the South, that, independently of phraseology, there is such an idiomatic difference in the structure of the national dialects of England and Scoland, that very good Scotch might be couched in the purest English terms, and without the employment of a single Scottish word.
                                                         (quoted from Tulloch 1985:164)

It should be noted that his model became very influential for some 20C authors such as Gibbon (8.7.1) who can be seen as following in Galt's footsteps.

8.4.6 *Ballads*
(Henderson 1983)

Traditional ballads originated as early as the 15C/16C, but they were systematically collected only in the 18C/19C, and are therefore best discussed in connection with the literature (and the collectors) of the time, as in the monumental collections by Percy (1765), Scott (1802-3) and Child (1882–98).

The language of the Scottish ballads has long been impressionistically described as 'mixed'. Thus the characterization by Henderson points out the problems but is linguistically quite vague:

> t108   ... the nature of 'ballad-Scots', the idiom in which these song-makers were operating – a flexible
>   formulaic language which grazes ballad English along the whole of its length, and yet is clearly
>   identifiable as a distinct folk-literary lingo ... It was ... the King James's Bible, which played a
>   vital part in stabilizing ballad-Scots, and facilitating a resourceful creative 'togetherness': a sort
>   5   of chemical fusion of two distinct but related ballad languages.   (in Daiches 1981:28)

The 'mixture' which deserves much closer scholarly attention appears to be a consequence of incomplete accommodation along three parameters:
1) modernization by successive replacement of archaic or obsolete words;
2) standardization by adaptation of regional dialects (NE, Borders) to Central Belt conventions or even anglicization;
3) literary 'improvement' by making the texts conform with metrical and stylistic preconceptions, or even composing new poems in the old style.

All these factors were certainly involved in Scott's edition of the *Border Ballads* (1802–3). "William Motherwell referred to (the rewriting) as 'the alembic established at Abbotsford for the purification of ancient Song'" and there are the caustic remarks by Margaret Laidlaw, the mother of the Ettrick Shepherd, who complained to Scott:

> t109   There was never ane o my sangs prentit till ye prentit them yoursel, and ye hae spoilt them
>   awthegither. They were made for singing an no for reading: but ye hae broken the charme noo,
>   and they'll never be sung mair   (both excerpts quoted from Henderson in Daiches, 1981:25)

It is still a matter of debate whether the original folk singers like Mrs Brown of Falkland (1747–1810), one of Child's major sources, recreated her texts at every singing (Henderson 1983:27); if this is so, no 'original' in style and language ever existed, and the quest for a purist Scots background would be futile.

Note that the street ballad (as opposed to the folk ballad and the artistic ballad) is only marginally recorded for Scots; it originated with the urbanization and industrialization of Britain – obviously too late for Scots to be used.

Ex 87   Can original ballads reworked by Scott be distinguished from those composed by him, on the basis of their language? (Tulloch 1980:61-3)

8.5 *Literary language 1832-1926*
8.5.1 *Introduction*

Scott's death and Carlyle's departure for London in 1832 ended a period in which Scotland had come to excel in the use of academic, cultivated English in written and spoken form; it had at the same time found niches for the vernacular to secure a hold at least in certain types of literature – however much the decline had now become irreversible for Scots even in speech, and this process was irresistibly spreading to the provinces. The still widespread competence in Scots – now definitely regarded as a dialect rather than a language – permitted a modest use in local newspapers after 1850 (cf. 9.5.1) and it determined the specific type of literature produced in Scots. With a few exceptions (8.5.5), the texts produced were provincial in at least one respect:

1) Some writers, most notably William Alexander for prose and Charles Murray for poetry (8.5.2), rediscovered the vital local dialect (both characteristically that of the NE) to deal with appropriate local topics. This decision was taken with the clear insight that no national norm of Scots was available, and that the usages of a living community presented a more forceful medium for poetic expression than an anaemic Burnsian quasi-standard that was increasingly becoming no-one's language.

2) Other writers, grouped together as the *whistle-binkie* school around 1840 and the *kailyarders* in the 1890s (8.5.3), used various degrees of authentic or stereotypical Scots, but did so for sentimental, backward-looking descriptions of unpolluted village life reflecting a lost golden age, and the language lost with it.

Both choices were rejected by writers like MacDiarmid (8.6.1) who thought that if Scots was worthy to survive it had to as a full national language, in concert with English, German, French etc. – at least as a poetic medium. For the linguist, these literary-cultural limitations of the type of Scots used in such 19C literature do not necessarily carry the same negative connotations. The *kailyarders'* language was no worse than Burns's where they made modest attempts at sociolinguistic realism, and the NE writers, making fewer compromises to a half-standard and to a supraregional readership, provide texts that are of immediate interest to the historical dialectologist and sociolinguist alike.

8.5.2 *Regional prose (William Alexander) and regional poetry (Charles Murray)*

William Alexander (1826-1894) was the most prolific and prominent journalist using Scots for newspaper reports (cf. 9.6.1). For his prose – both narrative and dialogue – he employed authentic local dialect and rejected the type of diction which was widely used and which is characterised by Donaldson as follows:

t110   The prevailing medium was a standardized 'book Scots'– sometimes called 'Sir Walter's
       Scotch' – a convention derived from the works of Burns and Scott and based upon the usage of
       the Central Belt. This had become familiar to generations of English and American readers ...
       and its prestige was such that it had apparently become an acceptable literary medium even for
5   non-Scottish writers. But the old standard was growing stale, and had never corresponded in
       many parts of the country with the language as people actually used it.   (1995b:3)

Donaldson states that this 'traditional Scots of the book' lost favour with Scottish writers, especially with those writing for the press. Therefore,

t111   all over Scotland a vigorous new demotic prose sprang into being whose distinguishing features
        were a passion for linguistic accuracy and a delight in the variety of the living language.
                                                                                    (1995b:ix)

Alexander's *Johnny Gibb* (1869-70, T54) is probably *the* outstanding specimen of a regional novel in Scots. After the serialized publication in the *Aberdeen Free Press*, Alexander became the paper's editor and continued his success with *Sketches of Life Among my Ain Folk* (1875). Writing for a newspaper, and local readers, the author chose to employ the living dialect:

t112   The language of *Johnny Gibb* represented a sophisticated attempt to achieve a scientific
        precision in lexis, syntax and idiom. Its orthographic inventiveness and vigour were intended to
        convey on the page with a high degree of accuracy the sound system of Lowland Scots in
        landward central Aberdeenshire...   (Donaldson 1995b:viii)

Alexander's book was a great success – in the NE – and was reprinted several times, a glossary being added from the third edition onwards.

    Charles Murray (1864-1941) was almost contemporary with Alexander; he achieved for poetry in NE Scots what the latter had done for prose. Murray started writing poetry in his native dialect in far-away South Africa where he spent some thirty years of his life. Though criticised (by MacDiarmid and others) for his parochialism, nostalgic attitudes and *kailyard* sentimentality, he remains the outstanding poet of his region, whose authentic language made him immensely popular and whose major collection of poems, *Hamewith* (1900, cf. T48), started a tradition setting off the NE from the dominating Central Belt. The two authors can, then, be rightly said to be points of reference for the vital tradition of writing dialect in the NE.

8.5.3 *The whistle-binkie school and the kailyard*

The popularity of Burns's poems and songs produced in the 19C not only the cult of Burns Nights (social gatherings celebrating the poet's birthday with speeches, recitations from his poetry and songs and usually a meal of haggis), but also gave rise to a spate of imitators. In Scotland, the most popular school has been labelled "Whistle-binkie" after the title of a first collection of poems published in 1832. "Most of the work was mawkishly pathetic and resounded with the sentimentality into which Scots vernacular verse had sunk in the mid and late 19th century" (Royle 1983:314). McClure, who also provides illustrative excerpts, aptly summarizes:

t113   What *Whistle-Binkie* offers for the most part is a domesticated Scots: the devitalised language
        of a people drained of confidence, and making of a specious and manufactured charm, humour
        and sentimentality a substitute, or a debased token, for a cultural identity. Confidence, that is, in
        the native language and its value as a mark of nationality. In other respects, confidence
   5   abounded, in the economic and industrial developments of Scotland's Victorian age; but a
        nation which was capable of doing nothing more worthy with the language of Burns, Scott,
        Hogg and Galt than *Whistle-Binkie* was not in a healthy state.   (2000:28)

Though poor in literary quality, the poems appear to have fulfilled a need for a growing reading public in the age of the Industrial Revolution. From these popular collections, there is a clear line that leads to the prose writings of the so-called *kailyard*.

The derogatory term 'kailyard' was coined in 1895 to characterize the work of a particular group of writers using Scots, and later on came to mean Scottish clichés or *kitsch*. Campbell (1981) lists four common characteristics of *kailyard* writings: an identifiable mostly rural locale, a sentimental depiction of usually past life, a moralizing 'healthy' attitude, and conservationist social values. The works of the most prominent *kailyard* authors, J.M. Barrie (1860-1937), S.R. Crockett (1859-1914) and Ian Maclaren (alias John Watson, 1850-1907), were all printed by the influential publisher W.R. Nicoll and – again – obviously fulfilled a need for nostalgic entertainment in an industrialized society.

The journalist, dramatist and novelist Barrie turned for inspiration to his native Kirriemuir (called "Thrums" in his writings), composing genre pieces about village life (collected as *Auld Licht Idylls*, 1888, and *Window in Thrums*, 1889), but outside Scotland became even more popular through his plays and especially *Peter Pan* (1904). The Galloway-born S.R. Crockett wrote over 40 novels, all quite popular, including the kailyard *Lilac Sunbonnet* (1896). Ian Maclaren was best known for his religious tracts (in English); his connection with the *kailyard* is through his collections of short stories programmatically named *Beside the Bonnie Brier Bush* (1894, T46), *The Days of Auld Lang Syne* (1895) and *Afterwards and Other Stories* (1899), as well as his novel, *Kate Carnegie and those Ministers* (1896), all set in the imaginary village Drumtochty.

The texts of these authors proved highly successful also outside Scotland, in the whole of Britain and in America, where they were sold in great numbers. The topics and the style met a popular demand, and the Scots elements used in them did not interfere with intelligibility for a public willing to put up with linguistic variation where it was appropriate for the genre.

Barrie's and Maclaren's texts, then, make obvious compromises for non-Scottish readers. Donaldson finds *Auld Licht Idylls* remarkable for "its minimalist approach to the vernacular, its notes on pronunciation, ... and glosses of elementary Scots words ... within the body of the text" (1986:146).

The dense Scots used in *Window in Thrums* is occasionally interrupted by glosses inserted in the text, such as "curran (number of) ...vent (chimney) ... chap (knock) ... silly (weak bodily)... thieval (stick with which to stir porridge) ... hod (hid) ... redd up (clean up) ... fleg (fright) ... deeve's (weary us)"; since these helps are somewhat irregular, it is difficult to say how much good they were toward the readers' understanding. The influence of the publishers in the process was summed up by Crockett who remarked: "We authors cannot always do just exactly what we would like. The publisher tells you to cut down the dialect because the English public does not understand it ..." (quoted from Donaldson 1986:147).

How far the authors stuck to sociolinguistic conventions is another question. Thus, in *Beside the Bonny Brier Bush* (T46), Maclaren has a letter written in Scots, biblical reflexion and a prayer, all slightly strange to find in broad Scots – considering the age-old dominance of English in these domains.

Although not normally classified as (urban) *kailyard*, J.J. Bell's *Wee Macgreegor* (1901) shares many features with the tradition. Relieving features of this serial novelette of a boy growing up in Glasgow are the humour and the intelligent depiction of class differences correlated with etiquette and proper linguistic behaviour: T50, which describes a visit to a well-to-do aunt, a fictional representative of *petit-bourgeois* Kelvinside, and the boy's misconduct are an excellent example of dramatized sociolinguistics.

Ex 88   Is the distinction between the domains of English for reflective and religious topics and Scots for narrative consistent in other kailyarders apart from Barrie?

8.5.4 *Reactions to the kailyard. Stevenson and George Douglas Brown*

The use of Scots for literary prose was, however, not exclusively left to Barrie and the *kailyard* in the late 19C. Two writers stand out for their achievement:

Robert Louis Stevenson (1850-94) wrote essays, criticism and travelogues before his world successes *Treasure Island* (1883), *Kidnapped* (1886), *Dr Jekyll and Mr Hyde* (1886), *The Master of Ballantrae* (1888) and the unfinished *Weir of Hermiston* (1896). Although most of his writing is in English, two outstanding tales show his expert use of Scots for narrative fiction: he included *Thrawn Janet* (T45) in his novel *The Merry Men* (1887) and *The Tale of Tod Lapraik* in *Catriona* (1893), in both cases using a 17C Scottish narrator to justify the use of Scots (similar to historical uses in Scott). Stevenson appears to have been very well satisfied with this linguistic 'experiment'. He wrote to Sidney Colvin in 1893: "He who can't read Scots can never enjoy *Tod Lapraik* (which) is a piece of living Scots; if I had never writ anything but that and *Thrawn Janet*, still I'd have been a writer" (*Letters* v:18). Apparently he found that the historical background and Covenanter context demanded Scots rather than English. However, in *The Maker to Posterity*

t114   Stevenson seems to accept the eventual disappearance of Scots as an inescapable, though
     regrettable fact –
     Few spak it than, an' noo there's nane.
     My puir auld sangs lie a' their lane,
5   Their sense, that aince was braw an' plain,
     Tint a'thegither,
     Like ranes upon a standing' stane
     Among the heather   (in *Underwoods*, 1887, quoted from McClure 2000:33-4)

George Douglas Brown's (1869-1902) *House with the Green Shutters* (1901, T49), whose setting, the village Barbie, is modelled on his native Ochiltree in Ayrshire. The book is one of the most forceful novels of his time; gone is the sentimental aspect of the idealistic, idyllic country-side of the kailyard tradition – decadence and destruction rule in Barbie. The language used is appropriate to the purpose. Where events are narrated by dialect speakers, the Scots can become quite dense, and the sociolinguistics of dialectal variation are carefully observed:

t115   "I' demned if he hasn't taken the Skeighan Road!" said Sandie Toddle, ... Toddle's accent was
a varying quality. When he remembered he had been a packman in England it was exceedingly
fine. But he often forgot.   (ch. 5)
"But what on earth has Wilson ta'en auld Jamieson's house and barn for? They have stude empty

5   since I kenna whan," quoth Alexander Toddle, forgetting his English in surprise.   (ch. 10)
"And by the way," said the parson, stooping to Scotch in his ministerial jocoseness, "how's auld
Tom, in whose class you were a prizewinner?"   (ch. 20)

Ex 89   Did Stevenson consider the time distance between him and the late 17C topics
by using archaic Scots?

8.6   *Hugh MacDiarmid and the Scottish Literary Renaissance*
8.6.1 *Hugh MacDiarmid*

Christopher Murray Grieve (pseud. Hugh MacDiarmid, 1892-1978) was born in
Langholm, speaking Scots as his native language. After several years as a journalist, he
started writing English poems (1923) before turning to Scots with the explicit aim to
create a new literary medium replacing the debased poetic diction and semi-standard
that had developed in the tradition of Burns, Scott and the *kailyard*. He proposed to
model this new type of Scots on the national language of the 'golden age' of Scots, on
the language of the makars. (He coined the slogan "Back to Dunbar!") As he stated
programmatically, he wanted "to adapt an essentially rural tongue to the very much
more complex requirements of our urban civilization" (*Scottish Chapbook* 1: 3, 1922).
This conviction was bound up with the political belief that Scotland needed a linguistic
identity to become an independent nation.

Taking up ideas of the Irish Renaissance (as formulated by Lady Gregory and Synge)
and recent modernist experiments by Joyce, he concentrated on poetical language,
creating an artificial style (dubbed 'Plastic Scots' by his opponents) . This was
composed of lexical elements taken from various sources, such as the works of the
makars, Jamieson's *Dictionary* (7.2) and several dialects and also containing new
coinages. Despite this linguistic mix, the poems written in this new medium in the
1920s are unanimously considered among the best poetry composed in Scotland in the
20C. In raising poetic diction to a standard equalling that of the major European
languages MacDiarmid objected to (and despised) parochialism, which he saw
expressed in both kailyard writers and authors using regional dialects, such as Charles
Murray's NE Scots. MacDiarmid's verdict was most forcefully expressed in 1925 when
he stated:

t116   His (Murray's) particular dialect is perhaps the poorest of them all and certainly the least capable
of being used to genuine poetic purpose (...). Aberdeenshire Scots is certainly the reverse of
'pure': *anything further* from the conceivable norm – anything more corrupt – it would be
difficult to find in any dialect of any tongue   (1925/1975:7, quoted from McClure 2000:22)

MacDiarmid's poems also stimulated a rethinking of the status of Scots in poetry among
many writers who had grown up speaking Scots natively (cf. 8.7.1). However, the
limitations of his approach were also evident; they serve to explain his ultimate failure:
1) As a consequence of its artificial and archaic provenience, his poetry was highly

intellectual, if not elitist, appealing to only few readers. There was also an obvious conflict with his political persuasions, and a decisive argument against any hope to make his diction acceptable to a wider audience. His partial failure to create a linguistic identity for the Scottish *people* is parallelled in his political career, since he was expelled from the Scottish National Party for his Communist leanings and then from the Communist Party because of 'nationalist deviation'.

2) Although MacDiarmid formulated his principles in a great number of articles written for the *Scottish Educational Journal* (MacDiarmid 1925), he never explained whether he intended to develop a full-purpose national language, and how to achieve and implement this aim.

3) His turning away from Scots as a literary medium in the 1930s was apparently determined by the fact that his poetry did not reach the masses, and was certainly inappropriate for international functions – a consideration that was of utmost importance when he came to write political propaganda in verse form (*Hymn to Lenin*, 1931, etc.).

If the Scottish Renaissance survived the defection of "the first founder of our fair language", it was because the aims of other authors were more realistic and more modest: with all their conservationist (or even revivalist) intentions, intelligibility was a major objective. Also, they clearly saw that it would be no use to reverse Muir's (²1982:8) dictum and make Scots "the language of the intellect".

We can do justice to MacDiarmid and those who followed him possibly only if we concede to poets what McClure is ready to admit in his affirmative evaluation:

t117   By unearthing the enormous store of almost or completely forgotten words from moribund spoken
       dialects and from earlier phases in the history of the written language, by reestablishing a vital link
       between the literature of the present and that of the Stewart period, and by restoring to Scots the
       ability to grow and regenerate itself from within by creative use of its existing lexical and
5   grammatical resources, the poets of the present century have successfully challenged the tacit
       assumption on which nearly all Scots writing since the seventeenth century had been based:
       namely, that the tongue in its written form can only reflect the linguistic resources and the social
       and cultural status of whatever spoken form and individual poet chooses to use.   (2000:20)

This approach is of course common practice in English or Irish writers like G.M. Hopkins or James Joyce (cf. McClure 2000:97).

Ex 90   Discuss the dangers in making Scots "the language of the intellect".

8.6.2 *The poets of the first phase of the Scottish literary Renaissance*
(McClure 2000:114-48)

The four poets selected by McClure to illustrate Scots poetic diction after MacDiarmid are ideal to evaluate early 20C achievements: Douglas Young (1913-73), Sydney Goodsir Smith (1915-75), Robert Garioch (1909-81) and Tom Scott (1918-95). Young's *Auntran Blads* (1943) was characteristically introduced by a poem in praise of Jamieson's *Dictionary* of 1808: "Frae Jamieson's muckle buik the words *tak wing*." No wonder, then, that his diction is tinged with archaisms, but his work documents "a poetic vision combining tradition and innovation, nationalism and cosmopolitanism" (McClure 2000:116).

Moreover, he is the author of one of the most convincing prose pieces, "In defence of 'Lallans'" (1948, T56) in which he justified his procedure. Similar to the complaints of Webster in 1789 who had found that the English language was already in decline, Young claimed in the *Epistle to John Guthrie*:

t118   But the Suddron's nou a sick man's leid,
       Alang the flattest plains it stots;
       Tae reach the hills his fantice needs
       This bard maun tak the wings o Scots.

           (quoted from McClure 2000:123)

Smith, born in New Zealand and educated in England, acquired his Scots through an intensive study of the great Scottish writers. McClure points out "a grave lack of artistic orderliness" (2000:124), a feature that might have been checked by a native speaker's *sprachgefühl*. Only in his later work did he become "one of the great synthesisers of Scots" (2000:126), thus McClure's apologetic note: "To denigrate Smith's medium as artificial would betray a truly amazing failure to appreciate the nature and value of literary creativity" (2000:132).

In contrast to Smith, Garioch's poetry has become quite popular, and the reason for this clearly is that "Scots was his mother tongue; and in his poetry he draws on the still-rich resources of a living community language" (McClure 2000:132-3). His diction shows a combination of literary Scots (*agley, caller, cranreuch ... spleuchan*) and 'demotic' speech (*bevvy, confab ... nyaff, plookie, rammy* etc., McClure 2000:133). Where he does not deliberately archaize his diction (as he does in particular in some translations), in many other poems "hardly a word would be unfamiliar to a reader with a basic knowledge of literary or spoken Scots" (McClure 2000:136).

Tom Scott is more difficult to approach: a blend of the historical Scots of the makars with "the mother-tongue of a community, not only affording the poet a fluent and expressive means of conveying his own thoughts but embodying that community's culture and code of values" (McClure 2000:141). Scott in his later work returned to his beginnings – using English as his poetic medium, a development similar to MacDiarmid's.

8.7   *'Modern choices'*
8.7.1 *Introduction*

In the later sociolinguistic context, a post-MacDiarmid writer's decision on which language is adequate for what literary purpose is, then, possibly more difficult to take than it has been for many years. One of the most relevant discussions of such problems, carried out *in Scots*, is a collection of short papers on "Our ain leid?" (McClure et al. 1981, cf. for instance T63-4). This decision is apparently determined by many factors, one of the most relevant being the literary genre chosen. It is obvious that for audiences who have great difficulties in reading Scots (whether they still speak it, and speak the variety represented, or not), short forms such as poems and short stories have a much greater chance of being accepted than long texts. In what follows, individual text types will therefore be discussed separately.

In particular, the question of how creative a writer is permitted to be as regards the coining of new words, reviving obsolete lexis and mixing the vocabulary of different local dialects has been a matter of permanent debate. MacDiarmid's answer was clearly that every liberty should be allowed, and Douglas Young's attitude was quite similar (T56, also cf. the quotation in Corbett 1999:159). By contrast, writers like J.K. Annand and less consistently, Robert McLellan, always found that intelligibility was highly important, and it would indeed be hard to imagine Annand's children's literature in innovative, experimental diction. William Neill, by contrast, believes in using words gathered from various sources for his translation of the *Odyssey*:

t119   Nane o the wards yaised in this buik are ootwith the Scots canon. I hae walit the wards I thocht
       best fittin tae echo the Greek, an in makkin yuiss o the hail ward-hoard that wes tae haund, I hae
       weill-kent fore-rinners frae the Scots tradeition an monie anither   (Neill 1992:10)

With due allowance for mixed styles, the choices for a literary writer may best be categorized in five options:

1) The use of a regional, rural living dialect, preferably from the NE or from Shetland (William Alexander, T44; William Tait, T59, or in the poetic work of Alexander Scott and Alastair Mackie, see McClure 2000:149-65); here authenticity of the representation has priority before considerations of supra-regional intelligibility and acceptability.

2) The use of synthetic Scots – the so-called *Lallans* – in the tradition of Hugh MacDiarmid, Sydney Goodsir Smith (T54), William Lorimer (T69b), William Neill, etc. It is characterized by a high density of lexical and orthographical Scotticisms and a great variability of the Scots vocabulary employed. Maximal distance from St E is intended – linguistic realism is not, nor is a standardization of the literary language. The acceptability and intelligibility of the individual elements and of the synthetic variety as a whole seem to be of secondary importance, as compared to the stylistic effects of the literary language.

3) The use of what may be called 'ideal' Scots (following Aitken 1984b), employed by authors such as Robert McLellan (T55 and T58) and J.K. Annand (T63, 69-71). The attribute 'ideal' refers to the writers' aims to standardise and institutionalise this variety. This is a major difference between *Lallans* and 'ideal' Scots, which are both marked by very high values for lexical and orthographical density and for the lexical variability of Scots. Easy intelligibility is thereby often sacrificed, while acceptability plays a major role. 'Ideal' vocabulary is not mixed; it is, on the contrary, very homogeneous. It is based on the spoken dialects of the authors, but 'aggrandized' (a term used by some of the authors themselves) by words acquired from traditional literary works in Scots. As a rule, 'ideal' Scots contains neither archaisms nor neologisms, nor localised items from outside the Central Belt, no slang or highly informal words, nor items socially marked for lower-class usage. Grammatical Scotticisms are restricted to those not found in stigmatized non-standard varieties of English. In this respect, 'ideal' Scots does not strive for maximal distance from St E: negative attitudes towards 'deviant' grammar seem to overrule other goals. Vocabulary and grammar appear as strictly 'respectable'. The question whether the Scots features on all linguistic levels may occur as 'overt Scotticisms' (Aitken 1984a:105-8) in real speech can serve as a gauge for the degree of respectability. On

the level of orthography, no particular local dialect is indicated. The spelling is based on traditional literary models (originating from the Central Belt), but is highly standardised. All Scots features belong to what is termed General Scots (cf. *SND* and the introduction to the *CSD*, p.xxxv): they are valid across all dialect regions and are not necessarily used but known by readers well-versed in the classics of Scottish literature. Standardisation is one of the major aims of the creators of 'ideal' Scots, because – just like the respectability of the lexical and grammatical items – it is one of the preconditions for the acceptance of Scots as a full and independent language.

4) The use of urban Scots, mainly from Glasgow or Edinburgh, predominantly for lighthearted, humorous texts or social criticism (Albert Mackie; Tom Leonard, T67; Tom McGrath; Steven Mulrine, T60, 61, 71; William McIlvanney, T62; and recently in Irvine Welsh's *Trainspotting*, T68). The diction is supposed to imitate real speech, including natural sociolinguistic behaviour. Thus, the density of Scots lexis is fairly low, the vocabulary is socially and locally marked and the pronunciation is indicated with the help of quasi-phonetic transcription which allows for a great degree of variation between standard and several non-standard spellings. This is reflected in particular in the frequent modification of weak forms of function words, which are usually left unchanged in 'ideal' Scots. There is no trace of standardization. The distance from St E is not an aim in itself but appears as a side-effect. The low density of Scots results in effortless intelligibility. In contrast, linguistic acceptability is of subordinate importance (this is particularly obvious from the frequent use of slang and taboo-words and of stigmatised grammatical features).

Each of these options has its limitations as regards genre, topic, expressiveness, and intended audience; some of the experimental uses have not proved to be thoroughly successful outside the obvious genres. These limitations have led various authors, at least from Galt onwards, to experiment with

5) the use of literary varieties in which the Scots element is reduced to a minimum. Lewis Grassic Gibbon, whose *Sunset Song* (1932) is justly praised as one of the major novels of the 20C, is characterised by Murison as follows:

t120   He will mingle in a few of the dialect words and idioms and try to make his adopted speech echo the tune patterns of his own native tongue. In other words, he will adopt a kind of compromise speech which will not be authentic dialect – but a basic English interwoven with enough of the vernacular to give it a sense of locality and the sound and stot of the Northeast voice ... This is
5   not what the purists and whole-hoggers like, but curiously enough it may result in something more like a classical Scots prose than the dialect *tours de force, Johnny Gibb* or, even more, *Eppie Elrick*, excellent as they are.   (Murison 1981:194)

8.7.2 *Poetry*

Poetical choices in the second half of the 20C are characterized more than before by a rich choice of options and fusions. Thus the diction of one of the leading figures, Alexander Scott, "is highly distinctive, even among the group of strongly individual ideolects of the mid-century makars; and one of its qualities is a subtle but pervasive North-Eastern flavour" (McClure 2000:149); his technical virtuosity being most audible in his use of onomatopoeia. McClure contrasts Alastair Mackie who "conveys his poetic vision with equal force in a realistic, down-to-earth Scots based on the mother tongue of generations of Aberdonians" (2000:157).

The voice of Glasgow, with excellent poetry written by Ian Hamilton Finley, Tom Leonard and Stephen Mulrine (cf. McClure 2000:166-78) is a new development which transformed a stigmatized urban dialect into a literary medium, its neglect of tradition partly illustrated by a phonetic transliteration, which had of course been used for humorous purposes before. McClure summarizes the situation with regard to Leonard's achievement:

t121   In some sense at least, later poems by Leonard suggest that an affirmative answer is actually
       called for: his work is a proclamation that the Glasgow working-class patois has appeared on the
       poetic scene with all its overtones of violence and brutality, and is no more to be trifled with
       than its speakers are in real life. The status of Glasgow demotic speech has always been, and
   5   remains, a vexed issue. A very common attitude – indeed, an orthodoxy – among teachers and
       school inspectors is that while the traditional rural dialects are worthy of at least nominal
       respect, the urban vernacular is merely "vulgar", "common", "slovenly" or "neither good
       English nor good Scots". Facts which sociolinguists and other language scholars can and often
       do cite, such as the grammatical self-consistency of the dialect, its innovative and expressive
   10 vocabulary, the merely contingent association of its distinctive pronunciation features with
       unattractive social conditions, the regularity and frequency with which urban sociolects develop
       in comparable circumstances elsewhere, make no impression on the deeply-ingrained, visceral
       dislike which the speech form commonly evokes among those who do not speak it.   (2000:171)

Another possible choice is the use of 'mainstream Scots' based on the language of the Central Belt. One of the writers who best succeeded in the genres of translation and children's literature is J.K. Annand (T69) whose audience of young readers made it necessary – as with Soutar's *Bairnsangs* of a generation before him[3] – to use, with great effect, a less dense Scots than was allowed to more experimental poets like A. Scott. Finally, regional diction continues to survive – in particular in the Northeast (such as in the work of Flora Garry, Sheena Blackhall and David Ogston; see McClure 2000:179-96) and in the very peripheral Shetland – where the sense of insular identity clearly makes up for the small number of speakers.

Different again the decisions for writers not aiming at 'high' literature: the translators of the German children's classic *Max und Moritz* (1865, T71) achieved racy, colloquial diction – regardless of the fact that versions were in the traditional broad dialects of Aberdeen and Shetland, in Glaswegian patter and in not too dense St Scots, permitting the reader, who cares to compare the excellent versions, insights into the expressiveness of parallel translations in four types of modern Scots (contrast for prose the versions of the "Christmas story", T69).

An obvious gauge to evaluate individual choices in poetic diction is to apply

---

[3]Compare Soutar's diary entry for 24 March 1932:

t122   I'm afraid these bairn-rhymes which I write from time to time must appear rather formidable for
       a child – yet what can one do? Even grown-ups in Scotland are children so far as their native
       tongue is concerned. All of us must wade through the vocabulary if we are to regain our lost
       heritage. (1932, quoted from McClure 2000:109)

McClure's measure of 'density' (1995h); this stimulating, but somewhat intuitive quantification, which classifies texts according to the two parameters of thin vs. dense and literary vs. colloquial and which leaves four possible combinations, was later refined for Scots drama by Lenz (1999). Authors are obviously torn between two divergent directions – *viz.* to base their texts on real Scots as it still exists and is easily understood by at least a section of the community, and to enrich their poetic diction by concepts and items taken from the literary tradition, from dictionaries, or from other dialects, or by creating new words by compounding, derivation and onomatopoeia. The second method entails the danger of not being accepted (or even understood) by many Scots (cf. McClure 1995h:173).

8.7.3 *Modern Scottish prose*

Readability must be a major concern for writers of dialect prose. Therefore, Scots tends to be restricted to dialogue or shorter pieces, or to be somewhat diluted. It is no surprise to find that there have been few novels in dense Scots since those written by William Alexander in the 19C (T44). The language of Sydney Goodsir Smith's novel *Carotid Cornucopius* (written in 1947) is so extravagant that it cannot be accepted as Scots at all. Authors like Robert McLellan (in his *Linmill Stories*, T58) or David Ogston have wisely chosen shorter narrative forms, producing collections of related short stories rather than novels.

McLellan is an excellent example of how the author's linguistic competence, the topic and genre, the intended audience and the variety of Scots chosen are interdependent. The rural background of his *Linmill Stories* and the perspective of a small boy required a natural, non-experimental diction – which McLellan acquired from his Linmill grandparents who (born around 1850?) belonged to a generation for whom English must have been quite a foreign language. The stories were originally written for the radio – which made it necessary for the listeners to understand the texts at first hearing. All the same, the language is surprisingly dense. The brevity of Annand's glossary disguises this fact, since he provides only a fraction of the words in need of translation for a non-Scottish readership. It is quite likely that a new radio production of the texts may no longer be feasible, since the intended audience – along with the necessary linguistic competence – no longer exists.

A variety cannot be regarded as a fully-fledged language unless it is used for expository prose as well as for fiction (Kloss [2]1978). It would be rash, however, to assume that the existence of non-fictional texts and a translation of the New Testament automatically raises a variety to the status of a full language. Experimental prose in Scots for various non-literary functions made a new start in the 1940s. It is represented mainly by reflexions on language like Douglas Young's defense of 'Lallans' (T56), the collection "Our ain leid?" (McClure *et al.* 1981, T63-4) and, in particular, various pieces written for *Lallans*, the journal of the 'Scots Language Society', which is entirely in Scots. The journal also includes genres ranging from book reviews to obituaries, and conference programmes. All this has shown that Scots is well equipped for such uses as far as lexis, syntax and style is concerned – but is lacking in acceptability in the general Scottish readership.

Among the most consistent attempts to extend Scots to scholarly prose are recent texts by Allan and Horsbroch. Allan was the first to discuss phonology and graphemics in Scots scholarly prose (1995), whereas Horsbroch's treatments of modern history document the flexibility of a language which many would have thought much too impoverished for such purposes. In particular, his contributions to the Belfast conference (Horsbroch 2000, 2001, cf. T73) are convincing illustrations of the socio-political situation of Scots in Scotland and Ulster described *in Scots*.

8.7.4 *Drama*
      (Lenz 1999)

In the performance of theatre plays, several channels other than language provide additional clues that aid the understanding of the plot; but only in rare cases is the overall effect of the whole event not dependent on the audience's comprehension of what is being said. As with prose, intelligibility of the language used on stage is usually of great importance to the author. Still, all major forms of literary Scots may be identified in modern plays. The least frequent of them is *Lallans*. A fairly clear example of the use of this variety in drama (rather than in poetry, where it is found most frequently) is Sydney Goodsir Smith's *The Stick-Up*: more than 20% of the vocabulary may be classified as Scots. This is composed from a great variety of local, social, stylistic and historical sources, supplemented by neologisms; about 50% of the words shared with English are spelt in a Scottish way, but the spelling does not imply a specific local pronunciation. The extraordinary character of the language is essential for the achievement of the intended – mainly poetic – effects: Scots is therefore deliberately foregrounded.

A much more dominant variety is 'ideal Scots'. Scots is treated as a separate language, often posed against St E as a variety of equal status. It is therefore deliberately not foregrounded. Examples are McLellan's *The Flouers o Edinburgh* (T55) and – in a more politically committed and therefore more strongly marked way – David Purves's *The Puddok an the Princess* (also cf. his translation of *The Tragedie o Macbeth*). In the former, Scots lexis makes up more than 17% of the vocabulary. About a third of the shared words have Scots spellings. These values are surpassed by far by the ones for *The Puddok an the Princess*: here the density of Scots lexis amounts to almost 33% and the orthographical density exceeds 50%.

The literary representation of an urban sociolect, usually Glaswegian, is at least equally influential for Scottish drama as 'ideal' Scots. Employed mainly in plays of the naturalist tradition, the language is intended to sound authentic and not to draw attention to itself. In this respect, urban Scots is not foregrounded. However, the deviance from St E as the only conventional written variety makes its use stand out for the readers (though not necessarily for the audience) of these plays. On stage this type of Scots sounds natural and appropriate for the type of characters represented. Tom McGrath's *The Hard Man* may serve as an example: Scots lexemes in this play add up to only 5% of the total and orthographical Scotticisms reach a density of about 17%.

These three 'model' varieties of Scots can appear in more or less distinct manifestations, but are also found in mixed forms and involving code-switching in some plays. Compare for example the mixed form in *The Rising* by Hector MacMillan (not particularly dense 'ideal' vocabulary combined with non-standardised spellings and many modifications of function words) and the co-existing varieties of Scots in *Mary Queen of Scots* by Liz Lochhead and *The Jesuit* by Donald Campbell.

Plays that are set in more remote areas, i.e. outside the Central Belt, but are nonetheless meant for supra-regional production, also use elements from 'ideal' and urban Scots rather than distinctly marked local or regional dialect features. Compare for instance Sue Glover's *Bondagers*, which is set in the Borders, or Donald Campbell's *The Widows of Clyth*, set in Caithness. Consequently, Glaswegian is the only clearly localized variety to be made out in the printed play texts. On stage, of course, the accents of the actors, which are not indicated in the spelling, but often prescribed in the stage directions, help localize the action.

Dense representations of clearly localized dialects of remote areas are also found in plays, but these are generally meant for the local community concerned. These texts are rarely printed and not performed outside the area in which they are set.

Ex 91   Illustrate the classification into three types of Scots also from lyrical poetry.

8.7.5 *Lighthearted shorter pieces*

As in other minority languages and dialects, Scots has long held an important position in humorous texts. While this tradition started in the Renaissance, it can be seen as having become especially important in the modern mass media (cf. 9.5.1 & 2), where newspaper cartoons such as *The Broons*, collections of jokes and anecdotes, and music hall productions have made Scots accept their vernacular – often in exaggerated distortions – where they would not have tolerated its use in more serious contexts.

9.1   *Anglicization*

The increasing influence of Southern English on Scots, mentioned repeatedly throughout this book, should be summarized in order to bring out the major strands of the
development and universal aspects of the encroachment of the H(igh) language on the
L(ow) variety.

In the early period, the surviving documents are largely limited to literary and administrational texts, which distorts the historical linguistic facts. However, we can certainly say that the feeling for Scottish identity expressed by a deliberate and purist use
of Scots, i.e. linguistic nationalism, was almost totally absent in Renaissance Scotland.
This is shown by

1) attitudes as illustrated by the late adoption of a name for the national language: until
   the early 16C the use of *Inglis* for both English and Scots stressed the identity of the
   two varieties; (1.4.1)

2) the inconsistency of people in authority, whether church leaders like Knox, monarchs
   like James VI, or printers of books, who wavered between Scots and English
   features, putting dogma, or intelligibility, above nationalistic considerations in their
   use of the mother tongue. It has, however, to be admitted that if the process of
   ausbau was difficult for EModE, it would have been much harder for a small
   language of a linguistically divided nation such as Scotland to achieve autonomy
   even if there had been sufficient support for implementing its own standard
   language.

What is bound to happen under such conditions is the emergence of diglossia, with
English at the H[igh] (formal, written) end, and Scots at the L[ow] (colloquial, spoken)
end, with a continuum likely to develop between them in due course.

Ex 92   Can we be sure that the use of the term 'English' always indicates 'Non-Scots'
            in sources after 1600?

9.1.1 *Anglicization before 1707*

The large-scale identity of the lexis and syntax of Scots and English made their
identification as parts of one linguistic system possible, and many English elements
were indeed seen as a potential alternative for 15C poets, serving

a) to indicate their *imitatio* of Chaucer's or Lydgate's style;
b) to enrich the rhetorical quality of their texts;
c) to use rhyme words or equivalents appropriate for metrical needs;
d) to fill lexical gaps (cf. Douglas' enumeration, T8).

On the other hand, texts could easily be Scotticized if there was a reason for doing so.
This process is what happened in Murdoch Nisbet's adaptation of Purvey's version of
the Wycliffite *New Testament* (c1520) and possibly in the transmission of James I's
Kingis Quair (8.1.2), as well as in all administrational texts. Tulloch (1989:7-10) shows
that Nisbet Scotticized mainly the spelling and inflection of his ME model and
translated only a few words. A sprinkling of Scots features on top of a text conceived as
English is also found in James VI's letters to Elizabeth I (T17), which are intended to

be understood by the addressee, but are given a Scottish veneer, coming from the Edinburgh court. This process could, then, be easily reversed, since it involved a cosmetic operation of a more or less mechanical exchange of spellings and morphology. Devitt (1989, cf. 2.7), who analysed the anglicization in various text types (but failed to see the superficiality of the adaptation), concentrated on five features which have long been known to be diagnostic of 'Scotsness':

1) relatives (*quh-* vs. *wh-*),
2) preterites and second participles (*-it* vs. *-ed*),
3) indefinite articles (*ane* vs. *a*),
4) negative particles (*na* vs. *no, nocht* vs. *not*), and
5) first participles (*-and* vs. *-ing*).

Although the limitations of her approach (which fails to take into account the anglicization of lexis and syntax, e.g. in the acceptance of *do* support) are evident, the statistics produced exhibit a convincing picture of the spread of English-derived patterns between 1530 and 1659, the curves having almost reached completion by 1620. This neatly confirms what is known from cultural history, and from the evidence of individual texts (cf. fig. 14).

Even the monarch was no exception; the anglicization of later versions of James VI's handwritten advice to his son, originally in quite dense Scots (*Basilicon Doron*, T18), happened for at least two reasons:

1) James had become more aware of the possibility of a political union of England and Scotland, and came to stress the cultural and linguistic unity of the two parts rather than insisting on the divergence; the fact is clearly evident from his phrasing in the manuscript version, but made much more explicit in the London print of 1603 (T18).
2) The text was printed in 1599 in Edinburgh by the English printer Waldegrave, who apparently introduced English features (likely to be sanctioned by the king).

After his arrival in London, James apparently tried to shed his Scottishness as thoroughly as possible – successfully in his writing (see his *Counterblaste to Tobacco*), but only incompletely in his speech.

Documents such as the Education Act of 1616 (T20) and the *Dundonald School Regulations* (cf. Görlach 1991:387-9) show how slowly even official documents were purged of Scots features – one wonders what kind of English would be taught in Scotland, if even the Regulations were written in such mixed language. Even the grammarian Hume, who should have had a firm grasp of the differences between Scots and English and a clear concept of linguistic correctness (based on English norms), failed to produce a homogeneous text (cf. T21).

Although in the late 17C little prestige appeared to be left for public uses of Scots, the picture was not yet monochrome. George Mackenzie, Lord Advocate from 1677 to 1689 found that Scots was an ideal medium for pleading – apparently because of its articulate pronunciation and rich special lexis. He claimed in his essay *What Eloquence is fit for the Bar*:

t123   English is fit for haranguing, the French for complimenting, but the Scots for pleading. Our
        pronunciation is like ourselves, firy, abrupt, sprightly and bold; their greatest wits being
        employ'd at Court, have indeed enrich very much their language as to conversation, but all ours
        bending themselves to study Law, the chief Science in repute with us, hath much smooth'd our
    5   language, as to pleading ... their language is invented by Courtiers ... but ours by learn'd men,
        and men of businesse, and so must be massie and significant.   (quoted from Corbett 1999:96)

There is a trace of this high reputation of Scots (or rather broad ScE pronunciation) still
left in accounts of Edinburgh lawyers before 1750–60.

Ex 93   Apply Devitt's tests to T12, T13 and T21.

9.1.2 *Anglicization 1707-1832*

The full acceptance of the English norms in writing was complete by 1700. When
Scotland in 1707 lost what remained of her political independence, there was
consequently no change in the use of English in administration and in the written
language of the schools and the church. A new start was, however, made when educated
urban Scotsmen came to accept the *spoken* norms of English as well. In the early 18C,
Sir Robert Sibbald distinguished three 'languages' in Scotland:

t124   that Language we call Broad Scots, which is yet used by the Vulgar ... in distinction to the
        Highlanders Language, and the refined Language of the Gentry, which the more Polite people
        among us do use   (quoted from McArthur 1992:894-5)

This development almost coincided with a growing desire for correctness in speech in
England which peaked, but certainly did not start with, Sheridan's *General Dictionary*
of 1780 and Walker's *Pronouncing Dictionary* of 1791 (cf. Görlach 2001a:89-92).
However, it is a remarkable new development that literati in the provinces, in particular
in Ireland and Scotland, became watchdogs of such correctness in the metropolitan
language. The fact was repeatedly commented on by the contemporary observer Kenrick
(1773), who states that the Irish and Scots in particular attempted to fix a normed
pronunciation, whereas the English saw less urgency for doing so.

There is an easy explanation of such seeming contradiction: at a time when correct
pronunciation was, at least for formal occasions, defined as a form as close to spelling
as possible, it gave a natural advantage to those who acquired English as a second
language or dialect by learning it from books. James Buchanan was affected by this
situation as he was also one of the most perceptive observers when he commented:

t125   In the English Tongue, as in all living Languages, there is a double Pronunciation; one cursory
        and colloquial, the other regular and solemn. The cursory Pronunciation, as the learned Mr.
        Samuel Johnson observes, is always vague and uncertain, being made different in different
        Mouths by Negligence, Unskilfulness, or Affectation. The solemn Pronunciation, though by no
    5   Means immutable and permanent, is yet less remote from the Orthography, and less liable to
        capricious Innovation. We shall observe, however, that although the best Speakers deviate least
        from the written Words, yet the more precise and severe Part of the solemn Pronunciation is
        seldom used in ordinary Conversation: For what may be suitable and becoming in a Pulpit,
        Desk, or on the Stage, or in other public Declamations, would often be exploded as formal and
   10   pedantic in common Discourse.   (1762: 58-9; also quoted in Jones 1995:4)

In the 18C, the notion of a superiority of cultivated English over Scots prevailed, which was seen as a reduced speech form lacking formal registers, grammatical precision and (largely) rhetorical refinement. This meant that – if Scotsmen wanted to catch up with educated Englishmen – they would have to adopt the prestigious, refined, expressive English, recently brought to stylistic perfection by Augustan writers like Addison and Swift, and regulated by lexicographers like Johnson and grammarians like Lowth. This was the universally accepted conclusion. It is expressed in such statements as Sir John Sinclair's:

t126   During the reign of James the First, the Scotch and English dialects, so far as we can judge by
comparing the language of the writers who flourished at that time, were not so dissimilar as they
are at present. Time, however, and commerce, joined to the efforts of many ingenious men, have
since introduced various alterations and improvements into the English language, which, from
5   ignorance, inattention, or national prejudices, have not always penetrated into the north. But the
time, it is hoped, will soon arrive, when a difference, so obvious to the meanest capacity, shall
no longer exist between two countries by nature so intimately connected. In garb, in manners,
in government, we are the same; and if the same language were spoken on both sides of the
Tweed, some small diversity in our laws and ecclesiastical establishments excepted, no striking
10   mark of distinction would remain between the sons of England and Caledonia.
                                                          (1782:9-10; also quoted in Jones 1995:5)

Unsurprisingly, Scots interferences were most conspicuous in public use. Correctness was, according to Sylvester Douglas, most important for persons in the following professions:

t127   In the pulpit, at the bar, or in parliament, a provincial phrase sullies the lustre of the brightest
eloquence, and the most forcible reasoning loses half its effect when disguised in the
awkwardness of a provincial dress. A certain cast of burlesque is thereby communicated from
the manner of the speaker to this matter, and the misapplication or erroneous pronounciation of
5   some particular word often produces a ludicrous ambiguity   (1779, quoted from Jones 1991:99)

Their predicament was, of course, that proper guidance was lacking for those eager to acquire impeccable English:

t128   A Scotchman ... must often be at a loss to assign the English equivalent, and frequently may
only substitute one barbarism for another. Many phrases, from false analogies, or the abuse of
general rules, will appear to him provincial which in truth are not so; and others, which are, he
will be unable to discover, or will not reject, because supported by the authority of some obscure
5   or obsolete English author.   (Douglas 1779, quoted from Jones 1991:101)

In pronunciation, problems were most grievous where ScE diverged, but English spelling was ambiguous, and the incorrect option might be chosen (as in the case of the two <o>'s in *horse* and *hoarse*, Kohler 1966). Word stress was also a major problem, because spelling was no help whatsoever; James Buchanan (1757) cautioned not to stress *súccess, aliénat, aliénable, difficult, démocracy, excéllency, embarráss* and *intelligible*.

The (imperfect) assimilation of Scottish speakers towards English was also noticed south of the Border. Samuel Johnson was of course biased against Scotland and the Scots, but his estimate about the situation in Edinburgh before he set out for the Hebrides in 1773 reflects the state of anglicization in Scottish speech:

t129   The conversation of the *Scots* grows every day less unpleasing to the *English*; their peculiarities
        wear fast away; their dialect is likely to become in half a century provincial and rustick, even to
        themselves. The great, the learned, the ambitious, and the vain, all cultivate the *English* phrase,
        and the *English* pronunciation, and in splendid companies Scotch is not much heard, except now
    5   and then from an old Lady.   (quoted from Tulloch 1980:174-5)

E. Topham, another English observer, stated:

t130   But their pronunciation and accent is far from agreeable: it gives an air of gravity, sedateness,
        and importance to their words, which [...] in common conversation seems dull, heavy, stupid,
        and unharmonious. [...]
        The inhabitants of this place, who are acquainted with the English, are sensible of this, and
    5   endeavour to speak like them [...] and the Professors of the College [...] strive to shake off the
        Scotch pronunciation as much as possible.   (1776, quoted from Pollner 1985:32)

Tobias Smollett, himself a Scotsman, made the Scotsman Lismahago express a similar
view:

t131   a North-Briton is seen to a disadvantage in an English company, because he speaks in a dialect
        that they can't relish, and in a phraseology which they don't understand. He therefore finds
        himself under a restraint, which is a great enemy to wit and humour.
                              (*Humphrey Clinker* 1771, p.199, quoted from Blake 1981:120)

A generation before these two statements, the Select Society (founded in 1754)
expressed its purpose of "promoting the reading and speaking of the English language
in Scotland", and justified it by reasons given in the Regulations:

t132   As the intercourse between this part of GREAT-BRITAIN and the Capital daily increases, both
        on account of business and amusement, and must still go on increasing, gentlemen educated in
        SCOTLAND have long been sensible of the disadvantages under which they labour, from their
        imperfect knowledge of the ENGLISH TONGUE, and the impropriety with which they speak
    5   it.
        Experience hath convinced SCOTSMEN, that it is not impossible for persons born and educated
        in this country, to acquire such knowledge of the ENGLISH TONGUE, as to write it with some
        tolerable purity.
        But, with regard to the other point, that of speaking with propriety, as little has been hitherto
    10 attempted, it has generally been taken for granted, that there was no prospect of attempting any
        thing with a probability of success; though, at the same time, it is allowed to be an
        accomplishment, more important, and more universally useful, than the former.
                                                        (1761; quoted in Jones 1995:9-10)

Many Scotsmen were of course aware of what they were about to lose. Alexander Ross
complained about the unnecessary neglect of the *auld leid* in 1768:

> Speak my ain leed, 'tis gueed auld Scots I mean;
> Your Southren gnaps I count not worth a preen.
> We've words a fouth, that we can ca' our ain,
> Tho' frae them now my childer sair refrain,
> An' are to my gueed auld proverb confeerin,
> Neither gueed fish nor flesh, nor yet sa't herrin.   (Ross 1935 (1938):11)

Even one of the great anglicizers, James Beattie in his tribute to Alexander Ross,
complained that

t133   Since Allan's (Ramsay) death naebody cared
        For anes to speer how Scotia fared ...
        For frae the cottar to the laird
        We a' rin South ...

And this is although the Scots language is worth cultivating:

> Our countra leed is far frae barren,
> It's even right pithy and aulfarren ...

The loss was felt even though the language shift was restricted to standard uses, by accepting Southern English as the norm in formal speech. The contrast may be compared to conditions in Ancient Greece, whereby Attic (the refined language of Edinburgh, the 'Athens of the North') coexisted with Doric, the rustic, unpolished but genuine idiom of the provinces. This feeling of a diglossia is expressed in Edwin Muir's famous dictum of English being the language of the intellect, and Scots the language of the heart (Muir [2]1982:8). Sir Henry Mackenzie expressed this feeling as early as 1780 as follows:

t134   ... the old SCOTTISH dialect is now banished from our books, and the ENGLISH is substituted
        in its place. But though our books be written in ENGLISH, our conversation is in SCOTCH ...
        When a SCOTSMAN therefore writes, he does it generally in trammals. His own native original
        language, which he hears spoken around him, he does not make use of; but he expresses himself
    5   in a language in some respects foreign to him, and which he has acquired by study and
        observation.   (1780:174, quoted from Jones 1995:13)

However, it is quite clear that what was here 'suppressed' (in Jones's 1995 terms) was not braid Scots but broad ScE. The fact is quite clear from statements like Alexander Scott's who – using a reformed spelling – gives us one of the few testimonies of contemporary ScE pronunciation (quoted under 3.4.4 above).

What happened in educated Edinburgh circles is well-illustrated by authors' and university professors' efforts to purge their texts of all provincial traces (T30-1), and the employment of language teachers to achieve impeccable correctness in speech. In a modern text, the situation is forcefully described by McLellan in his *Flouers o Edinburgh* (T55 – and, closer to the times of the shift, in various novels by Scott, cf. Tulloch 1980).

By 1800, the desire to speak proper English had apparently penetrated deep into the province. The minister of Peterhead in Aberdeenshire characterized the language of his parishioners in 1795 as follows:

t135   The language spoken in this parish is the broad Buchan dialect of the English, with many
        Scotticisms, and stands much in need of reformation, which it is hoped will soon happen, from
        the frequent resort of polite people to the town in summer.
                        (*The Statistical Account of Scotland*, 1795, quoted from Aitken 1979a:97)

It is only natural that this process continued. Thus, the *Second Statistical Account of Scotland* of 1845 says about Banff:

t136   Among the higher and better educated classes the English language may be heard spoken in
        tolerable purity both as to idiom and pronunciation: there are few who cannot express
        themselves in English, still fewer who do not familiarly understand it when spoken to them.
        Unmixed Scotch is never to be heard. The most common dialect is a mixture of Scotch and
5   English, the Scotch used being of the somewhat vicious kind, known, I believe, by the name of
        the Aberdeenshire. The Scotch, however, is gradually wearing out. Every person remembers the
        frequent use, in former years, of terms and phrases that are now seldom to be heard but among
        the older and more secluded. Even however in what is called by courtesy speaking English or
        using English words there is often a sore lack of the genuine English pronunciation.
                                                                (quoted from Aitken 1979a:97-8)

For many speakers (and writers) the acquisition of English must have been in the form
of a relexification. Galt has a very insightful remark on this process in an essay written
in 1803:

t137   At home, from his Mother and me, he learned to read and write. His pronunciation was not
        correct, as may well be supposed: but it was deliberate and significant, free from provincial
        peculiarities, and such as an Englishman would have understood; and afterwards, when he had
        passed a few summers in England, it became more elegant than what is commonly heard in
5   North Britain. He was early warned against the use of Scotch words and other similar
        improprieties; and his dislike to them was such, that he soon learned to avoid them; and, after
        he grew up, could never endure to read what was written in any of the vulgar dialects of
        Scotland. He looked at Mr Allan Ramsay's poems, but he did not relish them.
                                                                (quoted from Tulloch 1980:175)

An inevitable consequence was that social upstarts overdid their attempts at anglicizing
their speech (and in consequence became the butt of satire). The stereotypical 'refayned
eccent' of the middle-class areas of Morningside in Edinburgh and Kelvinside in
Glasgow is explained by such remedial efforts, as is a long list of satirized literary
characters which range from Aunt Purdie (T50) to Charles Gilchrist (T55). As other
varieties, Scots has various expressions to refer to persons showing off their linguistic
refinement: *knapping* or *speaking pan loaf*.

The educated Scots in their quest for formal correctness also had to pay a price –
Webster in 1789 appears to have been one of the first critics, foreshadowing more
widespread concern in 19C England, when he stated:

t138   a very learned Scotch gentleman once acknowledged to me "that the Scotch writers are not
        models of the pure English stile". Their stile is generally stiff, sometimes very awkward, and not
        always correct... The Scotch writers now stand almost the first for education; but perhaps no
        man can write a foreign language with genuin purity.   (1789:32-3)

Ex 94   What does "with tolerable purity" mean in the Regulations above?

Ex 95   What can we deduce from the fact that Gavin Douglas' *Aeneid* in Ruddiman's
             edition as well as Burns's poems in the Edinburgh edition (1787) were
             accompanied by extensive glossaries?

9.1.3 *The anglicization of the Highlands*

In spite of such moves as projected in the Education Act of 1616 (T20), English did not make any notable progress in the Highlands before the 17th century, with a final blow being dealt to Gaelic culture and language in 1746. Contacts with the Lowlands were few, which explains the relative stability of the Celtic Border and the restricted influence of Scots (1.6.5). English came in gradually and some parish schools were already active in English in the early 18th century. When the dissolution of Highland society came after Bonnie Prince Charlie's abortive claim and the suppressed Jacobite rebellion of 1745, English was enforced through various channels, the schools in particular. Despite inevitable interferences from the Gaelic mother tongue, especially in the first generation of speakers, the language was clearly closer to St E than varieties used by most Lowlanders. An early observer such as Samuel Johnson noted:

t139   Those Highlanders that can speak English, commonly speak it well, with few of the words, and
        little of the tone by which a Scotchman is distinguished. Their language seems to have been
        learned in the army or the navy, or by some communication with those who could give them
        good examples of accent and pronunciation. By their Lowland neighbours they would not
5   willingly be taught; for they have long considered them as a mean and degenerate race.
                                                                    (quoted from Tulloch 1980:319)

The influence of Scots on the newly imported English is, then, slight, and Highland English and Island English do not justify an inclusion in a book on Scots (cf. Shuken 1985, Sabban 1985a). On the other hand, the immigration of Gaelic speakers into Lowland Scotland had considerable impact on local forms of Scots – though not so much reflected in the lexicon, except in border areas. Wilson (1915:11) noted that the pronunciation of Dunning differed notably from that of Crieff; both places are in Lower Strathearn, but Crieff is much closer to the Highland Line and was apparently much more affected by immigration of Gaelic speakers in the 19C.

Ex 96   How can we explain the assertion that "the best English is spoken in Inverness"?

9.2   *Language planning*

Language planning usually aims at standardizing varieties and thereby also raising their prestige in the process; it is normally undertaken by committees authorized by governments and the like, in four more or less distinct steps:
1) Code selection – a variety must be chosen, on the basis of its geographical range, number of speakers and social status as well as intelligibility and degree of existing *ausbau*, that offers itself for standard functions.
2) Codification – the language must be standardized, i.e. existing variation be reduced (or made functional) and the result fixed in form of a grammar and a dictionary.
3) Elaboration – the codified language must be adapted to its intended societal functions, e.g. the range of registers must be increased, the vocabulary modernised, etc.

4) Implementation – the new norms must be spread through institutions such as schools, the media, with whatever persuasion or force is necessary for the general popular acceptance the newly codified language.

Experience has shown that however laborious and time-consuming steps (1)-(3) may be, the crucial test comes with (4), which often fails.

Language is part of a nation's identity, but the desire to be distinct, and to take upon oneself the necessary steps to develop national linguistic norms, varies from one community to another. In particular, it is decisive in how far the variety planned to be codified is still the common medium of the users (as it is, e.g., the case with Lëtzebuergesch in Luxembourg). In societies in which the local speech-form has become a minority variety, language planning, on top of the existing difficulties, also includes efforts of language revitalization (as for Low German and Scots). For the Scottish situation the four general points mentioned above may be specified as follows:

1) The choice is between a) the most widely spoken local form, Glaswegian, which is, however not socially acceptable as a national norm (often despised as 'gutter Scots'), b) NE dialect ('Doric') as the most vital regional form, which is too isolated and deviates from the varieties of the Central Belt too much to be accepted, c) East Central Scots, the language of a great amount of literature, and d) Lallans, the artificial-archaic poetical language, which lacks speakers.

2) Codification would seem to be comparatively easy once the variety has been selected; however, the endless discussions about Scots orthography (cf. McClure 1995c) warn us that agreement might be difficult to reach.

3) Elaboration has been tried for various special registers. The problem here is that much of the lexis needed is in the technical registers which tend to draw their vocabulary from neo-classical coinages. Solutions for Scots could be to be content with a local pronunciation of these international terms or to translate them (as in, say, Icelandic; cf. isolated instances of this method in Scots, such as *yearhunner* for *century*, *owerset* for *translate*). While the first method does not provide enough distance from English, the second produces words which tend to sound too strange to be accepted.

4) As has often been stated, institutions in Scotland are not consistently willing and not yet capable to put reform proposals into practice, nor are attitudes of the majority of Scots in favour of such moves.

The problems here sketched are similar to those faced by, e.g., Caribbean creoles (cf. Görlach 1991b). To create non-English norms and implement them would not only be against the wishes of the population, but it would also be very expensive – and cut the affected communities off from the speakers and writers of the world language.

Ex 97   Summarize the vital distinction between Scots on the one hand and Lëtzebuergesch and Jamaican Creole on the other as regards the chances of the implementation of a new national language.

The case of Ullans (2.3.4) is most spectacular, but only an extreme example of what happens in the elaboration of a neglected variety to make it adequate for the modern needs of standard language. The discussion of Scots in Scotland has been dis-proportionately concerned with spelling – without a solution that is both acceptable and adequate. More recently, however, texts written by Allan, Horsbroch and Macafee have brought the problems back to mind, by not only discussing them on a theoretical level, but also using Scots as a medium: only thus can the real problems be made visible.

It is quite clear that literary texts, though subject to similar problems of 'density' of minority language use as expository texts are, rely much less on acceptability and implementation. Experiments can easily be tolerated if readers are willing to recognize superior poetic qualities; the status of Lorimer's *New Testament* possibly takes a middle position here between literary and expository prose. A tentative classification of registers and types of Scots tried for them might look as follows (allowing for a more or less rather than a yes-no decision in the categorization):

Type of Scots	Expository Prose	Literary Prose	Poetry
Thin or diluted	B. Kay t1, 2	Moir (narrative) T40 S.G. Smith	Burns
Relexified	Telfer T73	Gibbon, cf. T56/77	?
Dense	Horsbroch T73	Moir (dialogue) T40 McLellan T58	A. Scott
Experimental	Ullans T75	Milne Lorimer? T69	MacDiarmid

Note that code-switches are common when it comes to sub-genres (dialogue vs. narrative in novels, main text vs. reflexion in Burns etc.).

9.3 Scots in education
(MacGillivray 1997, Niven & Jackson 1998)

The times after compulsory education was introduced in Scotland in 1872, and when Her Majesty's Inspectors roamed the countryside to see to it that 'proper' English replaced the 'ugly, slovenly, debased' dialects, were not encouraging for either English and or Scots dialects. Since Scots was not recognized as a separate language, there was no room for it in the curriculum, neither as a school subject nor as a medium. It is significant that even literature written in Scots was largely neglected in Scottish schools, curricula and teachers concentrating on mainstream works in English. Although Burns, Scott and a few other Scottish classic writers could not be entirely neglected, the exclusive focus on teaching literacy in St E led to linguistic difficulties with the comprehension of Scots in literature, which deterred many pupils (and teachers) from more intensive study. Under these conditions, proposals to increase at least the proportion of reading Scots texts were hard to implement, not to mention speaking and writing the *auld leid*.

How tentative suggestions to increase the Scottish component were even twenty years ago is illustrated by the report of the Scottish Central Committee on English, *Scottish Literature in the Secondary School* (Edinburgh: HMSO, 1976), a book which provides well-argued proposals for expanding at least the reading of Scottish classical authors. Attitudes appear to be changing, however, more recently (cf. Lorvik 1995 whose interviews of 100 secondary school teachers of English show that current viewes are surprisingly positive). In 1992, the *Scots Language Resource Centre* (SLRC) was founded as a branch of the *Scots Language Society*. Its main aims are to further the interest in Scots, promote its status, provide teaching materials and a contact network for teachers willing to teach Scots. It is also lobbying for government support of Scots. A new report, *Scottish Culture and the Curriculum* (Review of Scottish Culture Group, 1998), advocates outspokenly the teaching of more Scottish culture in schools. It demands the teaching of Scots so clearly that the *Scottish Consultative Council on the Curriculum* (SCCC), which instigated this review in 1996, came under pressure from the Labour government (fearing support for the SNP, which was at the time leading in Scotland). As a consequence, they called for a revised, toned-down version of the report, before it was published and submitted to the Education Department.

For one thing, toleration of local speech has grown, and there have been attempts at increasing the active use of the local dialect. The current national guidelines for English Language for all levels published by the Scottish Office Education and Industry Department include the distinct demand for teaching language and dialect awareness and appreciation. The examination board for the new 'Higher Still' qualification (introduced in 1999) made the choice of at least one Scottish text compulsory for the subject English. Scottish teaching authorities, however, have to overcome not only the problems of teaching a non-standardised variety; they also meet with reservations from both teachers, many of whom are not native speakers of Scots (especially those coming in from England), and parents, who often object to their children getting in touch with Scots at school.

From the 1990s onward, there have been moves to make the teaching of at least a passive knowledge of Scots and some knowledge about its history and sociolinguistic situation a compulsory rather than just an optional part of teacher training in Scotland. Teaching authorities are trying to raise the awareness that teachers all over the country in any other than the most middle-class public schools are likely to be confronted with the use of Scots in their classrooms. In order to be able to deal with this situation without discouraging their pupils they must understand their speech form and know about systematic differences from St E.

The practical problems of teaching more Scots in schools are, however, enormous. Purves, himself one of the proponents of such policies, sees the situation quite realistically:

140   It is difficult to see how any of the surviving dialects can effectively be taught in Scottish schools. None of them has an extensive literature and none of them, except Shetlandic, a contemporary published grammar which could be used as a basis for instruction in Scots. Furthermore, most teachers in Scotland are not native to the Scottish dialect area in which they
  5   teach.   (Purves 1997a:3)

Still, the amount of material available for active use and teaching of Scots has increased over the last decade: especially in the field of vocabulary, gaps are closing with the *Scottish National Dictionary Association* (SNDA) having published various smaller dictionaries, most recently the nation-wide bilingual *Concise English-Scots Dictionary* (Macleod & Cairns 1993) and the two-way bilingual *Scots School Dictionary* (Macleod & Cairns 1996, also available on CD-ROM). The authors justify their effort as follows:

t141   The aim of this dictionary is to give as much help as possible ... to all who want to use the Scots language, from writers to schoolchildren, for creative work or just for pleasure. Scots has in recent years gained considerably in prestige and acceptance in the community. School pupils were formerly criticized or even punished for the use of their native language, but today's

5   educational policies are to encourage its use and also to arouse an interest in its long literary tradition.

                                                                        (1993:iv)

The SNDA is continually adding material to its database, and – via its *Scuil Wab* (part of its website and entirely in Scots) – is trying to involve schoolchildren in the search for unrecorded Scots words. In addition, there are other vocabulary projects like the one organised by the *Times Educational Supplement Scotland*, which collects word lists compiled by Scottish schoolchildren.

    The SNDA also released a spellchecker, called "CANNIESPELL" (1998) and a small grammar of Scots for the use in schools, entitled *Grammar Broonie* (Rennie *et al.* 1999). Along with other short grammars, which have started to appear from the mid 1990s, such as the one included in the AUSLQ's *Innin ti the Scots Leid* (Lovie *et al.* 1995), Kynoch's *Teach Yourself Doric* (1994), two publications on the internet in English (Eagle [2]1999, Young [2]1996) and the more substantial though still far from comprehensive work by Purves (1997a), also in English, these are the first serious, though patchy, often archaic and prescriptive, efforts to provide a basis for the actual teaching of Scots grammar.

    If Scots is to become a school subject in its own right, spelling is also in need of standardisation. A spelling committee was set up in 1996 (members include Alasdair Allan, Andrew Eagle, John Law, J. Derrick McClure, David Purves and John Tait) to work out a standard orthography.

    A more pressing problem is the want of material suitable for teaching, especially the younger classes. The teaching of Scots is better funded in the primary than in the secondary schools, but there the lack of texts is felt most severely. Efforts are being made by various organisations to redress the situation: the *Scots Language Society* and *Scotsoun* (who publish recordings of Scots texts) started off in 1983 with *Gleg*, a Scots tutorial for children taught through stories, poems and songs. In 1993, the SCCC joined in a partnership with all of Scotland's education authorities in the *Scottish Languages Project*, which subscribed to the aim to promote language awareness and the use of Scots, as well as Gaelic in primary and secondary schools. By 1996 the Project had published *The Kist*, an extensive anthology of texts combined with a collection of multimedia teaching materials, which is now used particularly in upper primary and lower secondary levels all over Scotland. The SLRC, *Scottish Book Trust* and a number of new small publishing houses such as the Scottish Children's Press in Edinburgh,

Watergaw at Newton Stewart/Dumfriesshire, Merlin Press at Scone and Argyll Publishing are now producing texts and tapes in Scots for schools, which are being distributed via a central agency, Scottish Book Source. These efforts are supported by various essay-writing and poetry competitions, notably in Shetland and in the Northeast, but also elsewhere in the Lowlands; projects involving life performances in Scots (preferably of pieces written by the pupils themselves) include the joint SLS and SLRC "Scots in Schuils" competition.

Such moves would appear to save what remains of bidialectalism. However, it would be naïve to expect too much too soon – even though attitudes to Scots in schools have been changing. In fact, a recent survey of the field (MacGillivray 1997) leaves the reader perplexed; the various proposals of how the teaching of Scots literature might be increased are not precise enough, especially since they often neglect the vital question of how much linguistic competence can be assumed to exist among pupils.

Ex 98   Many people have seen the tolerance of regional accents as a sufficient basis for a linguistic national identity. Do you agree?

Ex 99   Do you see any difference between revitalizing Scots and an English dialect, such as that of Yorkshire?

The study of Scots at university level has achieved a better footing. After a slow start in the 1970s, Scots language courses or sessions on Scots language taught along with Scottish Literature became common at various departments throughout Scotland in the 1990s, though apparently interest is receding again. Edinburgh University set up a Scots language degree, which is, however, no longer available. Several long-term projects have been established, for example the "Scots Teaching Research Network" (STARN) supported by the Glasgow School of English and Scottish Language and Literature, a joint project of three departments of that university. The School of Scottish Studies (Edinburgh) also contributes to the study of the language though it is dedicated mainly to other aspects of Scottish culture.

Scots as a medium for academic writing is still marginal as in the committed work undertaken by Allan (1975, 1998); also compare the new annual journal *Cairn. The Historie Jurnal in the Scots Leid*, which was launched in 1997. Alongside this official activity, the Aberdeen Universitie Scots Leid Quorum attempted to build a network of university-based Quorums.

9.4   Scots in the church
(Tulloch 1989)

The Reformation started to affect Scotland long before 1560, although this date is usually given as its 'official' beginning there. Corbett summarizes from Wright (1988):

t142   As early as 1533 Alexander Alesius, an exiled Lutheran, wrote a letter of protest to James V, in Latin, protesting the right of the people to hear the word of God in their mother tongue

                                                                              (Corbett 1999:56)

Knox commented on the situation as follows:

t143 And so by Act of Parliament [March 15th, 1543] it was maid free to all, man and woman, to reid
the Scriptures in thair awin toung, or in the Engliss toung; and so war all Actes maid in the
contrair abolished. This was no small victorie of Christ Jesus, feghting against the conjured
ennemyes of his verite; not small conforte to such as befoir war holdin in such bondage, that thei
5 durst not have red the Lordis Prayer, the Ten Commandimentis, nor Articules of thare faith in
the Engliss toung, but thei should have bene accused of heresye. Then mycht have bene sein the
Byble lying almaist upoun everie gentilmanis table. The New Testament was borne about in
many manis handes. We grant that some (allace!) prophaned that blessed wourd; for some that
perchance had never red two sentences in it, had it maist common in thare hand; they wold
10 chope thare familiares on the cheak with it, and say, 'This hes lyne hyd under my bed-feitt these
ten yearis.' Otheris wold glorie, 'O how oft have I bein in danger for this booke; how secreatlie
have I stollen fra my wyff at mydnycht to reid upoun it.' ... Then ware sett furth werkis in our
awin toung, besydis those that came from England, that did disclose the pryde, the craft, the
tyranny, and abuses of that Romane Antichrist.

(Life and Works of Knox, ed. D. Laing, quoted from Murray 1873:66)

However,

t144 the Bible's role in the Reformation in Scotland is in some ways a paradoxical one. The most
forceful Scottish champion of free access to the vernacular Bible [i.e. Alesius] himself wrote
nothing in English, let alone Scots. The Scottish Reformers relied on English translations, and
made no attempt to provide a Scots version. Nor did they succeed in having an English Bible (or
5 New Testatment) produced in Scotland until 1579, in a reprinting of the Geneva Bible with not
the slightest attempt at adaptation in vocabulary or spelling for a Scottish readership.

(Wright 1988:155, quoted from Corbett 1999:56)

The exclusive availability of the Bible in English has determined the restricted use of
Scots in the religious domain. When Knox and the Scottish reformers decided to accept
the Geneva Bible in 1560 and when it was made obligatory for households of a certain
income to have a copy of the book, this virtually also determined

a) that the terminology of religion including many of the idioms and sayings became
   more and more English (however much the pronunciation might be in broad Scots);

b) that English came to be regarded as the correct, standard written form of a language
   whose spoken, less prestigious (or even corrupt) variety was local Scots.

That traces of Scots remained in text types such as sermons is illustrated by a quotation
from Edinburgh of 1638:

t145 The Kirk of Scotland was a bony trotting Naig, but then she trotted sae hard, that never a man
durst ryd her, but the Bishops; wha after they had gotten on her back, corce-langled her, and
hopshaikled her, and when shee becam a bony paceing beast, they tooke great pleasure to ryde
on her. But their cadgeing her up and downe from Edenbrugh to London, and it may be from
5 Rome to, gave her sik a hett cott, that we have been these twall months by gane stirring her up
and downe to keep her frae foundrying.
Yea, they made not only ane Horse, but ane Ass, of the Kirk of Scotland. Hou sae? ko ye. What
meane ye by this? Ile tell you hou: they made Balaam's Ass of her. Ye ken well eneugh Balaam
was ganging ane unluckie gate, and first the Angel mett him in a broad way, and then the Ass
10 bogled and startled, but Balaam gote by the Angel, and till her and battand her sufficiently; that
was when Episcopacy came in, and then they gave the Kirk of Scotland her paiks. ....

(James Row, St Giles', Edinburgh, 1638, quoted from Murray 1873:72)

In contrast to other European nations in which the existence of a vernacular Bible strongly contributed to the establishment of a standard language, the reverse was true in Scotland. Knox was obviously concerned with Protestant dogma rather than providing the vernacular text in the national variety; however, two much-cited statements relating to language use in religious texts have often been overinterpreted and need to be seen in proper perspective. McClure's insightful interpretation is very helpful in this context:

t146   The suggestion that Knox could not understand Winzet's language is offered as an ironic excuse
       for the reformer, on the same level as an immediately preceding suggestion that he had perhaps
       been unable to read his handwriting.   (1995d:53)

This explains why Lyndsay's demand of 1554 (T11) to have all important religious texts translated into the vernaculars – even into 'Irische' – did not necessarily refer to a translation into Scots: English was apparently good enough to satisfy the qualification of a 'vulgar tongue' for Scotland!

It is quite obvious that the English of the Bible, and of the Book of Common Prayer adopted in the 17C, influenced all other text types in the field: sermons, prayers, religious reflexions would contain at least extensive quotations from these sources, and it is likely that even the pronunciation of religious texts – considering their formality and high prestige – would have been oriented at the written word long before imitation of English pronunciation became fashionable, and then expected or obligatory, in urban educated speech in 18C Scotland. The literary (much-quoted) illustration from Burns's *Cotter's Saturday Night* is significant: the language automatically changes into English when the old father reaches for the family bible.

Unsurprisingly, the history of Scots texts in the field is strikingly peripheral (Tulloch 1989), and the failures of the attempts to fill the gaps in the tradition are suggestive:

1) Nisbet's Bible translation of c.1520 was bound to fail (even if it had reached print) because it was not idiomatic Scots but a halfhearted adaptation of a ME text, and particularly because it was therefore based on the wrong textual tradition, *viz.* on the 'Catholic' *Vulgata* rather than on Greek and Hebrew sources.

2) 19/20C attempts at translating the Bible (usually small sections of it) were made for different purposes or by outsiders as aptly summarized by Tulloch (1992): Prince Bonaparte (1857) used a few verses for collecting dialect specimens (using Riddell, Henderson and Robson as translators), Waddell (1871) was a member of the Free Church until he joined the Church of Scotland three years before his death, and the dialectologist Murray was prompted to write a new version of a few passages in order to improve on Riddell. Smith was taken to the US when he was three years old and lived in Canada from 1837 to his death in 1917, and though his *New Testament* was published in Paisley in 1901, it clearly came from an outsider. Paterson devoted himself to the *Proverbs* only (1917) and Cameron (1921) translated, again in Australia, where he had emigrated after he was deposed as a minister. Alexander Borrowman was a minister in the Church of Scotland, but also a poet and an active member of the *Scots Language Society* which provided the stimulus for his translation of *Ruth* (1979).

3) The bleak story of religious texts is crowned by the major achievement of Lorimer's *New Testament in Scots* published posthumously in 1983. This *was* the text that the cultural history of Scotland had needed for a long time, but it came too late, for various reasons:

a) Lorimer himself was not a native speaker of Scots, and however perfectly he acquired the second dialect, the fact explains a certain intellectuality of the attempt, but it also illustrates that

b) there was little audience left for him to appreciate his achievement; the mere linguistic competence of church audiences was no longer sufficient to understand the text at first hearing.

c) Lorimer had secured no institutional support whilst alive, and the chances of having his version accepted as the basic text by the Church of Scotland were small when the translation was edited and published posthumously by his son, although attitudes towards Scots had become more positive in the 1980s than the 1960s.

d) In the secular society of the late 20C a biblical translation – even if it had been adapted for use in church and religious instruction – cannot be expected to have the influence on language use and norms the Renaissance Bibles had, and in this case the acceptance would have meant a revivalist experiment for most churchgoers in the first place.

Whatever the community language, the use of another language of formal, prestigious and archaic character is common in many societies. But it was *English* that has filled exactly this position in Scotland, and a Scots Bible would have gone a long way towards reversing the sociolinguistic situation.

Although the sales of Lorimer's translation would seem to suggest large readerships and widespread use in Scotland, it is not clear whether the book is not rather fulfilling the function of a badge of identity on middle-class book shelves. By contrast, Stuart's (1992) *tour de force* of rendering passages of the New Testament in Glaswegian, though it can be interpreted as bringing the Good News to the people in the language they speak, is frowned upon by many, the stigmatized variety not being considered appropriate for the genre.

9.5   Scots in the media
9.5.1 *Newspapers*
(Donaldson 1986)

In the 18C, the function of Scottish newspapers was not comparable with that of the London-produced press: distances and slow communication made papers printed in Scotland as provincial as those from Gloucester or Manchester. This was to change with the railway and the telegraph in the 19C. Linguistically, the newspaper (or even the literary periodical) was a middle-class affair, and strict adherence to St E was the norm.

Radical changes came about in the 1850s, after modern printing methods, cheap paper and, finally, the repeal of the Stamp Act in 1855 made it possible for many enterprises even in provincial towns to start business. The small and geographically restricted circulation of many of these new papers combined with coverage of local events, greater degrees of informality and openness to local speech forms. Unsurprisingly, then, we find a phase of Scots represented in a great variety of genres written in many dialects, often in improvised speech-based spellings (since no orthographic conventions existed). This flourishing vernacular tradition coincided with the heyday of the Yorkshire and Lancashire almanacs, both representing a stage in diglossia when the spoken forms were the almost exclusive medium of everyday communication and, in consequence, reading printed dialect aloud would connect with this situation. Readers would then be prepared to put up with the additional difficulties of making sense of strangely spelt texts – having been taught how to read and write exclusively in St E. Significantly, this was also the time when entire novels in dialect were successfully published, and it is again no surprise that the most prominent Scottish novelist of this tradition, William Alexander, was a journalist who contributed to this vernacular journalism. For a modern reader, the range of topics and genres that was possible in Scots, ranging from local events to reports from the Crimean War, is truly remarkable.

The number of potential readers of vernacular prose texts shrank in the same proportion to which spoken Scots decreased in the communities (and when possibly other factors had reduced the readers' willingness to put up with these linguistic 'experiments'). At any rate, there is no continuation in the 20C of this broad range of newspaper Scots – as there is not for Yorkshire almanacs, by and large, after 1930.

Newspapers in the 20C were open to discussions on the *auld leid* and texts written in it – but with a difference. The range of Scots texts dwindled to the informal, especially funny: the cartoon *The Broons* and the humorous dictionary *The Patter* (Munro 1985) provide outstanding examples of the popularity of texts which were short, witty, informal and certainly not meant as an alternative to writing in St E. Criticism of the state of the language and the literature written in Scots also had wide coverage, but most of this was in the language considered more appropriate for abstract reflections and reasonings – English. One of the most influential representatives of the *Scottish Literary Renaissance*, MacDiarmid, was a journalist, but in contrast to his poems of the period, his caustic articles on the state of the art written for the *Scottish Educational Journal* in 1925-27 (collected in MacDiarmid 1976) are all in English – it is only in a few letters *to him* that correspondents use some Scots. After 1945, the *Scotsman* and the *Scots Review* allowed much room for discussions on the future of Scots – Douglas Young's and Sydney Goodsir Smith's reflexions (T56-7) come from this source – but the energy and enthusiasm appears to have flagged and such contributions were only revived in more recent years.

The use of Scots seems to have been slowly increasing in all media throughout the 1990s, according to the observations of Stuart McHardy, previously director of the SLRC, on whose analysis (p.c.) the following summary is based. The national newspapers (*The Scotsman* and *The Herald*) take only a small part in the reintroduction of Scots to the print media. They have the occasional article written in Scots (usually on the state of the language) and sometimes publish Scots poetry; otherwise its use is restricted to headlines and short passages within articles, sometimes as reported speech, much of this being in a humorous vein. However, there seems to be an increased use of individual Scots words in general.

The *Press and Journal* (Aberdeen) has at least one or two articles in Scots every week and occasionally uses Scots reported speech. The *Sunday Post* continues to utilize Scots in its cartoons "Oor Wullie" and "The Broons" and employs 'overt Scotticisms' and bits of reported speech in its articles. The same organisation's monthly *Scots Magazine* has taken a specific stance with respect to Scots from the late 1990s: it carries regular articles on Scots and has at least one piece entirely in Scots (though not in a very dense variety) in every issue. Smaller local newspapers sometimes carry small pieces in Scots; for a while in 1997 the *Perthshire Advertiser* sported a weekly column in Scots, though in other smaller papers the use of Scots is at best sporadic.

The tabloids tend to use Scots only in humorous contexts and even that is rare, though it has become slightly more frequent over the last decade. In the case of the Sunday newspapers, apart from the *Sunday Post* cartoons, the use of Scots is again very sporadic, perhaps because the target audience of the indigenous papers tends to be very middle class. Occasionally, particular journalists make a point of supporting Scots, as was the case with Dorothy Grace-Elder, now a MSP, who used to be a columnist for the *Scotland on Sunday*.

One area illustrating the increasing use of Scots has been in the letters pages. Most of the letters published in Scots are from well-known language activists. In some cases, newspapers have actually started to restrict the number of Scots letters published, despite the growing amount of such material submitted.

Scots fares better in literary journals such as *Chapman* and *Cencrastus* and is used throughout in the magazine of the SLS, *Lallans*, published since 1973.

9.5.2 *Radio and television*

Scotland has had a fair share in the development of radio/TV, but owing to the centralization of the BBC in London, regional coverage was not as prominent as it might have been. As regards the language used, up to the 1940s the firm belief in the preferability of 'BBC English' left little room for local dialects, outside informal, chatty or humorous productions. Attitudes have eased a great deal since 1945, especially over the last two decades, and local accents are common now. From the mid-1990s, BBC Radio Scotland has even been following a deliberate policy of implementing distinctly Scottish voices, and while there seems to be no cohesive policy among commercial radio producers, in regions where Scots itself is strong (e.g. Fife, Aberdeenshire, Dundee and the Borders), the use of local Scottish accents is the rule. In call-in shows the presenter will even switch to Scots dialect, if prompted by the callers. Elsewhere, there has been little room for Scots. Radio plays in Scots, poetry and story readings and Burns Night's programmes are occasionally produced, but there has as yet been no attempt, however experimental, to expand the functions into new genres. The modern uses of Low German which is now even found in Radio Bremen's international news could have served as an example – whether we wish to evaluate this extension as a success or not.

However, even positive decisions for an extended use of Scots in the media would automatically raise the question of 'which' Scots. There *is* a great deal of Glaswegian on radio and TV (not only when local derbies of the two major soccer teams are reported). A discussion on "Future for the Doric", broadcast on Radio Scotland, 29 April 1993, showed the almost unanimous consent of the audience to increase the share for NE Scots – but the 'dialect speakers' demanding such an extension spoke with very broad accents, while having almost no traces of NE lexis left in their speech. It is quite clear that an alternative decision in favour of broadcasts in Lallans would meet with little support in Scotland.

The attitudes of television channels towards Scots have been very varied over the past few years. The BBC and Channel 4 have shown a greater commitment to the use of Scots than the Scottish Media Group's Scottish and Grampian stations, which is surprising given the latter's historic support of the NE Scots in its own area. Border Television, which covers both sides of the English/Scottish Border, seems to refrain totally from reflecting the local speech of either part of their audience. Despite this situation, some programmes, especially on the national channels, such as Billy Kay's *Scots: The Mither Tongue* (1986), concentrate on the use of Scots and they have been followed by educational programmes, involving the serious use of various types of authentic dialect speech. Other shows, however, have been at best patronising and were – at worst – considered offensive in their portrayal of Scots, as if taking it seriously would mark the presenters as in some way inferior. Comedy programmes make much use of Scots, and have always done so, often, but not necessarily, in the caricaturish and stereotyping vein found in the much discussed *Rab C. Nesbit* series, the 1960s *Parliamo Glasgow* sketches or Billy Connolly's shows in the 1970s. Scots drama on television (as on radio) is dominated by the Glaswegian variety.

Throughout the 1990s there has been a steady increase in the use of Scots in advertising in all the media. This is not at all restricted to advertising for specifically Scottish articles, such as malt whisky. There is, however, a tendency for this to be humorous, involving witty plays on words, etc. – but that is in line with the general approach of advertising in Britain.

9.6   *Outlook*

Scots has been proclaimed a dying language for many centuries from Boswell in 1764, Pinkerton in 1786 via Stevenson in 1887 to, no doubt, many more pessimistic observers in the year 2000. However, in many respects, it is more alive than most observers would have thought possible. But the writing on the wall has been there for all to see, and since national identity has not generally been connected with linguistic separateness in Scotland, and certainly not with Lowland Scots, the sociolinguistic drift points to a further erosion of the *auld leid*. This does not make the rich tradition a less stimulating topic to investigate for the historical linguist, but it will give the traditional dialectologist less scope for research (as has widely happened in Europe). Since urban varieties are, by contrast, certain to thrive, there will be more than enough compensation for linguists by concentrating on synchronic sociolinguistic analysis.

10   *Texts*

The selection of texts is intended to represent many different genres from various periods of the history of the Scots language. The texts are to serve as examples of the grammatical features described in the first part of this book, as well as to support my account of the changing attitudes and the external history of the language. For more comprehensive analyses of many of the older authors or grammatical and stylistic aspects of Scots in its various stages of development readers are advised to turn to editions of the STS. McCordick (1996) provides a large selection of texts, but these are obviously modernized and therefore not adequate for philological descriptions. I have tried to base the excerpts here chosen on original versions and scholarly editions; the sources are mentioned, together with a few introductory remarks on authors, language and the relevance of the text chosen. The limited space available made it impossible to provide as comprehensive a range of texts as I would have wished; where cuts had to be made I have also sadly done without texts easily available in anthologies and collected works – the virtual absence of texts by Burns is such a case. MacDiarmid was, alas, impossible to include. To a certain extent the selection was also determined by the willingness of publishers to give me copyright permission. In a small number of cases, I was not able to trace the copyright holders; I would like to apologise to them and hope they would have granted their permission for my project, if I had been able to contact them.

T1 BARBOUR, John, *The Bruce* (1375-77)

John Barbour (c1320-1395) – scholar and poet – was Archdeacon of Aberdeen (1357-1395), but it is not clear where he was born. His long patriotic epic The Bruce is the first extant substantial poem in Scots. His Brut and Stewartis Original are lost; the Legends of the Saints were erroneously ascribed to him.

     The excerpts illustrate two text-types: the prologue which reflects on the narrative process and ideal contents of narrative texts, and the heroic poem itself. The second extract describes the oppressions of the Scottish populace under English occupation and contains the famous passage on freedom.

Source: John Barbour, *The Bruce*, [1375-77], eds. Matthew P. McDiarmid & James A.C. Stevenson, Edinburgh: STS, 1980, vol.II, pp.1-2 (ll.1-36), pp.8-10 (ll.178-240).

   Storys to rede ar delitabill
   Suppos þat þai be nocht bot fabill,
   Þan suld storys þat suthfast wer
   And þai war said on gud maner
5 Hawe doubill plesance in heryng.
   Þe fyrst plesance is þe carpyng,
   And þe toþer þe suthfastnes
   Þat schawys þe thing rycht as it wes,
   And suth thyngis þe ar likand
10 Tyll mannys heryng ar plesand.
   Þarfor I wald fayne set my will
   Giff my wyt mycht suffice þartill
   To put in wryt a suthfast story
   Þat it lest ay furth in memory
15 Swa þat na tyme of lenth it let
   Na ger it haly be for ʒet.
   For auld storys þat men redys
   Representis to þaim þe dedys
   Of stalwart folk þat lywyt ar
20 Rycht as þai þan in presence war.
   And certis þai suld weill hawe prys
   Þat in þar tyme war wycht and wys,
   And led þar lyff in gret trawaill,
   And oft in hard stour off bataill
25 Wan gret price off chewalry
   And war woydyt off cowardy,
   As wes king Robert off Scotland
   Þat hardy wes off hart and hand,
   And gud schyr Iames off Douglas
30 Þat in his tyme sa worthy was
   Þat off hys price & hys bounte

In ser landis renownyt wes he.
   Off þaim I thynk þis buk to ma,
   Now God gyff grace þat I may swa
35 Tret it and bryng it till endyng
   Þat I say nocht bot suthfast thing. (...)

   Quhen Schyr Edward þe mychty king
   Had on þis wys done his likyng
   Off Ihone þe Balleoll, þat swa sone
40 Was all defawtyt & wndone,
   To Scotland went he þan in hy,
   And all þe land gan occupy
   Sa hale þat bath castell & toune
   War in-till his possessioune
45 [Fra Weik anent Orknay]
   To Mullyr snwk in Gallaway,
   And stuffyt all with Inglis-men.
   Schyrreffys and bail ʒheys maid he þen,
   And alkyn oþer officeris
50 Þat for to gowern land afferis
   He maid off Inglis nation,
   Þat worthyt þan sa rych fellone
   And sa wykkyt and cowatous
   And swa hawtane and dispitous
55 Þat Scottis-men mycht do na thing
   Þat euer mycht pleys to þar liking.
   Þar wyffis wald þai oft forly
   And þar dochtrys dispitusly
   And gyff ony of þaim þar-at war wrath
60 Þai watyt hym wele with gret scaith
   For þai suld fynd sone enchesone

To put hym to destruccione.
And gyff þat ony man þaim by
Had ony thing þat wes worthy,
65 As hors or hund or oþer thing
Þat war plesand to þar liking,
With rycht or wrang it have wald þai,
And gyf ony wald þaim withsay
Þai suld swa do þat þai suld tyne
70 Oþir land or lyff or leyff in pyne,
For þai dempt þaim efter þar will,
Takand na kep to rycht na skill.
A quhat þai dempt þaim felonly,
For gud knychtis þat war worthy
75 For litill enchesoune or þan nane
Þai hangyt be þe nekbane.
[Alas] þat folk þat euer wes fre,
And in fredome wount for to be,
Throw þar gret myschance and foly
80 War tretyt þan sa wykkytly

Þat þar fays þar iugis war,
Quhat wrechitnes may man have mar.
A, fredome is a noble thing,
Fredome mays man to haiff liking,
85 Fredome all solace to man giffis,
He levys at es þat frely levys.
A noble hart may haiff nane es
Na ellys nocht þat may him ples
Gyff fredome fail ȝhe, for fre liking
90 Is ȝharnyt our all oþer thing.
Na he þat ay has levyt fre
May nocht knaw weill þe propyrte
Þe angyr na þe wrechyt dome
Þat is cowplyt to foule thyrldome,
95 Bot gyff he had assayit it.
Þan all perquer he suld it wyt,
And suld think fredome mar to prys
Þan all þe gold in warld þat is.

T2 BLIND HARY, *Wallace* (1470s)

Blind Hary (c1440-c1495), since the 19th century also known as "Henry the Minstrel", was a travelling story-teller, though apparently well-educated, possibly from Linlithgow district. His heroic poem *Wallace* tells the story of this national hero during the Wars of Independence from a nationalist perspective (hostile comment on the pro-English drift of James III's policy).

The excerpt is from the very end of the book. It reflects on narration, claims that the story is true and taken from a Latin source. According to the traditional 'modesty formula', the author claims that he is "a burell man".

Source: Blind Hary, *Wallace*, [1470s], in: Matthew P. McDiarmid (ed.), *Hary's Wallace*, Edinburgh: STS, 1969, vol.II, pp.121-3 (Book XII, ll.1410-64).

(...) Off Wallace lyff quha has a forthar feill
May schaw furth mair with wit and eloquence;
5 For I to this has done my diligence,
Eft*ir* the pruff geyffyn fra the Latyn buk
Quhilk maist*er* Blayr in his tym wnd*yr*tuk,
In fayr Latyn compild it till ane end.
10 With thir witnes the mair is to *com*mend.
Byschop Synclar, than lord was off Dunkell,
He gat this buk and *con*fermd it him sell
15 For werray trew; thar-off he had no dreid,
Him selff had seyn gret part off Wallace deid.
His purpos was till haue send it to Rom,
20 Our fad*yr* off kyrk th*ar*on to gyff his dom.
Bot maist*er* Blayr and als Schir Thomas Gray,
Eft*er* Wallace thai lestit mony day;

25 Thir twa knew best off gud schir Wil
    ȝhamys deid
    Fra sextene ȝer quhill nyne and twentie
    ȝeid.

    Thocht this mater be no*cht* till all
30 plesance,
    His suthfast deid was worthi till awance.
    All worthi men at redys this rurall dyt,
    Blaym no*cht* the buk, set I be wn*per*fyt.
    I suld hawe thank, sen I no*cht* *tra*waill
35 spard.
    For my laubour na man hecht me
    reward.
    Na charge I had off king nor oth*ir* lord.
    Gret harm, I thocht, his gud deid suld be
40 smord.
    I haiff said her ner as the proces gais
    And fen ȝeid no*cht* for frendschip nor
    for fais.
    Costis herfor was no ma*n* bond to me.
45 In this sentence I had na will to le.
    Bot in als mekill as I rahersit no*cht*
    Sa worthely as nobill Wallace wro*cht*,
    Bot in a poynt I grant I said amys.
    Thir twa kny*cht*is suld blamyt be for
50 this:
    The kny*cht* Wallas, off Cragge ry*cht*wys
    lord,
    And Liddaill als, gert me mak wrang

    record.
55 On Allyrtoun mur the croun he tuk a day
    To get battaill, as myn autour will say.
    Thir twa gert me say that ane oth*ir* wys.
    Till mayst*er* Blayr we did sumpart off
    dispys.

60 Go nobill buk, fulfillyt off gud sentens,
    Suppos thow be baran off Eloquens.
    Go worthi buk fullfillit off suthfast deid,
    Bot in langage off help thow has greit
    neid.
65 Quhen gud makaris rang weill in-to
    Scotland
    Gret harm was it that nane off thaim the
    fand.
    ȝeit th*ar* is part th*at* can the weill
70 awance.
    Now byd thi tym and be a reme*m*brance.
    I ȝow besek off ȝour ben*e*uolence,
    Quha will no*cht* low lak n*o*cht my
    Eloquence.
75 It is weill knawin I am a burell man.
    For her is said als gudly as I can.
    My spreyt felis na t*er*mys of P*er*nase.
    Now besek god th*at* gyffar is of grace,
    Maide hell and erd and set the hewyn
80 abuff,
    That he ws grant off his der lestand luff.

T3   HENRYSON, Robert, *The Testament of Cresseid* (late 15th cent.)

Robert Henryson (c1420-1500) was a poet, teacher of law (possibly at the university of Glasgow about 1462) and later schoolmaster at Dumfermline; one of the 15C makars. Works: *The Testament of Cresseid* (a continuation of Chaucer's Troilus and Criseyde); *The Morall Fabillis of Esope*.

    The excerpt is from the beginning of the narrative poem. It reflects on the narrative process, praises Chaucer's work and relates how and why he started writing this poem (topos, cf. James I above).

Source: Robert Henryson, "*The Testament of Cresseid*" [late 15th cent.], in: Harvey, H. Wood, ed. *The Poems and Fables of Robert Henryson, Schoolmaster of Dunfermline*. Edinburgh: Oliver & Boyd, 1958, pp.106-7 (ll.36-70).

THE TESTAMENT OF CRESSEID

(...) I mend the fyre and beikit me about,
Than tuik ane drink, my spreitis to comfort,
5 And armit me weill fra the cauld thairout:
To cut the winter nicht and mak it schort,
I tuik ane Quair, and left all uther sport,
10 Writtin be worthie Chaucer glorious,
Of fair Creisseid, and worthie Troylus.

And thair I fand, efter that Diomeid
Ressavit had that Lady bricht of hew,
How Troilus neir out of wit abraid,
15 And weipit soir with visage paill of hew;
For quhilk wanhope his teiris can renew
Quhill Esperus rejoisit him agane,
Thus quhyle in Joy he levit, quhyle in pane.

20 Of hir behest he had greit comforting,
Traisting to Troy that scho suld mak retour,
Quhilk he desyrit maist of eirdly thing

Forquhy scho was his only Paramour.
25 Bot quhen he saw passit baith day and hour
Of hir ganecome, than sorrow can oppres
His wofull hart in cair and hevines.

30 Of his distres me neidis nocht reheirs,
For worthie Chauceir in the samin buik
In gudelie termis and in Joly veirs
Compylit hes his cairis, quha will luik.
To brek my sleip ane uther quair I tuik,
35 In quhilk I fand the fatall destenie
Of fair Creisseid, that endit wretchitlie.

Quha wait gif all that Chauceir wrait was trew?
Nor I wait nocht gif this narratioun
40 Be authoreist, or fenyeit of the new
Be sum Poeit, throw his Inventioun,
Maid to report the Lamentatioun
And wofull end of this lustie Creisseid,
And quhat distres scho thoillit, and
45 quhat deid.

T4 DUNBAR, William and KENNEDY, Walter, *The Flyting* (c1500)

This contest of abuse voices the antagonism of Lowlander and Highlander, illustrating the prejudice that Highlanders are dirty, poor – and bards. Kennedy's criticism is levelled against the bookish university man, sympathetic to the English. The wealth of abuse documents a great number of non-standard items not recorded in other text types; some of the words may well have been created ad-hoc.
Source: Priscilla Bawcutt, ed. *The Poems of William Dunbar*, 2 vols. Glasgow: Association for Scottish Literary Studies, 1998:201-3 (the entire poem runs to 554 lines).

Quod Kennedy to Dumbar
Dirtin Dumbar, quhome on blawis thow thy boist, (25)
Pretendand the to wryte sic skaldit skrowis;
Ramowd rebald, thow fall doun att the roist,
5 My laureat lettres at the and I lowis;
Mandrag, mymmerkin, maid maister bot in mows,
Thrys scheild trumpir with ane threidbair goun,
Say, '*Deo mercy*', or I cry the doun,
And leif thy ryming, rebald, and thy rowis.

10 Dreid, dirtfast dearch, that thow hes dissobeyit
My cousing Quintene and my commissar.
Fantastik fule, trest weill thow salbe fleyit.
Ignorant elf, aip, owll irregular,
Skaldit skaitbird, and commoun skamelar;
15 Wanfukkit funling, that Natour maid ane yrle,
Baith Iohine the Ros and thow sall squeill and skirle,
And evir I heir ocht of ʒour making mair.

Heir I put sylence to the in al pairtis.
Obey and ceis the play that thow pretendis,
20 Waik walidrag, and werlot of the cairtis,
Se sone thow mak my commissar amendis
And lat him lay sax leichis on thy lendis,
Meikly in recompansing of thi scorne,
Or thow sall ban the tyme that thow wes borne,
25 For Kennedy to the this cedull sendis.

Quod Dumbar to Kennedy
Iersche brybour baird, wyle beggar with thy brattis,
Cuntbittin crawdoun, Kennedy, coward of kynd,
Evill farit and dryit, as Densmen on the rattis,
30 Lyk as the gleddis had on thy gulesnowt dynd,
Mismaid monstour, ilk mone owt of thy mynd,
Renunce, rebald, thy rymyng, thow bot royis.
Thy trechour tung hes tane ane Heland strynd;
Ane Lawland ers wald mak a bettir noyis.

35 Revin, raggit ruke, and full of rebaldrie,
Skitterand scorpioun, scauld in scurrilitie,
I se the haltane in thy harlotrie.
And in to vthir science no thing slie,
Off every vertew woyd, as men may sie.
40 Quytclame clergie and cleik to the ane club,
Ane baird blasphemar in brybrie ay to be,
For wit and woisdome ane wisp fra the may rub.

Thow speiris, dastard, gif I dar with the fecht.
ʒe, Dagone, dowbart, thairof haif thow no dowt.
45 Quhair evir we meit, thairto my hand I hecht,
To red thy rebald ryming with a rowt.
Throw all Bretane it salbe blawin owt,
How that thow, poysonit pelour, gat thy paikis.

With ane doig leich I schepe to gar the schowt
50 And nowther to the tak knyfe, swerd nor aix.

Thow crop and rute of tratouris tressonable,
The fathir and moder of morthour and mischeif,
Dissaitfull tyrand, with serpentis tung vnstable,
Cukcald, cradoun, cowart, and commoun theif,
55 Thow purpest for to vndo our lordis cheif
In Paislay, with ane poysone that wes fell,
For quhilk, brybour, ʒit sall thow thoill a breif.
Pelour, on the I sall it preif my sell.

Thocht I wald lie, thy frawart phisnomy
60 Dois manifest thy malice to all men;
Fy, tratour theif, fy, Ganʒelon, fy, fy!
Fy, feyndly front far fowlar than ane fen,
My freyindis thow reprovit with thy pen.
Thow leis, tratour, quhilk I sall on the preif,
65 Suppois thy heid war armit tymis ten,
Thow sall recry it, or thy croun sall cleif.

T5 DUNBAR, William, *Lament for the Makaris* (c1505)

William Dunbar (c1460-1520) was probably born in East Lothian, and possibly a student at St Andrews 1477-79, court poet from 1500, perhaps the most varied and creative of the Makars. His subject matter is wideranging and his mastery of stanza form and rhyme schemes noteworthy. Works: *The Flyting of Dunbar and Kennedy* (T4); *The Tretis of the Twa Mariit Wemen and the Wedo*; various satires, religious poems and aureate allegories. The text is a memorial to the dead makars of Scotland and England. It is of particular importance because it refers to various poets and thereby helps with the dating of their works.

Source: William Dunbar, "Lament for the Makaris" [c1505], in: W. Mackay Mackenzie, ed. *The Poems of William Dunbar*. London: Faber & Faber, 1932, pp.20-3.

LAMENT FOR THE MAKARIS
"Quhen He Wes Sek"

I that in heill wes and gladnes,
Am trublit now with gret seiknes,
And feblit with infermite;
    Timor mortis conturbat me.

5 Our plesance heir is all vane glory,
This fals warld is bot transitory,
The flesche is brukle, the Fend is sle;
    Timor mortis conturbat me.

The stait of man dois change and vary,
10 Now sound, now seik, now blith, now sary,
Now dansand mery, now like to dee;
    Timor mortis conturbat me.

No stait in erd heir standis sickir;
As with the wynd wavis the wickir,
15 Wavis this warldis vanite;
    Timor mortis conturbat me.

On to the ded gois all Estatis,
Princis, Prelotis, and Potestatis,
Baith riche and pur of al degre;
20   *Timor mortis conturbat me.*

He takis the knychtis in to feild,
Anarmit under helme and scheild;
Victour he is at all mellie;
    Timor mortis conturbat me.

25 That strang unmercifull tyrand
Takis, on the moderis breist sowkand,
The bab full of benignite;
    Timor mortis conturbat me.

He takis the campion in the stour,
30 The capitane closit in the tour,
The lady in bour full of bewte;
    Timor mortis conturbat me.

He sparis no lord for his piscence,
Na clerk for his intelligence;
35 His awfull strak may no man fle;
    Timor mortis conturbat me.

Art-magicianis, and astrologgis,
Rethoris, logicianis, and theologgis,
Thame helpis no conclusionis sle;
40   *Timor mortis conturbat me.*

In medicyne the most practicianis,
Lechis, surrigianis, and phisicianis,
Thame self fra ded may not supple;
    Timor mortis conturbat me.

45 I se that makaris amang the laif
Playis heir ther pageant, syne gois to
    graif;
Sparit is nocht ther faculte;
    Timor mortis conturbat me.

He hes done petuously devour,
50 The noble Chaucer, of makaris flour,
the Monk of Bery, and Gower, all thre;
    Timor mortis conturbat me.

The gude Syr Hew of Eglintoun,
And eik Heryot, and Wyntoun,
55 He hes tane out of this cuntre;
    Timor mortis conturbat me.

That scorpion fell hes done infek
Maister Johne Clerk, and James Afflek,

Fra balat making and tragidie;
60   *Timor mortis conturbat me.*

Holland and Barbour he hes berevit;
Allace! that he nocht with us levit
Schir Mungo Lokert of the Le;
    Timor mortis conturbat me.

65 Clerk of Tranent eik he hes tane,
That maid the Anteris of Gawane;
Schir Gilbert Hay endit hes he;
    Timor mortis conturbat me.

He hes Blind Hary and Sandy Traill
70 Slaine with his schour of mortall haill,
Quhilk Patrik Johnestoun myght nocht fle;
    Timor mortis conturbat me.

He hes reft Merseir his endite,
That did in luf so lifly write,
75 So schort, so quyk, of sentence hie;
    Timor mortis conturbat me.

He has tane Roull of Aberdene,
And gentill Roull of Corstorphin;
Two bettir fallowis did no man se;
80   *Timor mortis conturbat me.*

In Dumfermelyne he hes done roune
With Maister Robert Henrisoun;
Schir Johne the Ros enbrast hes he;
    Timor mortis conturbat me.

85 And he hes now tane, last of aw,
Gud gentill Stobo and Quintyne Schaw,
Of quham all wichtis hes pete:
    Timor mortis conturbat me.

Gud Maister Walter Kennedy
90 In poynt of dede lyis veraly,
Gret reuth it wer that so suld be;
    Timor mortis conturbat me.

Sen he hes all my brether tane,
He will nocht lat me lif alane,
95 On forse I man his nyxt pray be;
    Timor mortis conturbat me.

Sen for the deid remeid is none,
Best is that we for dede dispone,
Eftir our deid that lif may we;
    Timor mortis conturbat me.

T6 DOUGLAS, Gavin, *Virgil's Aeneid* (1515)

Gavin Douglas (c1474-1522), a poet, probably born in East Lothian and a student at St Andrews university, 1490-94, was born into a powerful family. He enjoyed court patronage all his life, held various church offices (Bishop of Dunkeld in 1515) and after involvement in political disputes died in exile in London. Douglas was the most learned of the Makars. Works: *The Palice of Honour* and the first Anglic translation of Virgil's epic, *The XIII Bukes of Eneados*, the most sustained long poem of quality of the time "writtin in the language of Scottis natioun" (I.103). Each of the 13 books is prefaced by an original prologue.

The excerpts are from the beginning of the work: an address to the reader and a prologue explaining that and why Douglas uses Scots: to widen the range of Scots, to communicate to a larger audience and to provide a contemporary means of understanding Virgil's poem. Furthermore it demonstrates which linguistic difficulties he encountered because of this choice and compares Scots and Latin.
Source: Gavin Douglas, *Virgil's Aeneid*. Translated into Scottish Verse, [1515], ed. David F.C.
    Coldwell, Edinburgh: STS, 1957 ('1972), vol.II, p.6-7 (ll.105-43), p.12-3 (ll.339-72).

(...) Quhat so it be, this buke I dedicait,
Writtin in the langage of Scottis natioun,
And thus I mak my protestatioun.
Fyrst I protest, beaw schirris, be ȝour leif,
5 Beis weill avisit my wark or ȝhe repreif,
Consider it warly, reid oftar than anys;
Weill at a blenk sle poetry nocht tayn is,
And ȝit forsuyth I set my bissy pane
As that I couth to mak it braid and plane,
10 Kepand na sudron bot our awyn langage,
And spekis as I lernyt quhen I was page.
Nor ȝit sa cleyn all sudron I refuß,
Bot sum word I pronunce as nyghtbouris doys:
Lyke as in Latyn beyn Grew termys sum,
15 So me behufyt quhilum or than be dum
Sum bastard Latyn, French or Inglys oyß
Quhar scant was Scottis – I had nane other choys.
Nocht for our tong is in the selwyn skant
Bot for that I the fowth of langage want
20 Quhar as the cullour of his properte
To kepe the sentens tharto constrenyt me,
Or than to mak my sayng schort sum tyme,
Mair compendyus, or to lykly my ryme.
(...) Besyde Latyn our langage is imperfite
25 Quhilk in sum part is the cauß and the wyte
Quhy that of Virgillis verß the ornate bewte
Intill our tung may nocht obseruyt be,
For thar be Latyn wordis mony ane
That in our leyd ganand translatioun haß nane
30 Less than we mynyß thar sentens and grauyte
And ȝit scant weill exponyt. Quha trewys nocht me,
Lat thame interprit "animal" and "homo"

T7 THE CHANCELLOR AND THRIE ESTATIS, *Letter to Henry VIII* (1522)

The official letter is a reply to an ultimatum. In 1522 (new style), i.e. not yet nine years after Flodden (1513), James V was still a minor and Scotland was governed by Scottish nobles (Lord Albany as the Governor, James Beaton as the Chancellor) opposing an English Queen Mother, Margaret. The strong alliance with France allowed Scotland to defy England, and resist Henry VIII's demands.

Source: *The Chancellor and Thrie Estatis of the Realme of Scotland*, "Letter to Henry VIII" [1522], repr. in: George Bruce and Paul H. Scott, eds. *A Scottish Postbag. Eight Centuries of Scottish Letters*. Edinburgh: Chambers, 1986, p.4 (source: Agnes Mure Mackenzie & James Kinsley, eds. *A Garland of Scottish Prose,* Edinburgh: Grant, 1956, p.153).

To Henry VIII   Edinburgh 11 February 1522

(...) Giff this your Querell be Just or Resonable God be the Juge, sen it may be na better, for we have alwais desirit and desiris to leiff with your Grace in gude Amyte and Pece, giff We may have it without extreme Inconvenientis. Howbeith
5 We ar resolute that, or We suld consent to do sa grete hurt to *the King* our Soverane Lord and the Common Weill of his Realme, sa grete Dishonour to our selff, and sa grete Wrang to our said *Lord Governour*, as to amove him furth of this Realme and leiff in Divisioun and dailie Truble amang our selff, as this lang tyme bipassit we have done, he being in France; We will with his Presence take
10 our Aventure of Pece or Were as sall pleys God to send it; Assuring Youre Grace that, for the Caus above specifyt, and utheris enew quhilk We sall schaw in tyme and Place, We nouther may nor will at requeist of Youre Grace, nor ony uthir Prince, consent nor suffer in ony maner that oure said *Lord Governour* depart furth of this Realme during the King oure Soverane Lordis Minorite and lesse Age.
15   And giff, for this Cause, We happin to be Invadit, quhat may we do bot tak God to oure gude Querell in Defens, and do as oure Progenitouris and Forbearis has bene Constrenyt to do, for the Conservatioun of this Realme heretofore.
      Geven under oure Soverand Lordis Prive Sele at Edinburgh the xi day of Februare the Yeir of God One Thousand Five Hundred and Twenty one Yeris.
20   Your humble Oratouris and Servandis with all lauthful service
            THE CHANCELLOR AND THRIE ESTATIS OF THE REALME OF SCOTLAND

T8 BELLENDEN, John, *The Chronicles of Scotland* (1531)

John Bellenden (Ballentyne, fl. 1533) was Archdeacon of Moray and canon of Ross. He translated (on the commission of James V) Hector Boethius' *Scotorum historiae* (this translation was used as the basis of the English version by John Harrison in EModE to form Book V of Holinshed's Chronicle of 1582, the form in which the Macbeth story was used by Shakespeare, cf. The excerpts printed in Görlach 1991a). Bellenden also translated Livy's *History of Rome* into straightforward Scots prose.
      The excerpt describes the plot against and murder of King James I in 1437 (the story about the lady-in-waiting is pure invention).

Source: John Bellenden (transl.), *The Chronicles of Scotland*, [1531], compiled by Hector Boece, eds. R.W. Chambers & E.C. Batho. Edinburgh: STS, 1936/41, pp.398-9.

(...) Piperden disconnfist in þis maner, King Iames tuke consultacion with his nobillis quhat was to be done aganis Inglismen, sen þai had violatt þe peace within þe trewis afoir contrackitt; and þerfor be avise of his nobillis he come with ane grete army to Roxburgh. And quhen he had lyin at þe sege of þe samyn, and þe house reddy to be
5 randeritt, þe Qwene come at þe post to þe army, schawand how sindry grete princes of þe realme war conspiritt aganis him. The King, aduerteist of þis conspiracionis, for fere of his life skalitt þe sege, and returnit to Perth. Þe principall of þis coniuracioun was his eme, Walter, Erle of Athoill. This Erle, desyrand to conquess þe croun, persuaditt afoir Duke Robertt, Governour, to slaye þe Duke of Rosaye afoir rehersitt,
10 and siklyke to slaye þe said King Iames his bruþer quhen he was bott Prince of Scottland, howbeit he was be providence of God deliueritt fra his tiranny in Ingland. This Erle of Athoill belevitt, quhen Duke Robert had puttt þame baith doun, to fynd ane new ingyne to haif distroyitt þe said Duke Robertt and his successioun. Becaus Duke Robertis sonnis war all distroyitt be þe Battell of Vernoll and iustice of þe said
15 King Iames, he persuaditt twa pert men, Robert Stewartt, his nepott, and Robertt Grahame. Þis Robert was afoir at þe Kingis horn for sindry grete offencis done be him aganis þe Kingis autorite, and had na thing in mair hattrent þan þe King. And þocht þair tresonabill devise was stoppitt sum thing be interuencioun of þe Qwene, ȝite becaus þe King knew nocht in speciall þe namez of þame quhilkis war on þis
20 wise conspiritt aganis him, he mycht þe less eschew þe tresoun devisitt aganis him. And þairfor þir vnhappy creatouris had þe mair espirance to bring þair cursit purposs to fyne, and come nocht lang eftir to þe Blak Freris of Perth, quhair þe King was lugitt for þe tyme, and corruppitt þe portaris and ischearis in sik maner þat þai gatt enteress in þe Kingis hall, and eftir þat come to þe durris of his invartt chalmer,
25 abyding þe cuming of ane of þe Kingis familiaris, quhilk was participant with þair tresoun, to gett enteress be þe samyn. In þe menetyme ane of þe Kingis seruandis, namytt Walter Stratoun, oppinnytt þe dure to ressaiff þe wyne to þe Kingis collacioun, and quhen he saw þame aufullye arrayitt at þe dure he cryitt "Tresoun!" with ane hiddeous schowte. Nochttheles, he was slayn in defence of þe dure. And in
30 þe menetyme, quhen þai war slayand him, ane ȝoung madyn, namyt Kathren Douglas, quhilk was eftir marijt apoun Alexander Lowell of Ballumby, stekitt þe dure; and becaus þe grete bar was hid awaye be ane tratoure of þair opinioun, scho schott hir arme in to þe place quhare þe bar suld haif passitt; and becaus scho was bot ȝoung, hir arme was sone brokkin all in schoyndre, and þe dure dongin vp be force,
35 throw quhilk þai enteritt and slew þe King with mony terribill woundis, and þe Quene hurtt. The remanent of his seruandis returnit at last in þe chalmer, and fand þe King bullerand in his blude, and ane Patrik Dunbar, bruþer to George, vmquhile Erle of Marche, left for dede in þe chalmer in his defence. (...)

T9   GAU, John, *The Richt Vay to the Kingdom of Heuine* (c1533)

John Gau (early 1490s-1553) was born possibly in Perth and (c1509-11) a student at the university of St Andrews; then he was as a Reformer exiled to Malmö (then under Danish rule) and moved to Copenhagen, where he died. *The Richt Vay to the Kingdom of Heuine* is the "first treatise in exposition and defence of the Reformed faith which appeared in the Scottish tongue" (Mitchell, xi). The catechetical treatise in prose form addressed at the laity is a translation of a Danish work from 1531.
    The excerpt represents the Lord's Prayer with a short introduction.
Source: John Gau, *The Richt Vay to the Kingdom of Heuine*, [c1533], ed. A.F. Mitchell, Edinburgh: STS, 1888, (ʳ1968), p.82.

Heir efter folouis the pater noster vith ane schort declaratione apone the same
The disciplis desirit at our lord Iesus Christ to leir thaime to pray (as Ihone did his disciplis) as S. Luc writis in his xi chaiptur in the quhilk ca. he techit thayme quhat thay suld pray and quhow thay suld persiueir and be constant in prayer / alsua he
5 techit thayme quhow thay suld pray and quat thay suld pray quhen he prechit the sueit sermond to thayme apone the montane (as S. Mathew vritis in his vi chaiptur) sayand quhen ze pray ze sal notht haiff mony vordis as ye paganis dwis for thay trow to be hard for thair mony vordis quhairfor ze sal notht dw as thay dw for zour fader in the heuine knawis quhat ze mister or ze desir ony thinge of hyme quhairfor ze sal
10 pray swa * Our fader thow quhilk is in ye heuine / thy nayme mot be hallowit / thy kingdome mot cum (to vsz) thy wil mot be dwne in ye zeird as it is in the heuine giff wsz this day our dailie breid / and forgiff wsz our dettis as we forgiff our dettours / and leid vsz notht in temptatione bot deliuer vsz fra ewil Amen / Heir off our Iesus Christis aune vordis ve leir quhow and quhat ve sal pray / the quhilk ii thingis ar
15 neidful to wsz to knaw.   *Quhou ve suld pray*   We sal noth haiff mony vordis bot we suld haiff our hart and thocht apone that quhilk we pray / ye fewer vordis ve haif ye prayer is ye better / and ye may vordis ve haiff without ye hart thairapone ye prayer is ye var / few vordis vith ane ardent desir of ye hart is ane crissine prayer mony vordis vith ye mwtht vithout ye hart is ane paganis prayier / quhairfor our lord said ze
20 sal notht haiff mony vordis.

T10   WEDDERBURN, Robert, *The Complaynt of Scotland* (1549)

Robert Wedderburn (c1500-1557), born in Dundee, was a student at St Andrews University, then a priest, later Reformer, and exiled to Germany (Wittenberg). Robert was the youngest of the three brothers who compiled the Gude and Godlie Ballatis. His authorship of the Complaynt is not generally accepted. *The Complaynt of Scotland* is a political treatise in the form of a dream allegory in which Dame Scotia calls upon her three sons (the Three Estates) to account for the divisiveness that has racked Scotland, to band together against England, and to advocate support for the auld alliance.
    The excerpts are from the Dedicatory Epistle, and the Prologue to the Reader, in which the author defends the use of Scots as a literary language – illustrated by his own work – rejecting the conventional Latin.
Source: [Robert Wedderburn], *The Complaynt of Scotland*, [1549], ed. A.M. Stewart, Edinburgh: STS, 1979, pp.1-2, 5-6, 12-4.

To the Excellent, Ande Illvstir Marie queen of Scotlande, the Margareit ande Perle of Princessis.

The immortal gloir, that procedis be the rycht lyne of vertu, fra ʒour magnanime
auansing of the public veil, of the affligit realme of scotlande, is abundantly dilatit
athort al cuntreis, throucht the quhilk, the precius germe of ʒour nobilite, bringis
nocht furtht alanerly, branchis and tendir leyuis of vertu: bot as veil it bringis furtht,
5 salutiffere & hoilsum frute of honour quhilk is ane immortal ande supernatural
medicyne, to cure & to gar conuallesse, al the langorius desolat & affligit pepil,
quhilkis ar al mast disparit of mennis supple, ande reddy to be venquest & to be cum
randrit, in the subiection ande captiuite, of our mortal ald enemeis, be rason that ther
cruel inuasions, aperis to be onremedabil. The special cause of our afflictione, hes
10 procedit, of thre vehement plagis, quhilk hes al maist succumbit oure cuntre in final
euertione that is to saye, the cruele inuasions of oure ald enemeis, the vniuersal
pestilens ande mortalite, that hes occurit mercyles amang the pepil: ande the
contentione of diuerse of the thre estaitis of scotland, throucht the quhilk thre plagis,
the vniuersal pepil ar be cum distitute of iustice policie ande of al verteus bysynes of
15 body ande saul. Ande nou illustir princes engendrit of magnanime genoligie, &
discendit of Royal progenituris, ʒour regement ande gouernyng, ande alse ʒour
honorabil amplitude of verteouse dignite incressis daly, in the contenual auansing of
the deffens of oure cuntre quhar for ʒour heroyque vertu, is of mair admiratione, nor
vas of valeria the dochtir of the prudent consul publicola or of cloelia, lucresia,
20 penolope, cornelia, semiramis, thomaris, penthasillie, or of ony vthir verteouse lady
that plutarque or bocchas hes discriuit, to be in perpetual memore. for al thair nobil
actis ar nocht to be comparit to the actis that ʒour prudens, garris daly be exsecut,
contrar the cruel volfis of ingland. The quhilkz volffis are nocht the rauand sauuage
volffis of strait montanis ande vyild fforrestis that deuoris nolt ande scheip for ther
25 pray: bot rather tha ar dissaitful volfis quhilkis hes euir been oure ald enemeis. (...)
Thir vailʒeant actis of ʒour predecessours (illustir princes) ande ʒour grit prudens,
makkis manifest, that ʒour grace is ane rycht nobil, baytht of vertu ande of genoligie.
al thir thingis befor rehersit, i beand summond be institutione of ane gude zeil, hes
tane ane temerare consait, to present to ʒour nobil grace, ane tracteit of the fyrst
30 laubir of my pen bot ʒit i vas lang stupefact ande timide, for falt of ane peremptoir
conclusione, i nocht heffand ane perfyte determinatione, of quhat purpos or mater
that var maist necessair ande honest to be dilatit: than dredour ande schame beand
repulsit fra my melancolius cogitations, i began to reuolue the librarye of my
vndirstanding, ande i socht all the secreit corneris of my gazophile, ymaginant vitht
35 in the cabinet of my interior thochtis, that ther var na mater mair conuenient ande
necessair, for this present dolorus tyme, nor to reherse the cause ande occasione of
the onmersiful afflictione of the desolat realme of scotland. the quhilk desolatione
hes occurrit be the mischance, of fureous mars, that hes violently ocupeit the
domicillis of tranquil pace that sueit goddes of humaine felicite. the quhilk tracteit i
40 hef dediet ande direckyt to ʒour nobil grace, in hope that ʒour grace vil resaue it as

humainly, as it var ane riche present of grit consequens. it vas the custom of perse,
that none of the subiectis durst cum in the presens of ther kyng, bot gyf tha brocht
sum gyft or present, to be delyurit til hym, efferand for ther qualite. the
historigraphours, rehersis of ane pure man of perse, quha be chance renconntrit kyng
45 darius. this pure man throucht grit pouerte, hed no thyng to present tyll his kyng,
efftir the custum of perse, quhar for he ran til ane reueire that ran neir by, & brocht
the palmis of his handis ful of that fresche vattir to the kyng for ane present. that
nobil kyng, persauand the gude vil ande hartly obediens of this pure man, he resauit
that litil quantite of cleen vattir as humainly, as it hed been ane riche present of gold,
50 ande he gart delyuir to the said pure man sex thousand peces of gold. and ane goldin
vattir lauar. fra this exempil cummis ane vlgare adagia, quhilk sais that quhen ane
pure man makkis ane sacrefeis, & throucht his pouerte he vantis ensens to mak the
seremons of his sacrefeis that sacrefeis sal be acceptabil befor the goddis, be cause
that he dois sa mekil, as his pissance maye distribute. (...)

T11 LYNDSAY, David, *Ane Exclamatioun to the Redar* (c1554)

Sir David Lyndsay (c1490-1555), born near Cupar (Fife), was a poet, dramatist and courtier from about
1511 (personal attendant to the young prince, later James V, knighted 1529 and created Lyon King of
Arms and royal ambassador). Though notable for various courtly poems, his fame mainly rests on the
first great Scottish play, *Ane Pleasant Satyre of the Thrie Estaitis* (1540). Because of his vigorous
championship of the rights of the poor, he gained enduring popularity, and continued to be widely read
in Scotland long after Henryson and Dunbar. His "Defense of the Vernacular" (as in Ane Exclamatioun
to the Redar) represents a type of praise of the mother tongue widespread in Renaissance Europe. *Ane
Dialogue Betuix Experience and ane Courteour* – also called *The Monarche* – is Lyndsay's last and
longest poem, which is an amalgam of his philosophy and an apologia pro vita sua.

The excerpt is from the first book of *The Monarche*. It follows after the *Epistle to the Reader*,
the *Prologue* and the first few exchanges between the Courtiour and Experience, defending the use of
the vernacular for a religious text.

Source: Sir David Lyndsay, *Ane Dialogue Betuix Experience and ane Courteour, Off the Miserabyll
Estait of the Warld* [The Monarche], [c1554], in: Douglas Hamer, ed. *The Works of Sir David
Lindsay of the Mount*, Edinburgh: STS, 1931, (ʳ1972), vol.I, pp.215-9, ll.538-631, 663-84.

ANE EXCLAMATIOUN TO THE REDAR,
TWYCHEYNG THE WRYTTYNG OF UULGARE AND MATERNALL LANGUAGE.

Gentyl Redar, haif at me non dispyte,
Thynkand that I presumptuously pretend,
In vulgair toung, so heych mater to writ;
Bot quhair I mys I pray the till amend.
5 Tyll vnlernit I wald the cause wer kend
Off our most miserabyll trauell and torment,
And quhow, in erth, no place bene parmanent.

Quhowbeit that diuers deuote cunnyng Clerkis
In Latyne toung hes wryttin syndrie bukis,

10 Our vnlernit knawis lytill of thare werkis,
   More than thay do the rauyng of the Rukis.
   Quharefore to Colȝearis, Cairtaris & to Cukis,
   To Iok and Thome, my Ryme sall be diractit,
   With cunnyng men quhowbeit it wylbe lactit.

15 (...) Off Languagis the first Diuersytie
   Wes maid the Goddis Maledictioun.
   Quhen Babilone wes beildit in calde,
   Those beildaris gat none vther afflictioun:
   Affore the tyme of that punyssioun
20 Wes bot one toung, quhilk Adam spak hym self,
   Quhare now of toungis thare bene thre score and twelf.

   Nochtwithstandyng, I thynk it gret plesour,
   Quhare cunnyng men hes languagis anew,
   That in thare ȝouth, be deligent laubour,
25 Hes leirnit Latyne, Greik, and ald Hebrew.
   That I am nocht of that sorte sore I rew:
   Quharefore I wald all bukis necessare
   For our faith wer in tyll our toung vulgare.

   (...) Sanct Ierome in his propir toung Romane
30 The Law of God he trewlie did translait,
   Out of Hebrew and Greik, in Latyne plane,
   Quhilk has bene hid frome ws lang tyme, god wait,
   Onto this tyme: bot, efter myne consait,
   Had Sanct Ierome bene borne in tyll Argyle,
35 In to Yrische toung his bukis had done compyle.

   Prudent sanct Paull doith mak narratioun
   Twycheyng the diuers leid of euery land,
   Sayand thare bene more edificatioun
   In fyue wordis that folk doith vnderstand,
40 Nor to pronunce of wordis ten thousand
   In strange langage, sine wait not quhat it menis:
   I thynk sic pattryng is not worth twa prenis. (...)

   The Propheit Dauid, Kyng of Israell,
   Compyld the plesand Psalmes of the Psaltair
45 In his awin propir toung, as I heir tell.
   And Salamone, quhilk wes his sone and air,
   Did mak his buke in tyll his toung vulgare.
   Quhy suld nocht thare sayng be tyll ws schawin
   In our language? I wald the cause wer knawin.

50 Lat Doctoris wrytt thare curious questionis,
   And argumentis sawin full of Sophistrye,
   Thare Logick, and thare heych Opinionis,
   Thare dirk Iugementis of Astronomye,
   Thare Medecyne, and thare Philosophye;
55 Latt Poetis schaw thare glorious Ingyne,
   As euer thay pleis, in Greik or in Latyne;

   Bot lat ws haif the bukis necessare
   To commoun weill, and our Saluatioun,
   Iustlye translatit in our toung Uulgare.
60 And als I mak the Supplicatioun,
   O gentyll Redar, haif none Indignatioun,
   Thynkand I mell me with so hie matair.
   Now to my purpose fordwart wyll I fair.

T12   KNOX, John, *History of the Reformation of Scotland* (1559-66)

John Knox (c1513-72), the Scottish reformer, was born in Haddington, East Lothian, and probably educated at St. Andrews. He became a Protestant in the early 1540s. After imprisonment by the French, he held ecclesiastical positions in England, escaped to the Continent under Mary Tudor, met Calvin at Geneva, and returned to Scotland in 1559, where he became the spiritual leader of a general Protestant revolt. Later he became minister of St. Giles', Edinburgh. Knox always favoured close religious and cultural links with England; his anglicized speech was criticized by some fellow Scotsmen. A Bible in Scots was obviously not his concern. One of his major works, the *History of the Reformation of Scotland in five books*, is a historical and autobiographical account of the principal events of Knox's lifetime and his part in them.

The passage describes a battle between French forces and the Scottish Protestant faction at Leith in late October 1559, when the council and the Catholic/French Queen Regent were fighting for supremacy.

Source: John Knox, *History of the Reformation of Scotland*, Book Second, 1558–1559, [c1559–66], in: David Laing, ed. *The Works of John Knox*, Edinburgh: James Thin, 1854 ('1966), vol.I, 457-9.

(...) It was verray appeiring, that amanges our selfis thair wes some treassoun. For when, upoun the first alarm, all man maid haist for releve of thair brethren, whome in verray deid we mycht have saved, and at least we mycht have saved the ordinance, and have keapt the Cannogait from danger; for we wer anis merched
5 fordwarte with bold curage, but then, (we say,) wes a schowt reased amonges our selfis, (God will discloise the traytouris one day,) affermyng "That the hole Frenche cumpanye war entered in at Leyth Wynd upoun our backis." What clamor and misordour did then suddanelie arryise, we list nott to expresse with multiplicatioun of wordis. The horsemen, and some of those that aught to have putt ordour to otheris,
10 ower-rod thair poore brethren at the enteress of the Netthir Bow. The crye of discomforte arose in the toun; the wicked and malignant blasphemed; the feable, (amanges whome the Justice Clerk, Schir Johne Bannatyne was,) fledd without

mercye: with great difficultie could thei be keapt in at the Weast Porte. Maister
Gavin Hammyltoun cryed with a lowd voce, "Drynk now as ye have browen." The
15 Frenche perceaving, be the clamour of our fray, followed, as said is, to the myddis of
the Cannogait, to no great nomber, bott a twenty or thretty of thair *infantes perdues*.
For in that meantyme the rest reteired thame selves with our ordinance. The Erle of
Ergyle and his men wer the first that stopped the fleying of our men, and compelled
the Porte to be opened efter that it was schoot. Bott in verray deid, Lord Robert
20 Stewarte, Abbot of Halyrudehouse, was the first that isched out. After him followed
many upoun the backis of the Frenche. At last cam my Lord Duck, and then was no
man mair frack nor was Maister Gavin Hammyltoun foirsaid. The Frenche brunt a
baikhouse, and tooke some spuilzie from the poores of the Cannogait. Thei slew a
Papist and dronken preast, named Schir Thomas Sklatter, ane aiged man, a woman
25 geving sowk and her child, and of oure soldiouris to the nomber of ten. Certane wer
tane, amongis whome Capitane Mowat was one, [and] Maister Charles Geddes,
servitour to the Maister of Maxwell.

The Castell that day schot ane schott at the Frenche, declairing thame thairby
freindis to us, and ennemy to thame; bott he suddanelie repented of weall-doing. The
30 Queyn glad of victorye, sat upoun the ramparte to salute and welcome hir victorious
suddartis. One brought a kirtill, one uther ane pettycote, the thrid, a pote or pane; and
of invy more then womanlie lawchtter, sche asked, "Whair bocht ye your ware? *Je
pense que vous l'aves achete sans argent.*" This was the great and motherlie cayre
whiche schee tooke for the truble of the poore subjectis of this realme.

35 The Erle Bothwell, lifted up in his awin conceat, be reassoun of this our
repulse and disconfitour, utterlie refused any restitutioun; and so within two dayis
after was his house spulzeid, in whiche war no thingis of ony great importance, his
evidentis and certaine clothing excepted. Frome that day back, the curage of many
was dejected. With great difficultie could men be reteaned in the towne; yea, some of
40 the greatast estimatioun determined with thame selfis to leave the interpryise.

T13   SKEYNE, Gilbert, *Ane breve descriptiovn of the pest* (1568)

Gilbert Skeyne (or Skene, c1522-99?) was born at Bandodle, Aberdeenshire and educated at
Aberdeen Grammar School and King's College, where he later became Professor of medicine (from
1556). From 1575 he practised in Edinburgh, and in 1581 he was appointed physician to James VI.
He wrote the earliest medical work in Scots published in Scotland. The text illustrates the difficulties of Scots terminology, but also the range of 16th-century Scots prose – and the need for such
texts for the less educated. (The excerpts are reproduced from the *English Experience* reprint series,
where the author is given as Sir John Skene (or Skeyne) – apparently Gilbert's brother, a lawyer –
and the date as 1586). The excerpts are from the prologue, and from the handbook-text itself. In the
first Skeyne apologises for the lack of rhetorical elegance and politeness in the text. He explains that
he uses "vulgar language" rather than Latin, because he wants his knowledge to become profitable
to the "unlernit", the "commoun and wulgar people". The second excerpt illustrates scientific prose
in the vernacular: a medical description of the plague.

Source: Gilbert Skeyne, *Ane breve descriptiovn of the pest*. Edinburgh: R. Lekprevik, 1568. STC
22626.5; facs. English Experience (reprint series) 415, 1971, sig. A2ʳ-A4ʳ.

ANE BREVE DESCRIPTIOVN OF THE PEST QVHAIRIN THE CAVSIS, SIGNIS
AND SUM SPECIALL PRESERUATION AND CURE THAIROF AR CONTENIT.
SET FURTH BE MAISTER GILBERT SKEYNE, DOCTOURE IN MEDICINE
TO THE READAR

Sen it hes plesit the inscrutabill Consall, and Iustice of God (Beneuolent readar) that
this present plaig and maist detestabil diseise of Pest, be laitlie enterit in this Realme,
it becummis euerie one in his awin vocatione to be not only most studious by
perfectioun of lyfe to mitigat apperandlie the iuste wrathe of God touart vs, in this
5 miserable tyme: Bot also to be maist curagius in suffering of trauail, for the
aduancement of the commoun weilth. I beand mouit in y part seand the pure of Christ
inlaik, without assistance of support in bodie, al men detestand aspectioun, speche,
or communicatioun with thame, thoucht expedient to put schortlie in wryte (as it hes
plesit God to supporte my sober knawlege) quhat becummis euerie ane baith for
10 preseruatioun and cure of sic diseise quhairin (gude readar) thou sall nather abyde
greit eruditioun nor eloquence, bot onlie tho sentence and iugement of the maist
ancient writaris in medicine expressit in vulgar langage without poleit or affectionat
termis. And howbeit it become me rather (quha hes bestouit all my Zouthe in the
Sculis) to had vrytin the samin in Latine, Zit vnderstanding sic interpryses had bene
15 nothing profitable to the commoun and wulgar people, thocht expedient and neidfull
to express the sam in sic langage as the vnlernit may be als weil satisfyit as Masteris
of Clargie. Quhilk beand acceptable and allowit be the Magistratis of this Noble
Burgh conforme to my gude mynde, sall God willing as occasioun and tyme sufferis
treit this samin argument at more lenthe, quhilk presentlie for vtilitie of ye pure, &
20 schortnes of tyme, is mouit to set furthe almaist rude and imperfite, nor doutand
gentill Readar, bot thou will appryse the samyn with siclyk mynd as the pure Wom-
anis oblatioun was apprysit be the Gude Lord, quha mot preserue the in the helthe of
Saule and bodie for euer & euer. So be it.

ANE COMPENDIOUS DESCRIPTIOUN OF THE PEST, CAP.1

25 Ane pest is the corruptioun or infectioun of ye Air, or ane venemous qualytie & maist
hurtfull Wapor thairof, quhilk hes strenthe and wikitnes abone al natural
putrifactioun & beand contractit first maist quietlie infectis the Spiritall partis of
mannis bodie, thairefter the humoris, puttand sairest at the naturall Humiditie of the
hart, quhilkis tholand corruptioun ane feuir mast wikit quietlie and theiflie strikis the
30 patient: quhais bodie exteriourlie apperis weil at eis, bot interiourlie is maist heuelie
vexit. Quhilk schortly may be descryuit. Ane feuerable infectioun, maist cruelle and
sindre wayis strikand doun mony in haist. Heirfor it is maist vehement & hait diseis
that may put at mannis bodie, & maist dangerous, because it is difficil to knaw all
thingis, quhilkis makis ane man propense to becum Pestilential. Alwais quhilk hes
35 the cause frome the Heiuins or corruptioun of Air, is properlie be maist learnit, callit
ane pest: and quilk is generit within vs or of vther causis is callit ane Malignant feuer.

T14   LINDSAY, Robert, *The Historie and Cronicles of Scotland* (1570s)

Sir Robert Lindsay of Pitscottie (c1532-80), a historian, was born near Cupar (Fife). His *Historie and Cronicles of Scotland* is a continuation of Boethius' *Scotorum Historiae*, or rather of Bellenden's translation of it (cf. T8), covering the period 1436-1575. It was first published posthumously in 1728, because of its bias against the House of Stuart. The first book of the Cronicles is a literal translation of Boethius, the rest an original prose compilation of historical accounts – the first in the vernacular.

Source: Robert Lindesay of Pitscottie, *The Historie and Cronicles of Scotland* [1570s], ed. Æ.J.G. Mackey, Edinburgh: STS, 1899, ('1966), vol.I, pp.196-8.

(...) This bischope had ane hieland man with him quha was his meist secreit serwand callit Makgregour quha happnit to be with the bischope in the pailzeoun with the king quhair he was at commoning at that tyme to spye and perceave quhair ane inglisman set the croun vp in keiping quhilk he wald faine haue beine in handis
5 withall. In the meintyme thair come ane fray in the kingis oist be discord of twa lordis quhilk the king wschit out and all his companie to stenche thir twa lordis of thair combat and tuilzie. This hielandman tareit and seand the pailzeoun and nane intill it and beheld and knew quhair the crowne was sett and sieand na man to spye him tuik the samyn and wand it in his playd and passit heistelie eftir his maister the
10 bischope quha was than loupand on hors to ryd his way becaus he saw the armyeis or feildis so nar vthir reddie to come and gif battell he thocht it was guid to him to be away nor in plaice. Bot incontinent the king come in and his lordis and zeid to the counsall bot he that keipit the crown mist the samyn incontinent and gart searche and seik bot it cuild nocht be gottin be na way. Thairfore they send proclamationis throw
15 the oist to gar stop all men that was passand ony way fra the oist to bring thame away quhill the crown war searchit and gottin againe. Amang the rest thay brocht the scoittis bischope againe and his hieland man with him quha was Inquyrit eftir his gaine cuming gif he knew ony thing of the kingis crowne or quha had teine it away quha purgit him selff richt effectuouslie that he knew it nocht nor tuk it nocht nor
20 nane of his as he beleiwit. Zit this bischope rememberit him that he had ane lous man with him in his companie callit Makgregour quhilk he suspectit gif ony thing war in missing it wald be found of tymes throw his handis. Thairfoire he callit him befor him and examinat him gif he knew of that croun or nocht or gif he had teine it bot incontinent the bischop knew be his cuntinance that he had the samyn. Thairfoir
25 incontinent [he] delyuerit him to the king and the lordis quha accusit him schairplie how he durst be so peirt for to mell with the honourabill croun of ingland to steill it or to tak it away. Quha ansuerit the king and the lordis againe in this maner as eftir follows – 'Schir and it be zour graces pleasour to gif me leiwe I will schew zou the veretie quhairfoir and quhy that I tuik zour croun and thocht to haue had the samyn
30 with me. Schir ze sall vnderstand that my mother pronusticatt quhan I was zoung and wad ding my brother and wald craib hir scho wald ding me and said that I wald be hangit as the leave of my foirbeiris was befoir me thairfoir I thocht one hir sayingis and tuik her to be ane trew woman zit I thocht that it sould be for na litill matter that I sould die that deid. It sould nocht be for scheip nor nolt nor hors nor meiris as my
35 foirbeiris did to steill and be hangit for. Bot I think it ane gret honour to my kin and freindis for the riche croun of Ingland that so mony honourable men hes laitlie dieit for, sum hangit sum heidit and sum murdrest and sum fecht to deid for luiffe of this

riche croun quhilk ze offerrit zour selff within this hour to die for or zour enemye harie gat it of zour heid. Be my faderis saull Schir gif me credence gif I had it in

40 scotland in blair in athole thair sould nevir ane of zou haue seine it fecht als as fast as ze will for it.' At thir wordis of this hieland man that cuild nocht speik guid inglis bot evirie word was ane mow that he spak quhilk causit the inglis lordis to lauche thairat and meid thame so mirrie and reioysit at his speikin that thay obtenit him graice frome the kingis handis and ane remissioun of that fault and depassit him and his

45 maister and convoyit thame out of the camp with saiff conduck to pas to Scotland.

T15 BUCHANAN, George, *Letter to Thomas Randolph* (1577)

George Buchanan (1506-82) was born at Moss (Stirlingshire), educated at the Universities of Paris and St Andrews and taught in Paris until appointed tutor of one of James V's natural sons in 1537. After a short stay in Scotland, he had to flee to England, France and then Portugal, because he was condemned as a heretic because of his satire against Cardinal Beaton. While imprisoned by the Inquisition he translated the Psalms into Latin. He returned to Scotland in 1560, where he was appointed tutor to Mary, Queen of Scots, inspite of his Protestant leanings. However, he soon distanced himself from the court and became moderator of the newly founded General Assembly of the Church of Scotland in 1567. 1570-78 he was Keeper of the Privy Seal and tutor to James VI. He remained a prominent leader of the Reformation movement until his death in 1582. Most of his works (tragedies, religious works, political treatises, a twenty-volume history etc.) were written in Latin; only two are in the vernacular, viz. *Ane Admonition Direct to the Trewe Lordis* and *Chamaeleon*, a satire.

The private letter chosen here is one of his two surviving vernacular ones. It is addressed to Thomas Randolph, the English Ambassador to Scotland, and is in surprisingly dense Scots, considering Buchanan's long stays abroad, his political/religious affiliations (cf. Knox) and the nationality of the addressee.

Source: George Buchanan, "Letter to Thomas Randolph" [1577], repr. in: George Bruce & Paul H. Scott, eds. *A Scottish Postbag. Eight Centuries of Scottish Letters*. Edinburgh: Chambers, 1986, p.5 (source: P. Hume Brown, ed. *Vernacular Writings of George Buchanan*. Edinburgh: STS, 1892, 58-9).

To Thomas Randolph   Stirling 25 August 1577

Maister, I haif resavit diverse letters frome you, and yit I have ansourit to naine of thayme; of the quhylke albeit I haif mony excusis, as age, forgetfulnes, besines, and disease, yit I wyl use nane as now, except my sweirness, and your gentilnes; and geif ye thynk nane of theise sufficent, content you with ane confession of the falt, w'out

5 fear of punitioun to follow on my onkindnes. As for the present, I am occupiit in writyng of our historie, being assurit to content few, and to displease mony thar throw. As to the end of it, yf ye gett it not or thys winter be passit, lippin not for it, nor nane other writyngs from me. The rest of my occupation is wyth the gout, quhilk haldis me besy both day and ny'. And quhair ye say ye haif not lang to lyif, I traist to

10 god to go before yow, albeit I be on fut, and ye ryd the post; praying you als not to dispost my hoste at New werk, Jone or Kelsterne. Thys I pray you, partly for his awyne sake, quhame I tho' ane gud fellow, and partly at request of syk as I dar no' refuse. And thus I take my leif shortly at you now, and my lang leif quhen God pleasis, committing you to the protection of the almy'ty. At Sterling xxv. day of

15 August, 1577.

Yours to command w' service,   G. Buchanan

T16 JAMES VI, "Ane Short Treatise Conteining Some Revlis and Cautelis to Be Obseruit and Eschewit in Scottis Poesie." (1584)

The importance of the text lies in the fact that it is the only treatment ever published on the topic in Scots (and that it was written by an active poet of royal status). It is a pity that James excluded rhetoric, and confined himself to metrical questions and the appropriate choice of verse types.
Source: *The Essayes of a Prentise, in the Art of Poesie*. Edinburgh: Vautroullier, 1584, Kij-iij, iv, Mi-ii; facs, ed. EE 209 (1969), also repr. in Smith (1904, I: 208-24).

The Preface to the Reader: The cause why (docile Reader) I haue not dedicat this short treatise to any particular personis, (as commounly workis vsis to be) is, that I esteme all thais quha hes already some beginning of knawledge, with ane earnest desyre to atteyne to farther, alyke meit with for the reading of this worke, or any
5 vther, quhilk may help thame to the atteining to thair foirsaid desyre. Bot as to this work, quhilk is intitulit, *The Reulis and cautelis to be obseruit & eschevvit in Scottis Poesie*, ze may maruell paraventure, quhairfore I sould haue writtin in that mater, sen sa mony learnit men, baith of auld and of late hes already written thairof in dyuers and sindry languages: I answer, That nochtwithstanding, I haue lykewayis writtin of
10 it, for twa caussis: The ane is, As for them that wrait of auld, lyke as the tyme is changeit sensyne, sa is the ordour of Poesie changeit. For then they obseruit not *Flovving*, nor eschewit not *Ryming in termes*, besydes sindrie vther thingis, quhilk now we observe, & eschew, and dois weil in sa doing: because that now, quhen the warld is waxit auld, we haue all their opinionis in writ, quhilk were learned before
15 our tyme, besydes our awin ingynis, quhair as they then did it onlie be thair awin ingynis, but help of any vther. Thairfore, quhat I speik of Poesie now, I speik of it, as being come to mannis age and perfectioun, quhair as then, it was bot in the infancie and chyldheid. The vther cause is, That as for thame that hes written in it of late, there hes neuer ane of thame written in our language. For albeit sindrie hes written of
20 it in English, quhilk is lykest to our language, zit we differ from thame in sindrie reulis of Poesie, as ze will find be experience. I haue lykewayis omittit dyuers figures, quhilkis are necessare to be vsit in verse, for twa causis. The ane is, because they are vsit in all languages, and thairfore are spokin of be *Du Bellay*, and sindrie vtheris, quha hes written in this airt. Quhairfore gif I wrait of thame also, it sould
25 seme that I did bot repete that, quhilk thay haue written, and zit not sa weil, as thay haue done already. The vther cause is, that they are figures of Rhetorique and Dialectique, quhilkis airtis I professe nocht, and thairfore will apply to my selfe the counsale, quhilk *Apelles* gaue to the shoomaker, quhen he said to him, seing him find falt with the shankis of the Image of *Venus* efter that he had found falt with the
30 pantoun, *Ne sutor vltra crepidam*.

I will also with zow (docile Reidar) that ze cummer zow with reiding thir reulis, ze may find in zour self sic a beginning of Nature, as ze may put in practice in zour verse many of thir foirsaidis preceptis, or euer ze sie them as they are heir set doun. For gif Nature be nocht the cheif worker in this airt, Reulis wilbe bot a band to
35 Nature, and will mak zow within short space weary of the haill airt: quhair as, gif Nature be cheif, and bent to it, reulis will be ane help and staff to Nature. I will end heir, lest my preface be langer nor my purpose and haill mater following: wishing zow, docile Reidar, als gude succes and great proffeit by reiding this short treatise, as I tuke earnist and willing panis to blok it, as ze sie, for zour cause. Fare weill.

T17   JAMES VI, *Letter to Elizabeth I* (1588)

James (1566-1625) was born in Edinburgh as the only son of Mary, Queen of Scots (executed in London 1587) and Lord Darnley, spent his childhood in Stirling under the tutelage of George Buchanan (cf. T17) and became James VI, King of Scots, in 1567. He succeeded Elizabeth I as James I King of England, (1603-1625), moved his court to London and after that visited Scotland only once. James is said to have been the most scholarly of the Scottish monarchs; he wrote an 'art of poesie' (the Reulis and Cautelis, T16) and a speculum principis (*Basilicon Doron* (cf. T18)). His *Daemonologie* (1587), a study of witchcraft, and *A Counterblaste to Tobacco* (1604) are both in impeccable English. The letter was written about one and a half years after his mother's execution. James is being very polite so as not to jeopardise the chances of his succession to the English throne.

Source: James VI, "Letter to Elizabeth I" [1588], in: J. Bruce, *Letters of Queen Elizabeth and King James VI of Scotland...*, London: Camden Society, 1849, no.31 (pp.53-4).

Madame and dearest sister, The suddaine pairting of this honorable gentleman, youre ambassadoure, upon thaise unfortunatt and displeasant neuis of his onkle, hes mouit me with the more haist to trace theis feu lynes unto you; first, to thanke you, as uell for the sending so rare a gentleman unto me, to quhose brother I was so farre
5 beholden; as also, for the tayce sending me such summes of money, quhiche, according to the league, I sall thankfullie repaye with forces of men, quhensoeuer youre estait sall so requyre, according as my last letter hath maid you certified; not doubting but, as ye haue honorable begunn, so ye uill follou foorth youre course touardis me, quhiche thairby I shall so procure the concurrence of all my goode
10 subjectis with me in this course as sall make my friendshippe the more steadable unto you. The next is to pray you most hairtly, that in any thing concerning this gentleman fallin out by the death of his onkle, ye will haue a fauorable consideration of him for my sayke, that he may not haue occasion to repent him of his absence at suche a tyme. All other things I remitt to his credite, praying you to thinke of me as of one
15 quho constantlie shall contineu his professed course, and remaine,

      Youre most louing and affectionat brother and cousin,   JAMES R.

Postcrip. I thocht goode, in kaice of sinistre reportis, madame, hereby to assure you that the Spanishe flete neuer entered uithin any roade or heauen within my dominion, nor neuer came uithin a kenning neere to any of my costis.

T18   JAMES VI, *Basilicon Doron* (1599-1616)

The text was originally intended as a set of rules for James' son Prince Henry, but was later expanded and employed as a statement of James' policies. It is extant in manuscript form (1599) and three successive printed editions (1599, 1603 and 1616), which show increasing anglicization. The excerpts are on language (recommendation of "a naturall & plaine forme", that is neither dialect nor inkhorn language).

Source: James VI, *Basilicon Doron*, [1599], *MS Royal* (1599) and Waldegrave print (1603) in: James Craigie, ed. *The Basilicon Doron of King James VI*. Edinburgh: STS, 1944, vol.I, pp.28-31, 127, 179; London (1616) in: *James I, King of Great Britain, The Workes of the Most High and Mighty Prince James*, By the Grace of God Kinge of Great Brittaine France & Ireland Defendor of ye Faith &c.. London: James Montagu, 1616 (*Basilikon Doron*: pp.137-89), repr. in: Charles Howard McIlwain, ed. *The Political Works of James I*. New York: Russell & Russell, 1965, pp.13, 35, 46; and Waldgrave print (1599) in: *James I, Basilicon Doron, 1599*. facs. Menston: Scolar, 1969.

MS Royal 1599: The next thing that ye haue to take heade to is, youre speiking & langage, quhairunto I ioine youre gesture, sen action is ane of the cheifest
5 qualities that is requyred in ane oratoure, for as the tounge speakis to the eares sa dois the gesture speake to the eyes of the auditoure, in baith youre speiking & youre gesture then use a
10 naturall & plaine forme not fairdit uith artifice, for as the frenshe men sayes, rien conterfaict fin, bot escheu all affectate formis in baith, in youre langage be plaine, honest, naturall,
15 cumlie, clene, shorte & sententiouse escheuing baith the extremities alsueill in not using a rusticall corrupt leid, nor yett booke langage & penn & inkorne termes, & least of all mignarde &
20 æffeminate termis

Waldegrave 1599: The next thing that ye haue to take heede to, is your speaking & language, whereunto I ioyne your gesture, sen actione is one of the
5 chiefest qualities that is required in an oratour, for as the tongue speaketh to the eares, so doth the gesture speake to the eies of the auditoure. In both your speaking and your gesture then, vse a
10 natural & plaine forme, not fairdit with artifice: for (as the French-men saie) *Rien counterfaict fin*: But eschewe al affectat formes in both. In your language bee plaine, honest, naturall, comely,
15 cleane, short, and sententious; eschewing both the extreamities, aswell in not vsing a rusticall corrupt leid, nor yet booke-language, and Pen and Inkehorne tearmes, and least of all, mignarde and effeminate tearmes

London 1616: The next thing that yee haue to take heed to, is your speaking and language; whereunto I ioyne your gesture, since action is one of the
5 chiefest qualities, that is required in an oratour: for as the tongue speaketh to the eares, so doeth the gesture speake to the eyes of the auditour. In both your speaking and your gesture, vse a
10 n[a]turall and plaine forme, not fairded with artifice: for (as the French-men say) *Rien contre-faict fin*: but eschew all affectate formes in both. In your language be plaine, honest, naturall,
15 comely, cleane, short, and sententious, eschewing both the extremities, aswell in not vsing any rusticall corrupt leide, as booke-language, and pen and inkehorne termes: and least of all mignard
20 and effœminate tearmes.

Waldegrave 1603: The next thing that ye haue to take heede to, is your speaking and language; whereunto I joyne your gesture, since action is one
5 of the cheefest qualities, that is required in an oratour: for as the tongue speaketh to the eares, so doth the gesture speake to the eies of the auditour. In both your speaking and
10 your gesture, vse a naturall and plaine forme, not fairded with artifice: for (as the French-men say) *Rien contre-faict fin*: but eschewe all affectate formes in both. In your language be plaine,
15 honest, naturall, comelie, cleane, short, and sentencious: eschewing both the extremities, aswell in not vsing any rusticall corrupt leide, as booke-language, and pen and inke-horne tearmes:
20 and least of all mignarde & effœminate tearmes.

T19 MELVILLE, James, *Scotland* (1601)

The author (1566-1614) was professor at St Andrews with strong Presbyterian views. His mixture of
Scots and English spellings and inflexions and the almost random nature of his orthography seem
particular noteworthy in a time of linguistic change and coming from a highly educated man (who may
have been more efficient in writing Latin). Cf. Cusack's notes 1998:270-2.
Source: "James Melville: Scotland 1601" (National Library of Scotland Manuscript Advocates 34.4.15,
        p.121) edited as *The Diary of Mr James Melvill* (Bannatyne Club 34, Edinburgh 1829); the
        excerpt is from Cusack 1998:268/1-32.

Sa seiking resolution cairfullie of my God what to do/ a cusing of my awin name/ of
his awin frie mocion and accord offerit to me/ be the assistence of God to put me
saiff in Bervik w^{t}in twenti foir houres be sie/ To this also my vncle Roger and vther
frinds aggreit sa efter consultation at my God and finding of his warrand in my hart
5 I concludit to go. albeit no^t w^{t}out grait tentationes and mikle heavines/ yit on the part
reioysing y^t God gaiff the hart to leaue natiue countrey house and sweit lowing new
maried wyff and all for the loue of him and his Chryst. This my Cusing being a
mariner conducit a bott to carie a Town of his portage wyn about to Carell/ and
decking me vpe in his se attyre betymes in the morning about the Simmer solstice/
10 tuk me in down vnder dondie as a shipbroken sie man, and rowing about behouit to
go to the heavin of Sttandr/ to los a certean of skleatt steanes/ and because it was law
water ~~and~~ we behoued to ly a whyll in the road till the water grew/ whare the bott
wanting ane owerlaft/ the seall was cassen ower hir ta end and ther I leyed vpe lest I
shuld be spyed of sum shipes rydding besyde/ bot w^{t}in short space partlie be rokking
15 in the sie and partlie for want of eare I grew sa extream seik/ y^t manie {a} tyme I
besaught my Cowsing to sett me a land/ schesin rather ane sort of dethe for a guid
cause nor sa to be tormented in a stinking holl. and yit whowbeit it was extream
peanfull/ I gatt ther notable medicin of vomitine quhilk was a preseruatiue to my
helthe all y^t yeir. Sa coming hard to the steppes of the Archbishops peare at Sttandr//
20 we lossit our skleattes and tuk in viuers and rowit out agean immediatlie and cam y^t
night to Pitmillie burn mouth wher I gead a land and reposit me in my sie abbit/ and
efter offers of grait kindnes be the Lard/ and furnitour of a rubber of stark merch eall/
betymes in the morning we rowit out about the ness/ the day was hat/ ther was bot
twa men in the bott/ by twa Cusings of myne w^t my selff/ of these twa we haid an at
25 our deuotion/ the vther was the awner of the bott and verie euill affected/ bot the hat
rowing and the stope w^t the stark eall laid besyd him/ maid him atteans to keaue ower
a slipe/ and it pleisit God to send a prettie pirhe of weund wherby getting on a seall
vpon hir or ever our schipper wakned we was a guid space besouth the May/ wha
seing he could no^t mend him selff was fean to yeild and agrie w^t his merchant for a
30 hyre to Bervik.

T20 ANON., *Education Act* **(1616)**

The Act is based on the Statutes of Iona, drawn up by Andrew Knox, Bishop of the Isles in 1609 and signed (under the pressure James VI and I) by many Highland chiefs, obliging them to adhere to the 'true religion', to send their sons to school in the Lowlands to learn English and to obey the King in all causes. The background to these Statutes – the King's suspicion of Highland culture, the link drawn between Gaelic and barbarity and the wish to replace Gaelic by English – surfaces clearly in the Education Act, which was ratified by the Privy Council in 1616. It "was the first piece of educational legislation after the reformation, but many parish schools had already been established and it may be that the real purpose of this act was merely to encourage their extension in the Highlands" (Donaldson [2]1974:178). The Act contains an explicit stricture on the barbarity of Gaelic not found in the Statutes.
Source: David Masson, ed., *Register of the Privy Council of Scotland*, vol x. Edinburgh: Register
House, 1891: 671-2; here from Görlach 1991a:384-5.

Forsamekle as, the kingis Majestie haveing a speciall care and regaird that the trew religioun be advanceit and establisheit in all the pairtis of this kingdome, and that all his Majesties subjectis, especiallie the youth, be exercised and trayned up in civilitie, godlines, knawledge, and learning, that the vulgar Inglishe toung be universallie
5 plantit, and the Irishe language, whilk is one of the cheif and principall causis of the continewance of barbaritie and incivilitie amongis the inhabitantis of the Ilis and Heylandis, may he abolisheit and removit; and quhairas thair is no meane more powerfull to further this his Majesties princelie regaird and purpois than the establishing of scooles in the particular parrocheis of this kingdome whair the youthe
10 may be taught at the least to write and reid, and be catechiesed and instructed in the groundis of religioun; thairfore the Kingis Majestie, with advise of the Lordis of his Secreit Counsall, hes thocht it necessar and expedient that in everie parroche of this kingdome, whair convenient meanes may be had for interteyning a scoole that a scoole salbe establisheit, and a fitt persone appointit to teache the same, upoun the
15 expensis of the parrochinnaris according to the quantitie and qualitie of the parroche, at the sight and be the advise of the bischop of the diocie in his visitatioun; commanding heirby all the bishoppis within this kingdome that thay and everie ane of thame within thair severall dioceis deale and travell with the parrochinnaris of the particular parrocheis within thair saidis dioceis to condescend and aggree upoun
20 some certane, solide, and sure course how and by quhat meanes the said scoole may be interteyned. And, gif ony difficultie sall arryse amongis thame concerning this mater, that the said bishop reporte the same to the saidis Lordis, to the effect thay may tak suche ordour heiranent as thay sall think expedient. And that letteris be direct to mak publicatioun heirof, quhairthrow nane pretend ignorance of the same.
25   Forsamekle as the Kingis Majestie, with advise of the Lordis of his Secreit Counsall, hes found it verie necessair and expedient for the better establisheing of the trew religioun that childrene be catechesed and educate in the knowledge of the groundis thairof frome thair tender yeiris; and seeing mony parentis ar so careles and negligent in that point as thair childrene, being ather altogidder ignorant or cairleslie
30 instructed, ar quhen thay come to aige easilie pervertit and drawne to Poperie, – thairfore his Majestie, with advise foirsaid, hes commandit and ordanit, and by thir presentis straitlie commandis, chairges, and ordanes, all and sindrie parentis to use the ordinar meanes of instructing thair young childreen, to present thame to thair

ordinar pastour at all usuall tymes of catechiesing and examinatioun, and to bring
35 thame to the bishop of the diocie at everie visitatioun within the parroche to be tryed
and confirmed be him, under the panes particularlie underwrittin, to be incurrit *toties*
quoties be everie persone that sall failyee to present thair childrene to the bischop at
his visitatioun as said is: that is to say, be everie nobilman fourty pundis, be every
barone fourty merkis, and be everie inferiour persone twenty merkis or lesse
40 according to the meanes of the said persone: and that letteris be direct to mak
publicatioun heirof, quhairthrow nane pretend ignorance of the same.

T21   HUME, Alexander, *Of the Orthographie and Congruitie of the Britan Tongue* (c1617)

Alexander Hume (c1555-c1630) was educated at Dunbar, became a student at St. Andrews and Oxford,
and a schoolmaster at Bath, Edinburgh (headmaster of the High School) and Dunbar. He was also a
grammarian (*Grammatica Nova* 1612; *Of the Orthographie*, c1617), writer on theological
controversies, and the author of Protestant poetry and some nature poems. His *Orthographie* exhibits
a thorough Anglicization of his native Scots, of which mainly spelling features remain.
      The two excerpts from the school-grammar of English represent the dedication to King James
VI and I (see above) and a part of a chapter from the second book "Of the Congruitie of our Britan
Tongue" – a traditional attempt at applying grammatical categories to the English language.
Source: Alexander Hume, *Of the Orthographie and Congruitie of the Britan Tongue*, [c1617], ed.
      Henry B. Wheatley, London: EETS, [3]1891, pp.1-3, 28-9, 31.

DEDICATION

To the maest excellent in all princelie wisdom, learning, and heroical artes, JAMES,
of great Britan, France, and Ireland, King, Defender of the faeth, grace, mercie,
peace, honoure here, and glorie herafter.

5   May it please your maest excellent *Majestie*, I, your grace's humble servant,
seeing sik uncertentie in our men's wryting, as if a man wald indyte one letter to
tuentie of our best wryteres, nae tuae of the tuentie, without conference, wald agree;
and that they quhae might perhapes agree, met rather be custom then knawlege, set
my-selfe, about a yeer syne, to seek a remedie for that maladie.
10   (...) Quhil I thus hovered betueen hope *and* despare, the same Barret, in the
letter E, myndes me of a star *and* constellation to calm al the tydes of these seaes, if
it wald please the supreme Majestie to command the universitie to censure and
ratifie, and the schooles to teach the future age right and wrang, if the present will
not rectius sapere. Heere my harte laggared on the hope of your *Majestie's*
15 judgement, quhom God hath indeued with light in a sorte supernatural, if the way
might be found to draue your eie, set on high materes of state, to take a glim of a
thing of so mean contemplation, and yet necessarie. Quhiles I stack in this claye, it
pleased God to bring your *Majestie* hame to visit your aun Ida. Quher I hard that your
Grace, in the disputes of al purposes quherwith, after the exemple of *the* wyse in
20 former ages, you use to season your moat, ne quid tibi temporis sine fructu fluat, fel
sundrie tymes on this subject reproving your courteoures, quha on a new conceat of
finnes sum tymes spilt (as they cal it) the king's language. Quhilk thing it is reported
that your *Majestie* not onlie refuted with impregnable reasons, but alsoe fel on

Barret's opinion that you wald cause the universities mak an Inglish grammar to
25 repres the insolencies of sik green heades. This, quhen I hard it, soe secunded my
hope, that in-continent I maed moien hou to convoy this litle treates to your
Majestie's sight, to further (if perhapes it may please your *Grace*) that gud motion. In
school materes, the least are not the least, because to erre in them is maest absurd. If
the fundation be not sure, the maer gorgiouse the edifice the grosser the falt. Neither
30 is it the least parte of a prince's praise, curasse rem literariam, and be his auctoritie to
mend the misses that ignorant custom hath bred. (...)

Accept, dred Soveragne, your pover servantes myte. If it can confer anie thing
to the montan of your Majesties praise, and it wer but a clod, use it *and* the auctour
as your's. Thus beseeking your grace to accep my mint, and pardon my miss,
35 commites your grace to the king of grace, to grace your grace with al graces spiritual
and temporal.   Your *Majesties* humble servant, Alexander Hume.

OF THE CASE OF THE NOUN (CAP. 5)

1. Case is an affection of a noun for distinction of person; As, the corner stone fel
on me; stone is the nominative case. The corner of a stone hurt me; stone is the
40 genitive case. quhat can you doe to a stone; stone is the dative case. he brak the
stone; it is the accusative case. Quhy standes thou, stone! it is the vocative. and he
hurt me with a stone; it is the ablative case.
2. This difference we declyne, not as doth the latines and greekes, be terminationes,
but with noates, after the maner of the hebrues, quhilk they cal particles.
45 3. The nominative hath no other noat but the particle of determination; As, the peple
is a beast with manie heades; a horse serves man to manie uses; men in auctoritie
sould be lanternes of light.
4. Our genitive is always joyned with an-other noun, and is noated with of or s.
5. With of, it followes the noun quhar-with it is joined; as, the house of a good man
50 is wel governed.
6. With s it preceedes the word quherof it is governed, and s is divyded from it with
an apostrophus; As, a gud man's house is wel governed.
7. This s sum haldes to be a segment of his, and therfoer now almost al wrytes his
for it, as if it wer a corruption. But it is not a segment of his; 1. because his is the
55 masculin gender, and this may be fœminin; As, a mother's love is tender; 2. because
his is onelie singular, and this may be plural; as, al men's vertues are not knawen. (...)

OF THE TYME OF THE VERB (CAP. 9)

1. Tyme is an affection of the verb noating the differences of tyme, and is either
present, past or to cumm.
60 2. Tyme present is that quhilk now is; as, I wryte, or am wryting.
3. Tyme past is that quhilk was, and it is passing befoer, past els, or past befoer.
4. Tyme passing befoer, quhilk we cal imperfectlie past, is of a thing that was
doeing but not done, as, at four hoores I was wryting; Quhen you spak to me I was
wryting, or did wryte, as lillie expoundes it.
65 5. Tyme past els is of a thing now past, quhilk we cal perfectlie past; As, I have written.
6. Tyme past befoer is of a thing befoer done and ended; as, at four hoores, or quhen
you spak to me, I had written.
7. Tyme to cum is of that quhilk is not yet begun; As, at four houres I wil wryte.

T22   FERGUSSON, David, *Scottish Proverbs* (1641)

David Fergusson (c1525-1598), a clergyman, was born in Dundee and became one of the earliest
reformers (from 1560 minister at Dunfermline). The Proverbs were compiled in the latter half of the
16th century and published posthumously in 1641: the earliest known collection of Scottish proverbs
containing 911 items (arranged alphabetically), many of which are traceable to Latin or Greek sources,
but can also be found in the works of English and Scottish medieval poets and the Bible. The excerpts
are from the sections H and I.
Source: David Fergusson, *Scottish Proverbs* [From the Original Print of 1641], ed. Erskine Beveridge,
          Edinburgh: STS, 1924, pp.40-1, 64-5.

Edition of 1641:	Manuscript:
He is a weak horse that may not bear the saidle.	He is a weak hors that may not bear the sadle
He that borrows and bigs, makes 5 feasts and thigs, drinkes and is not dry, these three are not thirftie.	He that borrowes & bigges, maks feasts & thiggs, drinks and is not dry thir thrie ar not thrifty
He is a proud Tod that will not scrape his own hole.	He is a proud tod quho wil not scraip his awin holl
10 He is wise when he is well, can had him sa.	He is wyse that quhen he is weil can hold him so
He is poore that God hates.	He is poor quhom God hates
He is wise that is ware in time.	He is wise quho is war in tyme
He is wis that can make a friend of a 15 foe.	He is wise quho can mak a freind of a foe
Hair and hair, makes the cairles head baire:	Hair and hair maks the carle beld
Hall binkes are sliddrie.	Hall binks ar sliddrie
He is not the best wright that hewes 20 the maniest speals.	He is not the best wright quho hewes moniest spails
He that evil does, never good weines.	He that evell does never good weins
Hooredome and grace, can never byde in one place.	
25 Hee that compts all costes, will never put plough in the eard.	He that counts all costs wil never put pleugh in the earth.
(...)	(...)
I have a good bow, but it is in the castle.	It is a pet quhilk wil not cling
30 It is hard to fling at the brod, or kick at the prick.	It is hard to fling at the brod
	It is hard to kick at the prick
Ilk man mend ane, and all will be mendit.	Ilkane mend on & al wil be mended
It is a sairie collope that is tain off a 35 Capone.	It is a shamed collop is gotten of a capon

Ill bairnes are best heard at home.

It is ill to wakin sleeping dogs,

Ill hirds makes fat wolffs.

It is hard to wife, and thrive in a
40   year.

It is good sleeping in a heal skin.

It is not tint that is done to friends.

It is ill to draw a strea before an
          auld cat.

Ill bairnes ar best hard at home

It is ill to waken sleiping dogs

Ill hirds maks fatt wolfs

It is hard to wyve & thryv in on yeir

It is good sleeping in a whol skin

It is not tint that is don to a freind

It is ill to draw ane strae befor ane
          old cat

T23 ANON., *The Minute Book of Tyninghame* (1634)

Entries in the Minute Book of Tyninghame (East Lothian) kirk session, 5 January, 1634, concerning a complaint of slander [implying witchcraft] by Beatrice Milton in Belpotis against Alexander Congilton, shepherd, who denied the slander. The excerpt is interesting for the consistent use of Scots spellings in the 1630s, whilst largely indistict as far as lexis is concerned. Compare other documents in Cusack for even more irregular spellings and mixtures of Scots and English.
Source: Facsimile and transcription in Simpson 1973; item 27.

Item the said day bitriche Milton in belpotis compleinit vpon alexander congiltone shiphird in belpotis that he had slanderit hir affirming hir to be the caus of hir dauchteris seiknes and lykwyse scho said he affirmit that scho was the cause that his cow did cast calff The said alexander congiltone being lawfullie summonit and callit
5 on compeir it and accusit heirof denyit the same, and affirmit that he having slaine ane swyne, his wyff (as scho was wont to do at vther tymis) sent in to the said bitriche Miltoun ane peice thairof with some puddingis that same day, and that efter is dauchter did come back againe fra the said bitrichis hous to his hous withe the said flesche his vther dauchter became verie seik till neir eving till the cow came hame,
10 his cow growing seik and casting calff his dauchter was therefter haill and that tw corbeis did cry about the hous...

T24 PITCAIRNE, Archibald, *The Assembly* (1692)

Archibald Pitcairne (1652-1713), poet and dramatist, was born in Edinburgh, the son of a merchant. He studied law and medicine and became a founder-member of the College of Physicians in Edinburgh, where he taught medicine and became a very famous physician. However, his career was disrupted by his Jacobite sympathies and his publicly pronounced atheism. His play *The Assembly – a satire on the hypocrisy of the General Assembly* – was written in 1692 and is at least partly in Scots, but due to its sharp criticism of the ministry of the Church of Scotland it was not printed (and probably not performed) before 1722 (in London). It is one of the very few dramatic texts in Scots handed down from the 17th century; indeed, it is the only Restoration comedy treating Scottish material written by a Scots author. The excerpts from two of the recurring scenes representing sessions of the Assembly are taken from the second edition, which is said to be a textually and typographically "corrupt text of the play" (Tobin 1974:13). This second edition is prefaced by a key , which identifies the fictitious character with their real counterparts.
Source: Pitcairne, Archibald. [2]1752. *The Assembly: or; Scotch Reformation. A comedy.* As it was acted
          by the persons in the drama. Done from the original manuscript written in the year 1692.
          [Edinburgh].

Act II, Scene iii. (pp.22, 25)

A Church. The Committee.

Mod. – Brethren, it has pleased God, of his good pleasure, to allow us another
opportunity to shew our zeal in his work. Well, call in the curate with his
petition, and dispatch him; but let us first resolve what answer to give.

Sol. – Resolve, Moderator, to grant them nothing at all; for give them an inch, and
5   they'll take a span.

R. Elder – I jeedge it guid, and for sekeerity of the Protestant religion, that nae
keerate get leave to set his fitt within this bigging.

Mod. – Mr Salathiel, what say you?

Sal. – *Bona certe.* Moderator, if you have a mind to hear what he has to say, 'tis best
10   to call him in; but, if otherways, I think it is e'en best he be not called in.

Turb. – I say, Moderator, if he beis admitted withing these walls, let him not come
near any of us: "Touch not the unholy thing, saith the Lord!" Let us not salute
him, or give him any testimony of respect or favour.

R. Elder – Or jeestice, moderator, for it would offend guid.

15 *Mod.* – Well, shall we call him, that he may come in?

R. Elder – Yes, but see the doors be nae apened to him. [...]

Mod. – Now, brethren, it may be the cause of lamentation for us, this day, to see that
the statesmen do not go on hand in hand with us in the work of the Lord.

Cov. – It sets them well, indeed, to be as far foreward in the cause of God as his own
20   servants: Na, Moderator, if they keep sight of us, and be ready at our call, we
shall seek nae mair of them.

Sal. – Alas! Moderator, they are so far from that, they now seem to have turn'd their
backs on us. What! have they not, by act of parliament, taken the very thunder-
bolt of excommunication from us? Have they not taken away all the civil and
25   temporal effects of it?

Rul. Elder – Fat ha' they deen? If that be true, we are but a beik of bees without
stangs.

Cov. – Indeed, brother, you say very right: What will malignants care for curses, if
we can do nae mair? You ken the're better at that than we are. Nay, herry
30   them, and shame them, was the auld gate o't.

Sal. – But, Moderator, what was my Lord Whigridden, and the rest of our elders who
are members of parliament, doing when that act pass'd?

Mod. – In truth, they cannot be blam'd in it, because it would have looked prelatic-
like in them to have watch'd and guarded that the kirk sustained nae prejudice;
35   you know that was a reson given for prelates their being in all courts:
Moreover, they knew, that if any such act were made, it was an impious law,
and of itself null, and of nae force. – But, my Lord, what say you for yourself?

Lord Whigridden – We have now reason to lament with Jeremiah, and with David to
sing, "Except the Lord do build the house, etc." The kirk of Scotland in (my
40   Lord) my father's time, was so fortified with cannons, pikes and guns, that
there was no surprising of her; but now she's like a garden without either dyke
or fence: We are left to ouselves every way, and ye know that's a hard case:

For who could have thought, that, in so good an act as that rescinding several
wicked acts of parliament, as that for keeping the 29th of May, etc. they should
45   have foisted in these wicked acts anent excommunication? For, to tell the
truth, I never considered more of an act than the title, and that I thought
sounded well enough: But I have since been consulting with Sir William
Littlelaw, a lawywer, a friend of ours, who tells me, that the claim of right will
secure us well enough as to that.

50 *R. Elder* – If we be nae otherways sekeered, bot be the claim of right, we've a cald
coal to blaw at: I wad anes see to sekeere the quintra frae free quarters, and a'
the rest of the abeeses mentioned in't, and then we may expect sume guid o't;
but guid seeth, Moderator, Sir William Littlaw had nae a's wits about him fan
that claim was drawn, and sae's seen o't the day; for they say he takes fits.

T25 RAMSAY, Allan, *Elegy on Maggy Johnston* (1712)

Allan Ramsay (1684-1758) was a poet and editor of middle Scots poetry, traditional Scottish songs and
ballads. He was born in Leadhills, Lanarkshire, and in 1700 apprenticed to a periwig maker in
Edinburgh. Later he opened a bookshop and the first circulating library in Britain, and in 1736 a
playhouse. Both his orginal works and his efforts as an editor demonstrate his intense commitment to
the Scottish literary heritage; he had a great influence on the subsequent Vernacular Revival.

The text is a mock elegy to a tavern keeper – one of Ramsay's witty and humorous poems in
Scots, i.e. of the most successful genre of his vernacular poetry. He also wrote poems in English in the
then fashionable Augustan style, but he stressed the importance of using Scots in his poetry and
attempted to show the versatility of Scots (e.g. by translating Horace's *Odes*). However, the effect of
his successful use of Scots in a limited range of genres confirmed the belief among the educated classes
that the vernacular as a literary language was restricted to the comic, low-brow poetry and pastoral
romance.

Source: Allan Ramsay, "Elegy on Maggy Johnston, who died anno 1711" [1712], in: Alexander
    Manson Kinghorn & Alexander Law, eds. *Poems by Allan Ramsay and Robert Fergusson*,
    Edinburgh: Scottish Academic Press, 1974, pp.3-6.

Auld Reeky! Mourn in sable hue,
Let fouth of tears dreep like May dew.
To braw Tippony bid adieu,
   Which we, with greed,
5 Bended as fast as she cou'd brew.
   But ah! she's dead.

To tell the truth now Maggy dang,
Of customers she had a bang;
For lairds and souters a' did gang
10   To drink bedeen,
The barn and yard was aft sae thrang,
   We took the green.

And there by dizens we lay down,
Syne sweetly ca'd the healths arown,
15 To bonny lasses black or brown,
   As we loo'd best;
In bumpers we dull cares did drown,
   And took our rest.

When in our poutch we fand some clinks,
20 And took a turn o'er Bruntsfield-Links,
Aften in Maggy's at Hy-jinks,
   We guzl'd scuds,
Till we could scarce wi' hale out drinks
   Cast aff our duds.

25 We drank and drew, and fill'd again,
   O wow but we were blyth and fain!
   When ony had their count mistain,
           O it was nice
   To hear us a' cry, Pike ye'r bain
30   And spell ye'r dice.

   Fou closs we us'd to drink and rant,
   Until we did baith glowre and gaunt,
   And pish and spew, and yesk and maunt,
           Right swash I true;
35 Then of auld stories we did cant
           Whan we were fou.

   Whan we were weary'd at the gowff,
   Then Maggy Johnston's was our howff;
   Now a' our gamesters may sit dowff,
40   Wi' hearts like lead,
   Death wi' his rung rax'd her a yowff,
           And sae she died.

   Maun we be forc'd thy skill to tine?
   For which we will right sair repine;
45 Or hast thou left to bairns of thine
           The pauky knack
   Of brewing ale amaist like wine?
           That gar'd us crack.

   Sae brawly did a pease-scon toast
50 Biz i' the queff and flie the frost;
   There we gat fou wi' little cost,
           And muckle speed,
   Now wae worth death, our sport's a'lost,
           Since Maggy's dead.

55 Ae simmer night I was sae fou,
   Amang the riggs I geed to spew;
   Syne down on a green bawk, I trow
           I took a nap,
   And soucht a' night balillilow
60   As sound's a tap.

   And whan the dawn begoud to glow,
   I hirsled up my dizzy pow,
   Frae 'mang the corn like wirricow,
           Wi' bains sae sair,
65 And ken' nae mair than if a ew
           How I came there.

   Some said it was the pith of broom
   That she stow'd in her masking-loom,
   Which in our heads rais'd sic a foom,
70   Or some wild seed,
   Which aft the chaping stoup did toom,
           But fill'd our head.

   But now since 'tis sae that we must
   Not in the best ale put our trust,
75 But whan we're auld return to dust,
           Without remead,
   Why shou'd we tak it in disgust
           That Maggy's dead.

   Of warldly comforts she was rife,
80 And liv'd a lang and hearty life,
   Right free of care, or toil, or strife
           Till she was stale,
   And ken'd to be a kanny wife
           At brewing ale.

85 Then farewell Maggy douce and fell,
   Of brewers a' thou boor the bell;
   Let a' thy gossies yelp and yell,
           And without feed,
   Guess whether ye're in heaven or hell,
90   They're sure ye're dead.

           Epitaph
   O rare Maggy Johnston

T26 RAMSAY, Allan, *The Gentle Shepherd* (1725)

The pastoral genre is represented by Ramsay's verse drama, written in a mixture of English and Scots (with Scots spoken by the rustic characters), composed within an English Augustan framework. The play is set in the Pentland Hills outside Edinburgh, immediately after the Restoration of 1660, i.e. it is not as removed from reality as could be expected from a romantic, pastoral drama. The play was immensely successful and occasioned a number of contemporary English translations.

Source: Allan Ramsay, *The Gentle Shepherd* [1725], in: Burns Martin & John Walter Oliver, eds. *The Works of Allan Ramsay*, Edinburgh: STS, 1953 (¹1972), vol.II, pp.225-8.

Phonetic transcription: see Grant & Dixon 1921:204-5.

Act II., Scene I.

A snug Thack-house, before the Door a Green;
Hens on the Midding, Ducks in Dubs are seen.
On this Side stands a Barn, on that a Byre;
A Peat-stack joins, and forms a rural Square.
5   *The House is* Glaud's; *– there you may see him lean,*
And to his Divot-Seat invites his Frien'.

GLAUD and SYMON.

Glaud – Good-morrow, Nibour *Symon,* – come, sit down,
　　　　And gie's your Cracks. – What's a' the News in Town?
10　　They tell me ye was in the ither Day,
　　　　And sald your *Crummock* and her bassend Quey.
　　　　I'll warrant ye've coft a Pund of Cut and Dry;
　　　　Lug out your Box, and gie's a Pipe to try.
Symon – With a' my Heart; – and tent me now, auld Boy,
15　　I've gather'd News will kittle your Mind with Joy.
　　　　I cou'dna rest till I came o'er the Burn,
　　　　To tell ye things have taken sic a Turn,
　　　　Will gar our vile Oppressors stend like Flaes,
　　　　And skulk in Hidlings on the Heather Braes.
20 *Glaud –* Fy, blaw! – Ah! *Symie,* ratling Chiels ne'er stand
　　　　To cleck and spread the grossest Lies aff hand,
　　　　Whilk soon flies round like Will-fire far and near:
　　　　But loose your Poke, be't true or fause, let's hear.
Symon – Seeing's believing, *Glaud,* and I have seen
25　　*Hab,* that abroad has with our *Master* been;
　　　　Our brave good *Master,* wha right wisely fled,
　　　　And left a fair Estate, to save his Head:
　　　　Because ye ken fou well he bravely chose
　　　　To stand his Liege's Friend with Great MONTROSE.
30　　Now *Cromwell's* gane to *Nick;* and ane ca'd MONK
　　　　Has play'd the *Rumple* a right slee Begunk,
　　　　Restor'd King *CHARLES,* and ilka thing's in Tune:
　　　　And *Habby* says, We'll see Sir WILLIAM soon.

Glaud – That makes me blyth indeed; – but dinna flaw:
35   Tell o'er your News again! and swear till't a';
         And saw ye *Hab*! And what did *Halbert* say?
         They have been e'en a dreary Time away.
         Now GOD be thanked that our Laird's come hame,
         And his Estate, say, can he eithly claim?
40 *Symon* – They that hag-raid us till our Guts did grane,
         Like greedy Bairns, dare nae mair do't again;
         And good Sir *William* sall enjoy his ain.
Glaud – And may he lang; for never did he stent
         Us in our thriving, with a racket Rent:
45   Nor grumbl'd, if ane grew rich; or shor'd to raise
         Our Mailens, when we pat on *Sunday*'s Claiths.
Symon – Nor wad he lang, with senseless saucy Air,
         Allow our lyart Noddles to be bare.
         Put on your bonnet, Symon; – *Tak a Seat.* –
50   *How's all at hame? – How's* Elspa? – *How does* Kate?
         How sells black Cattle? – What gie's Woo this Year? –
         And sic like kindly Questions wad he speer.
Glaud – Then wad he gar his *Butler* bring bedeen
         The nappy Bottle ben, and Glasses clean,
55   Whilk in our Breast rais'd sic a blythsome Flame,
         As gart me mony a time gae dancing hame.
         My Heart's e'en raised! Dear Nibour, will ye stay,
         And tak your Dinner here with me the Day?
         We'll send for *Elspath* too – and upo' sight,
60   I'll whistle *Pate* and *Roger* frae the Height:
         I'll yoke my Sled, and send to the neist Town,
         And bring a Draught of Ale baith stout and brown,
         And gar our Cottars a', Man, Wife, and We'an,
         Drink till they tine the Gate to stand their lane.
65 *Symon* – I wad na bauk my Friend. his blyth Design,
         Gif that it hadna first of a' been mine:
         For heer-yestreen I brew'd a Bow of Maut,
         Yestreen I slew twa Wathers prime and fat;
         A Firlot of good Cakes my *Elspa* beuk,
70   And a large Ham hings reesting in the Nook:
         I saw my sell, or I came o'er the Loan,
         Our meikle Pot that scads the Whey put on,
         A Mutton-bouk to boil: – And ane we'll roast;
         And on the Haggies *Elspa* spares nae Cost;
75   Sma' are they shorn, and she can mix fu' nice
         The gusty Ingans with a Curn of Spice:
         Fat are the Puddings, – Heads and Feet well sung.

T27 RAMSAY, Allan, *Dedication to Proverbs* (1737)

In 1737 Ramsay published A Collection of Scottish Proverbs; the dedication to this volume was here
chosen to illustrate his use of Scots for a text-type which would have been expected to be written in
English. It is addressed to the country people of Scotland – rather than to the anglicized polite society
of Edinburgh (– a justification for his choice of the vernacular?).
Source: Allan Ramsay, "Dedication" to *A collection of Scots proverbs*, [1737], in: Alexander M. Kinghorn
    & Alexander Law, eds. *The Works of Allan Ramsay*, Edinburgh: STS, 1972, vol.V, 61-2.

TO THE TENANTRY OF SCOTLAND,
FARMERS OF THE DALES, AND STORE - MASTERS OF THE HILLS.

Worthy Friends,
THE following Hoard of *Wise Sayings*, and Observations of our Forefathers, which
have been gathering through mony bygane Ages, I have collected with great Care,
and restored to their proper Sense, which had been frequently tint by Publishers that
5 did not understand our Landwart Language, particularly, a late large Book of them,
fou of Errors, in a Stile neither *Scots* nor *English*. Having set them to Rights, I could
not think them better bestowed than to dedicate them to YOU, wha best ken their
Meaning, moral Use, Pith and Beauty. Some amang the Gentle Vulgar, that are *mair
nice than wise*, may tartle at the Braidness, or, (as they name it) coarse Expressions.
10 But that is not worth our tenting; a brave Man can be as meritorious in Hodden-gray
as in Velvet.
    As nathing helps out Happiness mair than to have the Mind made up with right
Principles, I desire you for the thriving and Pleasure of your and yours, to use your
Een and lend your Lugs to these good *auld Saws*, that shine with wail'd Sense, and
15 will as lang as the Warld wags. Gar your Bairns get them by Heart; let them have a
Place amang your Family-Books; and may never a Window Sole through the Country
be without them. On a spare Hour, when the Day is clear, behind a Ruck, or on the
green Howm, draw the Treasure frae your Pouch, and enjoy the pleasant Companion.
Ye happy Herds, while your Hirdsell are feeding on the flowery Braes, you may
20 eithly make your sells Master of the haleware. How usefou will it prove to you, who
(have sae few Opportunities of common clattering) when ye forgather with your
Friends at Kirk or Market, Banquet or Bridal? By your Proficiency, you'll be able, in
the Proverbial Way, to keep up the Saul of a Conversation, that is baith blyth and
usefou.
25   Since Dedicators scantly deserve that Name, when they dinna gar the Praises
of their Patrons flow freely through their Propine, I should be reckoned one of little
Havins to be jum in that Article, when I have sic good Ground to work upon, and leal
Verity to keep me frae being thought a Fleecher; wherefore, since *Lacking breeds
Laziness, and Praises breed Pith*, I scruple not to tell you that you are the Props of
30 the Nation's Profit. It is you that are the Storekeepers of Heaven's Bountiths. Frae
your Barns and Byres we enjoy the necessaries of Life; ye not only nourish your
sells, but a' the idle and insignificant; ye are the Bees that make the Honey, that
mony a Drone licks mair of than ye do. How nither'd and hungry wad the gentle

Board look without the Product of your Riggs and Faulds? How toom wad the
35 Landlord's Coffers be, if ye didna rug his Rent frae the Plough-gang and the green
Sward? How naked wad we a' be obliged to skelp without your Lint-sheaf and Woo-
pack? And alake, how sair wad it harden the braw Lad and bonny Lass's saft Looks,
were they obliged to labour for their ain Meat and Claiths? Ye take that Burden aff
their Backs by laying ilka Thing to their Hand *like a peel'd Egg*, while they without
40 Toil reap the Bennisons of your Care.

I cou'd rin on with a thousand Articles to your Commendation, were they not
clear to ilka ane whase Saul is not Sandblind or purfled with Pride. Wherefore, since
I am sure that a' whase Regard is Praise, respect you, I shall conclude with wishing
you the happy Seed-time and blyth Kirn, the plentyfou Increase of your Nowt and
45 Sheep, laiden Riggs and crowed Heights, generous and kindly Lairds, and rowth to
pay their Rents, Peace and Love in your Families, with a numerous, bonny and stout
Affspring to succeed your sells, with o'ercome to serve their King and Country by
Sea and Land, with the Spirit of their bauld Forbears, wha never fail'd to prove as a
brazen Dike, in Defence of their Nation's independent Honours and ancient Renown.
50   I am, Men and Brethren, Your affectionate Friend, and humble Servant,
Edin. Octob. 15, 1736.   Allan Ramsay.

T28 MRS McLINTOCK, *Receipts for Cookery and Pastry Work* (1736)

Nothing is known about the author, but her collection is the first known cookery book written by a
Scotswoman for a Scottish audience and published in Scotland (1736). There appear to be only few
Scots features in the language of the book, apart from a few lexical items. Whether this is because a
local tradition of cookery recipes with distictive linguistic traits failed to evolve in Scotland, or because
the genre "cookery book" was taken over wholesale from England in the 18th century, seems
impossible to say.
Source: *Mrs. McLintock's Receipts for Cookery and Pastry Work*, [1736, facs.], ed. Iseabail Macleod,
        Aberdeen: UP, 1986, pp.6-7, 32.

XVII. *To make Short Bread*.
Take a Peck of Flour, put three lib. of Butter in among a little Water, and let it
melt, pour it in amongst your Flour, put in a Mutchkin of good Barm; when it is
wrought divide it in 3 Parts, roll out your Cakes longer than broad, and gather it on
the Sides with your Finger, cut it through the Middle, and job it on the Top, then fend
5 it to the Oven.

XCVIII. *To make Geil of Rasps*:
Break them with the Back of a Spoon, wring them through a clean Cloth, to every
Mutchkin of the Juice of Rasps, take half a Mutchkin of the Juice of red Rizers to
make it geil, and to every Mutchkin of Juice 1 lib. of Sugar, clarifie it with the White
10 of an Egg, boil it up to Sugar again, put in your Juice, set it on a clear Fire, skim it
well, boil it half a Quarter of an Hour, and put it into your Geil-glasses.

T29   HUME, David, *Scoticisms* (1760)

David Hume (1711-76), the philosopher and historian, was born in Edinburgh and studied law and philosophy at Edinburgh University, followed by literary and philosophical studies in France (1734-9). On his return to Scotland he settled in Berwickshire until taking up diplomatic service in 1746. From 1751 he spent most of his time in Edinburgh. His writings comprise various philosophical works (which often reflected his religious scepticism and thereby prevented him from acquiring an exalted academic position) and his five-volume *History of England*. Although his philosophical views (continuing and extending John Locke's empiricism) were opposed to those of his contemporaries who are generally seen as the representatives of "the Scottish Enlightenment", he is often subsumed under this label, and certainly shared their linguistic ideal, i.e. complete anglicisation of the speech of educated Scotsmen. He is said to have circulated his manuscripts requesting to have all Scotticisms removed. The following text is a list of such Scotticisms.

Source: David Hume, "Scoticisms" [1760], in: Thomas Hill Green & Thomas Hodge Grose, eds. *David Hume, The Philosophical Works in Four Volumes*, London, 1882, vol.IV, pp.461-4.

(...) *Notice* should not be used as a verb. The proper phrase is *take notice*. Yet I find Lord Shaftesbury uses *noticed*, the participle: and *unnoticed* is very common. *Hinder to do*, is *Scotch*. The *English* phrase is, *hinder from doing*. Yet Milton says, *Hinder'd not Satan to pervert the mind*. Book IX.

	SCOTCH.	ENGLISH.
5	Conform to	Conformable to
	Friends and acquaintances	Friends and acquaintance
	Maltreat	Abuse
	Advert to	Attend to
10	Proven, improven, approven	Prov'd, improv'd, approv'd
	Pled	Pleaded
	Incarcerate	Imprison
	Tear to pieces	Tear in pieces
	Drunk, run	Drank, ran
15	Fresh weather	Open weather
	Tender	Sickly
	In the long run	At long run
	Notwithstanding of that	Notwithstanding that
	Contented himself to do	Contented himself with doing
20	'Tis a question if	'Tis a question whether
	Discretion	Civility
	With child to a man	With child by a man
	Out of hand	Presently
	Simply impossible	Absolutely impossible
25	A park	An enclosure
	In time coming	In time to come
	Nothing else	No other thing
	Mind it	Remember it
	Denuded	Divested
30	Severals	Several
	Some better	Something better

Anent	With regard to
Allenarly	Solely
Alongst	Along

35   Yet the *English* say both amid, amidst, among and amongst.

Evenly	Even
As I shall answer	I protest or declare
Cause him do it	Cause him to do it

Yet 'tis good *English* to say, make him do it

40 Marry upon	Marry to
Learn	Teach
There, where	Thither, whither
Effectuate	Effect

This word in *English* means to effect with pains and difficulty

| 45 A wright | A Carpenter |

Yet 'tis good *English* to say a wheel-wright

Defunct	Deceast
Evite	Avoid
Part with child	Miscarry
50 Notour	Notorious
To want it	To be without a thing, even though it be not desirable
To be difficulted	To be puzzled (...)

T30   BEATTIE, James, *Scotticisms* (1779)

James Beattie (1735-1803), poet and philosopher, born in Kincardineshire as the son of a shopkeeper. He studied at Marischal College, Aberdeen, and taught at Aberdeen Grammar School, later at Marischal College (from 1760-90). He was a friend of Lord Monboddo's and frequent visitor to London; his poetry is in the then fashionable Augustan style.

The following text, "which was produced originally for his students, who had 'no opportunity of learning English from the company they kept'" (Royle), indicates the linguistic ideal of the intellectuals of that time: 'correct' Augustan English. The list was first published anonymously in Aberdeen in 1779 as *A List of Two Hundred Scotticisms*. It was reissued in Edinburgh in 1787 in a greatly enlarged and more systematic form under the title of *Scoticisms* [sic], arranged in alphabetical order, designed to correct Improprieties of Speech and Writing. In 1797 another edition was published, likewise in Edinburgh, which was preceded by a lecture on elocution by Hugh Blair, recommending clear and careful enunciation, and correct voice modulation. The words and expressions stigmatized as Scotticisms by Beattie can be characterized as Scots lexical items for which English substitutes are suggested, variant forms of shared lexical items, lexical items which are used in a different sense in Scots and English, and variants in grammatical usage. Many of these Scotticisms have become part of the standard language. None of them belong to the category of today's stereotypical Scots. Some represent technical terms in Scottish jurisprudence, and some of the forms cited are part of the general

non-standard language of the period and are not peculiarly Scots (as Beattie himself recognizes). (Information taken from Frank 1994:57).
Source: James Beattie, *Scoticisms [sic], arranged in alphabetical order, designed to correct Improprieties of Speech and Writing*. Edinburgh: William Creech, 1787, pp.115-8.

WHEN Paris was in his *twentieth and fourth* year, three goddesses are said to have *waited of* him, as he was *laying* on the side of a mountain; each of whom promised him some good thing, if he would pronounce her the fairest. He gave judgment *in favours* of Venus. Soon after he went to Greece, where he *see'd* Helen, the *prettiest*
5 woman of *these* days, who was *married on* Menelaus King of Sparta. This Helen *has been* a very worthless woman; for, without *thinking shame*, she went off with Paris, taking with her *severals* of her attendants, and much wealth: and yet Menelaus was a good-natured man, and she could not pretend that he had ever *disabused* or *maltreated* her. Though *difficulted* how to act, he did not succumb under her
10 misfortune; for he knew he could not be the *better of* that. He sent *timeous* notice to his brother Agamemnon; who *summonsed* all the neighbouring princes to a conference, *anent* the injury done by Paris. After having *deliberate* long, and heard Menelaus *narrate* the whole affair, and *adduce* evidence sufficient to *instruct* his assertions, they saw, that, *conform* to the notions of honour which then prevailed, it
15 was *simply impossible* to *evite* a war. *These* who were present chose Agamemnon for their leader; and undertook to cause the other princes, *how soon* they could meet with them, *homologate* the choice: for my *share*, said Menelaus, if I had it in my *offer* to have the chief command, I would decline it. Letters were *wrote* to every city of Greece; Paris was abhorred for his ingratitude to a King who had behaved to him
20 with the utmost *discretion*; the *whole Greeks* were made soldiers, none were *exeemed*; even the *tender* and the old behoved to serve, *notwithstanding of* their infirmities: and they who refused were *incarcerated*, and not LIBERATE till long *thereafter*. And the people were the more incensed at this injury, *that* there had been an old grudge between the Asiaticks and Europeans, as *Herodot notices* in the
25 beginning of his history; *where*, if I *mind* right, he *condescends upon* other *iniquous* proceedings, not unlike the crime of Paris, which we may well imagine would not be forgotten on this occasion. But, if the following story be true, I must, for my share, blame the Greeks for their cruelty, as well as the Trojans for their injustice. A poor Trojan, who was a *widow*, and a very *tender man*, had been ten months or *thereby*, an
30 *indweller* in Sparta, and was now ill with a *chronical sore head*, much *distressed* with an inward *trouble*, and so *dull*, that he could not hear a word, they grievously *maltreated*, though he *pled* his innocence, and they had nothing *relevant* to urge *again* him. (...)

T31 MAYNE, John, "Glasgow. A Poem." (1783)

The poem invites comparison, in style and content, with Fergusson's "Auld Reekie" – written at a time when, before the building of Edinburgh's New Town, it was Glasgow that was well redd up, clean and generally prosperous.
Source: *The Glasgow Magazine and Review*, Dec. 1783: 153; cf. Hook & Sher 1995: 207-10.

The Glasgow Enlightenment

HAIL, GLASGOW! fam'd for ilka thing
That heart can wish or siller bring;
Lang may thy canty *musics* ring,
    Our sauls to chear;
5 And Plenty gar thy childer sing,
    Frae year to year:

Within the tinkling o' thy bells,
Wow, Sirs, how mony a thousand dwells!
–Where they get bread they ken themsels,
10   But I'll declare,
They're ay weil clad in gude bein shells,
    And fat and fair.

If ye've a knacky son or twa,
To Glasgow College send them a';
15 Whare, for the gospel, or the law,
    Or classic lair,
Ye'll find few places hereawa'
    That can compare:

There they may learn, for sma' propine,
20 Physician, Lawyer, or Divine:
– The gem that's buried in the mine
    Is polish'd here,
Till a' its hidden beauties shine,
    and sparkle clear. –

25 In ilka house, frae man to boy,
A'hands in GLASGOW find employ:
E'en maidens mild, wi' meikle joy,
    Flow'r lawn and gauze,
Or clap wi' care the silken-soy,
30   For Lady's braws.

Look thro' the town; – the houses here
Like royal palaces appear!
A' things the face o' gladness wear, –
    The markets thrang, –
35 Bus'ness is brisk, – and a's asteer
    The streets alang.

"Tween ane and twa, wi' gawsy air,
The MERCHANTS to the Cross repair;
And tho' they shine like Habobs there,
40   Yet, weil I wat,
Commerce engages a' their care,
    And a' their chat:

Thir wylie birkies trade to a'
The Indies and America;
45 Whate'er can mak' ae penny twa,
    Or raise their pride,
Is wafted to the Broomielaw,
    On bony Clyde.

Yet, after a', shou'd burghers fail,
50 And fickle Fortune turn the scale;
Tho'a' be lost in some hard gale,
    Or rocky shore,
The Merchant's House maks a' things hale
    As heretofore.

55 – O Sirs! within but little space,
This GLASGOW's turn'd an unko place!
Here Piety, in native grace,
    Abounds in store;
And Beauty's saft enchanting face,
60   Wi' gowd galore.

Whae'er has daner'd out at e'en,
And seen the sights that I hae seen!
For strappan Ladies, tight and clean,
　　　May safely tell
65 That, search the kintry, *Glasgow green*
　　　Will bear the *belle*:

There ye may find, beyond compare,
The bluiming rose and lily fair;
The killing smile, beswitching air,
70　　　The virt'ous mind,
And a' that Bards hae fancy'd rare
　　　In woman kind.

But what avails't to you or me
How bony, gude, or rich they be?
75 –Shou'd ane attempt, wi' langing eie,
　　　To mak' his maen,
They'd, scornfu', thraw their heads a-jee,
　　　Nor ease his pain. –

If ony simple Lover chuse
80 In humble verse his joe to ruise,
The eident *Porters* ne'er refuse,

　　　For little siller,
To bear the firstlings o' his muse,
　　　Wi' caution, till her.

85 But waesuck for the *Chairmen* now,
Wha ne'er to a day's wark dught bow;
Sair will her lazy *nainsel* rue,
　　　Wi' heavy granes,
That e'er our streets were lin'd anew
90　　　Wi' gude plane stanes:

Whan Writer lads, or Poets bare,
Frae Ball or Play set hame their Fair,
Their lugs'll no be deav'd nae mair
　　　(When pursie's tuim)
95 Wi' '*Bony Lady, shuse a shair!*
　　　Ye'll fyle ye're shuin.'

– O GLASGOW! may thy bairns ay nap
In smiling Plenty's gowden lap;
And tho' their daddies kiss the cap,
100　　　And bend the bicker,
On their auld pows may blessings drap,
　　　Ay thick and thicker.

T32   FERGUSSON, Robert, *To Andrew Gray* (1773)

The poet Robert Fergusson (1750-74) was born in Edinburgh, of parents who had their roots in Aberdeenshire. Schooled at Edinburgh and Dundee, he left St. Andrews University without a degree in 1768, to work as a clerk in Edinburgh supporting his mother and sister. His poems were, from 1771 on, published by Walter Ruddiman. Illness and acute depression forced him to give up his job; he died in Edinburgh Bedlam. Fergusson left 33 poems in Scots (and 50 in English), some of which had a great influence on Burns; in particular, he gave Burns the confidence and freedom to write in a colloquial, self-expressive Scots. Fergusson's poem is of the same genre as Burn's "Epistle to W.S. Ochitree" but much denser Scots than Burns's text.
Source: Robert Fergusson, "To Andrew Gray" [1773], in: M.P. McDiarmid, ed. *The Poems of Robert Fergusson*, Edinburgh: STS, 1956, vol.II, pp.152-4.

To ANDREW GRAY.

Nae langer bygane, than the streen,
Your couthy *letter* met my ein;
I lang to wag a cutty speen
　　　On *Amond* water;
5 And claw the lips o' truncher tree'n
　　　And tak a clatter.

"Frae *Whistleha*" your muse doth cry;
Whare'er ye win I carena by;
Ye're no the laird o' *Whistledry*,
10　　　As lang's ye can,
Wi' routh o' reekin *kail* supply
　　　The inward man.

You'll trow me, *Billy*, kail's fu' geed
To synd an' peerify the bleid;
15 'Twill rin like ony scarlet reid,
   While *patt* ye put on,
Wi' *wethers* that round *Amond* feed,
   The primest mutton.

Ane wad maist think ye'd been at *Scoon*,
20 Whan kings wure there the Scottish crown;
A soupler or mair fletching loun
   Ne'er hap'd on hurdies,
Whan *courtier's tongues* war' there in tune,
   For *oily* wordies.

25 Can you nae ither theme divine
   To blaw upon, but *my* engyne?
At *nature* keek, she's unco fine
   Redd up, and braw;
And can gie scouth to muses nine
30   At *Whistle-ha*.

Her road awhile is rough an' round,
An' few poetic gowans found;
The stey braes o' the muses ground
   We scarce can crawl up;
35 But on the tap we're light as wind
   To scour an' gallop.

Whan first ye seyd to mak a *riddle*
You'd hae an unco fike an' piddle,
An ablins brak aff i' the middle,
40   Like *Samy Butler*:
'Tis ein sae wi' *Apollo's* fiddle,
   Before we wit lear.

Then flegna at this weary practice,
That's tane to get this wyly nack nice;
45The eidant muse begins to crack wise,
   An' ne'er cry dule:
It's *idleseat,* that banefu' black vice,
   That gars her cool.

Andrew, at *Whistleha,* your ein
50May lippen for me very sien:
For barley scones my grinders grien.
   They're special eating;
Wi' bizzin cogs that ream abien,
   Our thrapple weeting.

55Till than may you had hale and fier,
That we to *Maltman's browst* may steer,
And ilka care and ilka fear
   To dogdrive ding;
While *cheeh* for *chow* we laugh and jeer;
60   And crack and sing.

R. FERGUSSON. Edinburgh, June 23, 1773.

T33 BURNS, Robert, *Epistle to W.S. Ochiltree* (1785)

Robert Burns (1759-96), the poet, was born at Alloway, Ayrshire. He worked as a farmer and flax-dresser, and from 1789 as an excise officer in Dumfries. His first collection of poems was published at Kilmarnock in 1786, which brought immediate success to the 'heaven-taught ploughman' (a term coined by Henry Mackenzie in a review of these poems in The Lounger 1786, although Burns was rather well-educated and widely read). He composed songs about love, nature, friendship, and nationalism, and refashioned others, and in 1790 wrote his master-piece "Tam O'Shanter". Burns is Scotland's national bard (even though he also wrote poems in English); he has had immense influence on Scots writing in Scotland and N. Ireland, and on dialect poetry in England and Germany (Hebel, Groth). His texts have widely influenced the English-speaking world's concept of the Scots language – although the language used in his poems somewhat compromises towards English.

   In this verse epistle to William Simpson Ochiltree the speaker/writer claims to express his "thoughts in plain, braid Lallans". The patriotic poem is about Scotland's poets, her countryside, history and the enlightenment.

Source: Robert Burns, "To W. S*****n, Ochiltree" [1785], in: Robert Burns. *Poems Chiefly in the Scottish Dialect*. Kilmarnock: John Wildon, 1786, pp.208-17.

May – 1785.

I Gat your letter, winsome Willie;
Wi' gratefu' heart I thank you brawlie;
Tho' I maun say't, I wad be silly,
    An' unco vain,
5 Should I believe, my coaxin billie,
    Your flatterin strain.

But I'se believe ye kindly meant it,
I sud be laith to think ye hinted
Ironic satire, sidelins sklented,
10   On my poor Musie;
Tho' in sic phraisin terms ye've penn'd it,
    I scarce excuse ye.

My senses wad be in a creel,
Should I but dare a *hope* to speel,
15 Wi' *Allan*, or wi' *Gilbertfield*,
    The braes o' fame;
Or *Ferguson*, the writer-chiel,
    A deathless name.

(O *Ferguson*! thy glorious *parts*,
20 Ill-suited *law*'s dry, musty arts!
My curse upon your whunstane hearts,
    Ye Enbrugh Gentry!
The tythe o' what ye waste at *cartes*
    Wad stow'd his pantry!)

25 Yet when a tale comes i' my head,
Or lasses gie my heart a screed,
As whiles they're like to be my dead,
    (O sad disease!)
I kittle up my *rustic reed*;
30   It gies me ease.

Auld COILA, now, may fidge fu' fain,
She's gotten *Bardies* o' her ain,
Chiels wha their chanters winna hain,
    But tune their lays,
35 Till echoes a' resound again
    Her weel-sung praise.

Nae *Poet* thought her worth his while,
To set her name in measur'd style;
She lay like some unkend-of isle
40   Beside *New Holland*,
Or whare wild-meeting oceans *boil*
    Besouth *Magellan*.

Ramsay an' famous *Ferguson*
Gied *Forth* an' *Tay* a lift aboon;
45*Yarrow* an' *Tweed*, to monie a tune,
    Owre Scotland rings,
While *Irwin, Lugar, Aire* an' *Doon*,
    Naebody sings. (...)

Fareweel, 'my rhyme-composing' brither!
50We've been owre lang unkenn'd to ither:
Now let us lay our heads thegither,
    In love fraternal:
May *Envy* wallop in a tether,
    Black fiend, infernal!

55While Highlandmen hate tolls an' taxes;
While moorlan herds like guid, fat braxies;
While Terra firma, on her axis,
    Diurnal turns,
Count on a friend, in faith an' practice,
60   In ROBERT BURNS

POSTSCRIPT.

My memory's no worth a preen;
I had amaist forgotten clean,
Ye bad me write you what they mean
65   By this *new-light*,*
'Bout which our *herds* sae aft hae been
    Maist like to fight.

In days when mankind were but callans,
At *Grammar, Logic*, an' sic talents,
70They took nae pains their speech to balance,
    Or rules to gie,
But spak their thoughts in plain, braid
    lallans,
    Like you or me.

T34 BURNS, Robert, *Letter to William Nicol* (1787)

Burns's letter to his former schoolmaster is a playful tour de force, since the use of Scots for private
letters is otherwise not recorded for Burns, nor indeed for other contemporary writers.
Source: Robert Burns, "Letter to Mr William Nicol, Master of the High School Edinburgh" [1787], in:
John Delancey Ferguson, ed. *Letters of Robert Burns*, Oxford: Clarendon Press, 1931, pp.94-5.

Carlisle 1st June 1787 – or
I believe the 39th o' May rather

Kind, honest-hearted Willie,

I'm sitten down here, after seven and forty miles ridin, e'en as forjesket and
5 forniaw'd as a forfoughten cock, to gie you some notion o' my landlowper-like
stravaguin sin the sorrowfu' hour that I sheuk hands and parted wi' auld Reekie.–

My auld, ga'd Gleyde o' a meere has huchyall'd up hill and drown brae, in
Scotland and England, as teugh and birnie as a vera devil wi' me. – It's true, she's as
poor's a Sang-maker and as hard's a kirk, and tipper-taipers when she taks the gate
10 first like a Lady's gentlewoman in a minuwae, or a hen on a het girdle, but she's a
yauld, poutherie Girran for a' that; and has a stomach like Willie Stalker's meere that
wad hae digeested tumbler-wheels, for she'll whip me aff her five stimparts o' the
best aits at a down-sittin and ne'er fash her thumb. – When ance her ringbanes and
spavies, her crucks and cramps, are fairly soupl'd, she beets to, beets to, and ay the
15 hindmost hour the tightest. – I could wager her price to a thretty pennies that, for twa
or three wooks ridin at fifty mile a day, the deil-sticket a five gallopers acqueesh
Clyde and Whithorn could cast saut in her tail. –

I hae dander'd owre a' the kintra frae Dumbar to Selcraig, and hae forga her'd
wi' monie a guid fallow, and monie a weel-far'd hizzie. – I met wi' twa dink quines
20 in particlar, ane o' them a sonsie, fine fodgel lass, baith braw and bonie; the tither
was a clean-shankit, straught, tight, weel-far'd winch, as blythe's a lintwhite on a
flowerie thorn, and as sweet and modest's a new blawn plumrose in a hazle shaw. –
They were baith bred to mainers by the beuk, and onie ane o' them has as muckle
smeddum and rumblegumtion as the half o' some Presbytries that you and I baith
25 ken. – They play'd me sik a deevil o' a shavie that I daur say if my harigals were
turn'd out, ye wad see twa nicks i' the heart o' me like the mark o' a kail-whittle in
a castock. –

I was gaun to write you a lang pystle, but, Gude forgie me, I gat myself sae
noutouriously bitchify'd the day after kail-time that I can hardly stoiter but and ben.
30   My best respecks to the guidwife and a' our common friens, especiall Mr & Mrs
Cruikshank and the honest Guidman o' Jock's Lodge. –

I'll be in Dumfries the morn gif the beast be to the fore and the branks bide hale.

– Gude be wi' you, Willie! Amen –
ROBT BURNS

T35   KEITH, Charles, *An Address in Scotch* (1788)

The poem is a lament about the general loss of Scots in favour of the fashionable English. It was
presented as a prologue to Andrew Shirrefs NE Scots drama Jamie and Bess.
Source: Charles Keith, "An Address in Scotch" [1788], in: Andrew Shirrefs. *Poems chiefly in the
Scotch Dialect*, Edinburgh: Shirrefs, 1790, pp.xxiv-xxvii.

AN ADDRESS IN SCOTCH,
on the decay of that Language, written by a Gentleman of distinguished literary
Merit, (the Author of *Farmer's Ha'*), and spoken by Mr Briarly, previous to the
Representation of *Jamie and Bess*, January 12th 1788.

Auld honest SCOTA's slighted sair,
Her plain guid speech can please nae mair;
But we're new-fangl'd ilka hair,
    An' that's our shame,
5 For we're ay seeking what is rare
    And far frae hame.

We had our bards in days o' yore,
Wha in poetic flights could soar,
And wi' their pipes mak ilka shore
10   Fu' sweetly sound;
But our ain lays are now no more
    In Scota found.

Our DRUMMONDS and MONTGOMERIES then,
Were perfect masters of the pen,
15 Our DOUGLASSES and RAMSAYS, *men*
    O' rarest merit,
Wha chaunted ay in pauky strain,
    Wi' canty spirit.

Young FERGUSON in our ain days,
20 Began to sing in hamel lays,
But, bright and fleeting as a blaze,
    He left the warl';
O! he, dear swain, exceeds a' praise
    O' wife or carl.

25 Alack-a-day! sin' he is gone,
Poor Scota now in vain will moan,
Nae thing can for his loss atone,
    Her heart to hight;
Wi' him the *Muses* every one
30   Ha'e ta'en their flight.

There's nae *Mecenas* o' this age,
That loves the *Caledonian* page,
Nane but wad rise into a rage,

    Gin ony swain
35 Wad dare to seek their patronage
    In hamely strain.

This pride, O wherefore now-a-days?
And why forsake our ain sweet lays?
It is enough to gar fowk gaze,
40   And won'er sair,
To hear that *Scotsmen* sae dispraise
    Their guid auld lear.

SCOTA's daft sons are sair to blame,
That e'er they followed sic a scheme,
45 For *Scots* is neither flat nor lame;
    And, Sirs, consider,
When we had *kings* and *courts* at hame,
    They spake nae ither.

Tho' Southern lads ha'e sweetly sung,
50 Sic as a MILTON, POPE or YOUNG,
We needna quit our mither tongue,
    Not yet think shame
That we were *frae auld Scota* sprung,
    That dainty dame.

55 But *Fashion* now, light-headed fair,
Does meikle mischief brood and care;
She gars us play the fool fu' sair,
    Wi' a' her might,
Else fowk wad ne'er ha'e lear'd the air
60   Their speech to slight.

For a' my anger and chagrin,
Whilk ha'e maist thrown me i' the spleen,
On gentle fowks o' Aberdeen
    I cast nae blots,
65 For LADS and LASSES *there*, I ween,
    Speak *guid auld Scots*.

T36   SCOTT, Sir Walter, *The Twa Corbies* (1802)

Sir Walter Scott (1771-1832), poet and novelist, was born in Edinburgh, son of a wealthy and cultivated family, and became an advocate in 1792. Family connections, and prolonged stays in the Borders as a child and young adult, sparked off his interest in Border history and legend. As a consequence he started collecting ballads in the Borders (published as *The Minstrelsy of the Scottish Border*, 1802-3 with the assistance of John Leyden, Richard Heber, William Laidlaw and James Hogg). The first two volumes were printed by James Ballantyne in 1802; and a third volume, which included ballad imitations by himself, Lewis and others, was published in 1803. In subsequent editions, changes were made in the ballad texts, by way both of amendment and of additions, the arrangement was altered and the notes were improved and supplemented. Though entitled "Minstrelsy of the Scottish Border", it included ballads and other pieces which had no special connection with the borders either of Scotland or England. Most of the versions published by Scott were of a composite character. Unlike Percy, he obtained several traditional copies of most of the ballads and constructed his versions partly by selecting what he deemed the best reading of each (cf. Ward & Trent, et al. *The Cambridge History of English and American Literature*. New ed.: New York: Bartleby.com, 2000.)

   Scott contrasts "The Twa Corbies" with an English ballad called "The Three Ravens", which sets out from the same situation but comes to the opposite conclusion.

Source: Sir Walter Scott, *Minstrelsy of the Scottish Border*, London: Alex. Murray & Son, 1869
   (reprint of the original edition), p.369.

THE TWA CORBIES.

As I was walking all alane,
I heard twa corbies making a mane;
The tane unto the t'other say,
"Where sall we gang and dine to-day?"

5 "In behint you auld fail dyke,
I wot there lies a new slain knight;
And naebody kens that he lies there,
But his hawk, his hound, and lady fair.

"His hound is to the hunting gane,
10 His hawk, to fetch the wild-fowl hame,
His lady's ta'en another mate,
Sa we may mak our dinner sweet.

"Ye'll sit on his while hause-bane,
And I'll pick out his bonny blue een:
Wi' ae lock o' his gowden hair,
We'll theek our nest when it grows bare.

"Mony a ane for him makes mane,
But nane sall ken where he is gane;
O'er his white banes, when they are bare,
The wind sall blaw for evermair." –

T37   SCOTT, Sir Walter, *The Heart of Midlothian* (1818)

After 1805, Sir Walter Scott started drafting novels which were published anonymously from 1814 onwards. Many dealt with Scottish history, such as *The Heart of Midlothian* (1818), but others had no specifically Scottish subject (e.g. *Ivanhoe* 1820, *Kenilworth* 1821). The practice of using Scots of various styles for the Scottish characters of his novels has introduced many readers worldwide to the language, but also frozen the function of literary Scots prose in this auxiliary use.

   The excerpts chosen from *The Heart of Midlothian* illustrate Scott's attempts at representing the Scots speech of different social groups, a Highlander's English with the traditional stereotypes, and some of the often-encountered comments on the Scottish language.

Source: Sir Walter Scott, *The Heart of Midlothian*, [1818], ed. W.M. Parker, London: Dent, 1965,
   pp.207, 490, 487, 242, 249, 294-5, 295-8.

Pronunciation: cf. phonetic transcription of a different extract from this novel in Grant & Dixon
   1921:222f.

Note by Scott concerning the language of nobles in 1737:

The Magistrates were closely interrogated before the House of Peers, concerning the particulars of the Mob, and the *patois* in which these functionaries made their answers, sounded strange in the ears of the Southern nobles. The Duke of Newcastle having demanded to know with what kind of shot the guard which Porteous
5 commanded had loaded their muskets, was answered naïvely, "Ow, just sic as ane shoots *dukes* and *fools* with." This reply was considered as a contempt of the House of Lords, and the Provost would have suffered accordingly, but that the Duke of Argyle explained, that the expression, properly rendered into English, meant *ducks and water-fowl*. (p.207)

10   *Court Scots*:

"You are quite right," replied the Duke. "She is a Scotchwoman, and speaks with a Scotch accent, and now and then a provincial word drops out so prettily, that it is quite Doric, Mr. Butler."

"I should have thought," said the clergyman, "that would have sounded vulgar in
15 the great city."

"Not at all," replied the Duke; "you must suppose it is not the broad coarse Scotch that is spoken in the Cowgate of Edinburgh, or in the Gorbals. This lady has been very little in Scotland, in fact – She was educated in a convent abroad, and speaks that pure court-Scotch, which was common in my younger days; but it is so generally
20 disused now, that it sounds like a different dialect, entirely distinct from our modern *patois*."

Notwithstanding her anxiety, Jeanie could not help admiring within herself, how the most correct judges of life and manners can be imposed on by their own preconceptions, (...). (p.490)

25   *Highlander's speech*:

"Teil ane petter to ony ped in the kintra," answered the Captain. "And ye had petter tell your father, puir body, to get his beasts a' in order, and put his tamn'd Cameronian nonsense out o' his head for twa or three days, if he can pe so opliging; for fan I speak to him apout prute pestial, he answers me out o' the Pible, whilk is not
30 using a shentleman weel, unless it be a person of your cloth, Mr. Putler." (p.487)

Edinburgh citizen:

"Heard ye ever the like o' that, Laird?" said Saddletree to Dumbiedikes, when the Counsel had ended his speech. "There's a chield can spin a muckle pirn out of a wee tait of tow! Deil haet he kens mair about it than what's in the declaration, and a
35 surmise that Jeanie Deans suld hae been able to say something about her sister's situation, whilk surmise, Mr. Crossmyloof says, rests on sma' authority. And he's cleckit this great muckle bird out o' this wee egg! He could wile the very flounders out o' the Firth. – What garr'd my father no send me to Utrecht? – But whisht, the Court is gaun to pronounce the interlocutor of relevancy." (p.242)

40   *Old Presbyterian*:

He sate down on the other side of Dumbiedikes, wrung his hand hard, and whispered, "Ah, Laird, this is warst of a' – if I can but win ower this part – I feel my head unca dizzy; but my Master is strong in His servant's weakness." After a moment's mental prayer, he again started up, as if impatient of continuing in any one
45 posture, and gradually edged himself forward towards the place had just quitted. (p.249)

Jeanie Deans in Northern England:

Hitherto she had been either among her own country-folk, or those to whom her bare feet and tartan screen were objects too familiar to attract much attention. But as
50 she advanced, she perceived that both circumstances exposed her to sarcasm and taunts, which she might otherwise have escaped; and although in her heart she thought it unkind, and inhospitable, to sneer at a passing stranger on account of the fashion of her attire, yet she had the good sense to alter those parts of her dress which attracted ill-natured observation. Her checked screen was deposited carefully in her
55 bundle, and she conformed to the national extravagance of wearing shoes and stockings for the whole day. She confessed afterwards, that, "besides the wastrife, it was lang or she could walk sae comfortably with the shoes as without them; but there was often a bit saft heather by the road-side, and that helped her weel on." The want of the screen, which was drawn over the head like a veil, she supplied by a *bon-*
60 *grace*, as she called it; a large straw bonnet, like those worn by the English maidens when labouring in the fields. "But I thought unco shame o' mysell," she said, "the first time I put on a married woman's *bon-grace*, and me a single maiden."

With these changes she had little, as she said, to make "her kenspeckle when she didna speak," but her accent and language drew down on her so many jests and gibes,
65 couched in a worse *patois* by far than her own, that she soon found it was her interest to talk as little and as seldom as possible. She answered, therefore, civil salutations of chance passengers with a civil courtesy, and chose, with anxious circumspection, such places of repose as looked at once most decent and sequestered. She found the common people of England, although inferior in courtesy to strangers, such as was
70 then practised in her own more unfrequented country, yet, upon the whole, by no means deficient in the real duties of hospitality. She readily obtained food, and shelter, and protection at a very moderate rate, which sometimes the generosity of mine host altogether declined, with a blunt apology, – "Thee hast a lang way afore thee, lass; and I'se n'er take penny out o' a single woman's purse; it's the best friend
75 thou can have on the road." (pp.294-5)

Being seduced into betraying our heroine's confidence thus far, we will stretch our communication a step beyond, and impart to the reader her letter to her lover.

"MR. REUBEN BUTLER, – Hoping this will find you better, this comes to say, that I have reached this great town safe, and am not wearied with walking, but the better
80 for it. And I have seen many things which I trust to tell you one day, also the muckle kirk of this place; and all around the city are mills, whilk havena muckle wheels nor mill-dams, but gang by the wind – strange to behold. (...) I wish, Mr. Butler, I kend

onything that wad make ye weel, for they hae mair medicines in this town of York
than wad cure a' Scotland, and surely some of them wad be gude for your
85 complaints. If ye had a kindly motherly body to nurse ye, and no to let ye waste
yoursell wi' reading – whilk ye read mair than eneugh with the bairns in the schule
– and to gie ye warm milk in the morning, I wad be mair easy for ye. Dear Mr.
Butler, keep a good heart, for we are in the hands of Ane that kens better what is
gude for us than we ken what is for oursells. I hae nae doubt to do that for which I am
90 come – I canna doubt it – I winna think to doubt it – because, If [sic] I haena full
assurance, how shall I bear myself with earnest entreaties in the great folk's
presence? But to ken that ane's purpose is right, and to make their heart strong, is the
way to get through the warst day's darg. The bairns' rime says, the warst blast of the
borrowing days couldna kill the three silly poor hog-lambs. And if it be God's
95 pleasure, we that are sindered in sorrow may meet again in joy, even on this hither
side of Jordan. I dinna bid ye mind what I said at our partin' anent my poor father
and that misfortunate lassie, for I ken ye will do sae for the sake of Christian charity,
whilk is mair than the entreaties of her that is your servant to command,

JEANIE DEANS."

100   This letter also had a postscript. – "Dear Reuben, (...) Ye will think that I am
turned waster, for I wear clean hose and shoon every day; but it's the fashion here for
decent bodies, and ilka land has its ain land-law. Ower and aboon a', if laughing days
were e'er to come back again till us, ye wad laugh weel to see my round face at the
far end of a strae *bon-grace*, that looks as muckle and round as the middell aisle in
105 Libberton Kirk. But it sheds the sun weel aff, and keeps unceevil folk frae staring as
if ane were a worrycow. I sall tell ye by writ how I come on wi' the Duke of Argyle,
when I won up to Lunnon. Direct a line, to say how ye are, to me, to the charge of
Mrs. Margaret Glass, tobacconist, at the sign of the Thistle, Lunnon, whilk, if it
assures me of your health, will make my mind sae muckle easier. Excuse bad spelling
110 and writing, as I have ane ill pen."

    The orthography of these epistles may seem to the southron to require a better
apology than the letter expresses, though a bad pen was the excuse of a certain
Galwegian laird for bad spelling; but, on behalf of the heroine, I would have them to
know, that, thanks to the care of Butler, Jeanie Deans wrote and spelled fifty times
115 better than half the women of rank in Scotland at that period, whose strange
orthography and singular diction form the strongest contrast to the good sense which
their correspondence usually intimates. (pp.295-8)

T38 HOGG, James, *The Brownie of Bodsbeck* (1818)

James Hogg (1770-1835), poet and novelist, was born on a farm near the Border (Ettrick Forest) and therefore named 'The Ettrick Shepherd'. He had little formal education but was strongly influenced by Border ballads, history, fairy-lore, legends and the Old Testament. He helped Sir Walter Scott with the collection of Border ballads, and after unsuccessful attempts at farming, went to Edinburgh in 1810, where he started his literary career by writing (and publishing) poetry, ballads and songs and later prose. His first novel *The Brownie of Bodsbeck*, a historical novel set in the 17th cent. after the defeat of the Covenanters, was published in 1818 and *The Private Memoirs* and *Confessions of a Justified Sinner*, his most famous work, in 1824. His Scots speaking narrator in the latter novel expanded the use of Scots in prose.
Source: James Hogg, *The Brownie of Bodsbeck*, [1818], ed. D.S. Mack, Edinburgh: Scottish Academic Press, 1976, p.141.

"Now do you just pe holding your paice for a fery less time, for you must halways pe spaik spaiking, without knowing fat to say, unless I were putting it into your haid. I haif tould ould Simon Glas Macrhimmon, who knows all the pedigrees from the creation of the world, and he says that te Lheadles are all Macphersons; for, in the
5 days of Rory More of Ballindalloch and Invereshie, tere was te Gordons, who would pe making grheat prhogress on te Sassenach, and tere went down wit Strabogie of te clan Ahnderson, and te clan Grhaham, and one Letulloch Macpherson of Strathneshalloch, vit as bould a clan after her as any and mhore; and they would pe toing creat might upon the Sassenach, and they would pe killing her in tousands, and
10 ten she cot crheat lhands out of King Robert on te Bhorder, and Letulloch tey called her *Leadlea*, and te Sassenach she called her *Little*, so that all tese are of Macpherson, and you may pe te chief, and te forward son of te crheat Strathneshalloch himself. Now tat I would pe te tog, and te shame, and te tisgrhace, not to help my owhn poor clansman and prhother out of te evil, tat would pe worse
15 eneuch; and te ting tat I would pe asking of you is tis, tat you will always look upon a Macpherson as a prother until te end of te world, and pe standing py her as long as tere is peing one trop of plood in your whole poty."
"Gude faith, serjeant," says I, "I never was sae happy as to find, that the man to whom I hae been sae muckle obliged is sic a noble disinterested chiel; an' there's my
20 hand, I'll never gie up the cause of a Macpherson, if he's in the right." (...)

T39 GALT, John, *Annals of the Parish* (1821)

The novelist John Galt (1779-1839) was born in Irvine, Ayrshire, educated in Greenock, and worked as a businessman and merchant in London, on the continent and in Canada. Between 1820 and 1823 he wrote six novels for serial publication in *Blackwood's Magazine*, among them *Annals of the Parish* (1821), *The Provost* (1822) and *The Entail* (1823). These examined the changes that were radically altering Scottish country life (including the language shift from Scots to English in provincial towns); a large number of novels dealing with major social political and economic issues of the day followed. In *The Entail* he includes Scots dialogue in the manner of Scott, but in parts of *The Annals* and *The Provost* (both set in Dalmailing, a fictitious village in Ayrshire) he also attempts to introduce Scots rhythm and expressions outside the dialogues.

The excerpt from illustrates Galt's narrative style: the narrator – the elderly minister of the village – is not omniscient, but a character in his own story: someone who is/was likely to speak Scots and try to write English, but who produces many lexical, idiomatic and morpho-syntactic Scotticisms and sometimes even uses Scots spellings (supposedly unwittingly?).
Source: John Galt, *Annals of the Parish*, [1821], Edinburgh: James Thin/Mercat Press, 1980 (facs. of the 1895 edition published by Macmillan and Co.), pp.8-9.

(...) I have now to speak of the coming of Mrs. Malcolm. She was the widow of a Clyde shipmaster, that was lost at sea with his vessel. She was a genty body, calm and methodical. From morning to night she sat at her wheel, spinning the finest lint, which suited well with her pale hands. She never changed her widow's weeds, and
5 she was aye as if she had just been ta'en out of a bandbox. The tear was aften in her e'e when the bairns were at the school; but when they came home, her spirit was lighted up with gladness, although, poor woman, she had many a time very little to give them. They were, however, wonderful well-bred things, and took with thankfulness whatever she set before them, for they knew that their father, the bread-
10 winner, was away, and that she had to work sore for their bit and drap. I daresay, the only vexation that ever she had from any of them, on their own account, was when Charlie, the eldest laddie, had won fourpence at pitch and toss at the school, which he brought home with a proud heart to his mother. I happened to be daunrin' by at the time, and just looked in at the door to say gude-night: It was a sad sight. There
15 was she sitting with the silent tear on her cheek, and Charlie greeting as if he had done a great fault, and the other four looking on with sorrowful faces. Never, I am sure, did Charlie Malcolm gamble after that night.

I often wondered what brought Mrs. Malcolm to our clachan instead of going to a populous town, where she might have taken up a huxtry-shop, as she was but of a
20 silly constitution, the which would have been better for her than spinning from morning to far in the night, as if she was in verity drawing the thread of life. But it was, no doubt, from an honest pride to hide her poverty; for when her daughter Effie was ill with the measles – the poor lassie was very ill – nobody thought she could come through, and when she did get the turn, she was for many a day a heavy
25 handful; – our Session being rich, and nobody on it but cripple Tammy Daidles, that was at that time known through all the country-side for begging on a horse, I thought it my duty to call upon Mrs. Malcolm in a sympathising way, and offer her some assistance, but she refused it.

'No, sir,' said she, 'I canna take help from the poor's-box, although it's very true
30 that I am in great need; for it might hereafter be cast up to my bairns, whom it may please God to restore to better circumstances when I am no to see't; but I would fain borrow five pounds, and if, sir, you will write to Mr. Maitland, that is now the Lord Provost of Glasgow, and tell him that Marion Shaw would be obliged to him for the lend of that soom, I think he will not fail to send it.' (...)

T40   MOIR, David Macbeth, *The Life of Mansie Wauch* (1828)

David Macbeth Moir (1798-1851), poet and novelist (pseud.: Mansie Wauch), was born at Musselburgh, East Lothian, and studied medicine at Edinburgh; he went into practice in Musselburgh and spent the rest of his life in his home town. He was a regular contributor to *Blackwood's Magazine*, contributing poetry, editorial work and the serial *The Life of Mansie Wauch* (1824-28). This fictitious autobiography of the pawky small-town tradesman, with its humorous caricatures of life in a small Scottish town, anticipates the novels of the 'kailyard' that were to follow later on in the century.

The excerpt is part of the earlier chapters about his family and his childhood. When getting into a story which involves him emotionally, the narrator's style clearly shifts away from the standard.

Source: Mansie Wauch [pseud. of David Macbeth Moir], *The Life of Mansie Wauch, Tailor in Dalkeith. Written by Himself*. Edinburgh: Blackwood, 1828; the excerpt is taken from Grant & Dixon 1921:284.

Pronunciation: cf. the phonetic transcription in Grant & Dixon 1921:285 reproduced on p.99.

Then up and spak the red-headed laddie: "It's no fair; anither should hae come by this time. I wad rin awa hame, only I am frighted to gang out my lane. Do ye think the doup of that candle wad carry i' my cap?"

"Na, na, lad; we maun bide here, as we are here now. Leave me alane? Lord safe
5   us! and the yett lockit, and the bethrel sleeping with the key in his breek pouches! We canna win out now though we would," answered I, trying to look brave, though half frightened out of my seven senses: "Sit down, sit down; I've baith whisky and porter wi' me. Hae, man, there's a cawker to keep your heart warm; and set down that bottle," quoth I, wiping the sawdust affin't with my hand, "to get a toast; I'se warrant
10 it for Deacon Jaffrey's best brown stout."

The wind blew higher, and like a hurricane; the rain began to fall in perfect spouts; the auld kirk rumbled and rowed, and made a sad soughing; and the branches of the bourtree behind the house, where auld Cockburn that cut his throat was buried, creaked and crazed in a frightful manner; but as to the oaring of the troubled waters,
15 and the bumming in the lum-head, they were past all power of description. To make bad worse, just in the heart of the brattle, the grating sound of the yett turning on its rusty hinges was but too plainly heard. What was to be done? I thought of our both running away; and then of our locking ourselves in, and firing through the door; but who was to pull the trigger?
20   Gudeness watch over us! I tremble yet when I think on it. We were perfectly between the de'il and the deep sea – either to stand still and fire our gun, or run and be shot at. It was really a hang choice. As I stood swithering and shaking, the laddie flew to the door, and, thrawing round the key, clapped his back to it.

T41   ANON., 'Maansie o' Slushiegarth', *"Letter to the Editor"* (1838)

The local newspaper was an important medium in 19th-century Scotland. Produced and read locally, it represented distinctly Scottish popular culture. It was not restricted to news, but contained all kinds of text-types: serial novels, jokes, historical accounts, anecdotes, biographical articles etc., and vernacular Scots was used in many of these. Regular features of the popular press were columns contributed by pseudonymous vernacular correspondents, who used the dialect of the region.

The Orkney and Shetland Journal was compiled and written in London, though edited by a Shetlander. "Maansie", one of its vernacular correspondents, wrote shortly after Isaac Pitman's suggestions for an orthographic reform were published; these aimed to introduce a "rational system of orthography in which the same combination of sounds would under similar circumstances always be represented by the same combination of symbols". (Donaldson 1986, p.54). The ideas were taken up and experimented with in texts like Maansie's, who, for example, 'spells out' "many of the leading features of the Shetland dialect with its intriguing mixture of Scots and Norn elements [...], including replacement of the consonant 'th' (absent from Norn) by 'd' or 't' [...]; various devices to show the modified Shetland 'o' vowel, as in 'Lurick/Lerwick', 'shoe/she', and 'fock/ folk'; and the tendency to insert a 'y' sound between the initial consonant and a vowel, as in 'cyuntry/country'." (Donaldson 1986, p.55).

Source: 'Maansie o' Slushiegarth', "Letter to the Editor" in *Orkney and Shetland Journal* [1838], in: William Donaldson, *Popular Literature in Victorian Scotland. Language, Fiction and the Press.* Aberdeen: UP, 1986, p.55.

Diel hae me in da warld be na just gaen gyte! Da Lurick fock shuttin' wi' cannon, an' lightin' a der collies an' caandles an' dennerin' an' drinkin' an' rejoisin' aboot a fule ting o' a stemmer shipp itt da Queen is sent ta carry da jantry's letters ivery ook to da sooth! Fule moniments itt dey irr! What gude 'ill dis stemmer shipp doe ta wiz poor
5 fock? Will shoe mak meal ony shaper? Truggs! am fear'd shoe'll doe nae gude ava''cept helpin' wirr jantry ta gaing awa' ta da sooth wi' less spewin'. Na, na, I aye said itt nae gude wid come o' new fangled tings an it 'ill shune come to pass itt dis stemmer i'll mak kye an' sheep an' butter an' eggs an' a' kinds o' cyuntry proddick muckle dearer. Forby da scores an' dizzens an' maybe hunders o' idle jaantin' bodies
10 it'll be commin' frae da sooth, just lek da locusts itt cam da Egypt davoorin' da substance o' da laand! An de'll be tellin' wiz itt kens sae muckle better itt wi' shud hae rodds an' packets an' ferry boats an' inns, and muckle mair nonsense, just ta help dem ta rin o'er an' devoor wiz in a shorter time. Deil cut dem aff!

T42 ANON., 'Peter Hardie', *"Letter to the Editor"* (1858)

This text is a similar piece of 'correspondence' by another pseudonymous staff member, this time of a mainland newspaper, the *Aberdeen Free Press*. It "shows a number of features of mid-northern Scots" (Donaldson 1986, p.55).

Source: 'Peter Hardie', "Letter to the editor" in *Aberdeen Free Press* [5 Nov 1858], in: William Donaldson, *Popular Literature in Victorian Scotland. Language, Fiction and the Press.* Aberdeen: UP, 1986, p.55.

MAISTER AEDITUR, – Twa weeks syne a corryspondent o' yours ca'd attention to the bells, an', as it is usual wi' a' sic-like, spak some sense, an' a gude dael o' nonsense aboot them. I dinna mean, hooever, to reply to him, nor to nae ither body in parteekler, but jist to express my nain sentiments o' the subject. An' firstly, that
5 we've gotten a set o' gweed bells, I think, is past dispute... tho'... I wud add that... the lug requares some trainin to appresheate it ... there's been cry – a'maist bairnly, Sir, in its natur – for tunes playit. Noo, Sir, tak ye my word for't playin' teens upo' bells, is something an'alygous... to playin' teens upo' the fiddle wi' yer fingers instead o' the bow – a vera awkard means to an unsatisfactory result ... I thochtna muckle ... at
10 first, but noo, Sir, fan I've lockit my choppie door, an' am stappin' awa hame at nicht – (gin the weather binna a' the waur) – ye may see me stannin' up in rapt attiteed at ilka ither point to hear the legitimat bell-meesick. An' as my lug, an' the young lads at the ropes, get better trained, so proportionately does my enjoyment grow.

T43 ANON., *"Family Dialogues. Household Taxation"* (1850)

In the 19th century Scots was often used as an anti-language, in order to enliven dialogues by a non-standard speaker – apparently because it was considered to be easy to imitate.

Source: Anon., "Family dialogues. Household taxation.– No.I". In: *The Working Man's Friend*. II:25, 1850, pp.372-5.

> *Philip Freeman. Mrs. Freeman. John (the son). Jane (daughter). Andrew Binks (a neighbour).*
>
> *Mrs. F.* – I am glad, Andrew, you have come to talk to Philip here. These letters from America seem to run betwixt him and his wits.
>
> *Andrew B.* – Hoot! toot! Breetun's the best kintra after a's said an dune; be ye sure o'that mistress!
>
> 5 *Philip F.* – You had better hear some of the contents of the letter before you agree upon a verdict.
>
> *Andrew B.* – Weel, let's hear. (...)
>
> *Andrew B.* – Think ye every chiel that gangs ower sea, fa's intil sich a seam as that? (...)
>
> 10 *Jane* – I can't understand that, father.
>
> *Philip F.* – By-and-by, Jane, you will understand it all; but youngsters must be patient and learn.
>
> *Andrew B.* – Toots! It's a' nonsense and clish-ma-claver! Gin ye had eggs a dozen for a bawbee, wages would come doon in the same proportion; so ye wad be just
>
> 15   where ye started!
>
> *Philip F.* – That I deny, friend Andrew.
>
> *Mrs. F.* – Ye deny, Philip; but can ye give any reason for denying it? (...)
>
> *Andrew B.* – Laugh at the Edinbro' reviewers! Heard ye iver the like of that? You're jokkin' mon, or else ye've gaen clean wud! (...)
>
> 20 *Andrew B.* – Haud ye there, Philip! Do ye think to bamboozle us that gate, mon? (...)
>
> *Andrew B.* – Gin it be secret, how come ye to ken what was stated? (...)
>
> *Andrew B.* – Dinna ye disparage oatmeal parridge, Maister Freeman! (...)

T44 ALEXANDER, William, *Johnny Gibb of Gushetneuk* (1871)

The novelist William Alexander (1826-94) was born in Chapel of Garioch, Aberdeenshire. He was a ploughman, later a journalist and editor of the *Aberdeen Free Press*. His novel *Johnny Gibb of Gushetneuk* first appeared in serial form, 1869-70, and went through several book editions. It is claimed to contain the most authentic representation of rural Northeastern Scots of the 19th century; also cf. his *Sketches of Life Amang my Ain Folk* (1875) and another serial novel, *The Laird of Drammochdyle* (1865, ed. by William Donaldson in 1986).

The excerpt illustrates the very dense rural Aberdeenshire Scots in the dialogue (contrasting this with the English narrative). Even the quotations from the Bible are scotticised. The passage was chosen because the highly philosophical content of the conversation – though held as it is by an old farmer couple (i.e. persons likely to speak broad NE Scots) – stretches the literary conventions and the range of uses of Scots.

Source: William Alexander, *Johnny Gibb of Gushetneuk*, [1871], Edinburgh: David Douglas, [8]1884, pp.321-3. (New ed.: 1995, ed. William Donaldson. East Linton: Tuckwell).

Pronunciation: cf. the phonetic transcription of a different passage from this novel in Grant & Dixon 1921:322f.

(...) "Weel," said Johnny, with an air of more than his ordinary gravity, "I've been thinkin' 't owre, a' up an' doon. It's a queer thing fan ye begin to leuk back owre a' the time byegane. The Apos'le speaks o' the life o' man as a 'vawpour that appeareth for a little, and than vainisheth awa';' an' seerly there cudna be a mair nait'ral
5 resem'lance. Fan we begood the pilget here thegither, wi' three stirks, an' a bran'it coo,'t cam' wi' your providin', the tae side o' the place was ta'en up wi' breem busses an' heather knaps half doon the faul'ies, an' the tither was feckly a quaakin' bog, growin' little but sprots an' rashes. It leuks like yesterday fan we hed the new hooses biggit, an' the grun a' oon'er the pleuch, though that's a gweed therty year
10 syne. I min' as bricht 's a paintet pictur' fat like ilka knablich an' ilka sheugh an' en' rig was."

"An' ye weel may, man, for there's hardly a cannas breid upo' the place but 's been lawbour't wi' yer nain han's owre an' owre again to mak' it."

"That's fat aw was comin' till. Takin' 't as it is, there's been grun made oot o' fat
15 wasna grun ava, an' there it is, growin' craps for the eese o' man an' beast – Ou ay, aw ken we've made weel aneuch oot upon 't; but it 's nae i' the naitur' o' man to gyang on year aifter year plewin, an' del'in', an' earin, an' shearin the bits o' howes an' knowes, seein' the vera yird, obaidient till 's care, takin' shape, an' sen'in' up the bonny caller blade in its sizzon, an' aifter that the 'fu' corn i' the ear,' as the Scriptur'
20 says, onbeen a kin' o' thirl't to the vera rigs themsel's."

"Weel, a bodie *is* wae tae think o' lea'in' 't."

"Ay, ay; but that's nae a'. Gin fowk war tae leuk at things ae gate we wud be wae to pairt wi' onything 't we hae i' the wardle. But here's oorsel's noo 't 's toil't awa' upo' this place fae youth-heid to aul' age, an' wi' the lawbour o' oor nain han's made
25 it's ye may say – Gushetneuk the day's nae mair fat Gushetneuk was fan we cam' here nor my fit 's a han' saw. Sir Seemon ca's 'imsel' laird o' 't; but Sir Seemon's deen nae mair to the place nor the man o' France. Noo, you an' me can gae roun an' roun aboot it, an' wi' a' honesty say o' this an' that – 'Here's the fruit o' oor lawbour – that'll bide upo' the face o' the earth for the eese o' ithers aifter we're deid an'
30 gane.' Noo, this is fat I canna win at the boddom o' ava. I'm weel seer it was never the arreengement o' Providence that the man that tills the grun an' spen's the strength o' 's days upon't sud be at the merciment o' a man that never laid a han' till't, nor hardly wair't a shillin' upon't, to bid 'im bide or gyang."

T45 STEVENSON, Robert Louis, *Thrawn Janet* (1881)

Robert Louis Stevenson (pseud. Lewis Balfour) (1850-94), novelist and poet, was born and educated at Edinburgh, trained as a lawyer, he became a prolific writer of plays, travel accounts and novels (his first, *Treasure Island*, was published in 1881 as a serial in a magazine; it was followed by Kidnapped 1886, *The Strange Case of Dr Jekyll and Mr Hyde* 1886, *Catriona* 1893). He travelled extensively and his ill health later forced him to leave Scotland for warmer climates; he eventually settled in Samoa. He began his literary career by contributing essays and criticism to various magazines. Much of his prose writing is in Standard English, but the second book of his collection of poems, *Underwoods* (1878), is in Scots; there are a few Scots tales (sometimes inserted within novels), and the long short story *The Merry Men* (1887) and his last novel (*The Weir of Hermiston*), published fragmentarily after his death in 1896, contains some of the finest dialogues in Scots by a 19th-century novelist.

The excerpt is from "Thrawn Janet", a short story about diabolic possession, set in a fictitious small town in Fife in 1712. After a short introduction, the English speaking/writing narrator hands over to an unspecified member of the community, who then recounts the story in the local variety of Scots (Fite). The minister's language is Standard English, as would be expected, and the speech of the women is not in any way more densely Scots than the narrative.
Source: Robert Louis Stevenson, "Thrawn Janet" [1881], in: Kenneth Gelder (ed.), Robert Louis Stevenson. *The Scottish Stories and Essays*. Edinburgh: UP, 1989, pp.72-4.

This atmosphere of terror, surrounding, as it did, a man of God of spotless character and orthodoxy, was a common cause of wonder and subject of inquiry among the few strangers who were led by chance or business to that unknown, outlying country. But many even of the people of the parish were ignorant of the
5 strange events which had marked the first year of Mr. Soulis's ministrations; and among those who were better informed, some were naturally reticent, and others shy of that particular topic. Now and again, only, one of the older folk would warm into courage over his third tumbler, and recount the cause of the minister's strange looks and solitary life.

10   Fifty years syne, when Mr. Soulis cam' first into Ba'weary, he was still a young man – a callant, the folk said – fu' o' book-learnin' an' grand at the exposition, but, as was natural in sae young a man, wi' nae leevin' experience in religion. The younger sort were greatly taken wi' his gifts and his gab; but auld, concerned, serious men and women were moved even to prayer for the young man, whom they took to
15 be a self-deceiver, and the parish that was like to be sae ill-supplied. It was before the days o' the moderates – weary fa' them; but ill things are like guid – they baith come bit by bit, a pickle at a time; and there were folk even then that said the Lord had left the college professors to their ain devices, an' the lads that went to study wi' them wad hae done mair an' better sittin' in a peat-bog, like their forebears of the
20 persecution, wi' a Bible under their oxter an' a speerit o' prayer in their heart. There was nae doubt onyway, but that Mr. Soulis had been ower lang at the college. He was careful and troubled for mony things besides the ae thing needful. He had a feck o' books wi' him – mair than had ever been seen before in a' that presbytery; and a sair wark the carrier had wi' them, for they were a' like to have smoored in the Deil's
25 Hag between this and Kilmackerlie. They were books o' divinity, to be sure, or so they ca'd them; but the serious were o' opinion there was little service for sae mony, when the hail o' God's Word would gang in the neuk o' a plaid. Then he wad sit half the day and half the nicht forbye, which was scant decent - writin', nae less; and first they were feared he wad read his sermons; an' syne it was proved he was writin' a
30 book himsel', which was surely no' fittin' for ane o' his years an' sma' experience.

Onyway it behoved him to get an auld, decent wife to keep the manse for him an' see to his bit denners; an' he was recommended to an auld limmer – Janet M'Clour, they ca'd her – an' sae far left to himsel' as to be ower persuaded. There was mony advised him to the contrar, for Janet was mair than suspeckit by the best folk in
35 Ba'weary. Lang or that, she had had a wean to a dragoon; she hadnae come forrit* for maybe thretty year; and bairns had seen her mumblin' to hersel' up on Key's Loan in the gloamin', whilk was an unco time an' place for a God-fearin' woman.

Howsoever, it was the laird himsel' that had first tauld the minister o' Janet; an' in
thae days he wad hae gane a far gate to pleesure the laird. When folk tauld him that
40 Janet was sib to the de'il, it was a' superstition by his way o' it; an' when they cast
up the Bible to him an' the witch of Endor, he wad threep it doun their thrapples that
thir days were a' gane by, an' the de'il was mercifully restrained.

Weel, when it got about the clachan that Janet M'Clour was to be servant at the
manse, the folk were fair mad wi' her an' him thegither; an' some o' the guidwives
45 had nae better to dae than get round her door-cheeks and chairge her wi' a' that was
ken't again' her, frae the sodger's bairn to John Tamson's twa kye. She was nae great
speaker; folk usually let her gang her ain gate, an' she let them gang theirs, wi'
neither Fair-guid-een nor Fair-guid-day; but when she buckled to, she had a tongue
to deave the miller. Up she got, an' there wasna an auld story in Ba'weary but she
50 gart somebody lowp for it that day; they couldna say ae thing but she could say twa
to it; till, at the hinder end, the guidwives up an' claught haud of her, an' clawed the
coats aff her back, and pu'd her doun the clachan to the water o' Dule, to see if she
were a witch or no, soom or droun. The carline skirled till ye could hear her at the
Hangin' Shaw, an' she focht like ten; there was mony a guidwife bure the mark o'
55 her neist day an' mony a lang day after; an' just in the hettest o' the collieshangie,
wha suld come up (for his sins) but the new minister!

"Women," said he (an' he had a grand voice), "I charge you in the Lord's name to
let her go."

Janet ran to him – she was fair wud wi' terror – an' clang to him, an' prayed him,
60 for Christ's sake, save her frae the cummers; an' they, for their pairt, tauld him a' that
was ken't, an' maybe mair.

"Woman," says he to Janet, "is this true?"

"As the Lord sees me," says she, "as the Lord made me, no' a word o't. Forbye the
bairn," says she, "I've been a decent woman a' my days."

65 "Will you," says Mr. Soulis, "in the name of God, and before me, His unworthy
minister renounce the devil and his works?"

Weel, it wad appear that when he askit that, she gave a girn that fairly frichit them
that saw her, an' they could hear her teeth play dirl thegither in her chafts; but there
was naething for it but the ae way or the ither; an' Janet lifted up her hand an'
70 renounced the de'il before them a'.

"And now," says Mr. Soulis to the guidwives, "home with ye, one and all, and
pray to God for His forgiveness." (...)

T46 MACLAREN, Ian, *Beside the Bonnie Brier Bush* (1890s)

Ian Maclaren was one of the most popular 'kailyard' writers; his sentimental stories of Scottish village
life "took Britain and America by storm, and well over a million copies were rapidly sold" (blurb).
Whereas the contents and style of these backward-looking texts were strongly criticized, e.g. by
MacDiarmid, the language used can seem quite authentic. The excerpts here chosen come from three
text types less commonly associated with the use of Scots: religious reflexion, prayers and private
letters. It is likely that the author here overstepped sociolinguistic plausibility in his attempt to use
Scots for emotional contexts. The excerpts come from the 1977 edition, Edinburgh: Albyn Press, pp.
66, 85, 67).

"I will show you what I hef done, for she hass been a black shame to her name."

He opened the Bible, and there was Flora's name scored with wavering strokes, but the ink had run as if it had been mingled with tears.

Marget's heart burned within her at the sight, and perhaps she could hardly make
5 allowance for Lachlan's blood and theology.

"This is what ye hev dune, and ye let a woman see yir wark. Ye are an auld man, and in sore travail, but a' tell ye before God ye hae the greater shame. Juist twenty years o' age this spring, and her mither dead. Nae woman to watch over her, and she wandered frae the fold, and a' ye can dae is to tak her oot o' yir Bible. Wae's me if
10 oor Father had blotted out oor names frae the Book o' Life when we left His hoose. But He sent His ain Son to seek us, an' a weary road He cam. A' tell ye, a man wudna leave a sheep tae perish as ye hae cast aff yir ain bairn. Yir worse than Simon the Pharisee, for Mary was nae kin tae him. Puir Flaor, tae hae sic a father."

"Who will be telling you that I was a Pharisee?" cried Lachlan, quivering in every
15 limb, and grasping Marget's arm.

"Forgie me, Lachlan, forgie me. It was the thocht o' the misguided lassie carried me, for a' didna come tae upbraid ye." (...)

Then the minister asked Burnbrae to pray, and the Spirit descended on that good man, of simple heart:
20   "Almichty Father, we are a' Thy puir and sinfu' bairns, wha wearied o' hame and gaed awa' intae the far country. Forgive us, for we didna ken what we were leavin' or the sair hert we gied oor Father. It was weary wark tae live wi' oor sins, but we wud never hev come back had it no' been for oor Elder Brither. He cam' a long road tae find us, and a sore travail He had afore He set us free. He's been a gude Brither
25 tae us, and we've been a heavy chairge tae Him. May He keep a firm haud o' us, and guide us in the richt road, and bring us back gin we wander, and tell us a' we need tae know till the gloamin' come. Gither us in then, we pray Thee, and a' we luve, no' a bairn missin', and may we sit doon for ever in oor ain Father's House. Amen." (...)

So Margret knew it would be well with Lachlan yet, and she wrote this letter:
30 "My Dear Lassie, – Ye ken that I wes aye yir freend, and I am writing this tae say that yir father luves ye mair than ever, and is wearing oot his hert for the sicht o' yir face. Come back, or he'll dee thro' want o' his bairn. The glen is bright and bonny noo, for the purple heather is on the hills, and doon below the gowden corn, wi' bluebell and poppy flowers between. Naebody 'ill ask ye where ye've been, or
35 onything else; there's no' a bairn in the place that's no' wearying tae see ye; and, Flora, lassie, if there will be sic gledness in oor wee glen when ye come hame, what think ye o' the joy in the Father's Hoose? Start the verra meenit that ye get this letter; yir father bids ye come, and I'm writing this in place o' yir mother. Margret Howe."

T47 ANON., *Thrums on the Auld String* (1890)

The tradition of the prize novelists (parodies of Disraeli etc.) was introduced into the magazine *Punch* by William M. Thackeray in 1847.

The excerpt represents the preface to and a passage from a parody of J.M. Barrie's 'kailyard' novels, which are set in the ficticious small town "Thrums", the model for which was Barrie's birthplace Kirriemuir (cf. the allusion of the pseudonym "J. Muir Kirrie").

Source: Anon. [pseud. J. Muir Kirrie], "Thrums on the Auld String" (Mr. Punch's Prize Novels, No. VI), in: *Punch, or the London Charivari*, Nov. 15, 1890, p.229.

"With this story came a glossary of Scotch expressions. We have referred to it as we went along, and found everything quite intelligible. As, however, we have no room to publish the glossary, we can only appeal to the indulgence of our readers. The story itself was written in a very clear, legible hand, and was enclosed in a
5 wrapper labelled, "Arcadia Mixture. Strength and Aroma combined. Sold in six-shilling cases. Special terms for Southrons. Liberal allowance for returned empties."

(...) After TAMMAS had finished boring half-a-dozen holes in the old sow with his sarcastic eye, he looked up, and addressed HENDRY MCQUMPHA.

"HENDRY," he said, "ye ken I'm a humorist, div ye no?"
10   HENDRY scratched the old sow meditatively, before he answered.

"Ou ay," he said, at length. "I'm no saying 'at ye're no a humorist. I ken fine ye're a sarcesticist, but there's other humorists in the world, am thinkin."

This was scarcely what TAMMAS had expected. HENDRY was usually one of his most devoted admirers. There was an awkward silence which made me feel
15 uncomfortable. I am only a poor Dominie, but some of my happiest hours had been passed on the pigsty. Were these merry meetings to come to an end? PETE took up the talking.

"HENDRY, my man," he observed, as he helped himself out of TAMMAS's snuff-mull, "ye're ower kyow-owy. Ye ken humour's a thing 'at spouts out o' its ain
20 accord, an' there's no nae spouter in Thrums 'at can match wi' TAMMAS." (...)

"Man, man, there's no nae doubt at ye lauch at havers, an' there's mony 'at lauchs 'at your clipper-clapper, but they're no Thrums fowk, and they canna' lauch richt. But we maun juist settle this matter. When we're ta'en up wi' the makkin' o' humour, we're a' dependent on other fowk to tak' note o' the humour. There's no nane o' us
25 'at's lauched at anything you've telt us. But they'll lauch at me. Noo then," he roared out, "'A pie sat on a pear-tree.'"

We all knew this song of TAMMAS's. A shout of laughter went up from the whole gathering. The stranger fell backwards into the sty a senseless mass.

"Man, man," said HOOKEY to TAMMAS, as we walked home; "what a crittur ye
30 are! What pit that in your heed?"

"It juist took a grip o' me," replied TAMMAS, without moving a muscle; "it flashed upon me 'at he'd no stand that auld song. That's where the humour o' it comes in."

"Ou, ay," added HENDRY, "Thrums is the place for rale humour."

On the whole, I agree with him.

T48 MURRAY, Charles, *The Whistle* (1906)

The poet Charles Murray (1864-1941), born at Alford, Aberdeenshire, worked with an Aberdeen engineering firm and in 1888 emigrated to South Africa where as an engineer, later employed in Government service. He returned to Scotland in 1924. During his stay in South Africa he began to publish his poems in NE Scots, some of which had appeared individually in various magazines before, in collected volumes, first in Aberdeen (the collections *Handful of Heather* in 1893 and the first edition of *Hamewith* in 1900) and later in London, starting with an expanded version of *Hamewith* in 1909, which became the basis of Murray's nationwide reputation, then *A Sough o' War* in 1917, In the *Country Places* 1920 and the posthumous *The Last Poems* 1969. Many of his poems, especially in *Hamewith*, celebrate – somewhat nostalgically – the rural past of his childhood, but others deal with wider social issues, such as the war poetry in *A Sough o' War*.

"The Whistle" first appeared in *Chambers' Journal* in 1906 and was then included in the expanded version of *Hamewith* in 1909. It is one of his most frequently anthologized and best known poems, reflecting the widespread fear of loss of cultural identity resulting from changes in the educational system following the education act of 1872. It is clearly localised rural Aberdeenshire in language (though less so than other poems by Murray), but the sentiment evoked found nationwide response.
Source: Charles Murray, "The Whistle" [1906], taken from Grant & Dixon (1921:319-9), with the
    phonetic transcription reproduced p.99.

He cut a sappy sucker from the muckle rodden-tree,
He trimmed it, an' he wet it, an' he thumped it on his knee;
He never heard the teuchat when the harrow broke her eggs,
He missed the craggit heron nabbin' puddocks in the seggs,
5 He forgot to hound the collie at the cattle when they strayed,
But you should hae seen the whistle that the wee herd made!

He wheepled on't at mornin' an' he tweetled on't at nicht,
He puffed his freckled cheeks until his nose sank oot o' sicht,
The kye were late for milkin' when he piped them up the closs,
10 The kitlin's got his supper syne, an' he was beddit boss;
But he cared na doit nor docken what they did or thocht or said,
There was comfort in the whistle that the wee herd made.

For lyin' lang o' mornin's he had clawed the caup for weeks,
But noo he had his bonnet on afore the lave had breeks;
15 He was whistlin' to the porridge that were hott'rin' on the fire,
He was whistlin' ower the travise to the baillie in the byre;
Nae a blackbird nor a mavis, that hae pipin' for their trade,
Was a marrow for the whistle that the wee herd made.

He played a march to battle, it cam' dirlin' through the mist,
20 Till the halflin squared his shou'ders an' made up his mind to 'list;
He tried a spring for wooers, though he wistna what it meant,
But the kitchen-lass was lauchin' an' he thocht she maybe kent;
He got ream an' buttered bannocks for the lovin' lilt he played.
Wasna that a cheery whistle that the wee herd made?

25 He blew them rants sae lively, schottisches, reels, an' jigs,
The foalie flang his muckle legs an' capered ower the rigs,

The grey-tailed futt'rat bobbit oot to hear his ain strathspey,
The bawd cam' loupin' through the corn to "Clean Pease Strae";
The feet o' ilka man an' beast gat youkie when he played –
30 Hae ye ever heard o' whistle like the wee herd made?

But the snaw it stopped the herdin' an' the winter brocht him dool,
When in spite o' hacks an' chiblains he was shod again for school;
He couldna sough the catechis nor pipe the rule o' three,
He was keepit in an' lickit when the ither loons got free;
35 But he aften played the truant – 'twas the only thing he played,
For the maister brunt the whistle that the wee herd made!

T49   BROWN, George Douglas, *The House with the Green Shutters* (1901)

George Douglas Brown (1869-1902), was born in Ochiltree, Ayrshire; the son of a farmer became a
student at Glasgow and Oxford. He worked as novelist and journalist. His main achievement, *The
House with the Green Shutters* (published under the pseudonym George Douglas) is in the tradition of
John Galt; it was written in opposition to the 'Kailyard', whose sentimental treatment of rural Scotland
had come to dominate Scots verse and prose in the second half of the 19th century.

The first excerpt from *The House with the Green Shutters* contains a conversation between the
"bodies" (the self-important inhabitants of the small town the novel is set in) and a short narrative in
Scots by one of the broadest speakers, who is prone to reminiscence. Brown characterises many of his
characters by special features – not necessarily Scots ones – in their speech (the Provost, for instance,
often lengthens his vowels, as in "pow-ers" or "wha-at", "ainything"; the deacon has a lisp, etc.).
According to their social status, the "bodies" speak with more or less obvious dialect features. The
second excerpt is a particularly dense piece of Scots narrative. The narrator usually speaks English with
rare idiomatic Scotticisms, but occasionally shifts more towards Scots.

Source: George Douglas Brown, *The House with the Green Shutters*, [1901], ed. Dorothy Porter,
Harmondsworth: Penguin, 1985, pp.72-3, 100.

"He's getting a big boy, that son of Gourlay's," said the Provost, "how oald will
he be?"

"He's approaching twelve," said Johnny Coe, who made a point of being able to
supply such news because it gained him consideration where he was otherwise
5 unheeded. "He was born the day the brig on the Fleckie Road gaed down, in the year
o' the great flood; and since the great flood it's twelve year come Lammas. Rab Tosh
o' Fleckie's wife was heavy-footed at the time, and Doctor Munn had been a' nicht
wi' her, and when he cam to Barbie Water in the morning it was roaring wide frae
bank to brae; where the brig should have been there was naething but the swashing
10 of the yellow waves. Munn had to drive a' the way round to the Fechars brig, and in
parts o' the road the water was so deep that it lapped his horse's bellyband. A' this
time Mrs Gourlay was skirling in her pains and praying to God she micht dee.
Gourlay had been a great crony o' Munn's, but he quarrelled him for being late; he
had trysted him, ye see, for the occasion, and he had been twenty times at the yett to
15 look for him, – ye ken how little he would stomach that; he was ready to brust wi'
anger. Munn, mad for the want of sleep and wat to the bane, swüre back at him; and
than Gourlay wadna let him near his wife! Ye mind what an awful day it was; the

thunder roared as if the heavens were tumbling on the world, and the lichtnin sent the
trees daudin on the roads, and folk hid below their beds and prayed – they thocht in
20 was the Judgment! But Gourlay rammed his black stepper in the shafts, and drave
like the devil o' hell to Skeign Drone, where there was a young doctor. The lad was
feared to come, but Gourlay swore by God that he should, and he garred him. In a'
the countryside driving like his that day was never kenned or heard tell o'; they were
back within the hour! I saw them gallop up Main Street; lichtnin struck the ground
25 before them; the young doctor covered his face wi' his hands, and the horse nichered
wi' fear and tried to wheel, but Gourlay stood up in the gig and lashed him on
through the fire. It was thocht for lang that Mrs Gourlay would die; and she was
never the same woman after. Atweel aye sirs, Gourlay has that morning's work to
blame for the poor wife he has now. Him and Munn never spoke to each other again,
30 and Munn died within the twelvemonth, – he got his death that morning on the
Fleckie Road. But, for a' so pack's they had been, Gourlay never looked near him."

Coe had told his story with enjoying gusto, and had told it well – for Johnny,
though constantly snubbed by his fellows, was in many ways the ablest of them all.
His voice and manner drove it home. They knew, besides, he was telling what
35 himself had seen. For they knew he was lying prostrate with fear in the open
smiddyshed from the time Gourlay went to Skeighan Drone to the time that he came
back; and that he had seen him both come and go. (...) Tam Brodie, the most brutal
among them, was the first to recover. Even he did not try to belittle at once, but he
felt the subtle discomfort of the situation, and relieved it by bringing the conversation
40 back to its usual channel.

"That was at the boy's birth, Mr Coe?" said he.

"Ou, aye, just the laddie. It was a' richt when the lassie came. It was Doctor
Dandy brocht *her* hame, for Munn was deid by that time, and Dandy had his place."

"What will Gourlay be going to make of him?" the Provost asked. "A doctor or a
45 minister or wha-at?"

"Deil a fear of that," said Brodie; "he'll take him into business! It's a' that he's fit
for. He's an infernal dunce, just his father owre again, and the Dominie thrashes him
remoresless! I hear my own weans speaking o't. Ou, it seems he's just a perfect
numbskull!"

50   "Ye couldn't expect ainything else from a son of Gourlay," said the Provost. (...)

(...) It is a cheese-making countryside about Barbie, and the less butter produced
at a cheese-making place – the better for the cheese. Still, a good many pounds are
often churned on the sly. What need the cheese merchant ken – it keepit the gudewife
in bawbees frae week to week – and if she took a little cream frae the cheese now and
than they werena a pin the waur o't, for she aye did it wi' decency and caution! Still
it is as well to dispose of this kind of butter quietly, to avoid gabble among ill-
speakers. Wilson, slithering up the back road with his spring cart in the gloaming,
was the man to dispose of it quietly. And he got it dirt cheap, of course, seeing it was
a kind of contraband. All that he made in this way was not much to be suree – three-
pence a dozen on the eggs, perhaps, and fourpence on the pound of butter – still, you
know, every little makes a mickle, and hained gear helps weel.* (...)

T50   BELL, John Joy, *Wee Macgreegor* (1901)

John Joy Bell (1871-1934), novelist and journalist, was born in Glasgow and sudied chemistry at Glasgow University. In spite of its urban setting, much of his work shows a 'kailyard' sentimentality. In his best known work, *Wee MacGreegor*, he gives a stylized picture of Glasgow working-class life seen through the eyes of a boy (though not narrated by him); this gave the book very wide appeal and it became one of the most widely read novels of its type. The colloquial language used in dialogues, though compromising with written English, is one of the early coherent sources of Glaswegian urban Scots which was being formed in the late 19th century.

The excerpt illustrates the contrast between the Glaswegian dialogue and the English narrative, and also parodies the efforts of Glasgow's prosperous bourgeouisie to sound 'refined'.

Source: J.J. Bell, *Wee Macgreegor*, [1901], London: Grafton Books, 1977, pp.30-6.

Pronunciation: cf. the phonetic transcription of a different passage from this novel in Grant & Dixon (1921:376f).

AUNT PURDIE'S TEA-PARTY

The Robinsons were on their way to take tea at Aunt Purdie's, and the anxious Lizzie was counselling her son regarding his behaviour at the table of that excellent lady.

'Noo, Macgreegor, ye're no' to affront me. Yer Aunt Purdie's rale genteel, an' awfu' easy offendit.'

5 'Dod, ay!'said John, 'ye'll ha'e to mind yer Q.P.'s the day, as the sayin' is.'

'Dod, ay!' said Macgregor.

'I've tell't ye dizzens o' times, Macgreegor, ye're no' to say that,' said his mother.

'I furgot, Maw.'

'If yer Aunt Purdie wis hearin' ye speak that wey she wud be sair pit oot. An',
10 John,' turning to her husband, 'ye sud be mair carefu' whit ye say afore the wean. He's jist like a paurrit fur pickin' up words.'

'Dod, ay!' said John seriously, 'I'll ha'e to be carefu', Lizzie.'

'Ye're a terrible man,' said his wife, frowning and smiling.

'Wull I get a tert at Aunt Purdie's?' inquired Macgregor.

15 'Ye'll see whit ye'll get when ye get it.' replied his mother. 'An' mind, Macgreegor, ye're no' to be askin' fur jelly till ye've ett twa bits o' breid an' butter. It's no mainners; an' yer Aunt Purdie's rale parteeclar. An' yer no' to dicht yer mooth wi' yer cuff – mind that. Ye're to tak' yer hanky an' let on ye're jist gi'ein yer nose a bit wipe. An' ye're no' to scale yer tea nor sup the sugar, if ony's left in yer cup
20 when ye're dune drinkin'. An' if ye drap yer piece on the floor, ye're no' to gang efter it; ye're jist to let on ye've ett it. An' ye're no'–'

'Deed, Lizzie,' interposed her husband, 'ye're the body to think aboot things!'

'Weel, John, if I dinna tell Macgreegor hoo to behave hissel', he'll affront me. It's maybe a sma' maitter to a man, John, but a wumman disna like to be pit oot afore her
25 guid-sister. An', John, ye're to try an' be discreet yersel', an' think afore ye mak' a bit joke – fur she's a rale genteel wumman, an' awfu' easy offendit.'

'But yer brither likes a lauch, Lizzie.'

'Ay, Rubbert's a herty man; but a' the same, John, ye're no' to gar him lauch abin his breith. An' yer no' to lauch yersel' if Macgreegor tries to be smairt.'
30 'A' richt, Lizzie,' said her husband good-humouredly.

'Dod, I'm thinkin' ye're jist aboot as feart fur me as fur the wean.'

'Havers, John! I'm no' finnin' fau't wi' you. It's jist that ye whiles furget yer –'

'Ma Q.P.'s.'

'Ay, yer Q.P.'s, as ye ca' it. I aye thocht Q.P.'s wis a kin' o' fit-ba'.'

35   Her husband was about to explain when Macgregor exclaimed that Aunt Purdie's dwelling was in sight.

'Ay, it's the third close,' remarked John, proceeding to plug his pipe with a scrap of newspaper. After that he pulled up his collar, tightened his tie, cocked his hat a little over one eye, winked at his wife, and chucked his little daughter under the chin.

40   'I wud just as shin be at hame, Lizzie.' he observed, as they turned into the close.

'Whisht, John! Mrs Purdie's a rale dacent wumman, an' – an' we needna wait ower lang. See if ye can gi'e Macgreegor's hair a bit tosh up. It's awfu' ill to lie.... Noo, John, ye'll gang furrit an' ring the bell. Mind, ye're to speir if Mrs Purdie is in afore ye gang ower the doorstep.'

45   'But she wudna ha'e askit us to wur tea if she had been fur gaun oot.' said John.

'Tits, man! D'ye no' ken Mrs Purdie keeps a servant lass, an' ye maun speir at her if her mistress is in. Mind, yer no' to say "it's a fine day," or onythin' like that; ye're jist to speir if Mrs Purdie's in. D'ye see?'

'Weel, weel, wumman, onythin' to please ye!' And John pulled the bell-handle. 'I
50 ken she's in,' he whispered. 'I hear her roarin' at somebody.'

'Sh! John. Jist dae whit I tell't ye.'

The door was opened and John bashfully repeated the formula.

'Will you please step in?' said the domestic, a small, rosy-cheeked girl, who still showed her ankles though she had put up her hair.

55   'Dicht yer feet, Macgreegor, dicht yer feet,' said Lizzie in a quick, loud whisper, 'See, dicht them on the bass.'

Macgregor obeyed with great vigour, and followed the others into the lobby.

'Paw, we've a brawer nock nor thon yin,' he remarked in a husky undertone, pointing at a grandfather's clock in a corner.

60   'Whisht!' said his mother nervously.

'Wull I pit ma bunnet in ma pooch, Maw?' asked the boy.

'Na, na! John, hing his bunnet up aside yer ain.'

Just then Mrs Purdie appeared and bade them welcome; and presently they were gathered in the parlour, wherein the table was already laid for tea. Mr Purdie was
65 getting on well in the world – his grocery establishment was gaining new customers daily – and Mrs Purdie was inclined, alas! to look down on her homely relatives, and to regard their manners and speech as vulgar, with the sole result that her own manners were frequently affected, while her speech was sometimes a strange mixture.

70   'And how are you to-day, Macgregor?' she asked the boy as they sat round the fire.

'I'm fine,' replied Macgregor, glancing at the good things on the table.

'Fine what?' said Aunt Purdie severely.

'Ye sud say, "Fine, thenk ye,"' whispered his mother, giving him a nudge.

75   'Fine, thenk ye,' said Macgregor obediently. 'I wis at the Zoo yesterday.'

'Oh, indeed! Was you? And what did you see at the Zoo?'

'Beasts, thenk ye,' said Macgregor.

'An' hoo's Rubbert?' asked Lizzie with some haste.

'Robert is keeping well, thank you; but he's sorry he cannot leave the shope this
80 evening. His young man was unfortunately rin over by an electric caur yesterday.'

'Oh, thae caurs!' said Lizzie. 'I'm aye feart fur Macgreegor gettin' catched, an'
comin' hame wantin' a leg.'

'Robert's young man got conclusion of the brain,' said Aunt Purdie with great
solemnity. 'He was carrying a dizzen of eggs an' a pun' of the best ham when the
85 melancholy accident occurred.'

'Dae ye tell me that?' exclaimed Lizzie. 'An' wis the eggs a' broke?'

'With two exceptions.' And Aunt Purdie went on to describe the accident in detail
to Lizzie, while John and Macgregor looked out of the window, and wee Jeannie,
who had been put on the floor to 'play herself,' found amusement in pulling to pieces
90 a half-knitted stocking which she discovered in a basket under the sofa. (...)

T51 CAMERON, Henry P., *Genesis in Scots* (1921)

Henry Paterson Cameron (1852-1921) was educated at Glasgow University and became minister of the
parish of Milton in 1879. He translated literary texts and wrote on religious matters (including a
History of the English Bible, 1885). After being deposed as minister and divorced in 1890, he
emigrated to Australia, where he ran a private school. In his exile he retained his interest in Scots,
compiled a glossary to the works of John Service, another Scottish writer living in New South Wales,
and translated Thomas à Kempis's *Imitation of Christ* into Scots in 1912; *Genesis* in Scots was
published in the year of his death. The translation of *Genesis* is based on the *Revised Version* and is
influenced by earlier translations, e.g. by Waddell and Paterson, and by the language of the traditional
canon of Scottish literature. Cameron draws on "vocabulary from Scots of all periods [and various
regions], although his basic vocabulary is taken from Modern Scots" (Tulloch 1989:66). "All this
produces a large and varied vocabulary, including both well-known and little-known Scots terms. [...]
In both grammar and spelling Cameron is a pretty consistent scoticiser [and] generally adheres to the
conventions of the modern literary standard and avoids regional forms" (ibd.). "He aims to differentiate
Scots from English as much as is possible within the conventions of Modern Scots spelling. Where he
departs from these conventions he looks to Older Scots for authority. [...] Overall, Cameron produces
a consistent, standardised, literary Scots heavily dependent on written sources rather than the
reproduction of actual speech of a particular place and time" (67) – similar to Lallans, the language of
the Scottish Literary Renaissance, although Cameron refrains from creating his own new words. "The
formality is increased by the frequent retention of the *Revised Version* word order and by the use of
quha and quhilk rather than the colloquial at." (67). He adds a glossary to his translation, in which he
identifies some of his sources.

The excerpts are taken from the preface and two chapters of the *Genesis*.

Source: Henry P. Cameron, *Genesis in Scots*. Paisley: Alexander Gardner, 1921, pp.1, 13-4.

PREFATORY NOTE

In his Preface to *The Kirk i' the Clachan* – a buik ilk ane suld read – Mr. Mitchell o'
Cramond says: "There's a cry in mony lands for the truth i' the mither tongue." And
noo, sin that "scraigh" gangs up frae the herts o' mony bairns o' Scotia in Australia
and ither pairts as weel, we hae try't in a daine wey till meet this lang for trewth be
5 translatin intill the mither tung ane o' the buiks o' the Bible. For whaur is trewth to

be fun gin it binna i' the Bible? Forby, it is the buik a Scotchman loes best.

    This Scotifiean o' "Genesis" is foondit apo' the Revised Version, and the idee o' "paragraphs" wes taen frae Prof. Moulton's *The Modern Reader's Bible* – a wheen bonnie wee vollumns, and a' vera guid.

10   The owther wad like till eik that the buik wes begoud and fineist i' the Australian "bush", – faur awa frae the curfuffle o' the warl and the smasherie o' weir – still-and-on e'en mids the eldritch yowlin o' the dingo, the rowtin o' nowte, the maein o' fe, and the schill crawin o' the "rooster", he haes hard athin his saul and abune them a' the "saft, couthie" müsick o' the Doric.

15   THE SCHUPPIN O' THE WARL

I' the ingang God schuppit the hevin and the erd. And the erd wes wust and vide; and the mirk happit the face o' the depe: and the Gheist o' God steerit apo' the face o' the watirs.

    And quo' God, Lat thar be licht: and licht wes. And God saw the licht, that it wes 20 guid: and God sinder't the licht frae the mirk. And God ca'd the licht Day, and the mirk He ca'd Nicht. And thar wes e'enin and thar wes mornin, ae day.

    And quo' God, Lat thar be a lift i' the mids o' the watirs, and lat it sinder the watirs frae the watirs. And God schuppit the lift, and sinder't the watirs whilk war aneath the lift frae the watirs whilk war abune the lift: and it wes sae. And God ca'd 25 the lift Hevin. And thar wes e'enin and thar wes mornin, a saicond day.

    And quo' God, Lat the watirs ablow the hevin be gaither't thegither ontill ae bit, and lat the histie lan kythe: and it wes sae. And God ca'd the histie lan Erd: and the gaitherin thegither o' the watirs ca'd He Seas: and God saw that it wes guid. And quo' God, Lat the erd fesh furth gerss, yirb giean seid, and frute tree giean frute eftir 30 its kin', whaurin is the seid o't, apo' the erd: and it wes sae. And the erd fotch furth gerss, yirb giean seid eftir its kin', and tree giean frute, whaurin is the seid o't, eftir its kin': and God saw that it wes guid. And thar wes e'enin and thar wes mornin, a thrid day.

    And quo' God, Lat thar be lichts i' the lift o' the hevin till sinder the day frae the 35 nicht; and lat thame be for witters and for saizzons and for days and yeir: and lat thame be for lichts i' the lift o' the hevin to gie licht apo' the erd: and it wes sae. And God made the twa muckle lichts, the muckler licht to rewl the day, and the wee'r licht to rewl the nicht: He made the starns als. And God set thame i' the lift o' the hevin till gie licht apo' the erd and till rewl owre the day and owre the nicht, and till 40 sinder the licht frae the mirk: and God saw that it wes guid. And thar wes e'enin and thar wes mornin, a fowrt day.

    And quo' God, Lat the watirs fesh furth rowthily the steerin craitur whilk haes life, and lat birds flee abune the erd i' the apen lift o' hevin. And God schuppit muckle whaals, and ilka leevin craitur that steers, whilk the watirs brang furth rowthily, eftir 45 thair kin's, and ilka weengit bird eftir its kin': and God saw that it wes guid (...)

T52   GARIOCH, Robert, *Purity or Smeddum* (1933)

Robert Garioch (pen-name of R.G. Sutherland) (1909-81) was born and educated in Edinburgh. Until his retirement in 1964, he was a teacher, and also worked as assistant lexicographer for the *Dictionary of the Older Scottish Tongue*. From 1971-73 he was writer in residence at the University of Edinburgh. He is celebrated as one of the major Scots poets of the 20th century, with a great talent for satire and parody. He admitted that his "writing in Scots was a protest against the encroaching anglicization of the Scots tongue. There was, though, a quality to his use of language that sprang directly from his use of living Scots as a child" (Royle, 294). His best poems are, like Robert Fergusson's, about his native Edinburgh, on which he also wrote a short play (*The Masque of Edinburgh* 1954). Garioch was also active as a translator into Scots from various languages.

The following text is an article for the *Scots Observer*, in which Garioch describes how he came to develop his own type of literary Scots. It is a very early example of expository prose writing in Scots, antedating texts of a similar type by Young and Smith (T56 and T57) by about fifteen years.

Source: Robert Garioch, "Purity or Smeddum – The Alternatives of Scottish Dialect". *Scots Observer* 18 Feb. 1933. Repr. *Lallans* 18, 1982, pp.5-8.

Some twaw-three years syne, when A first ettled ti write poetry in what A fondly ima-
gined ti be ma ain Edinburgh dialect, that is, in the very mainner in whilk the words
form thirsels within ma heid, or iver they are sorted up to suit the conversational tone
o braw leddies in a drawinroom, ir that o drucken cairters in a pub, accordin ti
5 whichiver phase o Society A may happen ti be sib wi at the moment, A fund masel
maistly sneered it iz yit anither synthetic Scot; an iz yit anither synthetic Scot A hae
been generally lauched it iver eftir. I wad therefore like ti say a word ir twaw anent ma
Edinburgh dialect in particular, an the Scottish tongue generally. Noo, it hiz aye
appeared ti me thit, gin ony Scottish speech wud be true an naiteral-like, it maun
10 follow the same development in the individual iz ony ither language ir dialect what-
soiver. Ony sort o hauf-educated buddy, ony man, that is, whaw hiz eneuch buik-leir ti
gar him ettle ti write somethin o his ain, maun develop his language bi the same
process; nae maitter whither he writes in Braid Scots ir in Standard English. This
process, ti ma wey o thinkin, begins in oor early childhood, when we first begin ti
15 parrot the soons spoken bi the folks roon aboot iz. The foond o oor tongue, therefore,
is accent: the wee bairn stammers oot his smaw speech in the accent o his ain fireside:
the accent thit will bide in his speech till his voice is heard nae mair. The words thirsels
hae less import than the accent in whilk they are spoken.

As the bairn grows in knowledge an in years, his mind becomes filled wi new ideas
20 thit maun be expressed in the general standard terminology, as the local mainner o
speakin canny cope wi the situation. At the skuil, forbye, the growin bairn maun read
Standard English words, an iz like iz no, will mak a stoot-herted, bit no ower successfy
attempt ti pronounce them accordin ti the standard wey o speakin. Finally, the later
development o the speech o ony individual whaw gaes aboot a bit an reads onything
25 thit he may git a haud o, involves the assimilation o aw kinds o words an phrases, ivery
yin o whilk, hooiver, is pronounced mair ir less in his ain local accent.

Noo, ti apply thae general considerations ti the case o the dialect o ma three
poems. A hae ettled in the first o them ti describe a wee laddie's adventure frae a
bairn's point o view, in the accent o a wee Edinburgh keelie. A'll no say it's juist as
30 bonny a dialect iz some thit A hae heard; bit thayr it is: A happened ti be brocht up in
it, an maun e'en tak it iz A find it.

BUCKIE-WIFE

Auld wife, auld wife, hae ye ony buckies?
Tippence wirth o buckies an
35   *Preens fir twaw!*
Tane fir me, an
The tither fir ma lassie-o
We'll buy a puckle buckies fir
Ti pick in Potterrow!

40   The second poem belangs ti the transition period, in whilk the growin bairn is
warslin awaw wi unkent tongues, an maistly findin it a gey sair fecht.

TRANSITION

A sit in a braw-built skill,
wi brawlike Doric pillars abuin ma heid,
45   *bit the words A read*
are Attic-English, though sair fornenst ma will,
fir ma teuch Scots tongue gaes cantier ower the rocks
o the clarty staucherin speech o ma Embro nurse
than it diz wi the saft sweet sooch o an English verse –
50   *bit the maister knocks*
wi the sair hard edge o his tawse on ma finger-tips,
an he gars me mooth smooth verse wi ma Northern lips:
"Shades of the prison-howse begin ti close
Upon the growin boy
55   *Bit he beholds the light an whence it flows –*
He sees i' in his joy."
"What's that he sees, young man?" the maister says –
"Itt, Sir" – the bluid burns dirlin in ma face –
bi' the bell sterts ringin, ringin, an A've gey suin fun ma feet
60   *in a bonny stoory gu'er, playin fi'baw in the street!*

The third poem is written in the mair ir less mature style o a man whaw hiz
widened the scope o his vocabulary through contact wi ither local dialects, an wi
Standard English works; the hale bein in a measure unified bi the original accent o
the individual, whilk maun modify the orthography ti some extent.

65   MODERN ATHENS

The waves o the toon wallow in broons an blaes
ower sivin hills, yince bonny eneugh, nae doot:
they cawd it Modern Athens in Ruskin's days,
an cluttered the Calton Acropolis up wi loot,
70   *auld moulit cannons captured the deil kens whayr,*
an ugly yisless tank, aw rust an scale;
whayriver they fun an acre ir twaw ti spare
they biggit on't – a stang, bit daftlike jail,
a wheen roon huts fir gliffin at the stawrs...
75   *Sine in yon public park,*

whit div thi dae bit stick a bit o wark
raxed frae the clean, cauld pagan art o Greece,
strang, shapely pillars, even here at peace
in aw thon awfy wilderness, twalve nuns, pure in thir true
80   *proportions, stand apairt*
frae aw thon birslin fortalice o guns;
apairt frae Burns's wee, roon cotton-pirn
(a pepper-pat, some cawd) an Nelson's butter kirn.

Bit the thing that A canny mak oot at aw, as A stare at the hale clamjamphrey,
85   *is the fact that it dizny offend me avaw, si noo ye'll jalouse whayr A've cam frae!*

A'm felt thit Scotland's sowl is deid
(barrin the railway posters),
bit A stand on an ugly, bit handy irin brig
thit loups abuin Halkerston's Wynd, whayr the station is noo,
90   *though A canny git leave ti stand fir the thrangs o folk*
bizzin aboot that wey, ye'd think ye'd nae richt ti be here;
an ma lugs are deeved wi the din o electric cawrs,
melled wi the ding an the clatter o brewers' cairts,
the deid, hard dunt o an illshod wheel on the stanes,
95   *an mixter-maxter tined in the hale stramush,*
the wheezin, reedy tune o an auld blin man
wha joogles wi yin o thae concerteeny things:
an whiles A hear an unco girnin dirge
scraped frae an auld cracked fiddle yince broken in twaw,
100   *sine clappit thegither an tied wi a hantle o string;*
he fiddles awaw wi a jouk o his sunbrunt pow,
twa legs he hiz, bit yin o thum's made o wud,
an he fiddles and driddles awaw, day in day oot,
aye the same tune, A MAN'S A MAN FIR AW THAT.
105   *Bit here as A stnad in the middle o sic a steer,*
A'm lowin an lowin wi pride, though A dinny ken why
(But an Embro man maun aye be prood o his toon)
A cin feel the widdle o lorries an beggars an dirt
tak a grup o ma hert, though awmist fornenst ma will;
110   *wi the swish o the tramway wires abuin ma heid*
oot frae the warld o machines A turn ma gaze
through the reeky haze
o the Canongait lums, ti whayr Erthur's sooty hill,
like a lusty weed
115   *blawn ti a brewery yaird, grows green thayr still;*
an somethin gars me ken in ma hert o herts
thit the city mauna be judged bi her Calton rags;
somethin thit bides in the midst o buses an cairts,
in the roar o exhausts an the peace o the Castle crags,

120 *the noisy poo'r o the new, and the micht o the auld:*
     it maun be the changeless sowl o the helpless toon
     sturrin ma hert, though gey sair hadden doon
     ti the stane an lime o a corp ower easy mauled;
     the spirit o Embro thit nae bad taste cin kill,
125 *we maun be prood o Modern Athens still!*

In aw three poems A hae ettled ti yase the function o accent in a mainner worthy o the importance thit it possesses, ti ma wey o thinkin, in the formation o ony form o the Scots tongue, bi writin doon the words as A wud naiterally pronounce them under ideal circumstances, wi as muckle phonetic accurancy iz ye cin manage withoot 130 yaising byornar alphabetic characters.

In conclusion, A wud apply this theory o the naiteral individual development o dialect ti the question o synthetic Scots. Ti ma mind, the only true and naiteral Scottish literature maun follow this development, an the mair advantage it taks o the widenin o scope afforded bi the later stages o that process, the richer a medium will 135 it produce. On the ither haun, naethin cud be mair artificial than ti gaun ti a fairmhoose wi a wee notebuik, notin doon the words iz thi tumble frae the lips o the fermer an his guid wife; subsequently connin them weel at hame, an manufacturin a poem accordin ti the limitations o the speech o siclike country buddies. A poem o this kind is mibby pure eneuch; bit like mony anither pure article, it's no muckle the 140 better for't.

T53   GIBBON, Lewis Grassic, *Smeddum* (1934)

The novelist Lewis Grassic Gibbon (James Leslie Mitchell, 1901-35), was born in Auchterless, Aberdeenshire, the son of a farmer; in 1909 the family moved to the Howe of the Mearns, which was to be the setting for *A Scots Quair*. He was educated in Aberdeenshire and Kincardineshire, worked as journalist in Aberdeen and Glasgow, served in army and air force from 1919-29 and travelled extensively in that period. Apart from various historical and anthropological books, he wrote seven novels in English. His major achievement, however, is the Scottish trilogy *Sunset Song* (1932), *Cloud Howe* (1933) and *Grey Granite* (1934), which were posthumously published as *A Scots Quair* (1946).

The following passage by Gibbon is taken from the short story "Smeddum". The spelling of words shared by Scots and English is English throughout, but here Gibbon uses much more Scots vocabulary and idiomatic word-order.

Source: Lewis Grassic Gibbon, "Smeddum" [1934], in: J.M. Reid (ed.), *Classic Scottish Short Stories*. Oxford: UP, 1989, pp.226-7.

She'd had nine of a family in her time, Mistress Menzies, and brought the nine of them up, forbye – some near by the scruff of the neck, you would say. They were sniftering and weakly, two-three of the bairns, sniftering in their cradles to get into their coffins; but she'd shake them to life, and dose them with salts and feed them up 5 till they couldn't but live. And she'd plonk one down – finishing the wiping of the creature's neb or the unco dosing of an ill bit stomach or the binding of a broken head – with a look on her face as much as to say *Die on me now and see what you'll get!*

Big-boned she was by her fortieth year, like a big roan mare, and *If ever she was bonny 'twas in Noah's time*, Jock Menzies, her eldest son would say. She'd reddish 10 hair and a high, skeugh nose, and a hand that skelped her way through life; and if

ever a soul had seen her at rest when the dark was done and the day was come he'd
died of the shock and never let on.

For from morn till night she was at it, work, work, on that ill bit croft that sloped
to the sea. When there wasn't a mist on the cold, stone parks there was more than
15 likely the wheep of the rain, wheeling and dripping in from the sea that soughed and
plashed by the land's stiff edge. Kinneff lay north, and at night in the south, if the sky
was clear on the gloaming's edge, you'd see in that sky the Bervie lights come
suddenly lit, far and away, with the quiet about you as you stood and looked, nothing
to hear but a sea-bird's cry.

20 But feint the much time to look or to listen had Margaret Menzies of Tocherty
toun. Day blinked and Meg did the same, and was out, up out of her bed, and about
the house, making the porridge and rousting the bairns, and out to the byre to milk
the three kye, the morning growing out in the east and a wind like a hail of knives
from the hills. Syne back to the kitchen again she would be, and catch Jock, her
25 eldest, a clour in the lug that he hadn't roused up his sisters and brothers; and rouse
them herself, and feed them and scold, pull up their breeks and straighten their
frocks, and polish their shoes and set their caps straight. *Off you get and see you're
not late*, she would cry, *and see you behave yourselves at the school. And tell the
Dominie I'll be down the night to ask him what the mischief he meant by leathering
30 Jeannie and her not well.*

They'd cry *Ay, Mother*, and go trotting away, a fair flock of the creatures, their
faces red-scoured. Her own as red, like a meikle roan mare's, Meg'd turn at the door
and go prancing in; and then at last, by the closet-bed, lean over and shake her man
half-awake. *Come on, then, Willie, it's time you were up.*

T54   SMITH, Sydney Goodsir, *Epistle to John Guthrie* (1941)

Sidney Goodsir Smith (1915-75) was born in Wellington, N.Z., the son of a future professor of
medicine at Edinburgh University, and came to Edinburgh in 1927. Though he was educated at English
private schools and at Oxford University, by 1940 he was writing poetry in Scots. "Although it was not
his native tongue, Smith evolved a poetic language based largely on the cadences of spoken Scots,
reinforced with a vocabulary garnered from the Middle Scots Makars. However artificial it might
appear in theory, Smith's language is always vibrantly alive and rich with the demotic strengths of
spoken speech." (Royle, 280). Love poems (*Under the Eildon Tree*, 1948), a description of Edinburgh
(*Kynd Kittock's Land*, 1965) and a verse play (*The Wallace*, 1960) make him "the most important
writer in the second generation of the Scottish Renaissance" (Royle 1983: 280; also cf. Hall 1982 and
Murison 1975).

In the "Epistle to John Guthrie", Smith reacts to a critic's attack on his use of Scots for poetry. He
justifies himself by pointing out the active use of Scots by the Edinburgh working class. He claims that
it can be heard everywhere in the city, and that he is only augmenting what is there, in order to create
an effective literary language – like many English poets before him. The subject being also the medium
of the poem, the language is "aggrandized" by the use of old and/or regionally restricted dialect words;
the spelling is fairly consistent in its attempt to scotticize shared words, and Smith (in contrast to, e.g.,
MacDiarmid) takes care not to use 'superfluous' apostrophes, while not trying to create a naturalistic
phonetic spelling, either (cf. also his "Defence of 'Lallans'", T57).

Source: Sydney Goodsir Smith, "Epistle to John Guthrie", in: *Collected Poems*. London: John Calder,
1975, p.13.

EPISTLE TO JOHN GUTHRIE
(who had blamed the poet for writing in Scots 'which no one speaks')

We've come intil a gey queer time
Whan scrievin Scots is near a crime,
"There's no one speaks like that", they fleer,
– But wha the deil spoke like King Lear?

5 And onyweys doon Canongate
I'll tak ye slorpin pints till late,
Ye'll hear Scots there as raff an slee –
Its no the point, sae that'll dae.

Ye'll fin the leid, praps no the fowth,
10 The words 're there, praps no the ferlie;
For he wha'ld rant wi Rabbie's mouth
Maun leave his play-pen unco erlie.

Nane cud talk lik Gawen Douglas writes,
He hanna the vocablerie,
15 Nor cud he flyte as Dunbar flytes –
Yir argy-bargy's tapsalteerie!

Did Johnnie Keats whan he was drouth
Ask "A beaker full o the warm South"?
Fegs no, he leaned acrost the bar
20 An called for "A point o bitter, Ma!"

But the Suddron's noo a sick man's leid,
Alang the flattest plains it stots;
Tae reach the hills his fantice needs
This bard maun tak the wings o Scots.

25 And so, dear John, ye jist maun dree
My Scots; for English, man, 's near deid,
See the weeshy-washy London bree
An tell me then whaes bluid is reid!

But mind, nae poet eer writes "common speech",
30 Ye'll fin eneuch o yon in prose;
His realm is heich abune its reach –
Jeez! wha'ld use ale for Athol Brose?

T55 McLELLAN, Robert, *The Flouers o Edinburgh* (1948)

Robert McLellan (1907-1985), born at Linmill, Lanarkshire, was a writer of short stories (a selection of which were published collectively in 1977 as the *Linmill Stories*, T58) and of plays in Scots (*Jamie the Saxt* 1937, *The Flouers o Edinburgh* 1948, etc.). He also wrote several plays in English, but they never reached the popularity of the ones in Scots. McLellan took up and carried on the impetus of the Scottish Renaissance, mainly as the most influential 20th-century playwright using Scots.

The Flouers o Edinburgh is one of McLellan's historical plays, set in 1760s 'enlightened' Edinburgh. It deals with the political conflict between two generations of the Scottish gentry: on the one hand the Scots-speaking, 'nationalist' group, adhering to conservative values, represented mainly by the older generation, who still have Culloden fresh on their minds; on the other hand there is the 'progressive', anglicised party of those who speak English, or want to learn it because of its prestige and political value. Much of the humour is derived from the contrast between English and Scots, the respective evaluations of the two varieties by the two groups, and from the abortive attempts of some of the 'progressive' characters to learn English. The excerpt illustrates the cultural/ political debate: Charles has just returned from the grand tour (which was financed by his father) speaking English and opposing all the ideas and values that are important to his father. Doctor Dowie is later to try and learn English, fail miserably and even shame himself and his friends by betraying his Scottish origin by his accent when in London.

Source: Robert McLellan, *The Flouers o Edinburgh*, in: *Collected Plays*. London: John Calder, 1981, vol.I, pp.174-9.

Charles – (*Surprised and not altogether happy*) Father!

Lord S – Leave us, Jock.

Jock – Aa richt, for a whilie, but I'll sune hae to come in and mask the tea, and there'll be mair folk comin to the door. (*Muttering as he goes to the kitchen*) Losh,
5   what a sicht. Mair lace nor a lassie.

Charles – The insolent dog! Did you hear him?

Lord S – Can ye blame the man?

Charles – Father! What do you mean?

Lord S – I said 'can ye blame the man?' Whan did ye stert to talk and dress like an
10   Englishman?

Charles – (*With a faint sneer*) Do you want me to talk and dress like the men here?

Lord S – Ye belang up here, dae ye no? Ye were born Scots.

Charles – I am British, father. The terms 'Scotch' and 'English' became obsolete with the Union.

15 *Lord S* – Did they? I'll wager ye winna fin mony Englishmen caain themselves British and stertin to talk and dress like Scotsmen.

Charles – Can you blame them? Their language is much more refined than ours, and their clothes infinitely more tasteful.

Lord S – Their language is faur ower refined, as they caa it, for oor vocal organs. Ye
20   may think ye mak no a bad shape at it, but compared wi a real Englishman ye're like a bubbly-jock wi a chuckie in its thrapple. As for yer claes, they wad sit weill on a lassie, but they're haurdly fit weir for a man. Hae they been peyed for?

Charles – Father!

Lord S – Hae they, I'm askin?

25 *Charles* – We can surely discuss that matter elsewhere.

Lord S – There are a lot o maitters we could discuss elsewhaur, but ye seem to tak gey
    guid care we dinna. What dae ye mean by comin hame efter three years awa
    withoot as muckle as a word to yer ain faither? What gart ye gang oot to Aberlady
    insteid o comin to my ludgin in the Toun? I suppose ye were ashamed to look me
30   in the face. (...)

(*He opens the door to reveal* Doctor Dowie) Ay, sir?

Dowie – My name's Dowie, Doctor Dowie. I'm the meenister o the parish o Dule. I
    hae a letter o introduction to Leddy Athelstane frae ...

Jock – (*Interrupting pleasantly*) Oh ay, ye'll hae written a book?

35 *Dowie* – Weill, sir.

Jock – Na, na, Doctor, dinna sir me. I'm juist the servant here. My name's Jock.

Dowie – I see. Weill, Jock, I'm the author o 'The Tomb'.

Jock – 'The Tomb'?

Dowie – A lang poem.

40 *Jock* – Oh, 'The Tomb'! Come awa in Doctor. Come awa in. There's a copy o 'The
    Tomb' on the table there. Leddy Athelstane likes to hae it aye to haund. She says
    there's naething like it if ye want a guid greit.

Dowie – (*Pleased*) Daes she say that?

Jock – She daes.

45 *Dowie* – The wark's weill kent, then, amang the Toun gentry?

Jock – It's the maist popular wark o its time in the English language. Davie Hume
    himsell said sae juist last week.

Dowie – Hume the Infidel! He couldna admire it.

Jock – Oh he daesna admire it, but he had to admit it was the maist popular wark o its
50   time.

Lord S – Gie Doctor Dowie a cup o tea, Jock, and haud yer tongue. Doctor Dowie,
    I'm Lord Stanebyres.

Dowie – I'm pleased to meet ye, my lord. Lord Stanebyres? Lord Stanebyres? Let me
    see. Was it 'An Essay on the Nature o Truith'?

55 *Lord S* – Na na, Doctor, ye're aff in the wrang airt. I'm the only man in Edinburgh wi
    the abeelity to haud a pen wha hasna written an essay on the nature o truith.

Dowie – (*Crestfallen*) Authors are common here, then?

Lord S – The Toun's fou o them, (*more kindly*) but there arena mony write poetry,
    Doctor, and nane has haen yer ain success.

60 *Dowie* – Is that a fact? I winna deny, my lord that I cam here sair bothert wi douts, for
    my wife keepit on aye sayin, 'Dan', she said, 'dinna be disappeyntit gin they pey
    nae heed to ye in Edinburgh, for it's a hotbed o genius.' I haurdly lippent on bein
    kent here at aa.

Lord S – Oh but ye're kent. Weill kent. Aa' ower the country. And I wadna woner but
65   ye're weill kent in England tae.

Dowie – I was wonerin that, for I hae letters o introduction to some folk in London.
    I was thinkin o gaun doun there at the end o the month. The Presbytery's granted
    me leave o absence for twa months traivel.

Lord S – I see. Weill, we can sune fin oot the poseetion doun in London. Chairlie!
70   (*CHARLES comes forward from the balcony looking disgusted.*) This is my son;
       Chairlie, this is Doctor Dowie, the author o 'The Tomb'. (*As they bow, CHARLES
       condescendingly, the DOCTOR rather awed.*) He's wonerin if his wark's weill
       thocht o in London.

Charles – Yes, Doctor. Your work enjoys a considerable reputation.
75 *Dowie* – (*Delighted*) Na!

Charles – Yes, a considerable reputation.

Dowie – (*Overcome*) Is that no juist miraculous aathegither.

Charles – Of course, I have heard criticisms.

Dowie – (*Alarmed*) Criticims?
80 *Charles* – Yes, but none from your own countrymen. Home the dramatist thinks very
       highly of it.

Dowie – (*Pleased again*) Daes he? Home the dramatist!

Charles – Yes. (*Showing off*) He says that Lord Bute thinks highly of it too.

Dowie – Lord Bute. Ye was haurdly think a man in his poseetion could spare the time
85   for poetry.

Charles – His critics say he spares too much.

Dowie – Oh? Sae he has his critics tae?

Charles – I am afraid so.

Dowie – Weill, weill. And mine are aa English, ye say?
90 *Charles* – Yes.

Dowie – Poets themsells, mebbe?

Charles – Some of them, yes.

Dowie – Jealous, dae ye think, because a Scotsman can bate them in their ain tongue?

Charles – (*Concealing his disdain with difficulty*) Perhaps. Not altogether.
95 *Dowie* – Ye think there's mebbe something in what they say?

Charles – Unfortunately, Doctor, there is something in what they say.

Dowie – And what dae they say?

Charles – They complain of faults in your rhyme.

Dowie – Fauts in my rhyme! But the Scots Magazine says my rhymes are impeccable.
100 *Charles* – The Scots Magazine may say so, Doctor, but you must allow Englishmen
       credit for a superior knowledge of correct pronunciation in their own language.
       They complain that your rhymes are faulty unless your lines are spoken as they
       would be by a Scotchman who had never crossed the Border.

Dowie – I dinna juist see.

Charles – I could find you an example. (...)

Charles – Yes. Doctor, have you ever been to England?

Dowie – Na.

Charles – I thought so. English as a spoken language is quite foreign to you.

Dowie – But I read naething else.

Charles – I said as a spoken language. You cannot possibly know how English words
       should sound. You have no right to write English poetry.

T56 YOUNG, Douglas, *Thochts Anent Lallans Prose* (1947)

Douglas Young (1913-73) was born in Tayport, Fife, and educated in India, Edinburgh, St. Andrews and Oxford. Poet, translator and nationalist activist, Young became a lecturer and professor at Scottish and American universities. Most of his poetic works are in Scots; they include three collections of poetry and translations from the Gaelic, Latin, French, German, Italian, Russian, Lithuanian, Chinese and Greek (cf. his translations of Aristophanes' comedies, *The Puddocks* and *The Burdies*, in particular). He is also notable for his editing of Scottish poetry. "His spelling practices were very much those which later came to be prescribed by the Scots Style Sheet." (McClure) His expository prose (critical, historical, political) is usually in English.

The following article is an exception. It is a response to the criticism directed at the representatives of the Scottish Literary Renaissance, viz. that they do not use their 'synthetic Scots' for prose and that they do not speak it (the implication being that it is not a 'real' language). In order to counter the criticism, Young couches his arguments (that there is Scots prose, but not in print and that is the fault of publishers and readers; that the writers of the Scottish Renaissance are mainly poets and not prose writers; that they do speak Lallans, but that there is not enough of it in public life; that the speaking of Scots has been discouraged for many centuries; that Lallans is an inherently poetic language, in contrast to English, which is inherently prosaic) in 'synthetic Scots', which he usually reserves for poetry and verse drama, thereby trying to disprove the criticism by means of a concrete example. (cf. T85 and T104 on the same subject).

Source: Douglas Young, "Thochts Anent Lallans Prose", in: *The Scots Review*, April, 1947, p.14. (repr. from *EWW* 1981:10-12).

The unco langamachie about the Braid Scots or Neo-Lallans verses that a curn young makars are scryvan the nou has at lang length dwyned awa frae the douce columns o Scotland's twa-penny diurnals, albeid its echoes are aye soundan on awa doun about the Antipodes, amang the marber haas o New Delhi, in Winnipeg, Wisconsin, and
5 Wimbledon, whaure'er the Caledonian diaspora wones and thinks lang til auld Scotia's buts-and-bens and the raucle leid that lang syne was the couthy mither-tung o Jock Tamson's bairns, binnae the Gaels amang them.

In this slud it sets weel tae tak ferrer a thocht pit forrit by the kenspeckle makar, Mr Norman McCaig, at speirt what wey the Lallans Makars dinna scryve Lallans
10 prose, what wey they dinna speak Lallans theirsels, and hou comes it that the *archipoeta plasticissimus*, Hugh MacDiarmid, has gien owre the Lallans and o late years indytes fecklie Suddron. Nae answer was prentit til Mr McCaig's speirs, sae I s' ettle here til answer him.

Trowth is that a wheen o the Makars scryve Lallans prose, namely Lewis Spence
15 and Hugh MacDiarmid, Albert Mackie and mysel. An auntran blad o their Lallans prose has been furthset and muckle thocht o by wycelike fowk, but a guid wheen has gane about only in handscrifts, because o the expense o prentin it. Monie diurnals are geyan sweirt tae prent oniething in Lallans prose, and I mysel hain a hantle o braw scrifts that hae had sentence o the orrabladcreel. Aiblins ae day I'll owregie them til
20 the Scots Fowk's Buikbield.

Forbye that, Lallans poetry doesna win sae muckle siller that furthsetters arena gleg at prentin buiks o Lallans prose. Makars mak verses whiles only for their ain pleisure, but ettlins at the scryvin o prose dwyne aff for want o a mengie o fowk likely tae read them, a "public." But mair: culd Mr McCaig expect aa the Makars tae
25 be prosaists forbye? Whaur's the prose o Shakespeare? Or o Mr McCaig?

Nanetheless, there is substance in Mr McCaig's thocht. Gin Lallans be a spontaneous leid for the makin o verses, gin Lallans verse-makin isna tae be an academic dilettante ploy like Greek elegiacs or Latin hexameters, the "Plastic" Makars maun uis the leid for ither purposes than poetry, namely for prose and for speakin.
30 Itherweys the vitality o the leid maun be tint.

Speakin Lallans comes natural tae maist o the Makars nou scryvan, the like o Lewis Spence and Albert Mackie, Helen Cruikshank and Schir Alexander Gray, Hugh MacDiarmid and the lave, albeid monie o the young anes want the fouth o langage o bygane bairntimes. I mysel spak Urdu as my first leid, but hae been
35 acquent wi spoken Lallans frae my airest years. Sae Mr McCaig's observe is a wee thing agley. For aa that, there's sense in it tae, because the speakin o Lallans nouadays is a gey shilpit thowless fushionless affair by the virrfu colloguies o the auld fowk. It's no muckle found for extendit discourse, frae the pulpit or the platform, the judge's bink or the professor's lectern.
40 The Gaelic has aye been uist for extendit discourse, and the Gaels hae nae bother scryvin prose about oniething or naething. But Lallans prose hasna evolved muckle frae the saxteenth yearhunder. At the stert, about 1500, the fouth o words i the Lallan leid was mair nor i the Suddron. Schir William Craigie scryves: – "In the sixteenth century, and especially in the first half of it, Scottish as a spoken and written
45 language stood on a level with English, and in some respects even stood higher. The first real blow to it came through the Reformation." (*The Scottish Tongue*, Cassell, 1924, p.4). But frae the Protestant victory o 1560 on, Suddron becam the leid o the Auld Kirk and aa its seceders and competitors; ministers threepit i the Suddron; prentit langamachies were i the Suddron, gin they werena i the Latin; the parliament-
50 fowk, the gentry, the respectable *intelligentsia*, and monie o the commontie beguid tae knap Suddron, and it is the makars and siclike gangrel-bodies and the warkan fowk that hae sauvit the Lallan leid ataa, aither for speakin or scryvin.

Prose isna sae easy scryvit i the Lallans as M. Jourdain thocht it i the French. Aamaist onie Frenchman can scryve a French prose that's a pleisure tae read, but nae
55 monie French makars can scryve poetry. It's the ither wey about i the Lallans. Lallans words bruik a potency, a penumbra o mystery, an auld-farrant souch, that maks them a wonderfu prime matter for poetry. The mair sae nou that poetry i the Suddron is kind o dwaiblie, and the Suddron leid aamaist seems forfochten for poetry, Scots makars hae nae inhibitions about scryvin verses in as fou a canon o Lallans as they
60 can maister, wi the aid o Jamieson's muckle wordbuik and aa the artifices and cantels o archaism, catachresis and neologism that Lallanophiles are aince mair uisan eftir twa yearhunders' mislippenin.

Matthew Arnold thocht that "by nothing is England more glorious than by her poetry." In our day the speak is become true o Suddron prose. A maister o the pen
65 can say oniething he likes wi the vast fouth o diction tae hand i the Suddron, a wonderfu hybrid plastic medium, mair expressive owre a hale gamut nor French, German, or Russian. O course, mair nor the half o Suddron as nou scryvit comes frae Latin and Greek ruits, and it wald be as legitimate for a Lallans prosaist til extend his fouth o words wi parallel upbiggins, but Suddron has duin the job aaready, and sae

70 bruiks nou a rowth and a perjinkness that Lallans wald tak monie bairntimes tae win at.
Lallans has verra near stuid still wi its prose sin Bellenden and Pitscottie. Schir
Walter Scott and John Galt, William Alexander and Robert Louis Stevenson,
Crockett and a wheen mair, hae scryvit novels that hae duin a bittock for the hainin
and the betterin o Lallans prose, but nane o them aa ettled at a total canon o Lallans,
75 the wey the upbiggers o the Norse Landsmaal or the Afrikaans wrocht lang and
eidentlie frae the ruits up while they had consummate a leid able for aa the purposes
o life and letters. Lewis Grassic Gibbon gaed aff the straucht smaa gate wi his
Lallanised Suddron, potent medium tho it is. The better wey wald be tae creep afore
ye flee, no tae ettle at owre lang a wark. Robert Kemp and Robert Maclellan hae
80 shawn what can be duin wi Lallans in stage-plays, whaur dialogue whiles gangs aff
intil extendit discourse, that comes near a richt prose. "The Ettrick Shepherd" scryvit
braw tales in a rowthy Lallans, and we hae seen a wheen guidlike smaaboukit novels
in wycelike aefauld Lallans by fowk nou livan, sae the prospect o a major
Renaissance o Lallans prose downa be thocht clean fantastic.
85   Endlins, what wey has Hugh MacDiarmid owregien Lallans for Suddron? First, I
speir back. Is it Suddron he nou scryves, or Panglossic? Neist, what for did Rilke in
his auld years owregie German for French? Because he had uised up aa the resources
o his ain native leid. I jalouse as part o the explanation for MacDiarmid's linguistic
tergiversation that he fand the Lallans forfochten. Wi speakin o't for extendit
90 discourse and the scryvin o't for aakind prose Lallans suld kep new virr, and the
Lallanders forbye.

T57 SMITH, Sydney Goodsir, *In Defence of 'Lallans'* (1948)

Like Young's text (T56), this passage of expository prose is a reaction to criticism of the use of
Lallans. In contrast to T56, it is written in Standard English, with Scots words included as quotations
only, sometimes with glosses immediately following (e.g. "auld-farrant"). At the end of the excerpt,
there is a Scots phrase, illustrating what Aitken terms "overt Scotticisms", used by Scottish speakers of
English to demonstrate their national/nationalistic attachment. (For biographical information on Smith
cf. T54).
Source: Sydney Goodsir Smith, "In Defence of 'Lallans'", in: *The Scots Review*, May, 1948, p.23.
   (Repr. from *EWW* 1981:10-12).

(...) Those who declare that the Scots or Lallans used by modern makars is either
artificial or archaic should take a stroll one day or one night down the Canongate, say,
and listen to the women in the food queues or the men in the howffs, or the bairns in
the causie; or take a hurl on an early morning tramcar with the men going to work; or
5 let them go across to Fife and spend a week-end at St. Monans or somewhere – but
not St. Andrews! (this is where we come to it); or go and bide in Breadalbane or
Strathdon or Kyle for a fortnight or so.
   Sticking to Edinburgh for the moment, let our hypothetical anti-plastician come
with me down the Canongate. There he will not have to go out of his way to hear such
10 words spoken as *antrin, smittel, waukrife, begrutten, wancanny* and so on, all of

which I have to explain in my glossary if I am compiling a collection of poems in which these words occur. These poems, containing such words will be perfectly understandable to the folk living in the sort of districts I have mentioned – the glossary is for the genteel who buy books of modern poetry. If, on the other hand, I
15 were to use such words as *hirsute, analogy, anomaly, dichotomy, prerequisite* or suchlike, my friends in the Canongate might very well accuse me, as they have done, of using "beuk-langage," which is just what the anti-plasticians say about Lallans when they call it "artificial".

Some critics will say "This is not the language you have spoken all your life, so
20 how can you write poetry in it?" But how does the critic know this? Maybe it was the language the poet thought in all his life. And anyway let the critic read, and read widely, and then say whether it can be poetry or not. There is far too much theorising and dogmatising about the anti-plasticians. Let them pree the puddens!

T58 McLELLAN, Robert, *The Pownie* (1960s)

The *Linmill Stories* are told in retrospect from the perspective of a young boy who is staying on his grandparents' farm over the summer. McLellan himself spent much of his childhood with his grandparents' in the Clyde valley. Those visits provided the inspiration for the *Linmill Stories* and helped him develop a firm grasp of early twentieth century West-Central rural Scots. The excerpt is from the first story of the published collection and illustrates the use of the same type of Scots for both narrative and dialogue.
Source: Robert McLellan, "The Pownie", in: *Linmill Stories*. Edinburgh: Canongate Publications, 1990, pp.1-2.

Linmill was a fruit ferm in Clydeside, staunin a wee thing back frae the Clyde road aboot hauf wey atween Kirkfieldbank and Hazelbank, close to Stanebyres Linn, ane o the Falls o Clyde the tounsfolk cam to see, drivin doun frae Hamilton in fower-in-haund brakes, whan the orchards were in flourish in the spring.
5 My grannie and granfaither bade in Linmill, and my minnie took me there for aa my holidays. I had been born there, my minnie said, and I wad hae been gled neir to hae left it, but that couldna be. My faither had his business in a toun.
It's queer that I can hardly mind a haet aboot the toun whaur I bade in my bairnhood, whan I can mind ilka blade o the Linmill grass. Ein whan I'm lost in the
10 praisent, and the ferm seems forgotten lang syne, things like the taste o a strawberry, or the keckle o a hen whan it's laen an egg, can bring the haill place back.
Juist the ither day I had a drink o soor douk. That brocht the ferm back tae, for juist by the scullery door, on yer wey oot frae the kitchen, there was a soor douk crock wi a tinnie hingin frae a nail abune it, and whan ye wantit a drink ye dippit in
15 the tinnie and gied the milk a steer, and syne helpit yersell. Syne ye syned the tinnie at the back entry, and pat it back on its nail.
I wasna juist shair o that scullery. The ae winnock that gied it licht was sae smoored wi ivy that the place was eerie, and whan I gaed in for a drink o soor douk I keekit ower my shouther aye for bogles, and whiles it was hard no to think that
20 bogles were there, for there were twa hams and a roll o saut fish hinging frae cleiks

on the ceilin, and whan ye saw them black against the licht they were haurdly cannie.
   But I couldna keep oot. There was a muckle bunker alang the waa neist the
kitchen, for hauding pats and pans, and that had a raw o drawers in it, and I wonert
aye what was in them; and on the ither side, against the waa neist the stable, there
25 was a wuiden stair, wi a press aneth it for hauding besoms, and that stair drew me tae.
   I gaed ower to the fute o it whiles and lookit up, but there was nocht to be seen. It
was as black as the inside o the press aneth it, and that was as black as nicht.

T59   TAIT, William J., *A Sonnet* (1964)

William J. Tait (1919-92) was born in Mid Yell, Shetland, graduated from Edinburgh University, and
worked as a teacher in Lerwick and in England. Various of his poems were locally published.
   This translation of this fifth poem of the cycle of "Sonnets pour Hélène" by Pierre de Ronsard
(French poet and statesman, 1524-85) is an experiment, aimed at widening the functional range of
Shetlandic Scots by using it to fit the traditional form of the sonnet. It replaces much of the original's
elegantly archaic flavour with a rural tone.
Source: William J. Tait, "A Sonnet" translated from the French of Pierre de Ronsard into Shetlandic,
   in: John J. Graham & T.A. Robertson, *Nordern Lichts. An Anthology of Shetland Verse & Prose*.
   Lerwick: Shetland County Council, 1964, p.43.

Some nicht whin du is aald, an, glansin on da brace,
Da caandle lichts dy wheel, weel set in ta da fire,
Nönin my sangs, du'll hark: "Whin I wis eence da vyre
O aa da laand; Ronsard, du rösed my boannie face."
5 Dan no a servant-lass at neebs ower her hap-lace,
An dovers ower oot-döne wi darg o hoose an byre,
Bit whin shö hears my name, her haand'll slip da wire,
An rise as if ta bliss dee, deathless be my grace.
Toh under fael my banes in some aeth-kent kirk-yard,
10 Among da michty skalds A'll tak my aese at last.
Ower da hert-stane du'll cooer, failed, croppen, nigh twa-fald
An graim ower my lost love, an dy prood disregard.
Live, if du'll ant me, noo! waitna till du's grown aald;
Gadder life's flooers afore dy day an dirs is past.

T60   MULRINE, Stephen, *Sonnet fur Helen* (1980)

The poet and translator Stephen Mulrine (b. 1937) was born in Glasgow and educated there and in
Edinburgh. He is a lecturer at the Glasgow School of Art. In the 1970s he was one of a group of young
Glasgow poets who used the dialect in some of their poems and plays.
   This rendering of one of Ronsard's "Sonnets pour Hélène" into Glaswegian is more of a adaptation
of the topic in terms of modern urban consciousness and idiom, than a literal translation. It changes the
tone of the original even more than Tait's version.
Source: Stephen Mulrine, "Sonnet fur Helen", translated from the French of Pierre de Ronsard into
   Glaswegian, in: Manfred Görlach (ed.), *Focus on: Scotland*. Amsterdam/Philadelphia: Benjamins,
   1985, p.233.

Wan a these nights when yir auld and done,
Wi yir knittin needles gaun lik stink,
Ye'll oapn these poems bi the fire n think,
'Ah must've been bewtiful when Ah wis young',

5 An some aul cronie'll luft her heid,
Noaddin away owre her purl n plain,
An cry oan hivven tae bless ma name
That sung yir praises fur aw tae read.

Bit Ah'll be under the grun six feet,
10 Giein the maggots a well-earned treat,
While you're up the lum, auld Nannie-goon,

Wishin ye'd hud merr sense it the time,
Thin tae curl yir lip it luv lik mine,
Cuz this is it, flower, Last Chance Saloon.

T61   MULRINE, Stephen, *The Coming of the Wee Malkies* (1967)

Mulrine's best-known poem is actually the first he wrote in Glaswegian Scots. The "Wee Malkies" are part of his childhood in Glasgow.

Source: Stephen Mulrine, "The Coming of the Wee Malkies", in: Edwin Morgan, ed. *Poems by Alan Hayton, Stephen Mulrine, Colin Kirkwood, Robert Tait*. Preston: Akros Publications, 1967, p.10.

THE COMING OF THE WEE MALKIES

Whit'll ye dae when the wee Malkies come,
if they dreep doon affy the wash-hoose dyke
an' pit the hems oan the sterrheid light,
an' play keepie-up oan the clean close-wa',
5 an' blooter yir windae in wi' the ba',
missis, whit'll ye dae?

Whit'll ye dae when the wee Malkies come,
if they chap yir door an' choke the drain,
an' caw the feet fae yir sapsy wean,
10 an' tummle thur wulkies through yir sheets,
an' tim thur ashes oot in the street,
missis, whit'll ye dae?

Whit'll ye dae when the wee Malkies come,
if they chuck thur screwtaps doon the pan,
15 an' stick the heid oan the sanit'ry man;
when ye hear thum come shauchlin' doon yir loaby,
chantin', 'Wee Malkies! The gemme's... a bogey!'
haw, missis, whit'll ye dae?

T62 McILVANNEY, William, *Docherty* (1975)

William Angus McIlvanney (b.1936) was born in Kilmarnock. Educated at Kilmarnock and at the
University of Glasgow, he became a schoolteacher, but in 1975 resigned to become a full-time novelist.
He has held creative writing classes at various Scottish and French universities.

The novel *Docherty* is set in Graithnock, an industrial town in the west of Scotland, "loosely based
on Kilmarnock as it was in the first quarter of the century" (Royle). Through the eyes of a young boy,
Conn Docherty, life in a small mining community is described. The picture is dominated by the
character of Conn's father, Tam, who is "possessed of his own sense of virtue and yet alive to a
knowledge of the working man's degraded place in society" – an almost stereotypical figure in Scottish
literature. The exerpt represents Conn's experience at school: his violent teacher, who tries to beat the
use of Scots out of his pupils, and Conn's own defiant reaction to this treatment (a situation, up to the
1970s often described in reports of teachers' attitudes towards their pupils native dialect).
Source: William McIlvanney, *Docherty*. Edinburgh: Mainstream Publishing, 1975, pp.108-13.

'Well, well, well. Who started it?'
On one of the floorboards an accentuation in the grain makes a road. It runs
winding, vanishes under Mr Pirrie's boot.
'It doesn't matter. You'll both be getting the same. What's wrong with your face,
5 Docherty?'
'Skint ma nose, sur.'
'How?'
'Ah fell an' bumped ma heid in the sheuch, sur.'
'I beg your pardon?'
10   'Ah fell an' bumped ma heid in the sheuch, sur.'
'I beg your pardon?'
In the pause Conn understands the nature of the choice, tremblingly,
compulsively, makes it.
'Ah fell an' bumped ma heid in the sheuch, sur.'
15   The blow is instant. His ear seems to enlarge, is muffed in numbness. But it's only
the dread of tears that hurts. Mr Pirrie distends on a lozenge of light which mustn't
be allowed to break. It doesn't. Conn hasn't cried.
'That, Docherty, is impertinence. You will translate, please, into the mother-
tongue.'
20   The blow is a mistake, Conn knows. If he tells his father, he will come up to the
school. 'Ye'll take whit ye get wi' the strap an' like it. But if onybody takes their
hauns tae ye, ye'll let me ken.' He thinks about it. But the problem is his own. It
frightens him more to imagine his father coming up.
'I'm waiting, Docherty. What happened?'
25   'I bumped my head, sir.'
'Where? Where did you bump it, Docherty?'
'In the gutter, sir.'
'Not an inappropriate setting for you, if I may say so.'
The words mean nothing. Only what happens counts. (...)
30   'Simpson first!' It is a ritual. He holds the strap in his right hand, drops it over his
shoulder, reaches back with his left hand, flexes the leather, begins. 'I will *not*. Have.

Violence. In my school.'

Four. Conn can prepare.

'Docherty!' One. Conn recites to himself: *Ah bumped ma heid in the sheuch.* Two.
35 *Sheuch.* 'You're getting as bad as your brother was.' Three. *Fat man.* 'I was glad to
get rid of him.' Four. Conn's hands drop, stiff as plaster-casts. 'Up, Docherty, up!
Two more for insolence.' Five. *Bastard.* He is watching for signs of tears. Six. *Big,
fat bastard.* (...)

While Miss Carmichael gave him sympathetic exemption from her questions, he
40 took a stub of pencil in his fingers. Slowly across a scuffed piece of paper a word
moved clumsily. Opposite it another word was manoeuvred and settled, the way he
had seen in a dictionary Miss Carmichael showed him. His hand shook as he did it.
It was a painful and tremulous matter, like an ant trying to manipulate stones. He sat
buried inside himself while the words spread themselves across the paper. Minutes
45 later, he was stunned into stillness, looking at the big awkward shapes they made
before him.

sheuch	*gutter*
speugh	*sparrow*
lum	*chimny*
50 *brace*	*mantalpiece*
bine	*tub*
coom	*soot*
coomie	*foolish man (Mr Pirrie)*
gomeril	*another foolish man*
55 *spicket*	*tap*
glaur	*muck what is in a puddle after the puddle goes away*
wabbit	*tired*
whaup	*curloo*
tumshie	*turnip*
60 *breeks*	*troosers*
chanty	*po*
preuch	*anything you can get*
I was taigled	*I was kept back for a more*
longer nor I	*longer time than I*
65 *ettled*	*desired.*

One side of the paper was filled. He didn't start on the other side because he now
wanted to write things that he couldn't find any English for. When something sad had
happened and his mother was meaning that there wasn't anything you could do about
it, she would say 'ye maun dree yer weird'. When she was busy, she had said she was
70 'saund-papered tae a whuppet.' 'Pit a raker oan the fire.' 'Hand-cuffed to
Mackindoe's ghost.' 'A face tae follow a flittin'.' If his father had to give him a row
but wasn't really angry, he said 'Ah'll skelp yer bum wi' a tealeaf tae yer nose
bluids.'

Conn despaired of English. Suddenly, with the desperation of a man trying to
75 amputate his own infected arm, he savagely scored out all the English equivalents.

On his way out of school, he folded his grubby piece of paper very carefully and
put it in his pocket. It was religiously preserved for weeks. By the time he lost it, he
didn't need it.

T63   ANNAND, J.K., *The Guid Scots Tongue* (1978)

James King Annand (1908-93) was born and educated in Edinburgh. As a schoolboy and editor of the
Broughton Magazine he edited some of the early work of Hugh MacDiarmid. He worked as a teacher
in Edinburgh and Whithorn, and was also a naval officer. He edited *Lallans* magazine from 1973-83,
and remained honorary president of the Scots Language Society until his death in 1993. His poetry is
remarkable for the colloquial ease with which he uses his native Scots, notably in children's verse and
in translations.

The article, printed here in full, which is about the scarcity of prose in Scots is itself a piece of
expository prose in Scots. Annand maintains that Scots is neither dead nor dying in spoken language or
in poetry, but needs strengthening in the field of prose writing, especially non-fictional prose. His essay
demonstrates that he thinks that the functional range of Scots is large enough to do that. (cf. D. Young,
T57, and S.G. Smith, T58, on the same topic).

Source: J.K. Annand, "The Guid Scots Tongue", in: *Idiom* vol.4, no.1, April, 1978.

THE GUID SCOTS TONGUE

The guid Scots tongue is gey sweir to cowp the creels. This lang while back folk hae
been scrievin that the leid is about to dee. Professor Ferrier, a hunder and fifty year
syne, when editin John Wilson's "Warks", thocht that Scots speech was "now nearly
obsolete" and that the *Noctes Ambrosianae* was "the last specimen of the national
5 language of Scotland which the world is ever likely to see". A hunder year syne,
Dean Ramsay was sae shuir that spoken Scots wad sune dee that he colleckit a wheen
Scots words and sayins thegither in his *Reminiscences* to mak siccar that they wadna
be tint for aye. But Scots, in baith its spoken and written forms, is no deid yet. It is
mebbe a bit thin on the grund in some airts, and no sae strang in ithers, but it's still
10 alive and kickin. Gang to onie cattle mairt or lamb sale and ye'll hear Scots in aa its
virr. Or tak your dram in a pub whaur colliers or fishermen foregether, and ye'll hear
the auld scots words and iedioms dirlin in your lugs.

Literary wark in Scots has never been wantin, even tho in the last three hunder
years or sae Scots has been uised maistly for verse. It's no that easy to come by guid
15 Scots prose. Scrievers hae for the maist pairt been content to hain it for reportin the
direck speak of the "lower orders" tho John Galt and Lewis Grassic Gibbon, ilkane
in his ain wey whiles wrote prose that had a rale Scots gou til't. But it could be
threipit that the only rale Scots prose scrievit in the last two hunder year is to be fund
in twa-three short tales by Scott and Stevenson.

20   Whit wey then sud we keep Scots alive? Gif we dinna gie a heeze til't, comin
generation'll no be able to enjoy the Scots poetry and sangs that are sic a treisored
pairt o our birth-richt. And we maun stert wi the young bairns. Nou that grannies are
owre thrang gangin out to their daily darg to bother that muckle wi their bairns'

bairns, it'll faa til the schuils to learn the bairns to be skeelie in the auld tongue, no
25 by threipin it doun their thrapples, but by giein them the chance to enjoy the rhymes
and tales that our grannies tellt us. Of course there'll be thrawnness on the pairt o
some mithers that want their bairns to "talk proper" but they can be won owre. Monie
parents I ken frae England and ither fremit pairts hae gotten quite a regaird for Scots
and hae been gey proud when their bairns hae colleckit Burns Federation prizes.
30 There is nae dout that thir hinder ten year or sae there has kythed a new interest in
Scots in the schuils and universities, even in the B.B.C. and the newspapers. A
wheen o our younger playwrichts hae been uisin Scots and get their plays pit on in
the theatre forby, and even prentit. Some o Robert McLellan's short stories hae juist
been published in buik form. New societies sic as the Association for Scottish
35 Literary Studies and the Scots Language Society hae been set up.

But maugre aa this steer, I jalouse that twa things are needfu afore Scots can win
the place it sud hae as a national leid. Firstlins, we bude to hae a hantle sicht mair
Scots prose nor is written the day. Poetry in Scots is aa richt in its wey, but withouten
a guid bouk o prose, Scots will ne'er win the standin it deserves. In the second place
40 we'll hae to set a standard spellin insteid o the awfu mish-mash we hae the day wi
ilka scriever spellin as it comes up his back. Folk hae ettled at this afore. In 1947 a
cleckin o poets drew up the Scots Style Sheet, and it was follied wi fair success for a
while, but it needs up-datin and a comatee set up at a confabble in Glesca last
backend is nou warkin on't. But it's a gey stey brae they breist, as I ken as an editor
45 that's been ettlin to coax writers to faa into line. The feck o them are thrawn cattle.

What are the odds on us ever gettin a guidly bouk o prose in Scots?

Let's tak a keek, first at the schuils, and syne at the growne folk. In schuil
magazines thir days there seems to be a want o stories or articles o a dacent length in
onie language. But nane-the-less this while back I hae come across in schuil
50 magazines frae a wheen airts the orra bit o weel-written Scots prose that showed the
scriever had a rowth o Scots words, and what's aiblins mair important, a guid grup o
Scots iediom. A bit mair encouragement in this airt frae teachers micht wark
wonders. Nae dout it is expeckin owre muckle to see a magazine halelie in Scots thir
days, but it cuid still be dune. Fifty year syne, eggit on by my wyce-like teacher o
55 English, I mysel edited an issue o the schuil magazine that was seivinty-seivin per
cent Scots.

When I turn til adult scrievin in Scots I'm mair hopefu nor I was five year syne.
When the Scots Language Society speired gif I wad tak on to edit a magazine in
Scots I had my douts. While there's nae want o bodies that'll gie an editor passable
60 verse, I could then count on the fingers o ae hand the folk I kent wad be able to gie
me ocht in prose. The day, eftir editin ten issues, I ken I can count on at the least
twenty-eicht folk that can gie me guid Scots prose, whether it be in tales, articles,
literary criticism or reviews. Forby, mair and mair folk are gleg to buy and read a
magazine that prents nocht but Scots. The prent-rin o *Lallans* has growne fower-
65 fauld sin it begoud, and there's no a back number left.

T64   GRAHAM, John J., *Wir ain aald language* (1981)

John J. Graham (b. 1921) was born and educated in Shetland, read English at Edinburgh University,
worked as a teacher in Shetland (headmaster of Lerwick Central School and of Anderson High School).
Graham has widely written in his native dialect, compiled the only modern dictionary of Shetlandic,
and has been contributor to the *New Shetlander* ("a major preserving and developing influence on
Shetland language and local culture" McClure), the (co-)editor of journals, an anthology and a grammar
of his dialect.

The following text is part of a contribution to a symposium on the present-day status of Scots in its
written form, which – according to the introduction of the group of essays – "probably [presents] the
first appearance of any academic work in Scots in an international scholarly journal" (the results of the
conference were printed in the international magazine English World-Wide). Graham writes about his
native dialect, its history and local use, calling it the mother tongue, but not claiming language-status
for it. The text is an unusual example of the use of Shetlandic for expository prose.

Source: John J. Graham, "Wir ain aald language. Writin ida Shetland dialect", in: McClure et al., "Our
ain leid? The predicament of a Scots writer", *EWW* 2, 1981, p.18.

Whan da Shetland poet Vagaland wrat da lines:
"Trowe wir minds wir ain aald language
Still keeps rinnin laek a tön",
he wis jöst sayin, in his ain wye, at you canna sinder tocht an tongue, da singer an da
5 sang.

Shetland's "ain aald language" has its röts awa back ida Norn tongue at wis
spokken in Shetland fae aboot da nint tae da seeventeent century. Da Scots fock at
cam among wis fae da sixteent century an on brocht der ain leid, an at da lang an da
lent da twa languages melled tagidder to mak da tongue we caa Shetlandic. While dis
10 wis gjaan on, anidder wye o spaekin an writin wis shapin da local speech. Dis wis
English – ösed by da Kirk, da laa-coorts an ida sköls. Hit cam ta be seen by
Shetlanders as da language o da tapsters – da big boags; an if Shetlanders wis ever ta
win oot o da bit an git on ida wirld dan dey wid hae ta learn ta spaek English tö.

Aa da sam dey didna laek onyane at pat on airs an knappit English whin among
15 der ain fock, an dey skyimpit onyane at pat on dis pan-loff wye o spaekin. So hit cam
aboot at Shetland fock got kinda reffled aboot der wye o spaekin. Dey laekit der
midder tongue wi hits waarm, hamely vynd an da wye hit seemed ta be pairt o da
everyday life aroond dem. But, for aa hits uncan löd, da English tongue wis lookit up
til, an hit wisna ony winder for da sköls dreeled hit ita da bairns at dey böst ta spaek
20 English if dey wir aaber ta win on ida wirld. An no only dat, da sköl-taechers,
ministers and laawirs wir wint ta nochtify da Shetland speech an mak a föl o onyane
at ösed it publicly.

Hit wisna till well trowe da nineteent century at Shetlanders tried der haand at
writin ida dialect – maistly poems, wi a antrin story noo an dan. Dey wrat aboot life
25 as dey kent it – aboot da sea an da laand, voar an hairst, blydeness an döl – da things
at's aye lyin closs ta fock's herts fae da aidge o Time.

As we aa ken, wirds gadder aboot dem a fouth o memories an associations, an wir
midder tongue abön aa haes a hantle o echoes fae wir past. Dis is a aacht ta dialect
writers, for da wirds dey öse dunna jöst spaek strecht an veev but geng deep doon ta
30 da hert o da reader.

An dan fobye, da dialect writer can mak his writin veev wi fresh images fae life
aroond him redder dan da asky abstractions at merr sae muckle moadern writin. (...)

T65 PURVES, David, *Review of 'Our Ain Leid?'* (1981)

David Purves, dramatist and translator, editor of the *Lallans* magazine. He is president of the Scots Language Society, translated *Macbeth* into Scots (1992), and is very interested in orthographical reform and standardization of the Scots writing system.

In the following text Purves reviews the group of articles published as "Our Ain Leid? The predicament of a Scots writer", of which two excerpts are printed above (T64-5). He summarizes the contents, but the main emphasis of his review is on the types of Scots the individual authors use. He himself adheres to very strict spelling conventions, which are to achieve maximal distance from English spelling , while at the same time paying attention to historical development and consistency.

Source: David Purves, Rev., "'Our Ain Leid?' in *English World-Wide*, 2:1, 1981", in: *Lallans* 17, 1981, pp.37-9.

This symposium haes an introduction in Inglish bi Derrick McClure en airtikils in Scots wrutten aince eirant for *English World-Wide* bi John Thomas Low, A.D. Mackie, J.K. Annand, John J. Graham en Derrick McClure. The'r a screid anaw bi Douglas Young, taen frae *The Scots Review* awa back in 1947, afore he turnt his back
5   foraye on Scotland. The fek o thir names is weill kent ti the reidars o *Lallans*.

A bodie micht luik ferr afore findan anither clekkin o wrytars mair qualified ti dael wi siccan a theme as this, en thegither thai hae gien us a guid lang sicht o the fikkils that forgether wi wrytin in Scots. The airtikil bi John Low is cryit, *Is Scots English? or is Scotch no juist orra English*, sae it kests dout on whuther it soud hae
10 been prentit in a journal cryit *English World-Wide*. Low daels wi the historical background ti the waesum state that Scots is in the-day en the effects on generations o bairns o the dounhaudin o thair naitral leid in the skuils. John J. Graham wrytes anent the fikkils o skreivin in the Shetland dialect, en the ither authors is maistlie taen up wi the biggin o a standart Scots, weill suitit for prose forby poetrie.
15   Atwein thaim, thai mainage ti cuiver maist sydes o this quaisten, but for aw that, sum streitches mak gey ill reidin. The spellin seistems uised reinge ferr abraid, but maist authors pey sum heed ti the aa-taa-baa tradeition estaiblisht bi the 1947 Scots Style Sheet. The fact o the maitter is that naebodie thir days kens naitral Scots weill aneuch ti mak a richt job bi himsell o raxan it for uiss in discursive prose. (Here A
20 maun faw back on the verb *rax*, for want o a better Scots wird for siccan notions as *develop* or *evolve*). We maun thole the fact that siccar founds, or guid historical models, is sair wantan for siccan a darg as this.

As regairds the style o leid uised, the airtikils in this symposium faws inti thrie sindrie clesses:
25   First we hae skreids wrutten in a literarie leid no unlyke that uised for the main corpus o poetrie wrutten in Scots sen the days o Allan Ramsay. This leid is foundit on spoken Scots bi skreivars that haes sum kennin o spoken Scots dialect. The airtikils bi John Low, J.K. Annand en A.D. Mackie is aw in this cless.

Saicont we hae the airtikil in the Shetland dialect bi John Graham, the jynt editor
30 o *The New Shetlander*. This wes in a cless bi itsell, for altho this leid haes the touk o naitral Scots, it is a sicht fremit bi onie Scots spoken on the mainland.

The airtikils bi Douglas Young en J. Derrick McClure is wrutten in what is whyles cryit 'synthetic Scots'. In tymes bygaen, sum o the wrytars that haes uised this leid

haes been dilettantes mair eydent in howkan up deid Scots wirds nor in takkan tent o
35 leevan practice. Douglas Young, for exampil, uised Inglish sets lyke *I*, *mysel*,
mystery, *by* for *bi* or *be*, *found* for *fund*, *written* for *wrutten*, alang wi auld-farrant
whigmaleiries lyke *virrfu*, *diurnals*, *orrabladcreel* en *langamachie*. Inglified leevan
Scots wirds en auld deid anes maks ill neibors.

A whein year syne, Sydney Goodsir Smith tellt me that the truibil wi the Scots
40 nation is that ilkane gangs his ain gait. Thir twa airtikils is a guid exampil o this faut.
Awbodie kens that an independent mynd is a guid thing, but no ti the lenth o makkan
up yeir ain leid as ye gang alang. In ma day, A hae seen a hantil Scots, but A fand
Derrick McClure's airtikil that ill ti reid, A coud haurlie feinish it at the ae
dounsittin; an A dinna say this kis A kent his faither. Aiblins naething in this warld
45 is impossibil, but that our weird in Scotland wul be ti wryte Scots wi sic phrases as,
*insufficient ti expleit aa the behuifs o a letterit commonweil in the hodiern period o
specialisit technical kennin*, maun be gey neir it.

It cam inti ma mynd whyle A wes reidan this airtikil that gin McClure haed been
wrytan about airiplanes, he micht hae cryit thaim *flichterbarraes*, as wes proponit a
50 whyle back bi a bodie whas name A forget. Sic an unnaitral leid is fair sindert frae its
ruits in speech en wha is gaun ti reid it? For a mercie, Douglas Young's leid is a
whein less outlin, but it kyths whyles ti hae been owreset frae Inglish.

Whatevir, aw this is no ti argie that prose in Scots, onie mair nor poetrie, soud dae
nae mair nor ettil ti represent the hamelie spoken Scots o the last twa hunder year, but
55 gin oniebodie is ti reid it, it maun be sib baith ti the Scots tung en the standart (mair
or less) literarie leid that haes been uised for poetrie in Scots frae Ramsay til Garioch.

Whyles the leid uised bi John Low is aiblins juist a sicht owre hamelie. He micht
hae duin better nor uise siclyke phrases as, *mannies in chairge o the Scotch
Education Depairtment*. A im no shuir, aither, that he soud hae uised the set,
60 *preservit*, raither nor *preserred*. The wirds, *serr*, *preserr* en *deserr* haes been uised
for hunders o years nou.

For aw thir girns, A wes rael gled for ti see sic mensefu airtikils in a sairius
international journal, en A im weill shuir that John Low, J.K. Annand en A.D.
Mackie haes the richt idaya in wrytan prose in a leid sib til naitral Scots. Wi the wull
65 ti dae it, a richt wyce-like prose micht be biggit on sic founds.

But whan aw said en duin, McClure haes his pynt o view. As wes said anent his
ferr frein in 'Beside the Bonnie Briar Bush,' *Dinna be haurd on Weelum MacLure,
for he's no been haurd wi oniebodie in Drumtochty*! For ma ain pairt, A wadna want
ti be owre sair on him, for A im shuir his lanesum warsils haes thair pairt ti pley in
70 the kythin o literarie Scots.

T66 ANON., *Street Interviews with Working Class Glaswegians* (1983)

The following is part of a "collage of street interviews [...] recorded by Haig Gordon and broadcast by Radio Scotland as a postscript to Stewart Conn's production of J. McGrath's [play] *The Game's a Bogey* [...]. The speakers are all clearly working class Glaswegians, but they vary in their degree of casualness." They speak about "unemployment, housin, and the inadequate response of the medical profession to problems such as alcoholism and depression" (Macafee, p.68). Govan is a very poor area in the west of central Glasgow. The original interview, i.e. the spoken basis of Macafee's transcription into "St E or [...] a modification of the local orthography" (p.54), are available on tape (accompanying Macafee's book).

Source: Caroline Macafee, "Street interviews with working class Glaswegians for Radio Scotland", in: *Glasgow*. Amsterdam: Benjamins, 1983, pp.68-70.

D.   Ah'm a painter. But the thing's in Glasgow now, it means to get a paintin job, which means travellin all over Glasgow; then again, that details bus fare (laughter), ye know what Ah mean. Well, Ah'm separated; Ah'm still payin maintainance; so it doesn't leave me much, by the time Ah pay digs, keep maself. You just can't do it
5 nowadays on the cost i livin, ye know. Mean, ye know, jist tae come fae here tae mebbe tae Cardonald or – that's twenty pence there an twenty – that's forty pence jist tae sign the Broo. Ah mean what Ah'm gettin is twenty three poun a week. That's me to support maself, an the rest i it, ye know. It's jist gettin worse, Ah think, ye know. There is, well, Ah mean, painter's job, but it means too, as Ah say, travellin, an
10 people sometimes don't want tae travel from their home tae get a job, ye know. But Ah think that'll have tae be the stage in the future, jist have tae take jobs elsewhere, ye know, because Govan – Govan's jist dead.

E. It's lik the bloody seige i Stalingrad, so it is. Aw the empty spaces!

C. Ah've been away for five years. Jist come back in February, an it's terrible. Ah'm
15 disgusted wi it. They say put your litter in a rubbish bin. Where's the rubbish bins, ye know (laughter). They put these plastic wans up an somebody comes up an puts a dog end in it, an it melts!

A.   Aw the life has went oot i this community, specially roon aboot Govan, cos see when they're takin aw these tenements away, they're leavin it liein for long enough.
20 An then they've discovered too late, it's easier to sand blast and redevelop the houses than it is to pull them away. An they've done it aw too late. Cos Ah lived in a – Ah'd a great wee hoose, jist over in Sharp Street, an they took that away. That was a san stone building. They took that away, an ye're in hooses noo – they say they're redevelopin them aw noo, an that's – but, as Ah say, they've discovered that too late.

25 E. Same as in the city, they're stickin them oot miles away oot intae the schemes: they're only bloody barracks. There was a scheme we stayed in, Pollock: they've only opened up a shoppin centre now. That's been up for the last therty year. Ah think there was only aboot – see at the most, to cater for aboot forty, fifty thousand people, there was only aboot a dozen shoaps. It's travel aw the time, an wi the buses,
30 the expenses oan the buses, it's slaughter noo.

B. Ah've heard it said aboot this errea that they're takin aw the anti-social tenants oot i everywhere else, an puttin them in the wan errea, where they can watch them.

Whether that's true, Ah don't know. But Ah mean, it seems tae be, for every wan good family, you've goat aboot fifteen bad yins.

35 D.   For a young chap here, his only ambition is tae get out of it, ye know. Or there he jist gets the same as the rest i us, ye know, unemployed, livin fae week tae week wi no hope, no moral – morale, like ye know. And Ah don't see any future for any young person here.

B. When Ah got intae trouble when Ah was ten years of age, it was for money, an it
40 was only for coppers. But now, at ten years of age, they're runnin aboot wi knifes – aboot here anyway. They're runnin aboot wi knifes an swords an God knows what else. 'Ve started very young about here. Seems tae be a different breed entirely. Seem tae be wilder. They're breakin intae places, it's only to destroy them, burn them down, things lik that, ye know.

45 F. Ah worked in the yairds for five year, but it was gettin that bad, ye know. Ye were gaun in, ye were daein nothin. It was borin, actually, ye know. Ye were actually turnin intae an alcoholic; actually takin drink in an drinkin it. That was how borin it was.

G. [the only female speaker:]   Ah found my doctor tae be most unco-operative an
50 most unhelpful. Ah went tae him on several occasions an told him that ma husband had become totally alcoholic. Ah tried tae explain tae him jist how badly it was affectin the home life; it was affectin ma nerves; it was affectin him as well. And Ah found the doctor to be just totally indifferent tae the whole situation. He much preferred to hand you a bottle of tranquillisers.

55 H.   Ah was takin the tranquillisers. They were makin me drowsy, ye know. They were makin me, Ah'd be walkin along the street an ye would think Ah had a drink in me; Ah'd be staggerin. So Ah jist got, Ah jist stopped takin them an tried tae do without them. He started giving me sleepin tablets, but, as Ah sayed, it was just makin me worse.

T67a LEONARD, Tom, *Honest* (1984)

Tom Leonard (b. 1944) was born and educated in Glasgow. After graduating from Glasgow University he worked in various jobs before becoming a full-time writer. "His reputation was made by his poems in Glasgow dialect, in which he made great use of local words and phrases and their pronunciation. Although at first reading they may seem unintelligible, owing to Leonard's reliance on the idioms of Glasgow speech, their meaning becomes apparent when they are read aloud so that the natural speech rhythms can break through" (Royle, 174). He also wrote a radio play (*If Only Bunty Was Here* 1979) and short fiction in Glaswegian, but much of his work is in English. His main subject is the matter of Glasgow and its people, presented from an ironic, humorous and unsentimental perspective.

The passage from the short story *Honest* represents the narrator's reflections on the relationship between speaking/thinking and writing. A speaker of non-standard English cannot write down exactly what he thinks or says, unless he wants either to draw attention to his style, or to create a comic effect. Therefore, this piece of fiction deals with the same problem as the discussion about the "predicament of a Scots writer" quoted above (cf. T63 and T64) and the other pieces on the use of Scots for prose writing printed in this collection (e.g. Young, T56, Smith, T57).

Source: Tom Leonard, "Honest", in: *Intimate Voices. Selected Work 1965-1983*. Newcastle: Galloping Dog Press, 1984, pp.72-4.

(...) It's about time a wrote sumhm aboot masell! But whut? Ah thought even, ach
well, jist write doon a lohta yir memories, then maybe they'll take some kinda shape,
anyi kin use that ti write a story wi, or a play, or a poem, or a film-script, or God only
knows whut, on thi fly. So that's whuta did. Didny mahtr thi order, jist day eftir day,
5 writn doon ma memories. N ad be busy writn it, thinkin, whut an incredible life av
hud, even upti noo. Then ad be thinkin, they'll no believe aw this hapnd ti me. Then
a looktitit, najistaboot threw up. It wiz nuthin ti day wi me at all. Nthi other people ad
be writin about, thi people ad met an that, it wuz nuthin ti day wi them either. It
might eveniv been awright, if you coulda said it was about me nthem meetin, but you
10 couldny even say that. It wiz jist a lohta flamin words.

But that's sumhm else. Yi write doon a wurd, nyi sayti yirsell, that's no thi way a
say it. Nif yi tryti write it doon thi way yi say it, yi end up wi thi page covered in
letters stuck thigithir, nwee dots above hof thi letters, in fact, yi end up wi wanna
they thingz yid needti huv took a course in phonetics ti be able ti read. But that's no
15 thi way a *think*, as if ad took a course in phonetics. A doant mean that emdy that's
done phonetics canny think right – it's no a questiona right or wrong. But ifyi write
down "doon" wan minute, nwrite doon "down" thi nixt, people say yir beein
inconsistent. But ifyi sayti sumdy, "Whaira yi afti?" nthey say, "Whut?" nyou say,
"Where are you off to?" they don't say, "That's no whutyi said thi furst time."
20 They'll probably say sumhm like, "Doon thi road!" anif you say, "What?" they
usually say, "Down the road!" the second time – though no always. Course, they
never really say, "Doon thi road!" or "Down the Road!" at all. Least, they never say
it the way it's spelt. Coz it *izny* spelt, when they say it, is it?

A fine point, perhaps. Or maybe it izny, a widny no. Or maybe a think it is, but a
25 also a think that if a say, "Maybe it izny" then you'll turn it over in your head without
thinkin, "Who does he think he is – a linguistic philosopher?" Or maybe a widny
bothir ma rump whether it's a fine point or it izny: maybe a jist said it fur effect in thi
furst place. Coz that's sumhm that's dawned on me, though it's maybe wanna they
thingz that yir no supposed ti say. An thirz a helluv a lohta *them*, when yi think about
30 it, int thir? But anyway, what's dawned on me, or maybe it's jist emergin fray ma
subconscious, is, that maybe a write jist tay attract attention ti ma cell. An that's a
pretty horrible thought ti emerge fray *emdy's* subconscious, coz thi nixt thing that
emerges is, "Whut um a – a social inadequate?" N as if that izny bad enough, thi nixt
thing that yi find yirself thinkin, is, "Am a compensatin for ma social inadequacy, 'by
35 proxy', as it were?" An thi nixt thing, thi fourth thing, that yi find yirself thinkin, is,
"If av committed maself, unwittingly, ti compensation 'by proxy', does that mean
that a sense a inadequacy, unwittingly, huz become a necessity?" An thi fifth, an thi
sixth, an thi seventh thingz that yi find yirself thinkin, are, "Whut if ma compensation
'by proxy' is found socially inadequate?" and "Ivdi's against me – a always knew it,"
40 and "Perhaps posterity will have better sense." (...)

T67b LEONARD, Tom, *Unrelated Incidents* (1984)

The following piece is the first from a cycle of poems called "Unrelated Incidents". It challenges the general stigmatisation of Glaswegian not only by using the speechform for his poetry (by traditional definition the field of love, though not of science) rather than "funny stuff" (although the poem is of course funny, but not in a music-hall comedy way; cf. the reference to Stanley Baxter), but also by sending the custodian of the "language of the intellect", i.e. St E down the lift-shaft.

Source: Tom Leonard, "Unrelated Incidents" ((1) "its thi langwij a thi guhtr"), in: *Intimate Voices. Selected Work 1965-1983*. Newcastle: Galloping Dog Press, 1984, p.86.

<pre>
       its thi lang-
       wij a thi
       guhtr thaht hi
       said its thi
    5 langwij a
       thi guhtr
       awright fur
       funny stuff
       ur
   10 Stanlea Bax-
       ter ur but
       luv n science
       n thaht naw

       thi langwij
   15 a thi
       intillect hi
       said thi lang-
       wij a thi intill-
       ects Inglish

   20 then whin thi
       doors slid
       oapn hi raised
       his hat geen
       mi a fare-
   25 well nod flung
       oot his right

       fit boldly n
       fell eight
       storeys
   30 doon thi
       empty
       lift-shaft
</pre>

T68   WELSH, Irvine, *Trainspotting* (1993)

Irvine Welsh, who lives in London, published *Trainspotting* in 1993; it became an immediate success, and has since been followed by a number of other novels and collections of short stories.

As an example of modern Edinburgh slang the text of this novel is only marginally Scots, the impoverished language leaving a few distinctively urban Scots elements in prepositions, negations and the like. The character of the speech comes across much more impressively in the film version.
Source: Irvine Welsh, *Trainspotting*. London: Minerva, 1994, pp.113-7.

"INTER SHITTY"

(...) The London train's fuckin mobbed. This really gits ma fucking goat, this. Ah mean, ye pey aw that fuckin dough fir a ticket, they British Rail cunts urnae fuckin shy, n then thir's nae fuckin seats! Fuck that.

5   Wir strugglin wi they cans n boatils. Ma cairry-oot's aboot tae burst oot the fuckin bag. It's aw they cunts wi backpacks n luggage... n bairns' fuckin go-carts. Shouldnae huv bairns oan a fuckin train.

– Fuckin mobbed man, Rents sais.

– The fuckin trouble is, aw they cunts thit uv booked seats. It's no sae bad bookin fae
10 Edinburgh tae London, capital fuckin cities n that, bit it's aw they cunts thit've booked fae Berwick n aw they fuckin places. The train shouldnae stoap n aw they places; it should jist be Edinburgh tae London, end ay fuckin story. If ah hud ma fuckin wey, that wid be it, ah kin fuckin tell ye. Some cunts ur lookin at us. Ah speak ma fuckin mind, whitivir any cunt sais.

15   Aw they booked seats. Fuckin liberty, so it is. It should be first fuckin come, first fuckin served. Aw this bookin seats shite... ah'll gie the cunts bookin fuckin seats...

Rents sits doon beside they two burds. Fuckin tidy n aw. Good fuckin choice by the rid-heided cunt!

– These seats ur free until Darlington, he sais.

20   Ah grabs the reservation cairds n sticks thum in ma tail. – Thir fuckin free the whole wey doon now. Ah'll gie the cunts bookin, ah sais, smilin at one ay the burds. Too fuckin right n aw. Forty quid a fuckin ticket. No shy they British Rail cunts, ah kin fuckin tell ye. Rents jist shrugs his shoodirs. The posey cunt's goat that green basebaw cap oan. That's gaun oot the fuckin windae if the cunt fuckin faws asleep,
25 ah kin fuckin tell ye.

Rents is tannin the voddy, n wir jist near Portybelly whin the cunt's awready made a big fuckin dent in it. Hates a voddy, that rid-heided cunt. Well, if that's the wey the cunt wants tae fuckin play it... ah grabs the J.D. n swigs it back.

– Here we go, here we go, here we go... ah sais. That cunt jist smiles. He keeps
30 lookin ower it the birds, thir likesay American, ken. Problem wi that rid-heided cunt is thit he's no goat the gift ay the gab is far is burds go, likes, even if the cunt dis huv a certain style. No likesay me n Sick Boy. Mibbe it's wi him huvin brars instead ay sisters, he jist cannae really fuckin relate tae burds. Ye wait oan that cunt tae make the first fuckin move, ye'll be waitin a long fuckin time. Ah fuckin show the rid-
35 heided cunt how it's done.

– No fuckin shy, they British Rail cunts, eh? ah sais, nudgin the burd next tae us.

– Pardon? it sais tae us, sortay soundin likes, 'par-dawn' ken?

– Whair's it yis come fae then?

– Sorry, I can't really understand you... These foreign cunts've goat trouble wi the
40 Queen's fuckin English, ken. Ye huv tae speak louder, slower, n likesay mair posh,
fir the cunts tae understand ye.

– WHERE... DO... YOU... COME... FROM?

That dis the fuckin trick. These nosey cunts in front ay us look roond. Ah stares
back at the cunts. Some fucker's oan a burst mooth before the end ay this fuckin
45 journey, ah kin see that now.

T69a   SMITH, William Wye, *The Christmas Story* (1901)

William Wye Smith (1827-1917) was born in Jedburgh and "was taken by his parents to the United
States in 1830 and to Canada in 1837. After being a school-teacher, businessman and journalist he
became, in 1865, a minister of the Congregational Church" (Tulloch 1989:54) and retired in 1907. He
published several books of poetry as well as his translation of the new Testament (part of which, *The
Gospel of Matthew in Broad Scotch,* was brought out in Toronto in 1898).

Smith's translation is based on the *Revised Version* of the New Testament. It is "the first
contribution of the Scots diaspora to the history of Scots Bible translation. [...] It was only to be
expected that the fervent nationalism of exiled Scots would lead them to preserve and adorn the tongue
of their childhood in this way" (Tulloch, 54). Smith uses literary Scots, following the classical
Ayrshire-Burns tradition, rather than his native Border Scots. According to the author, the work was
meant as a colloquial rendering of the original, and therefore he sees the informal status of Scots as a
merit and not as a "predicament", but its "language is by no means as consistently colloquial as his
comments suggest" (Tulloch, 55). He hoped that his translation might serve as a model for a future
standardisation of Scots, and consequently tried to confirm to already-existing standards and to be
consistent in the use of Scots forms.

Source: William Wye Smith, "The Christmas Story", in: *The New Testament in Braid Scots*. Paisley:
Alexander Gardner Ltd., n.d. [1901], pp.130-1.

Noo i' thae days it cam aboot thar gaed oot a decree frae Cesar Augustus that a' the
inhabiters o' his dominions soud be enrolled. And this enrollment was made whan
Quirinius was Governor in Syria. And a' war gaun to be enrolled, ilk ane till his ain
citie. And Joseph, as weel, gaed up frae Galilee, oot o' the citie o' Nazareth, intil
5 Judea, intil Dauvid's citie, whilk is ca'd Bethlehem; for that he was o' the hoose and
stock o' Dauvid: To be enrolled, wi' Mary his betrothed wife, wha was a mither-to-be.

And sae it was, that while they war thar, the days war fulfilled for her to bring
forth. And she brocht forth her son – her first-born – and row't him in a barrie-coat,
and laid him i' the manger, for that there was nae room for them i' the inn. And thar
10 war in the same kintra side herds bidin i' the fields, and keepin gaird ower their
flocks by nicht. And see! an Angel o' the Lord cam till them, and the glorie o' the
Lord glintit roond aboot them; and they war sair gliff'd. And the Angel said, "Be-na
gliff'd; for I bring ye gude tidins o' muckle joy to the hail warld! "For thar is born
t'ye this day, in Daivid's toun, a Saviour, wha is the Anointit Lord. And here is the
15 token for ye: ye'se fin' the bairn row't in a barrie-coat, lyin in a manger." And a' at
ance there was wi' the Angel a thrang o' Heeven's host, praisin God, and sayin,

"Glorie to God i' the heighest heights,
and on the yirth peace! Gude wull to men!"

And as the Angels gaed awa frae them to Heeven, the shepherds said ane till
20 anither, "Lat us gang noo to Bethlehem, and see this thing that has come aboot, that
the Lord has made kent till us!" And they gaed, makin haste, and fund Mary, and
Joseph, and the bairn lyin in a manger. And whan they saw it, they tauld abreid the
words that war tell't to them anent this bairn. And a' that heard it ferlied at the things
tauld them by the shepherds. But Mary keepit a' thae things, ponderin on them in her
25 heart. And the shepherds returned, giean glorie to God, for a' thae things they saw
and heard; e'en as it was tell't them. And whan the auchth day was come for the
circumceesion o' the bairn, his name they ca'd Jesus, whilk was sae ca'd by the
Angel 'or he was conceiv't i' the womb.

T69b LORIMER, William Laughton, *The Christmas Story* (1957-83)

William Laughton Lorimer (1885-1967), son of a minister, was born near Dundee and educated there
and at Oxford. He became Professor of Greek at St. Andrews University, and a regular contributor to
the *Scottish National Dictionary*. The translation of *The New Testament in Scots* direct from the
original Greek was made between 1961 and 1966, "ransacking all available oral and literary linguistic
sources", but building on the Scots he had acquired from his nurse. Unable to finish his project, he
handed over the remaining editorial work to his son, R.L.C. Lorimer, who published the complete book
in 1983. The translation was remarkably successful (2500 copies sold in a fortnight). Lorimer "believed
the New Testament was not written in Standard Greek. Secondly, he considered the different writers of
the New Testament had varying styles of Greek. Thirdly, he hoped that the Scots translation of the New
Testament could help revitalise the Scots language" (Tulloch, 1989:75). Accordingly, he devised various different styles of Scots for different sections and functions, and employed colloquial, stylistically
neutral and formal/literary language all in the one text.
Source: William Laughton Lorimer, "The Christmas Story", in: *The New Testament in Scots*.
Edinburgh: Southside, 1983, pp.101-2.

About this time the Emperor Augustus pat furth an edick ordeinin at aa the fowk
i the haill warld suid be registrate. This wis whan Quirínius wis Governor o Sýria, an
it wis the first time at siccan a thing hed been dune. Sae aabodie gaed tae be
registrate, ilkane til his ain toun, Joseph amang the lave.
5   He belanged til the stock an faimlie o Dauvit, an sae it wis tae Dauvit's Toun,
Bethlehem in Judaea, at he gaed doun frae Nazareth in Galilee for tae gíe in his
name, takkin Mary, at wis haundfastit til him, wi him. She wis boukin gin this; an
whan they war in Bethlehem, she cam til her time an brocht hame her first-born son.
She swealed the bairn in a barrie an beddit him in a heck, sin there wis nae room for
10 them intil the inn.
Nou, i that same pairt the' war a wheen herds bidin thereout on the hill an keepin
gaird owre their hirsel at nicht. Suddent an angel o the Lord cam an stuid afore them,
an the glorie o the Lord shíned about them, an they war uncolie frichtit. But the angel
said tae them: "Binna nane afeared: I bring ye guid news o gryte blytheness for the
15 haill fowk – this day in Dauvit's Toun a sauviour hes been born til ye, Christ, the
Lord! This gate ye s' ken it is een as I say: ye will finnd a new-born bairn swealed in
a barrie an liggin intil a heck."

Syne in a gliff an unco thrang o the airmies o heiven kythed aside the angel, gíein
laud tae God an liltin:
20   "Glore tae God i the heicht o heiven,
               an peace on the yird tae men he delytes in!"
     Whan the angels quat them and gaed back til heiven, the herds said til ither,
"Come, lat us gang owre-by tae Bethlehem an see this unco at the Lord hes made
kent til us". Sae they hied owre tae Bethlehem what they coud drive, an faund Mary
25 an Joseph there wi the new-born babe liggin intil the heck; an whan they saw him,
they loot fowk ken what hed been said tae them anent the bairn. Aabodie ferliet tae
hear what the herds tauld them, but Mary keepit aa thir things lown an cuist them
throu her mind her lane. Syne the herds gaed back tae their hirsel, praisin an ruisin
God for aa at they hed hard an seen; aathing hed been een as they war tauld.

T69c LOW, John Thomas, *The Christmas Story* (1985)

John Thomas Low (1908-82) was born in Edinburgh and educated there. Throughout his academic
career, and especially during the 24 years of teaching at Moray House College of Education, his
interests centred on English drama, and on Scots language and literature in Scottish schools. He
frequently contributed essays in Scots to *The Scotsman* and *Lallans*, and edited works by L.G. Gibbon,
R.L. Stevenson, and G.D. Brown.
     The following versions 70c-f were all commissioned in: Manfred Görlach (ed.), *Focus on:
Scotland*. Amsterdam: Benjamins, 1985, p.211.

     Noo in thae days the word gaed oot frae Ceasar Augustus, the high heid yin o aa the
     Roman warld, that aabody sud be taen accoont o to pey tax. (This was first brocht in
     noo whan Cyrenius was in chairge o Seeria.) They aa bude to gang to be taxed, ilka
     ane til's ain toun. Amang the lave, Joseph gaed up til Judea frae the tounie o
5   Nazareth in Galilee, i the citie o Dauvit, whilk is cried Bethlehem, (himsel bein o the
     strynd and sib tae Dauvit). We him gaed Mary his guidwife, promised til him and on
     the road. Whan they war bidan there, her time cam and she gied birth til a son, her
     first-born. She happit him up in his bairn's claes and laid him doon in a manger
     because there was naewye else for them in that hoose.
10   In that same kintra placie there war a puckle shepherd laddies in the park, lookan
     efter their hirsel in the deid o nicht, whan, o a suddenty, an angel cam doon to them,
     skinklan wi the glore o the Lord; and they were gey feart. Quo the angel: "Dinna be
     feart: keep a calm sough; for I hae speirins for ye that'll gie tae ye and aa the lave o
     mankind muckle heize to your speerits. For til ye in Dauvit's toun the day a Saviour
15   has been born that is Christ the Lord. And this is hoo ye'll ken him: ye'll come upon
     the bairn happit in's swaddlin-claes, liggan in a manger". Syne, o a suddenty, there
     war wi the angel a muckle thrang o heevanlie fowk praisan God and sayan:
          "Aa glore tae God heich abune's in Heevan,
               an on the yirth saucht and guid gree til aa mortal bodies".
20   Syne it cam aboot, efter the angels had gane back til Heevan, that the shepherd
     laddies said, the tane until the tither: "Come on nou: we maun gang richt til
     Bethlehem and see this ferlie that has befaaen, and whilk the Lord has acquent us
     wi". They skelpit on, and fand Mary and Joseph and the infant bairn liggan in a

manger. Whan they had a sicht o't, they telt aabody whit they had hard tell aboot the
25 bairn. Aa the fowk that were telt aboot it were fair dumfounert at the things the
shepherd lads had said. Mary mindit upon aa thir things and thocht owre them in her
hert. Syne the shepherd laddies gaed hame, giean praise and glore til God for aa the
ferlies that had befaaen: it had aa turned oot juist as had been foretelt. Whan, efter
aicht days, He was auld eneuch to be circumcised, He was gien the name Jesus, whilk
30 was the name gien til him be the angel afore he was cleckit.

T69d ANNAND, J.K., *The Christmas Story* (1985)

James King Annand (1908-93) was born and educated in Edinburgh. As a schoolboy and editor of the
Broughton Magazine he edited some of the early work of Hugh MacDiarmid. He worked as a teacher
in Edinburgh and Whithorn, and was also a naval officer. He edited *Lallans* magazine from 1973-83,
and remained honorary president of the Scots Language Society until his death in 1993. His poetry is
remarkable for the colloquial ease with which he uses his native Scots, notably in children's verse (cf.
Annand [5]1981, [3]1979 and c1979) and in translations (e.g. Annand 1985, 1978).
Source: J.K. Annand, "The Christmas Story", in: Manfred Görlach (ed.), *Focus on: Scotland*.
   Amsterdam: Benjamins, 1985, p.212.

And in thae days it was pitten oot by Caesar Augustus that ilka bodie soud pey his
stent. And ilka bodie gaed til his ain pairish to pey his stent. And Joseph, tae, gaed up
frae Galilee, oot o the toun o Nazareth, intil Judea, intil David's Toun that is cried
Bethlehem, for Joseph was o the kith and kin o David. Wi him gaed his guidwife
5 Mary, that was big-boukit wi bairn.
    And sae it cam aboot that while they were there the time cam for her lyin-in. And
she had a laddie-bairn, her first-born, and she happit him in swaddlins and beddit him
in a manger, for there was nae place for them at the inns. And in that same airt there
were hirds ootby takkin tent o their hirsels throu the nicht. And fegs, the angel o the
10 Lord cam on them, and the glore o the Lord skinkelt aboot them and they were gey
feart. And the angel spak til them and said: "Dinna be feart. For I bring ye guid
wittins o muckle joy for aa the folk. For there is born the day in David's Toun a bairn
to sain us, cried Christ the Lord. And this is hou ye sall ken him. Ye'll finnd the bairn
in swaddlins, beddit in a manger." And suddent there was wi the angel a menyie o the
15 heivinlie host praisin the Lord and sayin:
        "Glore be to God in the heichest,
            an on yirth peace and guid-will til aa men."
    And it cam aboot, as the angels were gane awa up til heivin, the hirds said, the
tane til the tither: "Lat us gang nou til Bethlehem and see this ferlie that has come to
20 pass, that the Lord has brocht to our ken." And they gaed incontinent, and fand Mary
and Joseph, and the bairn beddit in a manger. And when they had seen the bairn they
spreid abraid the wittins that had been tellt them anent the bairn, and aa them that had
ferlied at what they had been tellt by the hirds. But Mary kept mim, tho her hert was
full. And the hirds gaed awa, gie-in to God the glore and the praise for aa they had
25 hard and seen, juist as it had been tellt them.

T69e GARRY, Flora, *The Christmas Story* (1985)

The poet Flora Garry (1900-99) was born in New Deer in Aberdeenshire, and was educated at the local school and Peterhead Academy, and later at the University of Aberdeen. She taught at schools in Dumfries, Strichen and Glasgow. After her retirement she returned to her native North-East.
Source: Flora Garry, "The Christmas Story in Buchan", in: Manfred Görlach, ed., *Focus on: Scotland*.
   Amsterdam: Benjamins, 1985, p.215.

Noo, at at time it sae happent a decree gaed oot fae Caesar Augustus at the hale kent
wardle sid be registert. An this registration wis first cairriet oot fin Cyrenius wis the
governor o Seeria. An aabuddy gaed to be registert, ilky buddy till the place faar he
wis born. An Joseph gaed up fae Nazareth o Galilee, awa intil Judea, as far's Daavit's
5 toon caad Bethlehem (for he wis the same line as Daavit an cam o the same stock) to
be registered wi Mary, his promise't wife, fa wis expeckin. An this wis the wye o't,
at fin they war there, the time hid come for her lyin-in.

An the loonie wis born – her aulest – an she rowe't him up in his happin-claes an
laid him doon in a haik, because there wis nae room for him in the inn. Noo, in at
10 same country-side, there wis shepherds bidin ootside amo the parks an lookin eftir
thir flocks aa throwe the nicht. An – harken noo! – an angel o the Lord cam amo
them an the glorie o the Lord bleezt aa roon aboot thim an they war fair terrifiet. An
the angel said to thim: "Dinna ye be feart, for – look noo! – I'm fessin great,
winnerfu news tae you an tae the hale wardle. For this verra day in Daavit's toon
15 there wis born for ye a Saviour an He's Christ the Lord. An this'll be some guidance
till ye – ye'll fin the littlan rowe't up in his happin-claes an lyin in a haik". Syne, on
a suddenty, alang wi the angel cam a great steerin crood o the hosts o hivven praisin
God an sayin:

"Glorie ti God in the hichest hichts
20   an on earth peace, gweed-wull amo men".

An syne, fin the angels hid turnt roon an awa back ti hivven, the shepherds said,
the teen ti the tidder, "We'll tak the road noo – aye, as far's Bethlehem – an see this
unco thing at's come aboot, at the Lord's acquantit's wi". An they skyce't on an cam
upo Mary an Joseph an the littlan lyin in a haik. An fin they'd seen't, they pat the
25 wird roon till aa the folk aboot fit they'd been tell't aboot this bairn. An aabuddy
harknin marvell't at the things the shepherds tell't him. An Mary store't thim up an
trishert thim in her hert. An the shepherds gaed awa back hame, glorifeein an praisin
God for aathing they'd hard an seen, jist as it hid been tell't till them. An fin the
aachth day hid come for the circumceesin o the bairn, they caad him Jesus, the name
30 gien by the angel afore he wis conceivt in the womb.

T69f GRAHAM, John J., *Da Nativity Story* (1985)

John J. Graham (b. 1921) was born and educated in Shetland, read English at Edinburgh University, worked as a teacher in Shetland (headmaster of Lerwick Central School and of Anderson High School). Graham has widely written in his native dialect, compiled the only modern dictionary of Shetlandic, and has been contributor to the *New Shetlander* ("a major preserving and developing influence on Shetland language and local culture" McClure), the (co-)editor of journals, an anthology and a grammar of his dialect.
Source: John J. Graham, "Da Nativity Story in Shetlandic", in: Manfred Görlach, ed., *Focus on: Scotland*. Amsterdam: Benjamins, 1985, p.216.

An sae hit cam aboot, at dat time, at Caesar Augustus made a laa at everyane sood be taxed. (An da first uptak o dis tax wis whin Cyrenius wis governor o Syria.) An everyane göd ta be taxed ta his ain hameplace. An among dem, Joseph set oot fae da toon o Nazareth i Galilee an göd tae Judaea ta da toon whaar his forebears cam fae –
5 Bethlehem. An wi him wis Mary, da lass at he wis contractit ta mairry. An shö wis at da faain fit. An sae hit cam aboot at while dey wir dere her time wis come at shö wis gyaan ta cry. An shö hed a peerie boy an shö rowed him in a hap an laid him in a stall in a byre, for dey wir nae room ida ludgin-hoose.
An dey wir i dis sam neebrid shepherds keepin an ee apo der flocks trowe da
10 nicht. An didna a angel o da Loard appear afore dem in a glöd o licht, an dey wir braaly faerd. An da angel spak tae dem an said: "Dunna be faerd for I'm come wi windrous news ta you an every livin sowl. Fir dis day wis boarn, for you an fir aa mankind, a Saviour Christ da Loard. An dis is foo you sal ken him: you'll fin da bairn rowed in a hap lyin in a stall in a byre." An wi dat sam aa aroond dem appared
15 a great gadderi o angels rösin da Loard an sayin:
"Glory ta Goad ida heichest
An ipo da aert paece an gödwill tae aa mankind."
An dan da angels left dem an göd awa ta Heevin, an da shepherds said ta ane anidder: "We man geng owre ta Bethlehem an see fir wirsels da fairlies at da Loard
20 is löt on ta wis." An dey göd blödspring an fan Mary an Joseph, wi da bairn lyin in a stall. An whan dey saa it dey telt everyane dey fell in wi da news dey wir gotten fae da angels aboot da bairn, an everyane dey telt stranged at da shepherds' tale. But Mary keepit aathing bunavara. An da shepherds göd back ta da hills rösin da Loard for aa da windrous things dey hed heard an seen.

T70 ANNAND, J.K., *Private Letter* (1979)

This letter to Manfred Görlach is a response to the addressee's attempt at writing a private letter in Scots himself, using Scots as a foreign language. Annand points out a grammatical mistake, treating Scots as a standardized language, rather than a dialect. The rest of the letter deals with the translation of Wilhelm Busch's *Max und Moritz* into Scots, which Annand was asked to do, demonstrating that Annand is able to discuss technical matters in Scots, i.e. that the functional range of Scots is – as far as he is concerned – not limited compared to English.
Source: J.K. Annand, private letter, 1979.

Dear Maister Görlach,   26 December 1979

Thank ye kindly for your letter o the 13 December. It is patent that your Scots is
better nor it should be for yin that isna a native speaker. I can see me speirin at ye for
a spiel for the magazine *Lallans* yin o thir days, aiblins an article on your darg at the
5 Universitie sae faur as Scots is concerned, or on ony ither maitter ye wale. (Micht I
pynt out, houaniver, that ye are agley when ye scrieve "Hings frae this *yin* aipple-
tree!" Yin/ane is a noun or pronoun, and the form should be yae/ae.)

I'm blyde that ye like the feck o my ettle at the Scots verse version, even tho ye
hae richtly pynted out a wheen fauts that I hope I'll pit richt afore I come til the
10 hindmaist version. I'm sensible o that "extra unstressed syllable at the beginnings of
lines". I dout we Scots are heftit til the iambic tetrameter for "narrative verse" – tak
Burns's Tam o Shanter, or Walter Scott's Lays. Houevir I've ettled to pit the fauts
richt and thanks to your help I've managed it wi the feck o them.

I'm sendin ye the Zweite Streich in verse. Gif ye jalouse I'm on the richt wey o't,
15 I'll try to feenish the hail poem afore I send ye the prose translation. Dinna pey owre
muckle attention to my spellin o the same word in orra weys. That'll be pit richt afore
the ploy is played, and ye get the feenished poem. Ye'll hae noted that I tak liberties
wi the tenses o verbs, cheyngin present tense for past, and past for present. I dinna
think this maitters muckle, and it maks it that muckle easier to pit it as in rhythm and
20 rhyme.

Ye'll hae takken tent o the fack that I canna complete line 91. I canna find the
meanin o "abgerupft".

I hope ye hae had a guid Yule. And lang may your lum reek in the New Year!
Yours aye,   *James Annand*

T71   BUSCH, Wilhelm, *Max und Moritz: four translations into Scots by J.K. Annand, Steve Mulrine, J. Derrick McClure and Derrick Herning* (1986)

The four passages are excerpts from full translations of 418 lines commissioned by M. Görlach in
1981/2 for a collection of 14 renderings of the famous children's classic (1865). The four translations
are among the best ever attempted of the text (of over 300 documented); they permit interesting
comparisons of the potentials of the dialects used – the village setting of the story might be expected to
fit best with rural varieties, but Mulrine's racy Glaswegian rendering will convince sceptics that this
need not be so.

The authors come from very different backgrounds. J.K. Annand (1908-93) was one of the best-
known writers in Scots, which he used with natural ease, in his poems, his prose and his many excellent
translations. Stephen Mulrine (b. 1937) is one of the major Glasgow poets who used the urban
vernacular for various genres, whereas J.D. McClure (b. 1944) who has been teaching English and
Scots literature and language for many years at Aberdeen University, and Derick Herning (b. 1932), the
polyglot teacher of Anderson High School, Lerwick, since 1967, both wrote in a Scots dialect not their
own – but were helped by native speaking experts.

Source: *Wilhelm Busch, Max and Moritz in English Dialects and Creoles*, ed. Manfred Görlach.
Hamburg: Helmut Buske, 1986, pp.71-81.

a) J.K. Annand, *Dod and Davie*
(Lallans)
Third Ploy:
Goat the Teyler in the toun
was kent for miles and miles aroun.
Shiftin claes and Sabbath claes,
5 warm top-coats for wintry days,
lang-legg'd breeks and cutty cloaks,
weskits fou o handy pokes -
aa thir claes, or ocht bespak,
Teyler Goat richt weel could mak.
10 Skeelie, tae, to mend or patch,
cut them doun, add bits to match,
shew on buttons for your breeks,
had been tint or lowss for weeks;
hou or whar or what ye will
15 no a task owre ill to fill.
Maister Goat tuik't aa the same,
pleasin folk was aye his aim.
Freind he was to ilka chiel,
freinds they were to him as weel.
20 But our callants had a ploy
Goat the Teyler to annoy.
By Goat's hous there was a water
rinnin fast wi noisy blatter.
Sen the burn was no that big,
25 plank o wuid serred as a brig.
Dod and Davie, hertless craturs,
thocht to brek the brig in smaithers,
skrechan-skrachan! wi the saw
nearly cut the brig in twa.
30 Nou that darg is dune and by
suddent there is hard a cry!
"Billy Goat, come out!" they geck,
"Teyler, Teyler, meck, meck, meck!"
Maister Goat could tak a lot,
35 maistly he cared not a jot;
tholin thon frae onie cratur
gaed agin his better natur.
Pickin up his rule he tore
smertly throu the open door.
40 Yince agane the laddies geck
loudly at him, "Meck, meck, meck!"
Sune's he steps upon the brod -
crack! - brig flees aa owre the road.
"Meck, meck, meck!" agane they yatter.
45 Plop! the Teyler's in the water.

b) Stephen Mulrine, *Matt an Malkie*
(Glaswegian)
Thurd Terr:
Aw the folk fur miles aboot,
wantin troosers ur a suit,
wi weskit poackits rerr an haundy,
5 tails fur werrin oan a Sunday,
wurkin claes fur through the week,
jaikits, nicky-tams rale neat -
aw knew how tae come tae Boke,
Boke the Tailor aye could cope;
10 if claes need mendin, patcht ur sewn,
trooser buttons, say, pit oan,
frunt ur back, it disnae maitter,
Boke kin fix it, noo ur later,
any joab, without a hitch -
15 that's his role in life, tae stich.
Natcherally aw the folk
keep upsides wi Tailor Boke.
Matt an Malkie, bit, yon perr,
want tae see him terr his herr.
20 Anywey, ootside his door,
runs this burn wi a roar,
ablow a brig, made oot a plank
keepin feet fae gettin damp.
Matt an Malkie, busy aye,
25 cut the widden brig hauf-wey,
saw it through, a sneaky trick,
rizzle-razz! tae weaken it.
Then the minit that joab's done,
they shirrick Bokey, jist fur fun:
30 "Tailor, come oan oot, weh-heh!
stchupit goat-face, meh, meh, meh!"
Boke could staun a loat a cheek,
shrug it aff withoot a peep,
bit soon as thon perr stert tae laugh,
35 Bokey jis aboot goes daft,
grabs a yerdstick oot the hoose;
at the door, comes merr abuse:
"Meh, meh, meh!" he hears the noise -
shure enough, it's they bad boays.
40 Acroass the brig he belts, too true -
crack! the brig haufs right in two!
"Meh, meh, meh!" comes fae the bank -
splat! the tailor's doon the stank!

c) J. Derrick McClure, *Mac an Matthy*
   (Northeastern Scots)
Third Pliskie:
Ilkie bodie in the toon
kens aal Gait, the teylor loon.
Claes for Sabbath or the ouk,
5 warm quytes tae hap yer bouk,
queetikins an moggans lang,
weskits tee wi pooches strang,
tailie jaikets trig an braa,
Maister Gait cud mak em aa.
10 Hed ye ocht at needit sortin?
Ony duds tae cloot or shorten?
Hed ye e'er a button tint,
ruggit aff yer breeks ahint?
Foo or far or fit's tae dee,
15 fore or hint, fite'er it be,
Gait wad gledly sort yer claes -
yon's the darg o aa his days.
Sae, iss skeely, eident cheil
in the toon wes likit weel.
20 Mac an Matthy, tho - yon pair
thocht tae gar him rage an rair!
See, forenenst his fite door-steen
rins a burn wi cheerie creen.
Ere a buird wes pit tae lig
25 ower the watter for a brig.
Mac an Matthy tak a saa -
cut it hidlins near in twaa.
Bizzie-buzzie - sweirt ey're neen:
fegs, but fit a spite ey've deen!
30 Fin the briggie's sinnert, swythe
comes a scratch, a lant sae blythe:
"Teylor! Oot ye come, min! Heh!
Billy-Gait, ye! Meh, me, meh!"
Maister Gait can thole it aa,
35 ne'er a word he'll say ava.
Sic a jaa, tho, s' nae tae dree -
noo he's in a tirravee!
Up he lowps, his ellwann cleeks,
swippert throu his aal door-cheeks,
40 an he's seen rampadgin fair,
hearin "Meh, meh, meh!" eence mair!
On the brig his fit he pits -
Crack! the briggie braks tae bits!
"Meh, meh, meh!" soons oot bedeen -
45 Platch! an syne the teylor's geen!

d) Derick Herning, *Jarm an Jeemsie*
   (Shetlandic)
Plunkie Three:
Lamb da tailor i dat place,
wis of coorse a weel kent face.
Wirkin plags an Sunday stroods,
5 ooen breeks an cotts wi hoods,
weskits at hed muckle pooches,
wirset froaks an aaldwives mutches,
siclaek claes athoot a scam
wis shön made bi mester Lamb.
10 If a jeckit wis owre stret
or a pair o breeks wis spret,
if a sark wis lost a button
or a torn skirt needit cuttin,
didna maitter whaar da sklent,
15 back or foreside, nivver ent -
wark laek dis ta Lamb dey broucht,
aa day lang wi leid he wroucht.
Sae it wis at aa da fock
laekit mester Lamb a lock.
20 Jarm an Jeemsie nane da less
nyagg will gie him an distress.
Bi da hoose whaar bed dis man,
white wi froad, a mill burn ran.
Owre da burn dey wir a brig,
25 hit led owre fae hoose ta rig.
Jarm an Jeemsie wirk awa
foo o filska wi da saa.
Skritty skratt, da tötaks strive,
i da plank a holl dey rive.
30 Whin der clooky wark wis owre,
dey begöd ta rout an roar:
"Come doo oot, doo aalie lamb,
tailor, tailor, yaarm, yaarm, yaarm."
Skyimp or taant aald Lamb could dree,
35 hit wis herd his löd ta jee.
Bit ta hear what dey him caa'd
wis anyoch ta mak him mad.
Wi a bismar in his nev,
he da hoose in scad did lave.
40 Fir eence mair ta mak him barm,
dis pair gölbröl "Yaarm, yaarm, yaarm."
Whin he sprits noo on da plank,
brokken hit anaeth him sank.
Lood dey roar oot: "Yaarm, yaarm, yaarm",
45 jöst afore he comes ta harm.

T72   LORIMER, R.L.C., *Macbeth-Translation* (1992)

Robin L.C. Lorimer, the son of W.L. Lorimer, edited and published his father's Bible translation (cf. T69b) and followed his father's linguistic model when translating Shakespeare's 'Scottish play'. As a result the Lorimer version has more archaisms than Purves's adaptation, which makes it more like the original, but harder to stage.
Source: R.L.C. Lorimer, *Shakespeare's Macbeth Translated into Scots*. Edinburgh: Canongate, 1992, pp.25-7, p.92.

Gruoch [*readin*] They rencountered me the day we cam speed; and bi mais traist
    instruction I lairn that they have intil them mair nor mundane knawledge. Whan
    with lowing desire I socht further tae speir them, than made they themsels air, in
    whilk they vainished; and while yet I stude ferliein at it, wha suid come but
5   messages fra the King, hailsing me Thane of Cawdor; with whilk style the Weird
    Sisters had of before saluist me, and referred me til time on-coming with, 'Weill
    come, King that sall be!'
        With all whilks I have thocht weill til acquant thee, my maist luvit pairt-takker
    in gryteness, sae as thow micht nocht forfault thy skair of rejoicing throu unkenning
10   the gryteness hecht thee. – Lay thir things in-by thy hairt, an sae fare weill.
    Glammis ye'r ense, an Cawdor, an will be
    what ye've been hecht. Yit I misdout your naitur,
    o man-kin's mither-milk it's fulled owre fou
    tae cleik the shortest road. Ye'r keen o gryteness –
15   no scant o ambítion, but scant o th'illness
    o will tae gae wi'd. Ettlin tae mak out
    híelie, but haililie, ye'd ey play fair,
    an yit unfairlie win. Ye'd hae, gryte Glams,
    what cries, 'Thusgate ye maun du', gin ye'd hae'd,
20   an what, I dout, ye'r feart raither tae du,
    nor wiss suid no be dune. Heast, heast ye back, man,
    sae's I may pour my spírits in your lug,
    an wi the smeddum o my tungraik screinge
    aathing at hains ye frae the gowden gird
25   the Weirds, wi mair nor naitural assistance,
    seems tae hae crouned ye wi. (...)
    The vera corbie's rauk
    at crowps the weirdit coming-in o Duncan
    aneth my barmekin. C'awà, ye spírits
30   at waits on mortal thochts, reive me my sex;
    full my haill bouk frae heels tae heid pang-fou
    o fellon crueltie; thicken my blude;
    stap aff ingate an througate tae remord,
    sae's nane o naitur's auntrin conscience-stangs

35   can slack my ettle, nor mak trews twixt it
        an its effeck. Come, fin' my wumman's breists,
        an tak my milk for gaw, ye ill-deed-duers,
        whauriver in your unseen essences
        ye fettle naitur's deiviltrie. Come, nicht,
40   shroud ye yoursel in Hell's maist keir-black reek,
        latna my gleg knife see the wound it maks,
        nor lift keek throu the plaiding o the mirk
        an skreich, 'Haud sae!'

        Macbeth – Puir bitch. Gin she'd but díed some ither while,
45   ther' wad been time eneuch for sicna wurd.
        The morra an the morra an the morra
        creeps in wi huilie pass frae day tae day
        till the laist tick, tack, o clockit time,
        an aa wir days bygane hes lichtent fuils
50   their road til stourie daith. Whuff, cannle-dowp!
        Life's nocht but a scug gangin, a bauch actor
        at strunts an fykes his ae hour on the stage,
        syne downa be hard mair – nocht but a tale
        tauld bi an ídjot, gey loud-soundin, teenfu,
55   signifiein naething.

T73 HORSBROCH, Dauvit, *A Hairst For A Bit Screive: Written Historie in Scots*

Dauvit Horsbroch is a Research Fellow at the University of Aberdeen and a prominent Scots-language
activist.
        Convincing expositing prose in Modern Scots is rare; it has often been stated that to create such
registers will be one of the most difficult tasks in language planning. Horsbroch's text is a rare
exception which combines convincing arguments relating to the topic of this book with easy prose style
that does not affect us as laboured or artificial. Another attraction is that, though scholarly, it is close
to naturally spoken Scots – this was the impression when the author read his paper in Scots at the
Belfast Conference.
Source: Kirk & Ó Baoill 2001:188-9.

        The'r a whein problems wi *Robert the Bruce* bi Glenn Telfer. The batters proudlie
        intimate: "This is the first book on Bruce to be written in the Scots language since
        Barbour's *Brus* in 1376." Weil, this is misleadin becis buiks o historie –
        comprehendin the raign o Robert the Bruce – war bein wrutten in Scots as late as the
5   17t centurie. An even efter this, aulder texts war bein prentit again richt doun til oor
        ain days. Gin a bodie leuks haurd at the text o this buikie it winna staun up til a
        scance. In ma ain opeinion it faws short o bein clessifeed as Scots at aw. Here a bit
        extrack tae shaw whit A mean:

Bruce's very presence maun hae been disconcerting at times. Wheneer the question o
10 *kingship arose, Bruce woud be sitting there representing an alternative – regardless o whit*
he sayd or felt. That he stuck wi the Scots' cause is the important fact. We woud scarcely hae
a story o Scotland tae write o, neer mind Bruce himsel, if he steyed wi King Edward frae the
beginning or returnt tae him eftir Falkirk. Imagine Bruce on the English side during aa this
period and the haill south-west o Scotland an English fastness? Bruce's apparent lack o
15 *activity is, I believe, an illusion created bi oor lack o knawledge. Whit wes happening in*
Bruce's ain land and in the south-west in general was nae sideshow.

This – tae this bodie – is Suddron Scottified, an even the Scots is wersh. Even takin
Inglish wurds sic as *would* an taking the *l* awa daesna mak it Scots. Whaur is the
Scots *wad*, we main speir? But the eidiom, as faur as the lenth o this bit screive, is
20 Inglis. Tak sentences sic as: *The English wer jist too strang for the Scots tae risk*
anither battle wi them. Patentlie, *ower strang* is wantin here. Thir weys o wrytin
juist lowp up at Scots speakers. (...)

Whit is the richt register for wrutten academic Scots? Whit gait shuid we tak?
Shuid academic Scos marra academic Inglis, aw for lang-nebbit Latinate wurds, an
25 cauldrif tae the reader, or shuid it hae a style aw its lane? Is it in the tradeition o Scots
tae be mair couthrie, mair infurmal in style? Shuid academic Scots be the exack same
Scots that a bodie wad hear oot on the gait or shuid it differ fae it? Thir questions
haed tae be conseidered bi fowk in Aiberdeen whan thay firsgt brocht *Cairn*
thegither. An the answer; weil, the'r nae richt answer ava, ceptna get wrytin.
30 A'm sweirt tae uise the wurd *staunart* – tho A wad lyke tae feel free tae – in case
fowk deek for thair guns an don steil bunnets. Insteid A'll say conseistent general
Scots. Athoot this we canna howp tae set furth guid academic *or* admeinstrativ Scots.
The'r aye some bodies in Scotland that hauds the braith that Scots alane, amang aw
the leids o the warld, shuidna hae onie general staunart for heicher registers, becis
35 this, thay claim, wad kill the leid aff.

T74 ROBINSON, Christine and CRAWFORD, Carol Ann, *Specimens of spoken urban Scots* (2001)

The following excerpts come from recordings made from speakers from the biggest urban centres in
Scotland. Robinson & Crawford initially intended "to offer guidance to actors working on Scottish
accents", which meant that they "did not seek out the strongest examples but selected more mainstream
speakers who still exhibit the most typical features of each area" (2001:9). The transcripts from
interviews recorded in informal situations are accompanied by a sixty-minute CD, which rewards close
analysis, especially since characteristics of intonation, pitch, rhythm and stress which make up much
of what is felt to be Scottish today can be described on the basis of a substantial sample, and features
of each of the four speech communities can be contrasted with each other.

GLASGOW. *Nan*: My mother sent me to elocution lessons when A wis about seven
and A went tae ... eh this woman in Kirklee Street, right, and she had me sayin aw
this rubbish. Anywey. An then they had this big exhibition an A'd tae say this poem
an go up on this stage an A wis staunnin (th)ere. A wis shakin. You should have
5   heard me. A cannae even mind the poem noo [...] And (th)en years later ma mother
[...] went 'Tae think A actually peyed hauf a croon an hoor tae get you eh, you know,
elocution." A used to be all right for about two hoors after A came oot. See efter
that. That was it.   (2001:43-4)

EDINBURGH. *Jenny*: Oh the coat, that's it. the ... the coat. ma ... ma Auntie Phemie's
10 coat. It was this coat that my Auntie Phemie left us one time and it was a jaiket.
Well, she was a stout woman, ken, and there was pockets in this coat and it went
right doon. Well it was rare for stealin anythin. Pinchin. Carrot and turnip an aw the
rest o it and inside was pockets fae there right doon tae the flair, ken, and A used tae
wheel this barrae and it was ... it ... these great big wheels and A was aye terrified
15 [I'd reco...] that somebody would recognise me, ye ken, wheelin this barrae up the
Ferry Road. My grannie used to stey beside us and as I say my grannie didnae like
me. She just liked the laddies in the faimlie and it used to annoy me, ken, because eh
I used to dae aw the messages for the folk there, an the folk up the stair an aw the
rest of it. And it was Liptons in the Kirkgate. It was Liptons and the Buttercup and
20 all these old shops that was up there we used to go ... An (th)en was Crawfords. I've
got aw these pictures that's in that thingmie – Crawfords.   (2001:59)

DUNDEE. *Jean*: Beechwood wisnae far fae Lochee ... an there was a big ... em ...
Cox's Mill in Lochee and I could remember at the school, comin hame for yer lunch,
for yer denner an ... the ... queues o people just aa leavin the mills like, goin home
25 for their dinner you know and the ... the women wi their heidsquares on tae keep the
stoor off their heid, you know, aff their hair – I remember that. Cos the ... the Lochee
High Street would be full o workers, you know, and ye kent they were workers cos
they were dead busy, you know ... hurryin tae get hame and hurryin h ... tae get back
tae work.   (2001:68)

30 ABERDEEN. *Barbara*: It's a bittie hard actually, wi haen four jobs. But even though
[A've] got four jobs, part-time jobs, they dinna work up tae a full-time job even, cos
like (th)e creche, they're two and a half hours, the after school club is three and a
half hours, an ma cleaning job is one hour and then my under twelves is only ten
hours a month. [It's] still nae a forty hour wik.
35 We're nae allowed pets in oor hoose but we've got a snake. Shona had the snake and
she used tae get her lad tae gie it white fish. But I couldna get it tae eat. A'm gaun
'Oh no! It's gaun tae die'. So she bought a goldfish, aboot an inch and a half, say,
two inches lang. An she took it hame. An she put it in the snake's water bowl. 'S a
water snake. And she fed her little fish and she sat for two hours watchin this fish ...
40 snake never came oot an she went doon (th)e stairs again. When I came in she says,
'Ma, go on upstairs an see ma fish.' A saw her fish aa right. It was a great bump in
(th)e snake.   (2001:90)

T75 KIRK, John M., *Ullans neo-Scots* (2000)

John Kirk is a Lecturer in English at Queen's University Belfast. The text is from an information leaflet on employment by Belfast City Council; the Ullans version is accompanied by the English translation. Ullans is the revivalist attempt based on the rural Scots dialect spoken by some 100,000 speakers in N Ireland, expanded by neologisms, and recently extended to the register of formal written prose, as a consequence of official recognition as a minority language.
Source: John M. Kirk, "Two Ullans texts", in Kirk & Ó Baoill 2000:33-4, which also see for comment.

Bilfawst Citie Cooncil ... inlats fur ilkaboadie
Belfast City Council ... Opportunities for Everyone

1. Cud ye compluther we iz – yer ain sel?
Does your face fit?

5   2. Gin ye'r taakin o inlats fur darg wi Bilfawst Citie Cooncil, tha repone wud be 'ay'.
When it comes to employment opportunities with Belfast City Council, the answer is 'yes'.

3. Bilfawst Citie Cooncil – aareddie wi mair warkers nor near onie ither boadie in
10   tha citie - is ettled fur tae hae its inlats o darg apen til aaboadie.
Belfast City Council - already one of the city's biggest employers - is committed to making sure that its employment opportunities are open to everyone.

4. Nae metter quhar ye'r frae, an quhitiver fawks ye caa yer ain, sae lang as yer the tap boadie fur tha jab, ye wud compluther wi iz richtlie!
15   *Whatever your background, whatever community you come from, if you are the best person for the job, your face fits!*

5. We tak fowks on fur bein tha maist fit fur tha darg, an haein tha richt exams an siclike, sae gif ye houl ye'r on fur yin yae jab, we wud be blythe fur ye tae pit in fur it.
20   *We recruit on the basis of ability, qualifications and aptitude for work so if you think you could handle a particular post we would welcome your application.*

6. Tha Rax til Resydenters Ettlin wuz drew up fur tae skail thon thocht til aa oor resydenters sae as tha maist feck o aa soarts o fowk wull pit tharsels forrit fur jabs wi Bilfawst Citie Cooncil.
25   *The Community Outreach Programme has been designed to take that message to all our communities so that jobs within Belfast City Council will attract applications from the broadest possible base...*

7. ... quhilk airtins shud gie a heeze til tha Citie Cooncil's ettlin on preein the tap boadies fur tha richt jabs.
30   *... which will help the City council to find the best people for the best jobs.*

11   *References*

This list includes all works mentioned, or quoted from, in chapters 1-9. Sources of the main texts (T1-T75) are given in the individual introductions preceding the excerpts and are here not repeated. Bracketed figures refer to pages where the publications are mentioned; titles without such indication were considered so important that they seemed to justify the addition to my list of references.

Abercrombie, David. 1979. "The accents of Standard English in Scotland". In Aitken & McArthur, 68-81.

Adams, G. Brendan, ed. 1964. *Ulster Dialects: An Introductory Symposium*. Holywood: Ulster Folk Museum.

---. 1977. "The dialects of Ulster". In Ó Muirithe, 56-69.

Adams, James. 1799. *The Pronunciation of the English Language Vindicated from Imputed Anomaly and Caprice*. Edinburgh: for the author. Facs. Menston: Scolar Press, 1968 [EL 72]. [85-6]

Agutter, Alexandra. 1988a. "Standardisation in Middle Scots". *Scottish Language*, 7:1-8.

---. 1988b. "Middle Scots as a literary language". In Craig, 13-26. [116]

Aitken, Adam Jack. 1971. "Variation and variety in written Middle Scots". In A.J. Aitken, A. McIntosh & H. Pálsson, eds. *Edinburgh Studies in English and Scots*. London: Longman, 167-209.

---, ed. 1973. *Lowland Scots: Occasional Papers no. 2*. Edinburgh: Association for Scottish Literary Studies.

---. 1977. "How to pronounce Older Scots". In Aitken, McDiarmid & Thompson, 1-21. [82]

---. 1979. "Scottish speech: a historical view with special reference to the standard English of Scotland". In Aitken & McArthur, 85-118. [32, 68, 173-4]

---. 1980. "New Scots: the problems". In McClure, Aitken & Low, 45-66.

---. 1981a. "The Scottish vowel-length rule". In Benskin & Samuels, 131-57. [82-4]

---. 1981b. "The good old Scots tongue: does Scots have an identity?". In Haugen, McClure & Thompson, 72-90.

---. 1982. "Bad Scots: some superstitions about Scots speech". *Scottish Language*, 1:30-44.

---. 1983. "The languages of older Scots poetry". In McClure, 18-49. [141-2]

---. 1984a. "Scottish accents and dialects". In Trudgill, 94-114. [77, 93, 104, 107, 162]

---. 1984b. "Scots and English in Scotland". In Trudgill, 517-32. [162]

---. 1985. "Is Scots a language?". *English Today* 3:41-5.

---. 1987. "The extinction of Scotland in popular dictionaries of English." In R.W. Bailey, ed. *Dictionaries of English. Prospects for the Record of Our Language*. Ann Arbor: University of Michigan Press, 89-120. [114-5, 151]

---. 1990. "The lexicography of Scots" Art. 199a in F.J. Hausmann *et al*. eds. *Wörterbücher. Dictionaries. Dictionnaires*. Berlin: de Gruyter, II: 1983-7. [121-3]

---. 1996. *The Pronunciation of Older Scots*. Dunfermline: Robert Henryson Society/Scotsoun Publications.

--- & Tom McArthur, eds. 1979. *Languages of Scotland*. Edinburgh: Chambers.

---, Matthew P. McDiarmid & Derrick S. Thompson, eds. 1977. *Bards and Makars: Scots Language and Literature, Mediaeval and Renaissance*. Glasgow: UP.

---, Angus McIntosh & H. Pálsson, eds. 1971. *Edinburgh Studies in English and Scots*. London: Longman.

Aldis, Harry G. 1904. *A List of Books Printed in Scotland Before 1700*. Edinburgh; repr. with additions 1970.

Allan, Alasdair. 1995. "Scots spellin: ettlin efter the quantum lowp". *EWW* 6:63-104. [166, 180]

---. 1998. "New founs fae auld larachs: leid-plannin for Scots" unpublished University of Aberdeen PhD thesis. [57, 180]

Anon. 1784. *A General View of English Pronunciation: to which are added EASY LESSONS for the Use of the English Class*. Edinburgh. Facs. Menston: Scolar Press, 1968 [EL 9].

---. 1855. *Scotticisms Corrected*. London: Shaw.

Bailey, Richard W. & Manfred Görlach, eds. 1982. *English as a World Language*. Ann Arbor: University of Michigan Press.

Bailey, Richard W. & Jay L. Robinson. 1973. *Varieties of Present-Day English*. New York: Macmillan. [14]

Bald, M. 1926. "The anglicisation of Scottish printing". *Scottish Historical Review*, 23:107-15. [9]

---. 1927. "The pioneers of anglicised speech in Scotland". *Scottish Historical Review*, 24:179-93.

---. 1928. "Contemporary references to the Scottish speech of the sixteenth century". *Scottish Historical Review*, 25:163-79.

Barber, Charles. 1976. *Early Modern English*. London: Deutsch. ([2]1994, Edinburgh: UP). [36]

Barnes, Michael P. 1984. "Orkney and Shetland Norn". In Trudgill, 352-66. [20]

---. 1991. "Reflections on the structure and the demise of Shetland and Orkney Norn". In P.S. Ureland & G. Broderick, eds. *Language Contact in the British Isles*. Tübingen: Niemeyer, 429-60.

Barry, Michael V. 1982. "The English language in Ireland". In Bailey & Görlach, 84-133.

Bartlett, Christopher. 1992. "Regional variation in New Zealand English: the case of Southland". *New Zealand English Newsletter* 6:5-15. [67]

Basker, James G. 1993. "Scotticisms and the problem of cultural identity in eighteenth-century Britain". In J. Dwyer & R.B. Sher, eds. *Sociability and Society in Eighteenth-Century Scotland*. Edinburgh: Mercat Press, 81-95. [122]

Bauer, Laurie. 1997. "Attempting to trace Scottish influence in New Zealand English". In Schneider, II, 257-72. [67]

Baugh, Albert C. & Thomas Cable, [4]1993. *A History of the English Language*. London: Routledge & Kegan Paul. ([5]2002)

Bawcutt, Priscilla. 1976. *Gavin Douglas: A Critical Study*. Edinburgh: UP.

Beal, Joan. 1997. "Syntax and morphology". In Jones, 335-77. [93, 95, 100, 101, 105-6]

Benskin, Michael & M.L. Samuels, eds. 1981. *So Meny People, Longages and Tonges: Philological Essays in Scots and Medieval English Presented to Angus McIntosh*. Edinburgh: UP.

Björkman, Eric. 1900-02. *Scandinavian Loan Words in Middle English*. 2 vols. Halle: Ehrhardt Karras.

Bjørn, C., A. Grant & K.J. Stringer, eds. 1994. *Nations, Nationalism and Patriotism in the European Past*. Copenhagen: Academic Press.

Blake, N.F. 1981. *Non-Standard Language in English Literature*. London: Deutsch. [36, 148, 172]

Bliss, Alan, ed. 1979. *Spoken English in Ireland, 1600–1740*. Dublin: Dolmen Press. [3]

Bollard, John K., Frank R. Abate, Katherine M. Isaacs. [2]1997. *Pronouncing Dictionary of Proper Names*. Detroit, Mi.: Omnigraphics. [75]

Borrowman, Alexander S. 1979. *The Buik o Ruth and Ither Wark in Lallans*. Edinburgh: Gordon &Wright.

Brand, J. 1701. *A Brief Description of Orkney, Zetland, Pightland-Firth and Caithness*. Edinburgh.

Britain, David & Peter Trudgill. 1999. "Migration, dialect contact, new dialect formation and re-allocation: Canadian raising in England". *TPS* 97:2, 245-56. [64]

Brown, E. Keith & Martin Millar. 1980. "Auxiliary verbs in Edinburgh speech". *TPS*, 81-133. [104]

Buchan, Peter and David Toulmin. 1989. *Buchan Claik. The Saut and the Glaur o't. A Compendium of Words and Phrases from the North-East of Scotland*. Edinburgh: Gordon Wright. [124]

Buchanan, James. 1757. *Linguae britannicae vera pronunciatio*. London. Facs. Menston: Scolar Press, 1967 [EL 39]. [81, 171]

---. 1762. *The British grammar*. London. Facs. Menston: Scolar Press, 1968 [EL 97].

---. 1766. *An Essay Towards Establishing a Standard for an Elegant and Uniform Pronunciation of the English Language throughout the British Dominions*. London.

---. 1770. *A Plan for an English Grammar-School Education*. London.

Campbell, Ian. 1981. *Kailyard*. Edinburgh: Ramsay Head. [157]

Cardell, Kerry & Cliff Cumming. 1992/93. "Scotland's three tongues in Australia: Colonial Hamilton in the 1860s and 1870s". *Scottish Studies* 31:40-62. [65]

Catford, John C. 1957a. "The Linguistic Survey of Scotland". *Orbis* 6/1: 105-21.

---. 1957b. "Vowel systems of Scots dialects". *TPS*, 107-17.

Chambers, Jack K. & Peter Trudgill. 1980. *Dialectology*. Cambridge: UP.

Cheshire, Jenny, ed. 1991. *English Around the World: Sociolinguistic Perspectives*. Cambridge: UP.

Chirrey, Deborah. 1999. "Edinburgh: descriptive material". In: Paul Foulkes & Gerald Docherty eds. *Urban Voices. Accent Studies in the British Isles.* London: Edward Arnold, 223-9. [50]

Cleishbotham the Younger. 1858. *Handbook of the Scottish Language*. Edinburgh.

Corbett, John. 1997. *Language and Scottish Literature*. Edinburgh: UP.

---. 1999. *Written in the Language of the Scottish Nation. A History of Literary Translation into Scots.* Clevedon: Multilingual Matters. [3, 11, 12-4, 111, 147, 150, 162, 170, 180-1]

--- *et al.* fc. *Scottish Corpus of Texts and Speech (SCOTS).* Glasgow.

Craig, Cairns, ed. 1988. *The History of Scottish Literature.* 4 vols. Aberdeen: UP.

Craig, D. 1961. *Scottish Literature and the Scottish People 1680-1830.* London: Chatto & Windus.

Craig, Sir William G., ed. 1935. *Facsimiles of National Manuscripts of Scotland,* 1867-71. 3 vols. Southampton: Ordnance Survey Office.

---. 1950. "The language of MS ROYAL 18 Bxv". In *Basilikon Doron.* STS, 3rd series, 18:117-35.

Craigie, J., ed. 1948-58. *The Poems of King James VI.* STS, 2nd series.

Craigie, Sir William A. 1925. "The earliest records of the Scottish tongue". *Scottish Historical Review,* 22: 61-80.

---. 1939. "The language of the *Kingis Quair." Essays & Studies* 25: 22-38. [143]

---. A.J. Aitken, J.M. Templeton, H. Watson & J.A.C. Stevenson, eds. 1937-. *A Dictionary of the Older Scottish Tongue [DOST].* 8 vols. to *s(c)hake.* Chicago: University of Chicago Press; London: Oxford UP. [8, 34, 121, 123]

CSD see Robinson 1985

Cusack, Bridget. 1998. *Everyday English 1500-1700. A Reader.* Edinburgh: UP. [1, 6]

Daiches, David. 1981. *A Companion to Scottish Culture.* London: Arnold. [10, 22, 154]

Devitt, Amy J. 1989. *Standardizing Written English: Diffusion in the Case of Scotland 1520-1659.* Cambridge: UP. [53, 55-6, 97, 110, 169]

Dieth, Eugen. 1932. *A Grammar of the Buchan Dialect.* I: *Phonology – Accidence.* Cambridge: Heffer. [11, 40, 42, 46, 47, 87, 90]

Donaldson, Gordon. 1970. *Scottish Historical Documents.* New York: Barnes & Noble. (²1974, Edinburgh: Scottish Academic Press).

Donaldson, William. 1986. *Popular Literature in Victorian Scotland: Language, Fiction and the Press.* Aberdeen: UP. [4, 54, 59, 138, 157, 183, T41, T42]

---. 1989. *The Language of the People: Scots Prose from the Victorian Revival.* Aberdeen: UP. [4, 59]

---, ed. 1995a. *Johnny Gibb of Gushetneuk* (1871). East Linton: Tuckwell. [T44]

---, ed. 1995b. *My Uncle the Baillie* (1876-77). East Linton: Tuckwell. [155-6]

DOST see Craigie *et al.* 1937-

Eagle, Andrew. ²1999. *Wir Ain Leid. An Innin tae Modren Scots.* http://ourworld. compuserve.com/Homepages/K27 [179]

Eckhardt, Eduard. 1910–11. *Die Dialekt- und Ausländertypen des älteren englischen Dramas.* 2 vols. Louvain: Uystpruyst.

Ellenberger, Bengt. 1977. *The Latin Element in the Vocabulary of the Earlier Makars Henryson and Dunbar.* Lund: CWK Gleerup. [143]

Ellis, Alexander John. 1889. *On Early English Pronunciation.* vol. 5. London: Trübner. [42, 87]

Elphinston, James. 1766. *The Principles of the English Language Digested for the Use of Schools*. London.

---. 1786, 1787. *Propriety Ascertained in her Picture or Inglish Speech and Spelling Rendered Mutual Guides, Secure Alike from Distant, and from Domestic, Error*. 2 vols. London. [75]

---. 1790. *Inglish Orthoggraphy epittomized*. London: Ritchardson. Facs. Menston: Scolar Press, 1971 [EL 288].

---. 1795. *Minniature ov Inglish Orthoggraphy*. London: Ritchardson. Facs. Menston: Scolar Press, 1967 [EL 28].

Fenton, Alexander. 1959. "Proverbs and sayings of the Auchterless and Turriff area of Aberdeenshire". *Scottish Studies* 3:1, 39-71. [124]

--- & D.A. MacDonald, eds. 1994. *Studies in Scots and Gaelic: Proceedings of the Third International Conference on the Languages of Scotland, 1991*. Edinburgh: Canongate Academic.

Fenton, James. 1995. *The Hamely Tongue: A Personal Record of Ulster Scots in County Antrim*. Newtownards: Ulster Scots Academic Press, ²2000, Belfast: The Ullans Press. [124]

Ferguson, Charles A. 1959. "Diglossia". *Word* 15: 325-49.

Findlay, Bill, ed. 2002. *Frae Ither Tongues: The Use of Scots in Translation*. Clevedon: Multilingual Matters.

Flaws, Margaret & Gregor Lamb. 1996. *The Orkney Dictionary*. Kirkwall: The Orkney Language and Culture Group. [48, 124]

Forbes, Robert (transl.), "*Ajax His Speech to the Grecian Knabbs*, (transl. from Ovid's *Metamorphoses*, Liber XIII) attempted in Broad Buchans", to which is added, *A Journal to Portsmouth*, and a "Shop Bill", in the same dialect. Aberdeen: A. Brown & Co., Edinburgh: John Menzies & Co., 1869, pp.2-11.

Fox, Denton. 1966. "The Scottish Chaucerians". In D.S. Brewer, ed. *Chaucer and Chaucerians. Critical Studies in Middle English Literature*. London: Nelson, 164-200. [137, 143]

--- & William A. Ringler, eds. 1980. *The Bannatyne Manuscript*. National Library of Scotland Advocates' MS. 1.1.6. Facsimile edition. London: Scolar Press.

France, Peter & Duncan Glen, eds. 1989. *European Poetry in Scotland. An Anthology of Translations*. Edinburgh: UP. [12]

Francis, W. Nelson. 1983. *Dialectology: An Introduction*. London: Longman.

Geddes, John. [1978]. *Caithness Spoken. A Selection of Old Caithness Words and Expressions*. Michinhampton: the author. [124]

Gifford, Douglas *et al.*, eds. 2002. *Scottish Literature*. Edinburgh: UP.

Glauser, Beat. 1974. *The Scottish-English Linguistic Border*. Bern: Francke. [32, 40, 44]

---. 2000. "The Scottish/English border in hindsight." *IJSL* 145:65-78. [44]

Görlach, Manfred, ed. 1985a. *Focus on Scotland*. (VEAW G5). Amsterdam: Benjamins. [xi]

---. 1985b. "Scots and Low German: the social history of two minority languages". In Görlach, 19-36. [67]

---. 1987. "Lexical loss and lexical survival: the case of Scots and English". *Scottish Language*, 6:1-20; repr. in *Studies* 1990: 123-43. [112]

---. 1990. "The development of Standard Englishes". In Manfred Görlach, *Studies in the History of the English Language*. Heidelberg: Winter, 9-64.

---. 1991a. *Introduction to Early Modern English*. Cambridge: UP. [xi, 1, 6, 9, 11, 16, 30, 36, 57, 69, 70, 80, 81, 144]

---. 1991b. "Jamaica and Scotland - bilingual or bidialectal?". In M.G. *Englishes: Studies in Varieties of English 1984-1988* . Amsterdam: Benjamins, 69-89. [31, 67, 176]

---. 1995a. *More Englishes*. (VEAW G13). Amsterdam: Benjamins.

---. 1995b. *New Studies in the History of English*. Heidelberg: Winter.

---. 1995c. "Sociolinguistic determinants for literature in dialects and minority languages: Max and Moritz in Scots". In 1995a: 220-45.

---. 1995d. "Irish English and Irish culture in dictionaries of English". In 1995a: 124-63. [115]

---. 1995e. "Morphological standardisation: the strong verbs in Scots". In 1995b: 51-81. [7, 97]

---. 1997a. "Celtic Englishes?". In Hildegard L.C. Tristram, ed. *The Celtic Englishes*. Heidelberg: Winter, 27-54.

---. 1997b. "Language and nation: the concept of linguistic identity in the history of English." *EWW* 18:1-34. [2]

---. 1997c. *A Linguistic History of English*. London: Macmillan (German original 1974) [91]

---. 1998a. *Even More Englishes*. (VEAW G22). Amsterdam: Benjamins.

---. 1998b. *An Annotated Bibliography of 19th-century Grammars of English*. Amsterdam: Benjamins. [10]

---. 1998c. "And is it English?". In 1998a, 1-18. [33]

---. 1998d. "Text types and the history of Scots". In 1998a, 55-77. [38, 55-60]

---. 1999. *English in 19th-century England*. Cambridge: UP. [xi]

---. 2000. "Ulster Scots: a language?". In Kirk & Ó Baoill, 13-31. [63]

---. 2001a. *18th-century English*. Heidelberg: Winter. [xi, 60, 170]

---. 2001b. "Scots: the view from outside." In Kirk & Ó Baoill, 2001a: 181-94. [37, 68]

---. 2002a. *Explorations in English Historical Linguistics*. Heidelberg: Winter.

---. 2002b. "Correctness and the history of English". In 2002a:137-212.

---. 2002c. "The contribution of translation to the development of English". In 2002a:1-70. [12]

---. 2002d. *Still More Englishes* (VEAW). Amsterdam: Benjamins.

---. 2002e. "The problem of authentic language". In 2002d:17-47. [6]

Graham, John J. 1979. *The Shetland Dictionary*. Stornoway: Thule Press. ([4]1999). [48, 124]

---. & T.A. Robertson, eds. 1964. *Nordern Lichts. An Anthology of Shetland Verse and Prose*. Lerwick: Manson. [48]

Graham, William. 1977. *The Scots Word Book. English-Scots, Scots-English Vocabularies*. Edinburgh: Ramsay Head. [121]

Grant, A. 1994. "Aspects of national consciousness in medieval Scotland". In Bjørn, Grant & Stringer, eds., 68-95. [2]

Grant, William. 1913. *The Pronunciation of English in Scotland*. Cambridge: UP. [87]

--- & J. Main Dixon. 1921. *Manual of Modern Scots*. Cambridge: UP. [xi, 1, 87, 135, 148, T40, T48]

--- & David D. Murison, eds. 1931-76. *The Scottish National Dictionary [SND]*. Edinburgh: The Scottish National Dictionary Association. [8, 34, 121, 123]

Gregg, Robert J. 1964. "Scotch-Irish urban speech in Ulster". In Adams, 163-92.

---. 1972. "The Scotch-Irish dialect boundaries in Ulster". In M.F. Wakelin, ed. *Patterns in the Folk Speech of the British Isles*. London: Athlone, 109-39. [63]

---. 1985. *The Scotch-Irish Dialect Boundaries in the Province of Ulster*. Ottawa: Canadian Federation for the Humanities.

Gregor, Walter. 1866. *The Dialect of Banffshire with a Glossary of Words not in Jamieson's Scottish Dictionary*. London: Asher.

Grieg, J.Y.T., ed. 1961. *The Letters of David Hume*. Oxford. [4]

Häcker, Martina. 1999. *Adverbial Clauses in Scots. A Semantic-Syntactic Study*. Berlin: Mouton de Gruyter. [109]

Hagan, Anette I. 2002. *Urban Scots Dialect Writing*. Frankfurt/M.: Peter Lang.

Hamilton, Anne Marie. 1998. "The endurance of Scots in the United States". *Scottish Language* 17:108-18. [64]

Hardy, Buff. 1985. *Far's the Paper*. Aberdeen Journals. [47]

Hargreaves, Henry. 1981. "Patric Scot's medical book". In Benskin & Samuels, 309-21. [59]

Harris, John. 1984. "English in the north of Ireland". In Trudgill, 115-34.

---. 1991. "Ireland". In Cheshire, 37-50.

Hart, John. 1569. *An Orthographie, conteyning the due order and reason, howe to write or paint thimage of mannes voice, most like to the life or nature*. (London. STC 12890). Facs. Menston: Scolar Press 1969 [EL 209]; ed. B. Danielsson (Stockholm, 1955-63). [30]

Haugen, Einar, J.Derrick McClure, & Derrick Thompson, eds. 1981. *Minority Languages Today*. Edinburgh: UP.

Henderson, H. 1983. "'At the foot o' yon excellin' brae': the language of Scots folksong". In McClure, 100-128. [154]

Henderson, T. F. 1889. *Scottish Vernacular Literature*. London: Nutt.

Hewitt, David. 1987. "James Beattie and the languages of Scotland". In J.J. Carter & J.H. Pittock, eds. *Aberdeen in the Enlightenment*. Aberdeen: UP, 251-60.

---, ed. 1995. *Northern Visions. Essays on the Literary Identity of Northern Scotland in the Twentieth Century*. East Linton: Tuckwell. [47]

Hook, Andrew. 1999. *From Goosecreek to Gandercleugh. Studies in Scottish-American Literary and Cultural History*. East Linton: Tuckwell. [60, 64]

--- & Richard B. Sher, ed. 1995. *The Glasgow Enlightenment*. East Linton: Tuckwell.

Horsbroch, Dauvit, ed. 1997-. *Cairn. The Historie Jurnal in the Scots Leid*. Aberdeen: University.

---. 1999. "Scots as a European language 1500-1700". *Scottish Language* 18:1-16. [146]

---. 2000. "Mair as a sheuch atween Scotland an Ulster: twa policies for the Scots leid?". In Kirk & Ó Baoill, 133-41. [3, 166]

---. 2001. "A twalmonth an a wee tait forder". In Kirk & Ó Baoill, 123-33. [3, 57, 166]

Hubbard, T., ed. 1991. *The New Makars: The Mercat Anthology of Contemporary Poetry in Scots*. Edinburgh: Mercat Press.

Hudson, R.A. ²1996. *Sociolinguistics*. Cambridge: UP.

Hughes, G. Arthur & Peter Trudgill. 1987. *English Accents and Dialects*. London: Edward Arnold. (¹1979)

Jack, Ronald D.S., ed. 1971. *Scottish Prose 1550-1700*. London: Calder & Boyars.

---. 1981. "The prose of John Knox: a re-assessment". *Prose Studies*, 4:239-51. [144]

---. 1988. "Poetry under King James VI". In Jack, 125-38. [11]

---, ed. 1988. *The History of Scottish Literature*. vol. 1: *Origins to 1660*. Aberdeen: UP.

---. 1994. "Burns as Sassenach poet". In K. Simpson, ed. *Burns Now*. Edinburgh: Canongate, 150-66.

---. 1997a. "The language of literary materials: origins to 1700." In Jones, 213-66. [145]

---. 1997b. "Critical introduction: Where stands Scottish literature now". In R. Jack & P. Rozendaal, eds. *The Mercat Anthology of Early Scottish Literature 1375-1707*. Edinburgh: Mercat Press, vii-xxxix. [32]

---. 1998. "Which vernacular revival? Burns and the Makars". *Studies in Scottish Literature* 30, 9-17. [55]

Jackson, K.T. 1955. "The Pictish Language". In Frederick Threlfall Wainwright, ed. *The Problem of the Picts*. London: Nelson, p.129-69. [19]

Jakobsen, Jakob. 1921 (²1928). *Etymologisk Ordbog over det Norrøne Sprog på Shetland*. Translated as *An Etymological Dictionary of the Norn Language in Shetland*, 2 vols. London: David Nutt, reprinted New York: AMS Press, n.d. [124]

Jamieson, John. 1808. *An Etymological Dictionary of the Scottish Language*. Edinburgh: William Creech. [122, 126, 159, 160]

Jamieson, Robert. 1814. *Illustrations of Northern Antiquities from the Earlier Teutonic and Scandinavian Romances*. Edinburgh: James Ballantine. [37]

Johnson, Samuel. 1755. *A Dictionary of the English Language*. London. Facs. London: Times Books, 1983. [121]

Johnston, Paul A. 1984. "Variation in the Standard Scottish English of Morningside". *EWW* 5:133-85.

---. 1985. "The rise and fall of the Morningside/Kelvinside accent". In Görlach, 37-56. [52]

---. 1997a. "Older Scots phonology and its regional variation". In Jones, 47-111. [80, 82-3]

---. 1997b. "Regional Variation". In Jones, 433-513. [39]

Jones, Charles, ed. 1991. *A Treatise on the Provincial Dialect of Scotland, by Sylvester Douglas*. [1779] Edinburgh: UP. [87, 171]

---. 1993. "Scottish Standard English in the late eighteenth century". *TPS*, 9:95-131. [75]

---. 1995. *A Language Suppressed: The Pronunciation of the Scots Language in the Eighteenth Century*. Edinburgh: John Donald. [1, 58, 75-6, 87, 125, 128, 170-3]

---, ed. 1997a. *The Edinburgh History of the Scots Language*. Edinburgh: UP. [xi]

---. 1997b. "Phonology". In Jones, 267-334. [87]

---. 2002. *The English Language in Scotland. A Study Guide for Teachers*. Edinburgh: UP. [1]

Jones, Daniel, Peter Roach & James Hartman. [15]1997. *English Pronouncing Dictionary*. Cambridge: UP. [75]

Jumpertz-Schwab, C. 1998. *The Development of the Scots Lexicon and Syntax in the 16th Century under the Influence of Translations from Latin*. Frankfurt: Peter Lang. [144]

Jupp, James, ed. 1988. *The Australian People*. North Ryde, NSW: Angus & Robertson. [60, 65]

Kay, Billy.[2]1993. *Scots.The Mither Tongue*. Ayrshire: Alloway. ([1]1986). [1-2, 31, 186]

Kerr, R. D. ed. [1979]. *A Glossary of Mining Terms Used in Fife*. Kirkcaldy College of Technology for Fife Colleges. [124]

King, Ann. 1997. "The inflectional morphology of Older Scots". In Jones, 156-81.

King, Charles, ed. 1971. *Twelve Modern Scottish Poets*. London: Hodder & Stoughton. [76]

Kingsmore, Rona K. 1995. *Ulster Scots Speech: A Sociolinguistic Study*. Tuscaloosa: University of Alabama Press.

Kirk, John M. 1987. "The heteronomy of Scots with Standard English". In Macafee & MacLeod, 166-81.

---. 1997. "Ulster English: the state of the art". In H. Tristram, ed. *The Celtic Englishes*. Heidelberg: Winter, 135-79.

---. 2000. "Two Ullans texts". In Kirk & Ó Baoill, 33-44. [38, 120]

--- & Ó Baoill, eds. 2000. *Language and Politics. Northern Ireland, the Republic of Ireland, and Scotland*. Belfast: Queen's University. [38]

--- & --- eds. 2001a. *Language Links: The Languages of Scotland and Ireland*. Belfast: Queen's University. [38]

--- & ---. eds. 2001b. *Linguistic Policies for Northern Ireland, the Republic of Ireland, and Scotland*. Belfast: Queen's University. [38, 57]

Kist, The: Anthology, 1996. Scottish SCCC. Nelson Blackie [179]

Kloss, Heinz. [2]1978. *Die Entwicklung neuer germanischer Kultursprachen seit 1800*. Düsseldorf: Schwann (Scots, 256-63). [165]

Kniezsa, Veronica 1991. "*Scotica Pronunciatione*: sixteenth and seventeenth-century English authors on Scots". *Scottish Language*, 10:1-8.

---. 1997. "The origins of Scots orthography". In Jones, 24-46. [73]

Kohler, K.J. 1966. "A late eighteenth-century comparison of the 'Provincial Dialect of Scotland' and the 'Pure Dialect'". *Linguistics*, 23:30-69.

---. 1967. "Aspects of Middle Scots phonemics and graphemics". *TPS*, 32-61.

Kolb, Eduard. 1964. *Phonological Atlas of the Northern Region*. Bern: Francke.

Kratzmann, G. 1988. "Sixteenth century secular poetry". In Jack, 105-24.

Kuipers, C.H., ed. 1964. *Quintin Kennedy (1520-1564): Two Eucharistic Tracts. A Critical Edition*. Diss. University of Nijmegen.

Kynoch, Douglas. 1994. *Teach Yourself Doric*. Aberdeen: Scottish Cultural Press. [179]

---. 1996. *A Doric Dictionary. Two-way Lexicon of North-East Scots. Doric~English, English~Doric*. Aberdeen: Scottish Cultural Press. [124]

Labov, William. 2001. *Principles of Linguistic Change, 2. Social Factors*. Oxford: Blackwell. [52]

Lamb, Gregor. 1988. *Orkney Wordbook*. Birsay: Byrgisey. [48, 124]

LAS see Mather & Speitel

Leith, Dick. 1983. *A Social History of English*. London: Routledge & Kegan Paul. (²1995)

Lenz, Katja. 1996. "Modern Scottish drama. Snakes in Iceland – Drama in Scotland?". *ZAA* 44:301-16.

---. 1999. *Die schottische Sprache im modernen Drama*. Heidelberg: Winter. [165-6]

---. 2000a. "A proposed method of characterizing literary Scots – a study in dramatic texts". *Anglia* 118:185-216.

---. 2000b. "A 'peripheral' problem? The use of Scots in plays set outwith the Central Belt of Scotland". *Revista Canaria de Estudios Ingleses* 41:29-42.

---. 2002. "Losses and gains – the case of Scots in Scotland". In: Gerardo Mazzaferro, ed. *The English Language and Power*. Alessandria: Dell'Orso Editore.

Leonard, A.S. 1929. *The Doctrine of Correctness in English Usage 1700-1800*. Madison: University of Wisconsin Press.

Letley, Emma. 1988. *From Galt to Douglas Brown. 19th-century Fiction and Scots Language*. Edinburgh: Scottish Academic Press.

Lewis, C.S. 1954. *English Literature in the 16th Century*. Oxford: Clarendon. [142-3]

Lorvik, Marjorie. 1995. *The Scottish Lass Betrayed? Scots in English Classrooms*. Edinburgh: Consultative Council on the Curriculum. [178]

Lovie, Rod, Alasdair Allan, Davie Horsburgh [sic]. 1995. *Innin ti the Scots Leid / An Introduction to the Scots Language*. Aberdeen: Aiberdeen Univairsitie Scots Leid Quorum. [179]

Low, Donald A. 1974. "Introduction". In Donald A. Low, ed. *Robert Burns. The Critical Heritage*. London: Routledge, 1-57. [150]

---, ed. 1987. *Two Glossaries by Robert Burns: The Glossaries to the Kilmarnock and Edinburgh Poems*. Stirling: University of Stirling, Bibliographic Society.

Luke, David. 1982. *Jacob and Wilhelm Grimm. Selected Tales*. Harmondsworth: Penguin. [14]

Lunney, L. [Connolly]. 1994. "Ulster attitudes to Scottishness: the eighteenth century and after". In I.S. Wood, ed. *Scotland and Ulster*. Edinburgh: Mercat Press, 56-70.

Lynch, Michael. ²1992. *Scotland: A New History*. London: Pimlico. [14]

---. 1994. "National identity in Ireland and Scotland, 1500-1640". In Bjørn, Grant & Stringer, eds., 109-36.

Macafee, Caroline I. 1980. "Characteristics of non-standard grammar in Scotland"; 1992 http://www.abdn.ac.uk/-en1038/grammar.htm [95, 101, 103, 104, 105, 107]

---. 1983a. *Glasgow*. (VEAW T2). Amsterdam: Benjamins. [xi, 50, 51]

---. 1983b. "Sociolinguistic approaches to Scots language". *Scottish Language* 2:20-32. [53]

---. 1985. "Nationalism and the Scots Renaissance now". In Görlach, 1985a, 7-18.

---. 1992-3. "A short grammar of Older Scots". *Scottish Language*, 11-12:10-36. [101]

---. 1994a. *Traditional Dialect in the Modern World: A Glasgow Case Study*. Frankfurt: Peter Lang. [22, 32, 50, 52, 120]

---. 1994b. "Dialect erosion with special reference to urban Scots". In Fenton & MacDonald, 69-80. [32, 113]

---, ed. 1996. *A Concise Ulster Dictionary*. Oxford: UP. [63, 124]

---. 1997a. "Older Scots lexis". In Jones, 182-212. [125]

---. 1997b. "Ongoing change in modern Scots: the social dimension". In Jones, 514-50.

---. 2000. "The demography of Scots: the lessons of the Census Campaign". *Scottish Language* 19:1-44.

---. 2001. "Scots: hauf empty or hauf fu?" In Kirk & Ó Baoill, 159-68.

--- & Iseabail Macleod, eds. 1987. *The Nuttis Shell. Essays on the Scots Language presented to A.J. Aitken*. Aberdeen: UP.

McArthur, Tom, ed. 1992. *The Oxford Companion to the English Language*. Oxford:UP. [6, 170]

Macaulay, Ronald K.S. 1977. *Language, Social Class and Education. A Glasgow Study*. Edinburgh: UP. [50, 51, 88]

---. 1991. *Locating Dialect in Discourse: The Language of Honest Men and Bonny Lasses in Ayr*. Oxford: UP.

---. 1997. *Standards and Variation in Urban Speech*. (VEAW G20). Amsterdam: Benjamins.

MacCallum N., & D. Purves, ed. 1995. *Mak it New: An Anthology of Twenty-one Years of Writing in 'Lallans'*. Edinburgh: Mercat Press.

McClure, J. Derrick. 1980. "Developing Scots as a national language". In McClure, Aitken & Low, 11-41. [120]

---, ed. 1983. *Scotland and the Lowland Tongue. Studies in the Language and Literature of Lowland Scotland*. Aberdeen: UP.

---. 1987. "'Lallans' and 'Doric' in North-Eastern Scottish Poetry". *EWW* 8:215-34.

---. 1993a. "Varieties of Scots in recent and contemporary narrative prose". *EWW* 14:1-22.

---. 1993b. "Translation and transcreation in the Castilian period". *Studies in Scottish Literature* 26:185-98. [12]

---. 1994. "English in Scotland". In R.W. Burchfield, ed. *English in Britain and Overseas: Origins and Development*. (CHEL 5) Cambridge: UP, 23-93. [xi, 1, 14, 35, 87-8, 89, 101, 104, 106, 107, 110]

---. 1995a. *Scots and Its Literature*. (VEAW G14). Amsterdam: Benjamins. [54]

---. 1995b. "The concept of Standard Scots". In 1995a:20-36. (1979) [77]

---. 1995c. "The debate on Scots orthography". In 1995a:37-43. (1985)

---. 1995d. "Scottis, Inglis, Suddroun: language labels and language attitudes". In 1995a: 44-56. (1981) [5-6, 18, 29]

---. 1995e. "What Scots owes to Gaelic". In 1995a:68-85. (1986) [126]

---. 1995f. "Scots in dialogue: some uses and implications". In 1995a:86-106. (1983)

---. 1995g. "Language and genre in Allan Ramsay's 1721 Poems". In 1995a: 161-70. (1987) [149]

---. 1995h. "Scots and its use in recent poetry". In 1995a:171-89. (1979) [31, 165]

---. ²1997. *Why Scots Matters*. Edinburgh: Saltire Society. (¹1988) [1]

---. 2000. *Language, Poetry and Nationhood. Scots as a Poetic Language from 1878 to the Present*. East Linton: Tuckwell. [129, 159-64]

---. 2002. *Doric. The Dialect of North-East Scotland*. (VEAW T8). Amsterdam: Benjamins. [xi]

---, A.J. Aitken & John Thomas Low, 1980. *The Scots Language: Planning for Modern Usage*. Edinburgh: Ramsay Head.

---, *et al.* 1981. "Our ain leid? The predicament of a Scots writer". *EWW* 2:3-28; repr. in Görlach 1985a:181-201. [57]

---, *et al.* eds. 1983. *Scotland and the Lowland Tongue*. Aberdeen: UP.

--- & M.R.G. Spiller, eds. 1989. *Bryght Lanternis: Essays on the Language and Literature of Medieval and Renaissance Scotland*. Aberdeen: UP.

McCordick, David, ed. 1996. *Scottish Literature. An Anthology*. 2 vols. New York: Peter Lang. [187]

MacDiarmid, Hugh.1976. *Contemporary Scottish Studies*. Edinburgh: *Scottish Educational Journal* (Reprint of essays published in *SEJ* 1925-27). [159, 184]

McDiarmid, Matthew P. 1973. "Introduction" to *The Kingis Quair of James Stewart*. London: Heinemann. [143]

MacGillivray, Alan, ed. 1997. *Teaching Scottish Literature. Curriculum and Classroom Applications*. Edinburgh: UP. [177]

McGugan, Irene. 2001. "Scots in the twenty-first century". In Kirk & Ó Baoill, 29-35. [1, 3]

McIntosh, Angus. 1952. *Introduction to a Survey of Scottish Dialects*. Edinburgh: Nelson.

Mackie, A. 1881. *Scotticisms Arranged and Corrected, Solecisms Corrected*. London: Hamilton Adams. [121]

Mackie, Albert. 1978. *Talking Glasgow*. Belfast: Blackstaff.

---. 1984. *The Illustrated Glasgow Glossary*. Belfast: Blackstaff.

Macleod, Iseabail. 1998. "Scots dictionaries present and future". *Scottish Language* 17:10-15.

---, Pauline Cairns, Caroline I. Macafee & Ruth Martin, eds. 1990. *The Scots Thesaurus*. Aberdeen: UP. [116]

--- & Pauline Cairns, eds. 1993. *The Concise English-Scots Dictionary*. Edinburgh: Chambers. [125, 179]

--- & Pauline Cairns. 1996. *The Scots School Dictionary*. Edinburgh: Chambers. [119, 123, 179]

--- & Pauline Cairns. 1998. *The Electronic Scots School Dictionary*. Edinburgh: SNDA. [123, 179]

---, Ruth Martin & Pauline Cairns. 1988. *The Pocket Scots Dictionary*. Aberdeen: UP. [123]

--- & Aoughas MacNeacail. 1995. *Scotland: A Linguistic Double Helix*. Brussels: European Bureau for Lesser Used Languages. [1]

McLeod, Wilson. 1998. "Scotland's languages in Scotland's Parliament". *Scottish Affairs* 24:68-82. [3]

McNaught, D. 1901. "The rauchle tongue of Burns." *Burns Chronicle and Club Directory* II, 25:4-8. [49]

McNeill, P. & R. Nicholson, eds. 1975. *An Historical Atlas of Scotland*. St. Andrews: Atlas Commitee.

MacQueen, John, ed. 1970. *Ballatis of Luve. The Scottish Courtly Love Lyric 1400-1570*. Edinburgh: UP. [29]

MacTaggart, John. 1824. *The Scottish Gallovidian Encyclopedia*. London: the author; ²1981. Strath Tay: Clunie Press. [124]

Mapstone, Sally, ed. 2001. *William Dunbar, 'The Nobill Poyet'. Essays in Honour of Priscilla Bawcutt*. East Linton: Tuckwell. [6]

Marchand, Hans. ²1969. *The Categories and Types of Present-Day English Word-Formation*. München: Beck. [128]

Marwick, Hugh. 1929 (²1992). *The Orkney Norn. A Glossary, Preceded by a Historical Sketch*. Dunfermline: W. I. A. Murray. Originally published by Oxford UP. [124]

Máté, Ian. 1996. *Scots Language. A Report on the Scots Language Research carried out by the General Register Office for Scotland in 1996*. Edinburgh: General Register Office (Scotland). [3]

Mather, John Y. & Hans H. Speitel. 1975, 1977, 1986. *The Linguistic Atlas of Scotland*. 3 vols. London: Croom Helm. [43-4]

Mathews, Mitford Mcleod. 1931. *The Beginnings of American English. Essays and Comments*. Chicago: UP. [60]

Matthews, Constance Mary. 1966. *English Surnames*. London: Weidenfeld & Nicolson.

Melchers, Gunnel. 1985. "*'Knappin', 'Proper English', 'Modified Scottish'. Some language attitudes in the Shetland Isles*". In Görlach, 87-100.

Menzies, J. 1991. "An investigation of attitudes to Scots and Glasgow dialect among secondary school pupils". *Scottish Language*, 10:30-46. [51]

Meurman-Solin, Anneli. 1993a. *Variation and Change in Early Scottish Prose: Studies Based on the Helsinki Corpus of Older Scots*. Helsinki: Suomalainen Tiedeakatemia. [108, 146]

---. 1993b. "Introduction to the Helsinki Scots corpus". In M. Rissanen, M. Kytö & M. Pallander-Collin, eds. *Early English in the Computer Age: Explorations through the Helsinki Corpus*. Berlin & New York: Mouton de Gruyter, 75-82. [7]

---. 1993c. "Periphrastic and auxiliary *do* in early Scottish prose genres". In M. Rissanen, M. Kytö & M. Palander-Collin, eds. *Early English in the Computer Age: Explorations through the Helsinki Corpus*. Berlin & New York: Mouton de Gruyter, 235-51.

---. 1995. "A new tool: the Helsinki Corpus of Older Scots (1450-1700)". *ICAME Journal*, 19:49-62.

---. 1997. "Differentiation and standardisation in Early Scots". In Jones, 3-23. [34]

Miller, James. 1989. *The Grammar of Scottish English*. Part 4 of: James & Lesley Milroy, eds. *Regional Variation in British English Syntax*. Swindon: Economic and Social Research Council. [103, 105]

---. 1993. "The grammar of Scottish English". In J. Milroy & L. Milroy, eds. *Real English: The Grammar of English Dialects in the British Isles*. Harlow: Longman, 99-138. [93, 101, 106, 107]

--- & E. Keith Brown. 1982. "Aspects of Scottish English syntax". *EWW* 3:3-17. [104, 105, 107]

Milton, Colin. 1983. "From Charles Murray to Hugh MacDiarmid: Vernacular revival and Scottish Renaissance" in David Hewitt & Michael Spiller, eds. *Literature of the North*. Aberdeen: UP, 82-108. [4]

---. 1992. "Language, class and education in twentieth-century Scottish writing", *English World-Wide* 13:219-51.

---1995-96. "*Shibboleths of the Scots*: Hugh MacDiarmid and Jamieson's Etymological Dictionary of the Scottish Language", *Scottish Language* 14/15:1-14.

Moessner, Lilo. 1997. "The syntax of Older Scots". In Jones, 112-55. [99, 101, 107-8, 110]

Montgomery, Michael B. 1989. "Exploring the roots of Appalachian English". *EWW* 10:227-78. [64]

---. 1994. "The evolution of verb concord in Scots". In Fenton & MacDonald, 81-95. [95]

---. 2000. "The position of Ulster Scots." *Ulster Folklife* 45:86-107.

---. 2001. "British and Irish antecedents". In John Algeo, ed. *English in North America*. (CHEL 6). Cambridge: UP, 86-153. [60, 64]

--- & Robert J. Gregg. 1997. "The Scots language in Ulster". In Jones, 569-621. [23, 60, 62-3]

Muir, Edwin. 1936. *Scott and Scotland*. London: Routledge. (²1982, Edinburgh: Polygon). [160, 173]

Mulrine, Steven. 1985. "Poetry in Glasgow dialect". In Görlach, 227-35.

Munro, Michael. 1985. *The Patter: A Guide to Current Glasgow Usage*. Glasgow: Glasgow District Libraries. [120, 184]

Murison, David D. 1970. "The two languages of Scott", in A.N. Jeffares, ed. *Scott's Mind and Art*. London: Oliver & Boyd, 206-29.

---. 1971. "The Dutch element in the vocabulary of Scots." In Aitken *et al.*, 159-76.

---. 1972. "The Scottish National Dictionary". *University of Edinburgh Journal*, 25:305-89.

---. 1975. "The language of Sydney Goodsir Smith". In Norman MacCaig, ed. *For Sydney Goodsir Smith*. Loanhead: MacDonald, 23-29.

---. 1977. *The Guid Scots Tongue*. Edinburgh: Blackwood. (²1978). [49]

---. 1981. "Northeast Scots as a literary language". In William Donaldson & Douglas Young, eds. *Grampian Hairst. An Anthology of Northeast Prose*. Aberdeen: UP, 187-95. [151]

Murray, J.A.H. 1873. *The Dialect of the Southern Counties of Scotland*. London: The Philological Society. [35, 42, 44, 45, 55, 87, 95, 99, 128, 139, 181]

Murray, Mary. 1982. *In My Ain Words. An East Neuk Vocabulary*. Anstruther: Scottish Fisheries Museum. [124]

Mutschmann, Heinrich. 1909. *A Phonology of the Northeastern Scotch Dialect on an Historical Basis*. Bonn: Hanstein. [40, 42, 46, 87]

Neill, William. 1992. *Tales frae the Odyssey o Homer Owreset Intil Scots*. Edinburgh: Saltire Society. [162]

Nicolaisen, W.F.H. 1976. *Scottish Place-names: Their Study and Significance*. London: Batsford. [23-5]

---. 1977. *The Place-names of Scotland*. London: Batsford. [23-4]

Niven, Liz & Robin Jackson. 1998. *The Scots Language: Its Place in Education*. Edinburgh: Watergaw. [177]

Ó Muirithe, Diarmaid, ed. 1977. *The English Language in Ireland*. Cork: Mercier.

Phillipson, N.T. & R. Mitchison, eds. 1970. *Scotland in the Age of Improvement*. Edinburgh: UP.

Pollner, Claus Dirk. 1985a. *Englisch in Livingston. Ausgewählte sprachliche Erscheinungen in einer schottischen New Town*. Frankfurt: Peter Lang. [49, 172]

---. 1985b. "Linguistic fieldwork in a Scottish new town". In Görlach 57-68. [113]

---. 1985c. "Old words in a young town". *Scottish Language* 4:5-15. [52]

---. 1994. "The ugly sister - Scots words in Early Modern English dictionaries". In Dieter Kastovsky, ed. *Studies in Early Modern English*. Berlin: Mouton de Gruyter, 289-99. [114]

Preston, Dennis. 1989. *Perceptual Dialectology. Nonlinguists' Views of Areal Linguistics*. Dordrecht: Foris. [40,43]

Price, Glanville. 1984. *The Languages of Britain*. London: Arnold. [19, 21]

Purves, David. 1997a. *A Scots Grammar: Scots Grammar and Usage*. Edinburgh: Saltire Society. [101-4, 110, 178, 179]

---. 1997b. "MacDiarmid's use of Scots: Synthetic or natural?" *Scottish Language* 16: 82-7.

Ray, John. 1674. *A Collection of Words Not Generally Used ...* London (²1961); facs. Menston: Scolar Press [EL 145] [122]

Reid, Euan. 1978. "Social and stylistic variation in the speech of children". In Trudgill, 158-72. [50]

Rennie, Susan with Iseabail Maclod & Pauline Cairns. 1999. *Grammar Broonie. A Guide tae Scots Grammar*. Edinburgh: Scottish National Dictionary Association. [123, 179]

Review of Scottish Culture Group. 1998. *Scottish Culture and the Curriculum*. http://www.snp.org.uk/library/sccc/sccc1.htm

Riach, W.A.D. 1988. *A Galloway Glossary*. Aberdeen: Association for Scottish Literary Studies, Occasional Papers 7. [124]

Robertson, T.A. & John J. Graham. ²1991. *Grammar and Usage of the Shetland Dialect*. Lerwick: Shetland Times. [¹1952]. [47]

Robinson, Christine & Carol Ann Crawford. 2001. *Scotspeak. A Guide to the Pronunciation of Modern Urban Scots*. Perth: SLRC (with CD). [4, 7, 50, 90, 91]

Robinson, Mairi. 1973. "Modern literary Scots: Fergusson and after". In Aitken, 38-55.

---. 1985. *The Concise Scots Dictionary*. Aberdeen: UP. [xi, 8, 40, 123, 128-32]

Robinson, Philip. 1997. *Ulster Scots: A Grammar of the Traditional Written and Spoken Language*. Belfast: The Ullans Press. [63]

Rohlfing, Helmut. 1984. *Die Werke James Elphinstons (1721-1809) als Quellen der englischen Lautgeschichte*. Heidelberg: Winter. [75]

Romaine, Suzanne. 1979. "The language of Edinburgh schoolchildren: the acquisition of sociolinguistic competence", *Scottish Literary Journal*, Supplement 9, 54-60. [50]

---. 1980. "The relative clause marker in Scots English: diffusion, complexity, and style as dimensions of syntactic change". *Language in Society*, 9:221-47. [99, 109]

---. 1982a. *Socio-Historical Linguistics: Its Status and Methodology*. Cambridge: UP. [53, 99, 109-10]

---. 1982b. "The English language in Scotland". In Bailey & Görlach, 56-83. [52]

Ross, Alexander. 1935 (1938). *The Scottish Works of Alexander Ross, MA*. STS III:9. [172]

Royle, Trevor. 1983. *The Macmillan Companion to Scottish Literature*. London: Macmillan. [156]

Sabban, Annette. 1985a. "On the variability of Hebridean English syntax: the verbal group". In Görlach, 125-43. [175]

---. 1985b. "Overt and covert prestige: Evaluative boundaries in a speech community". In Görlach, 69-86.

Salmon, Vivian. 1999. "Orthography and punctuation". In Roger Lass, ed. *1476 to 1776*. (CHEL 3). Cambridge: UP, 13-55.

Sandred, Karl Inge. 1983. *Good or Bad Scots?* Stockholm: Almqvist & Wiksell.

Schneider, Edgar W., ed. 1997. *Englishes around the World. Studies in Honour of Manfred Görlach*. 2 vols. (VEAW G18-19). Amsterdam: Benjamins.

Scot, Alexander. 1779. *The Contrast: A Specimen of the Scotch Dialect. In Prose and Verse. According to the Latest Improvements; With an English Version*. Edinburgh (to be had of M. Drummond, ..., or of W. Creech). [75-6]

Scots Style Sheet. 1947. ed. by the Makars' Club. Repr. in King 1971:17-8 and Purves 1997:63-4.

Scott, Paul H. 1998. "The future of the Scots language". *Scottish Affairs* 24:83-9.

Sheridan, Thomas. 1780. *A General Dictionary of the English Language*. 2 vols. London: for J. Dodsley. Facs. Menston: Scolar Press [EL 50]. [170]

---. 1781. *A Rhetorical Grammar of the English Language*. Dublin. Facs. Menston: Scolar Press, 1969 [EL 146]. [82]

Shuken, Cynthia R. 1985. "Variation in Hebridean English". In Görlach, 145-58. [175]

Simpson, Grant G. 1977. *Scottish Handwriting 1150-1650. An Introduction to the Reading of Documents*. Aberdeen: UP.([2]1986) [11, 70, 73, 79]

Smith, G.G., ed. 1902. *Specimens of Middle Scots*. Edinburgh: W. Blackwell.

---, ed. 1904. *Elizabethan Critical Essays*. 2 vols. Oxford: UP. [137, T16]

SND see Grant & Murison, 1931-76.

SNDA. 1998. *Canniespell*. Edinburgh [179]

Speitel, Hans Henning. 1978. "The word geography of the Borders". *Scottish Literary Journal*, Supplement 6: 17-37.

--- & J.Y. Mather. 1968. "Schottische Dialektologie". In L.E. Schmitt, ed. *Germanische Dialektologie: Festschrift für Walter Mitzka*. Wiesbaden: Franz Steiner, 520-41.

Sprague, T.B. 1881. "On som differences between the speech ov Edinboro and London". *TPS*, 1880-1881, 106-16.

Staff Notes and Annotated Bibliography. 2001 (for English and Communication [Language]). Edinburgh: Learning, Teaching Scotland.

Stevenson, J.A.C. & I. Macleod. 1989. *Scoor-Oot: A Dictionary of Scots Words and Phrases in Current Use*. London: Athlone.

Strang, Barbara M.H.. 1970. *A History of English*. London: Methuen. [91]

Stuart, Jamie. 1992. *The Glasgow Gospel*. Edinburgh: St. Andrews Press. [183]

---. 1993. *Auld Testament Tales*. Edinburgh: St. Andrews Press.

Sutherland, Iain. [2]1996. *The Caithness Dictionary*. Wick: The Northern Times. [124]

Templeton, Janet M. 1973. "Scots: an outline history". In Aitken, 4-11.

Topham, E. 1776. *Letters from Edinburgh*. Edinburgh. [172]

Traynor, M. 1953. *The English Dialect of Donegal: A Glossary, Incorporating the Collections of H.C. Hart, etc*. Dublin: Royal Irish Academy.

Trotter, R. de Bruce. 1901. "The Scottish language". *The Gallovidian* 3/9:22-9. [95]

Trudgill, Peter, ed. 1978. *Sociolinguistic Patterns in British English*. London: Edward Arnold.

---, ed. 1984. *Language in the British Isles*. Cambridge: UP.

---. 1986. *Dialects in Contact*. Oxford: Blackwell. [34, 64]

Tulloch, Graham. 1980. *The Language of Walter Scott: A Study of his Scottish and Period Language*. London: Deutsch. [58, 119, 151, 172-4]

---. 1983. "The use of Scots in Scott and other nineteenth-century Scottish novelists". In J.H. Alexander & David Hewitt, eds. *Scott and His Influence*. Aberdeen: ASLS, 341-50.

---. 1985. "The search for a Scots narrative voice". In Görlach, 159-79. [153]

---. 1989. *A History of the Scots Bible with Selected Texts*. Aberdeen: UP. [57, 95, 138-9, 168, 180, T51]

---. 1997a. "Lexis". In Jones, 378-432. [65-6]

---. 1997b. "The Scots language in Australia". In Jones, 623-36. [65]

---. 1997c. "Scots as a literary language in Australia" in Schneider II: 319-34. [65-6]

Tytler, Alexander Fraser. 1790. *Essay on the Principles of Translation*. Edinburgh: William Creech; repr. London: Dent, 1907 (Everyman 168).

Walker, John. 1791. *A Critical Pronouncing Dictionary*. London. Facs. Menston: Scolar Press, 1968 [EL 117]. [81, 86]

Warrack, Alexander, ed. 1911. *Chambers Scots Dictionary*. London: Chambers. [42, 123]

Watson, George. 1923. *The Roxburghshire Word-Book*. Cambridge: UP. [124]

Webster, Noah. 1789. *Dissertations on the English Language*. Boston: for the author. Facs. Menston: Scolar Press 1967. [174]

Wells, John C. 1982. *Accents of English*. 3 vols. Cambridge: UP.

Wettstein, P. 1942. *The Phonology of a Berwickshire Dialect*. Bienne: Schüler. [45]

Wickens, Beatrice. 1980. "Caithness speech: Studying the dialect with the help of schoolchildren". *Scottish Literary Journal* 12:61-76; 14:25-36.

Williamson, I.K. 1982/83. "Lowland Scots in education: a historical survey". *Scottish Language* 1:54-77, 2:52-87. [10]

Wilson, Sir James. 1915. *Lowland Scotch, as Spoken in the Lower Strathearn District of Perthshire*. London: Oxford UP. [10, 42-3, 46, 87, 93, 102, 130, 175]

---. 1923. *The Dialect of Robert Burns as Spoken in Central Ayrshire*. Oxford: UP. [42, 46]

---. 1926. *The Dialects of Central Scotland*. Oxford: UP. [42, 87]

Wilson, William Morrice. 1993. *Speak o' the North-East*. NES Publications [privately published]. [124]

---. 1995. *Speak o' the North-East. Index/Glossary*. NES Publications [privately published]. [124]

Withers, C.W.J. 1979. "The language geography of Scottish Gaelic". *Scottish Literary Journal*. Suppl. 9:41-54.

---. 1984. *Gaelic in Scotland 1698-1981: The Geographical History of a Language*. Edinburgh: John Donald. [19]

Wittig, Kurt. 1958. *The Scottish Tradition in Literature*. Edinburgh & London: Oliver & Boyd.

Wright, D.F. 1988. *The Bible in Scottish Life and Literature*. Edinburgh: UP. [180-1]

Wright, John. 1905. *The English Dialect Dictionary*. 6 vols. London: Frowde. [42, 123]

Young, Clive. [2]1996. *The Scots Haunbuik*. http://umist.ac.uk/UMIST_CAL/Scots/haunbuik.htm

Young, Douglas. 1948. *'Plastic Scots' and the Scottish Literary Tradition. An Authoritative Introduction to a Controversy*. Glasgow: William Maclellan.

12 Indexes

12.1 Index of topics

12.2 *Index of names*

The index is somewhat selective; bold figures refer to the biographical information preceding the excerpts T1-75.

12.3 *Index of words*